D1526053

SCHOOL OF
ORIENTAL AND AFRICAN STUDIES
UNIVERSITY OF LONDON

THE UNEASY NARRATOR

The Uneasy Narrator

CHINESE FICTION
FROM THE TRADITIONAL
TO THE MODERN

HENRY Y. H. ZHAO

Senior Lecturer in Chinese Literature in the University of London

OXFORD UNIVERSITY PRESS

1995

Oxford University Press, Walton Street, Oxford OX2 6DP

Oxford New York
Athens Auckland Bangkok Bombay
Calcutta Cape Town Dar es Salaam Delhi
Florence Hong Kong Istanbul Karachi
Kuala Lumpur Madras Madrid Melbourne
Mexico City Nairobi Paris Singapore
Taipei Tokyo Toronto
and associated companies in
Berlin Ibadan

Oxford is a trade mark of Oxford University Press

Published in the United States
by Oxford University Press Inc., New York

British Library Cataloguing in Publication Data
Data available

Library of Congress Cataloging in Publication Data
Zhao, I-heng.
The uneasy narrator : Chinese fiction from the traditional to the
modern / by Henry Y. H. Zhao.
— (London oriental series ; v. 40)
Includes bibliographical references.
I. Chinese fiction—History and criticism.
I. Title. II. Series.
PL2415.Z43 1995 895.1'3009—dc20 94–47596
ISBN 0–19–713611–7

1 3 5 7 9 10 8 6 4 2

Typeset by Graphicraft Typesetters Ltd., Hong Kong
Printed in Great Britain
on acid-free paper by
Bookcraft Ltd.
Midsomer Norton, Avon

Acknowledgements

I would like to record my appreciation of the people and institutions who helped the writing of this book. The British Academy has repeatedly provided grants for research in China. The School of Oriental and African Studies of the University of London has all along kindly supported its revision and publication.

Many of my teachers, colleagues and friends gave me great help. Professor Cyril Birch of the University of California, Berkeley, read the earliest version of the book and he encouraged me to continue to work on it until publishable. Professor Samuel Cheung and Professor Eric Johannesson of Berkeley, Professor David Pollard of the Chinese University of Hong Kong and Dr Alison Bailey of the University of London read the text in different stages of its revision and stimulated me with their comments. Professor Yue Daiyun of Beijing University and Professor Wu Fuhui of the Modern Chinese Literature Achives in Beijing gave me invaluable advice on various problems. Professor Shen Dan of Beijing University and Dr Elly Hagenaar of the University of Leiden discussed with me in their works on the issue of reported speech in Chinese fiction which urged me to present my views better. Ms Susan Whimster gave the manuscript an extremely careful checking and helped me to tidy up the inconsistencies in references resulting from repeated revisions. In the last few years I have used much of the material in the book in my teaching at the School of Oriental and African Studies and in my lectures at Beijing University. The lively discussion with students of various nationalities often surprised me into new ways to improve my argument. I thank them all.

Contents

CONTENTS

How To Use the Appendixes

The present book draws support from a large number of fiction works in Chinese and from scholarly works both in Chinese and in English. In order to save space, and to facilitate reading and further research as well, three appendixes are provided at the end of the book.

Appendix I is a glossary supplying the Chinese original for personal names, titles of novels or story collections, and some special terms appearing either as pinyin romanization or as English translation in the text or in the footnotes, though not those only briefly mentioned in the footnotes.

Appendix II is a list of keys to the abbreviations in the text and the footnotes. Since abbreviations are used only when Chinese fiction works are quoted, the list, by providing publication details, also serves as a bibliography of primary sources.

Appendix III is, then, a bibliography of secondary sources. Works in Chinese are listed together with works in Western languages, to spare readers the trouble of guessing in what language the work might be.

INTRODUCTION

A Theoretical Outline

I

This study will limit itself to the relations between Chinese vernacular fiction and Chinese culture until the early twentieth century, without claiming the applicability of its analytical paradigm to the relations between fiction and culture in general, which nevertheless, does not mean that the present study will be so specific that it does not have any theoretical implications.

Since the greater part of the discussion will concentrate on the formal narrative features and period stylistics of Chinese vernacular fiction, it is perhaps advisable to map out my theoretical approach before the study starts, so that it will not be drowned in discussion of technicalities.

First of all, culture is regarded in this book as the summary of all discursive activities relevant to social life.[1] By 'discursive' I mean any activity of communication and signification. Socially relevant discursive activities cover a wide range, from art and literature, to customs and habits, to the execution of political power or the regulation of material production. In short, culture is the conglomeration of all meaning-production, transmission, and reception in a given society.

This huge body of cultural discursive activity has to be controlled by an interpretation system, i.e. ideology, which tries to ensure the expected interpretation of all discursive activities. Ideology, then, works as a normalizing system for culture. Formed for regulating the interpretative activities in society, it could, however, turn around to regulate meaning-production in society based on its own model.

As long as it functions effectively in normalization, any ideology can be regarded as reasonable. Ideology is supposed to provide answers to all queries about meaning—from cosmological problems to personal behaviours. Any partial ineffectiveness will be fatal as it leads to a lack

---

[1] It is said that there are over 100 definitions of culture, and no fewer definitions of ideology. Mine is only a tentative definition, aiming at an easier understanding of the relationship between fiction, culture, and ideology.

of confidence in the validity of the ideology to everything else. Around the turn of the twentieth century, for instance, Chinese ideology was unable to explain the disastrous inferiority in weaponry to the Western powers. Not entirely by accident, it was also at a loss to know how to continue to hold the narratorial control in vernacular fiction.

Such widespread doubt about ideological validity is usually called a cultural crisis. Whether the culture can survive the crisis depends on whether it can adjust its interpretative norms to the new situation. This, however, is not likely to take place without difficulty.

Among all the socially relevant discourses in a culture, the literary discourse, being an innovative violation of the linguistic norms, is the most likely to challenge the value-judgement norms. The complexity of production and interpretation of literary discourse may quite possibly force the smoothly polished surface of ideology in a society to crack, yielding all kinds of denormalized meanings that the culture would otherwise successfully smother.

Due to its inextricable bondage to language, literature is the most recalcitrant activity in culture. When a cultural crisis is incubating, literary discourse is probably the first to show the symptoms in the text.

These symptoms detected in the text, however, should not be taken as the reflected image of the contradictions within the ideology, because an ideology, having to be all-explaining, is supposed to contain no contradictions. Nor should the symptoms in the text be considered as the image of real social contradictions, because no text can hope to bypass ideology and reflect history directly.

The task of critical reading, e.g. the current study, then, is not to find the meaning supposedly hidden within the text, nor is it to reveal the meaning behind the distorted image of 'reality' in the text. Critical reading aims at laying bare the meaning of the text-distortion caused by the tension between culture and historical movement.

Here lies the reason why the study of the relations between Chinese fiction and Chinese culture in the early twentieth century is interesting: this was a period of prolonged crisis between a seriously weakening culture and an impatient literature. Various efforts to readjust the troubled relations between the two were made, only to aggravate the situation. Fiction, in the mind of many Chinese ideologues and writers, could help overcome the crisis and save the nation, and frequently in this century it has been made to serve that purpose. Ironically, this abuse of literature itself is, in my view, a symptom of the culture in crisis.

II

The narrator is, in any fictional text, an indispensable character who plays a special role. We can find, under critical examination, that he, though only a fictional being, enjoys some social-cultural connections beyond the control of the author. In other words, he can force the author to create him in a certain way. He can have such a character that, in comparison with him, the almighty creator that the author appears to be could turn out to be only a subject of limited power.

How could I assume the narrator as a person, and a male person at that? It is hard to determine the personality or the sex of the narrator if he does not show up in the text. But in the case of traditional Chinese fiction, the narrator is indeed a male person with a fixed role to play in the narrative. Besides, my discussion will show that he really has a powerful personality that justifies the anthropomorphic appellation.

It is, however, too much of a simplification to assume that a certain historical period will produce a certain type of narrator in fiction to match it. I only want to argue that to examine the narrator's personality, his position in the narrative scheme, his control over the narrative, and his rapport or conflict with the author, could yield significant insight into the complicated relationship between fiction and culture.

The narrator often seems to have a self-consciousness beyond the control of the authors: he is, in some periods, apparently comfortable in his job of narrating, but quite uneasy, even frustrated, at other times.

In those periods when he feels fully at ease in narrating, he is the God standing over the fictive narrated world, or rather, the plenipotentiary governor sent by the relatively stable culture to the narrated world. He does not seem to be disturbed by the inconsistency of the author's emotion, nor by the vicissitudes of the characters' fortunes. In the whole narrative scheme, he feels secure in his position, from where he can intervene in the narrated world in many ways, so that the unpredictable changes of the narrated world may be brought into the steady control of the interpretative system of the culture.

At other times, he is confident in organizing a rebellion in the narrated world against the fiction-producing world. He can try in the narrated world to subvert the order of the mainstream culture and install a whole set of new values not recognized by the mainstream culture. Often the author and the characters look nervous as if they are running into unpredictable dangers while the narrator remains staunch in the challenge so that the narrative coheres the deviant values.

Yet, in certain historical periods the narrator may show all kinds of uneasiness. He has neither a stable set of narrative devices to put the narrated world in order, nor an interpretative system to guide the narrative. He seems at a loss as to how to handle the various problems in narrating. He clings to the old way of controlling while knowing only too well that his conventional position in the narrative scheme is slipping away under his feet. The narrator's embarrassment may betray many things that the author is unable to tell us.

In our discussion we shall meet all three types of narrators.

With some generalization, we can say that the narrator in traditional Chinese fiction is more often than not of the first type—the comfortably domineering narrator; the narrator of the May Fourth fiction (1918–27) tends to be the second type—the confidently subversive narrator; the narrator in late Qing dynarty fiction at the beginning of the twentieth century is most probably the third type—the painfully uneasy narrator.

To go a step further, we find that the three narratorial situations may be said to be the result of three different kinds of relationships between Chinese fiction and Chinese culture.

As the title indicates, our discussion will concentrate on the unfortunately uneasy narrator in Chinese fiction at the beginning of the twentieth century. Later, after the May Fourth period, the narrator in Chinese fiction more or less reverts to uneasiness again, and is bogged down in it for as long as half a century. Our discussion, however, will end before he repeats his history.

PART ONE

Chinese Vernacular Fiction
Until the Early Twentieth Century

1

Chinese Vernacular Fiction

I

Traditionally, there were two types of fiction in China: literary-language (*wenyan*) fiction and vernacular (*baihua*) fiction. Since both were fiction, they were related in many aspects, and historians of Chinese fiction often discuss them in the same book or the same chapter.

Upon careful examination, however, they share little in common, except for some stock subject-matter.[1] Indeed they do not share even subject-matters. The two types of fiction were so different in their origins, in their course of evolution, in their formal characteristics, in the exertion of authorship, and in expected audience that they should be considered as two different genres. It would be hard to imagine a vernacular *Six Chapters of My Floating Life* (*Fusheng Liuji*), or a literary-language *Water Margin* (*Shuihu Zhuan*), not only because the literary language is too subtle and refined, or the vernacular too crude and copious, but because the two have entirely different narratological conventions and interpretative expectations.

It is not until the beginning of the twentieth century that the two kinds of fiction begin to reach out for each other, which is a topic this book is going to deal with.

For the sake of convenience, the term 'Chinese traditional fiction' denotes vernacular fiction in the present book, if not otherwise qualified. Fortunately, no works of significance in the literary language were produced after the last glorious performance in this genre in Pu Songling's *Strange Stories from Liaozhai* (*Liaozhai Zhiyi*, c.1680) and Ji Yun's *Notes in the Yuewei Hermitage* (*Yuewei Caotang Biji*, c.1799).[2] This makes our discussion simpler. Lin Shu's translation of Western fiction during the late Qing dynasty stimulated literary-language fiction

---

[1] e.g. the numerous novels about prostitution (*Xiaxie Xiaoshuo*) in the second half of the 19th cent. can be said to have continued a time-honoured tradition started by the Tang Dynasty literary-language fiction about prostitution.

[2] There were some noted imitators of Pu Songling and Ji Yun at the end of the 19th cent., e.g. Wang Tao with *Songyin Manlu* and Yu Yue in *Youtai Xianguan Biji*. None of them is of any literary merit.

so that it enjoyed a momentary recovery. This, again, will be addressed in our discussion.

The term vernacular fiction does not apply to the fiction works of the May Fourth New Literature even though those works are in the vernacular, since by that time the literary language was virtually ousted from literary practice, eliminating the antithesis between the literary language and the vernacular.

Another point concerning genres that has to be clarified here is that the works of the traditional vernacular fiction to be discussed in this book are mostly novels, while those of the May Fourth fiction are mostly short stories. There is then a danger that inappropriate comparisons might be made between the two different genres, as novels and short stories are definitely distinct from each other in aspects such as plot structure and time scheme. However, in most narratological characteristics—the main subject of this book—they are so similar that they can be considered two sub-genres under one heading.

Many scholars have tried to offer an explanation for the strange fortune of the Chinese vernacular short story, which, after enjoying spectacular blooming in the sixteenth century, disappeared from Chinese literature, yielding the stage to novels for the ensuing three centuries. Although the disappearance was not complete and there were more than thirty collections of vernacular short stories produced from the seventeenth to the nineteenth centuries, they are, on the whole, insignificant, attracting little attention then and now. The neglect of short stories became so serious that many of the sixteenth-century and earlier short story collections were lost, and were only rediscovered by modern scholars after the 1930s, many in Japan, and most were not reprinted until after the 1960s.[3]

Hu Shi argued that this disappearance was caused by the two eighteenth-century novels *The Scholars* (*Rulin Waishi*) and *Mirror for Flowers* (*Pinhua Baojian*), which succeeded in stringing short stories into a novel.[4] Lu Xun holds that the disappearance was due to the fact that in the eighteenth century short stories became too didactic to survive.[5] Meng Yao suggests that the achievements of the late Ming short

---

[3] Among them were one of the most important late Ming collections, Ling Mengchu's *The Second Collection of Amazing Stories* (*Erke Pai'an Jingqi*), of which the complete text of 40 stories was reprinted in 1960, and also the early Qing collections, Mengjue Daoren's *The Third Collection of Amazing Stories* (*Sanke Pai'an Jingqi*, repr. 1987) and Shengshui Aina Jushi's *Idle Talk under Bean Arbour* (*Doupeng Xianhua*, repr. 1961).

[4] Hu Shi 1929: book 2, ii. 167.   [5] Lu Xun 1956: viii., 89.

story were too great for later writers to compete with.[6] Apparently none of these probable causes was decisive. I would venture to say that the traditional short story was, generally speaking, a sub-genre that belongs to the early stage of Chinese vernacular fiction, and was bound to the rewriting mode characteristic of this period. Most of the short stories in late Ming collections were rewritten versions based on oral narrative, or on plays, or on anecdotes from historical writing. The pieces that we can recognize as the creative writing of the Ming compilers amount only to a small part of the total. It seems that the generic conventions of vernacular short stories had created the audience's expectation that when they picked up a short story collection, they could read old stories retold. That is why, I suggest, the vernacular short story did not survive the Rewriting period.

Vernacular short stories reappeared in the first decade of the twentieth century. Some late Qing fiction writers, especially the so-called 'Butterfly' writers, tried their hand at this sub-genre.[7] Those short stories, however, received little attention in comparison with the success of novels. Chinese literary critics at that time held that brevity was the distinguishing characteristic of Western fiction, whereas being enjoyably lengthy was a great advantage of Chinese fiction. Many of the the May Fourth writers acknowledged their indebtedness to two traditions: Western short stories (not many Western novels seem to have been carefully read by the May Fourth writers), and Chinese traditional vernacular novels (almost none of these writers mentioned Chinese short stories).

The serious result of this subgeneric separation is demonstrated in the fact that while most short stories of the May Fourth period were distinctly modern narratologically, the few novels of this period were more reminiscent of traditional Chinese novels. Both Zhang Ziping's *Fossils from the Alluvial Age* (*Bingchuan Qi Huashi*, 1922) and Yang Zhengsheng's *The Jade Girl* (*Yu Jun*, 1925) are very close to late Qing-Butterfly fiction. Jiang Guangci's *The Young Wanderer* (*Shaonian Piaopo Zhe*, 1925) reads like a vernacular rewriting of the late Qing writer Su Manshu's literary-language autobiographical novels. Except for a very few works such as Lao She's *Zhang's Philosophy* (*Lao Zhang de Zhexue*,

---

[6] Meng Yao 1966: 304.
[7] e.g. Wu Jianren's *Thirteen Stories by Jianren* (*Janren Shisan Zhong*); Liu Lengtie's *Lengtie Suimo*. Some of the Butterfly magazines, e.g. *Xiaoshuo Congkan* under Cheng Shanzhi's editorship, *Xiaoshuo Daguan* under Bao Tianxiao's editorship, carried short stories in almost every issue.

1926), no novel of the period can be counted as among the outstanding works of May Fourth fiction.

Since it appears that short stories and novels have in turn been the dominant genre in Chinese fiction, there will be no generic confusion in my comparing the major works of traditional fiction (mostly novels) and those of May Fourth fiction (mostly short stories). In fact, the shift from the dominance of novels to that of short stories is itself an important aspect of the drastic transformation of Chinese fiction early this century.

To redress the imbalance, I shall include in my discussion some late Ming short stories and some May Fourth novels despite the fact that they were not the major works of those periods.

II

The above generic discussion has already touched upon the problems of the periodization of Chinese vernacular fiction.

The pre-historical period—the period of oral narration—of Chinese vernacular fiction extended through many centuries. Mentions of oral narrative performance are found in poetry and literati essays (*biji*) since the mid-Tang (eighth to ninth centuries AD).[8] Written narratives started to be produced about five centuries later, in the Southern Song period (twelfth to thirteenth centuries AD), though we hardly have any texts dating with certitude from this period.[9]

The characteristic of the first period of Chinese fiction is a continuous rewriting by successive anonymous editors. Because of the lack of authorship, editorship asserted itself through repetition. This Rewriting period, beginning from the Southern Song, lasted for more than four centuries, until the end of the sixteenth century, some time between 1582 and 1602, when *The Goden Lotus* (*Jin Ping Mei*) was written.

[8] Hu Shiying in his voluminous study of *huaben* fiction tries to push the history of oral story-telling up to pre-Qin times, but he also acknowledges that story-telling as a regular genre of popular entertainment did not occur until the Tang Dynasty (Hu Shiying 1980: 12–25).

[9] The earliest extant written texts of vernacular fiction that can be dated more or less with certainty are *Five Fully Illustrated Pinghua* (*Quanxiang Pinghua Wuzhong*) and *Events in the Xuanhe Reign of Song* (*Da Song Xuanhe Yishi*), generally held to be Yuan-revised Song texts, and both eventually incorporated into other novels. However, Liu Dajie argues that among the *Five Fully Illustrated Pinghua*, the only probable intact Song text was the *Newly Compiled Pinghua on the Five Dynasties* (*Xin Bian Wudaishi Pinghua*) (Liu Dajie 1957: 462–4).

Some critics hold that *The Journey to the West* (*Xiyou Ji*, which was produced between 1550 and 1580, earlier than *Jin Ping Mei*) is the first masterpiece of creative writing by one author. However, research in recent years has found at least four earlier or contemporary novels, not counting dramatic versions, with more or less the same story and the same characters.[10] Thus *Jin Ping Mei* could be considered to stand at the threshold between the Rewriting period and the Creative period, as it is the first Chinese novel completely created by one author, even though its story evolves from an episode in an earlier novel *Water Margin* (*Shuihu Zhuan*). The fact that *Jin Ping Mei* later exists in several versions does not make it a work of the Rewriting period since those later versions, like those of many novels of the Creative period, are variations of the same text. The versions of the Rewriting period, on the contrary, are changed so much that they can hardly be considered to be of the same text.

The practice of rewriting persisted even after *Jin Ping Mei*—Feng Menglong's rewriting of *Subduing the Sorcerer* (*Pingyao Zhuan*) and *The Forgotten Text of the Sui History* (*Sui Shi Yiwen*) was done in the early seventeenth century. But Feng's rewriting of the two novels finalized their history of rewriting. Generally speaking the Rewriting period ended in the late sixteenth century, since after that time rewriting, though still practised, was no longer the major mode of fiction production.

In the following discussion I shall make use of the comparison between the two versions of *Jin Ping Mei* which seem to straddle on the two sides of the narratological threshold, one almost leaving the Rewriting period and the other embarking on the Creative period. A study of the *Cihua* version of 1617 and the *Chongzhen* version of the 1620s can serve to illustrate the difference in the conventions of the two

[10] The four novels are: the novel that provided the excerpt included in the *Yongle Encyclopedia*; the novel that provided the chapter reprinted in the Korean Textbook of Chinese Language *Pak tong sa on hae*; Zhu Dingchen's *Tang Sanzang Xiyou Shi'e Zhuan*; Yang Zhihe's *Xiyou Jizhuan*. The latter two might not be versions on which the present version of *The Journey to the West* is based. They at least prove that there were many rewritings of the same story in the Ming period. Some of the episodes in the novel may be traced back to ancient works such as *Shan Hai Jing*, *Hanwu Gushi*, *Baopu Zi*, and others, the earliest dated the 4th cent. BC.

Another novel, *The Investiture of Gods* (*Fengshen Yanyi*), was produced by Xu Zhonglin sometime between 1567 and 1619, almost at the same time as *Jin Ping Mei*, but it was definitely a rewriting. The predecessors for *The Investiture of Gods* are easier to identify: *Wuwang Fa Zhou Pinghua*—one of the earliest *Pinghua*, and the Li Jing stories in the archives of Dunhuang Caves, among others.

periods.[11] The *Chongzhen* version, which came out only a few years later than the 1617 *Cihua* version, seems to be a complete overhaul of the original version (which could be the *Cihua* version). The *Cihua* version retains a great deal of the conventions simulating oral perform-ance established during the Rewriting period, while the *Chongzhen* version deleted most of them, reducing the oral features in the narrative scheme to the generic minimum.

With *Jin Ping Mei* began the Creative period which brought Chinese fiction to its zenith in the seventeenth and eighteenth centuries when *The Scholars* (*Rulin Waishi*, c.1735) and *The Dream of the Red Chamber* (*Honglou Meng*, 1750–90) and other novels were written.

After the golden century of Chinese fiction, writers themselves felt that they could hardly hope to produce novels comparable with these masterpieces.[12] Mediocrity seemed to be stifling Chinese fiction all through the nineteenth century, and traditional Chinese fiction was ir-revocably in decline. Narratologically, Chinese fiction of the nineteenth century seems to be more or less a return to the rewriting mode, with a series of popular *Gong'an* (crime cases) novels like *The Cases of Lord Shi* (*Shigong An*, 1824), *Three Heroes and the Five Gallants* (*Sanxia Wuyi*, 1879), *The Cases of Lord Peng* (*Penggong An*, 1892), most of which have a number of recensions.

By the end of the Qing dynasty, around the turn of the twentieth century, however, traditional Chinese fiction enjoyed an unexpected revival, which lasted until after the fall of the Qing Dynasty, and its aftermath, the Butterfly fiction, continued well after the May Fourth Movement, and enjoyed a larger audience than the new writers until as late as the 1930s.[13]

Both the late Qing period and the May Fourth period were preceded by theoretical pronouncements. Liang Qichao's 1902 essay 'On the

[11] The extant versions of Jin Ping Mei basically belong to 2 lineages. One is Guben *Jin Ping Mei*, originally printed during the Chongzhen Reign (1621–8). In the early 1930s a different version—*Jin Ping Mei Cihua*—was discovered which purported to have been written by someone under the alias Lanling Xiaoxiao Sheng, and was printed in 1617 during the Wanli Reign. Until now, no proof has been found of an earlier printing of *Jin Ping Mei* than the *Cihua* edition, though the existence of hand-scribed copies of the novel was mentioned by noted scholars of the time.

[12] Yu Yue said in the preface to the novel *Seven Heroes and Five Gallants* (*Qixia Wuyi*): 'We are inferior to our ancestors not only in learning, or poetry, or prose. Even in drama and fiction, recent works are far inferior to those of the Qianlong and Jiajing reigns [1736–1820].'

[13] Link 1981: 8.

Relations Between Fiction and Mass Politics' ('Lun Xiaoshuo yu Qunzhi zhi Guanxi') for his magazine *New Fiction* (*Xin Xiaoshuo*) started the upheaval of late Qing fiction, while Hu Shi's 1917 essay 'A Modest Proposal for the Reform of Literature' ('Wenxue Gailiang Chuyi') written for the magazine *New Youth* (*Xin Qingnian*) was commonly held to be the starting-point of May Fourth fiction.

As for the date of the ending of the May Fourth period, I prefer the date suggested by the editors of the colossal *Omnibus of New Chinese Literature* (*Zhongguo Xin Wenxue Daxi*, 1932)—the year 1927—thus giving ten years to May Fourth fiction. It is a coincidence that the date fits neatly into the political chronology of modern Chinese history. If it was around 1927 that Lu Xun happened to lay down his fiction-writer's pen, and the leading May Fourth critic Shen Yanbing became the leading novelist Mao Dun, it is then not just politics that made 1927 the ending date of the May Fourth period. Hu Shi, as the editor of the Volume of Theory of the *Omnibus* complained, 'The New Literature so solemnly advocated by my friends and myself more than ten years ago has now come under attack from the new critics, and my friends and I have gradually been regarded as the last representatives of the outdated Victorian era.'[14] He felt that the history of Chinese literature entered a new period 'more then ten years' after he started to advocate the New Literature, and he was right. In a sense, this post-May Fourth period lasted for half a century, until the mid-1980s, and is beyond the current study. Nevertheless, the Epilogue of this book will briefly examine how Chinese fiction fared in the rest of the century, the course of which was more or less foreshadowed by our analysis, just as in the beginning part we shall review traditional Chinese fiction before the twentieth century.

The above discussion can be summed up in the following chart:

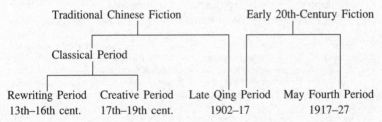

Traditional Chinese Fiction		Early 20th-Century Fiction	
Classical Period			
Rewriting Period	Creative Period	Late Qing Period	May Fourth Period
13th–16th cent.	17th–19th cent.	1902–17	1917–27

[14] Zhao Jiabi 1935: Volume I of Literary Theory 30.

In the chart, I venture to use some terms without providing sufficient justification, as they are mostly for the sake of convenience. For instance, though the term 'late Qing fiction' is generally accepted among students of Chinese fiction, it is obviously an anachronism, as here it also covers the six years after the fall of the Qing Dynasty in 1911 before the eve of the May Fourth period.[15] Fortunately, most of the important works which I shall discuss were produced before the fall of the Qing, leaving the period after the fall of the dynasty as an anticlimax.

My discussion is based mainly on the comparison of the four periods of Chinese fiction. But besides the vertical comparison, I shall also touch on the difference between the four major thematic types of traditional Chinese fiction, the four types first suggested by Lu Xun—the historical (*Jiangshi*), the heroic (*Yingxiong Chuanqi*), the fantasies (*Shenmo*), and the novel of manners (*Shiqing*).[16] The four major subjects appeared in the Rewriting period one by one, until mundane romances pushed Chinese fiction out of the Rewriting period into the Creative. Interestingly, the four major subjects reappeared in late Qing fiction, again one by one, with much shorter time-span, until the novel of manners put an end to traditional Chinese fiction with its enormous commercial success.

The Creative period of Chinese fiction coincided with the emergence of the Western neo-classical novel in the seventeenth and eighteenth centuries. The novel in the West was a rising genre at the time, gradually gathering impetus, and testing the limits of its power. Overlapping in time with the Creative period of Chinese fiction, they had much in common. Jaroslav Prusek, the eminent Czechoslovak scholar of Chinese literature, suggests that it is worthwhile making a parallel comparative study of Chinese fiction of this period with 'English literature at the beginning of the modern times, and particularly in the seventeenth and eighteenth centuries', and he concludes from the comparison that

[15] Some critics have suggested other terms, e.g. 'New Fiction', after the name of the influential first Chinese-fiction magazine founded by Liang Qichao in 1902. Jaroslav Prusek, for instance, uses the term in his discussion of late Qing fiction (Prusek 1980: 106–12) Yet this term does not cover the whole range of fiction in this period, and is not convenient anyway as it has to be put in quotation marks on every occasion. Prusek 1980: 106, 112, and *passim*.

[16] Lu Xun 1956: viii. *passim*. The terms used by Lu Xun are rendered in more or less the same way in this book as in Hsien-yi and Gladys Yang's translation of Lu Xun's *A Brief History of Chinese Fiction* (1957). There are, however, some terms where my translations differ from those of the Yangs. Explanations are not given on each such occasion, since the Chinese originals are provided in the text and also in the Glossary.

Chinese fiction was 'more penetrating or at least more profound'.[17] However, he does not explain why its penetrating and profound nature failed in the ensuing centuries to maintain its promise. My comparative study, concentrating more on cultural conditions, will perhaps lead to a different conclusion.

[17] Prusek 1980: 85. Etiemble seems to agree with this evaluation as he argues that *The Dream of the Red Chamber*, 'où le merveilleux et le réel sont intimement intégrés, est d'une psychologie qui ne déparerait pas un roman de Dostoievski,' and that after Wu Jingzi and Liu E's novels on the decline of Chinese society 'Faut-il penser . . . que l'Empire du Milieu était fort en retard sur l'Europe à cet égard et devait adopter le roman des barbares de l'Ouest?' (Etiemble 1974: 220)

2

Late Qing Fiction

I

In chapter 46 of *The Bureaucrats* (*Guanchang Xianxing Ji*), one of the few late Qing novels that is still read, an aged Imperial envoy refuses to accept a gift because it is a Western product. His lieutenant tries to persuade him, only to make him more annoyed. 'I am like a virtuous woman,' he says. 'who has remained chaste up to the age of sixty or seventy. Why should I lose my chastity at this late time?' (GCXXJ, 324).

The anecdote, though funny, is an appropriate illustration of the frustrated yet obstinate mind of the mandarin-literati power élite at the end of the last century, when the world's longest civilization was on the verge of disintegration under the military and commercial invasion of the Western powers.[1] The senility as well as the rigidity of Chinese culture made it less capable of coping with the situation. Its determination to stay uncontaminated, however, was destined to give way. The slow and gradual process of Westernization began with the importing of foreign weapons, and later foreign machines for the manufacture of weapons. The guideline for this officially controlled Westernization was 'Chinese Learning the Fundamental, Western Learning the Utilizable' (*Zhongxue Weiti, Xixue Weiyong*).

Repeated humiliations in the face of Western invasions, culminating in the total annihilation of China's Western-imported and Western-trained fleet in the Sino-Japanese War in 1895, and the foreign occupation of Beijing in the Boxer Rebellion of 1900, brought this officially endorsed 'utilizable westernization' to an end. The Chinese literati began seriously to consider what they should do in order to survive in the twentieth-century world.

Around the turn of the century, Chinese fiction experienced a miraculous reflowering after almost a century of mediocrity. The sheer

---

[1] The crisis should have come earlier, in the mid-19th cent., with the Opium War and the burning of the Imperial Summer Palace by the British and French forces. But the successful suppression of the Taiping Uprising and the Muslim Rebellion in the 1860s and 1870s created a false impression of a 'resurgence' of the Qing Dynasty. The sense of crisis did not reach the majority of the élite until the end of the 19th cent.

number of works of fiction produced in this period warrants attention. According to A Ying's catalogue, about 1,100 volumes of fiction (novels or short-story collections) were published at this time, as compared with a total of little more than 300 in the preceding seven centuries. In the year 1903 alone, for example, seventy-six volumes of fiction, either translations or original works, were published—more than the sum total of the previous half century. Late Qing fiction boasts more than 300 authors and translators and more than 100 magazines, solely or mostly devoted to fiction.[2]

Among the factors contributing to the flourishing of late Qing fiction, the most important was of course the modern media—newspapers and magazines.[3] The centre of this literary ferment was Shanghai, where literature benefited from the fast-growing publishing industry with modern printing facilities, and the new urban reading public. By this time fiction was in great public demand. Most late Qing novels were first serialized in fiction magazines before being printed in book form though many of them never appeared as books at all. In other words, a late Qing novel was most likely to have been published chapter by chapter before the author had even finished the whole book. Some more prolific writers could proceed with several novels at the same time so long as they managed to meet the respective deadlines.[4] This is a very important factor which accounts for many formal features of the fiction of this period.

Yet it would be misleading to think of late Qing fiction as something produced only for commercial purposes. On the contrary, its arrival was heralded as a serious search for a powerful weapon to save the nation, i.e. by something new in China—the evaluation of the cultural function of fiction.

[2] Zheng Fangze 1983: 392–400.
[3] The history of modern mass media in China is a short one. In 1862 an English journalist published *Shanghai Miscellany*, the first magazine in China. In 1872 the first Chinese newspaper in Chinese, *Shen Bao*, was founded in Shanghai by another Englishman. Beginning from the end of the last century, low-class tabloids for leisure reading began to mushroom in Shanghai. The first one, *Playful Paper (Youxi Bao)*, was founded by a leading late Qing novelist, Li Boyuan.
[4] Wu Jianren was said to be able to 'write thousands of words without even stopping to think about them', as he 'never made a draft' (Xin Xiang, 'Talking About Fiction' ('Shuo Xiaoshuo'), YYXS 1906, i). Li Boyuan was believed to be writing seven novels simultaneously, including his best novel *The Bureaucrats*, toward the end of his life. His novel *The Hell for the Living (Huo Diyu)* was left unfinished upon his death in 1906, and his two friends, Wu Jianren and Ouyang Juyuan, each contributed one chapter to finish the serialization.

The three most influential critical essays calling for a 'New Fiction' were Yan Fu and Xia Zengyou's 'Why *Guowen Bao* Adds a New Section of Fiction' ('*Guowen Bao* Fuying Shuobu Yuanqi', 1897), Liang Qichao's 'Introduction to the Translation and Printing of Political Fiction' ('Yiying Zhengzhi Xiaoshuo Xu', 1898), and 'On the Relation Between Fiction and Society' ('Lun Xiaoshuo yu Qunzhi Guanxi', 1902).[5] The last, being the most important critical essay on fiction in the late Qing, served as a *de facto* manifesto for the great boom of fiction production in the ensuing years. All the most important late Qing novels appeared (or rather, started being serialized) in the three years after the publication of the article, i.e. during 1902–4.

Literary historians today are generally shocked by the excessive exaggeration of these essays, in which the leading reformist theoreticians set the tone for late Qing fiction. In his 1902 manifesto Liang Qichao placed the blame for all the evils in Chinese society onto the previous 'unreformed' vernacular fiction:

Today our people are so frivolous, indulging in lust . . . and even abandoning themselves to immoral behaviour that runs rampant all over China. I say: this is because of fiction. Today outlaws are all over our country . . . and the Boxers went so far as to take over the capital and provoke foreign interference. I say: this is because of fiction. (Liang Qichao 1941: x. 7)

The main culprits in his accusation were unmistakably *The Dream of the Red Chamber* and *Water Margin*.[6] The new fiction he proposed was to perform a similar miracle in society, only this time a good one:

In order to make a new start for our nation, there must be a new start for fiction. In order to acquire a new morality, there must be a New Fiction; in order to establish a new religion, there must be a New Fiction; in order to practise a new politics, there must be a New Fiction. Even the new mind and the new personality have to rely on a New Fiction. Why? Fiction has an unbelievable power to mold the people. (*Ibid.* 9)

---

[5] Some scholars today hold that the earliest call for public attention to the social function of fiction was in 1872 with Lushao Jushi's preface to the translation *Xinxi Xiantan* (*Idle Talks about Strange Lands*). The 'translation' was actually a sinicized adaptation of parts of *Gulliver's Travels* and 'The Legend of Sleepy Hollow'. The preface, however, failed to attract any attention at the time.

[6] In his 1898 article mentioned above, Liang Qichao reviewed the whole history of Chinese fiction with contempt: 'Though listed among the nine strata, there have been hardly any good works of fiction. Novels about heroes are all on the *Water Margin* model, fiction on sexual relations all imitates *The Dream of the Red Chamber*. On the whole, they do nothing more than incite robbery or induce licentiousness. One after another, they all follow the same beaten track. That is why people of good taste despise fiction.'

This megalomaniac manifesto came as a shock to the Chinese mind, and provided a great impetus or at least an effective moral justification for fiction writing. Its basic argument virtually became the guideline for Chinese fiction till around 1907. Many critics followed Liang and pushed his re-evaluation of the importance of fiction to ridiculous extremes. Tao Youzeng, for instance, in his essay 'On the Power and Influence of Fiction' (1907) extolled fiction as 'the great wave that shakes the East and West ... the guideline for the development of the nation ... the ignition for the progress of learning ... the power line for the civilization of the society ... the great foundation of the prosperity of the nation'.[7]

Liang Qichao's claim that 'fiction is the highest genre of literature' was unprecedented in the history of Chinese culture. Before him, there were occasional high praises of vernacular fiction, e.g. Jin Shengtan's comparing *Water Margin* to *Zhuangzi*. But those were recommendations of individual works. As a genre, vernacular fiction was never highly esteemed before the late Qing.

However, Liang Qichao's dismissal of all previous Chinese works of fiction as harmful shows that he in fact has not misunderstood the role of fiction in Chinese culture. His endorsement of the so-called New Fiction was for a very practical purpose—to find an efficient propaganda tool for his reformist political movement. Popularization, then, was the foremost consideration in his favouring of vernacular fiction, and he did not even mention the need for a change in narrative form, as traditional fiction, in his view, was sufficiently effective in popularizing ideas.[8] He, and many others like him, did not realize that the New Fiction, traditional in form, would be new only in a very limited sense, and could easily relapse into the old mode.

This aim of popularization brought in a powerful conservative element—the readership, which is slower to change than the authors. Xu Nianci, editor of *Xiaoshuo Lin*, advised in his article 'My View on Fiction' ('Wo zhi Xiaoshuo Guan'):

I have seen young shop-assistants reading all day volumes of *The Three Kingdoms*, or *Water Margin*, or *The Tale of Tang* (*Shuo Tang*), or *The Tale of Yue Fei* (*Shuo Yue*), or even licentious novels, to kill time, pausing only when they have to attend to customers. No one reads new works, since the translations are

[7] A Ying 1960: 39.
[8] He himself, however, was a conscious experimenter in new fiction technique. His *The Future of New China*, though unfinished, was one of the most innovative fiction works of the late Qing.

full of weird foreign names that discourage readers, and the books written recently by Chinese writers have too many new terms that cannot be found in dictionaries. I insist that writers and translators publish books specially for these shop assistants on thin paper with Chinese bindings, with chapter-divisions of Chinese style, in vernacular language ... (XSL, 9, no. 10)

From his advice we can see how the serious concern with immediate popular appeal and social effect became a decisive force in preserving tradition.

Nevertheless, it would be rash to conclude that popular success was the sole reason why narratological conventions persisted in late Qing fiction. Some fiction works, having adopted, to different degrees, the new techniques learned from translated fiction, also became popular.

Late Qing fiction, as compared with eighteenth-century Chinese fiction, has suffered from a relatively low evaluation by students of Chinese fiction. But, in the early days of the May Fourth Movement, when modern Chinese fiction had not yet taken shape, several late Qing works of fiction were even envisaged as being part of a modern Chinese literature. This shows that late Qing fiction is not completely traditional in nature. There are some new elements in it that differ markedly from previous Chinese vernacular fiction.[9]

Hu Shi, in his essay initiating the May Fourth literary movement 'A Modest Proposal on the Reform of Literature' ('Wenxue Gailiang Chuyi') of January 1917 declared:

I have often said of today's literature that no work can be favourably compared with the world's first-rate literary works except for vernacular fiction (such as the novels by Wu Jianren, Li Boyuan and Liu E), because these works do not imitate ancient literature.[10]

His appraisal provoked a serious discussion among the May Fourth pioneers, not about the general estimation of late Qing fiction, but about which novels should be considered the best.[11]

---

[9] In the 1950s and early 1960s on Mainland China, under the slogan 'Favouring the Present but not the Past' (*Houjin Bogu*), a critical effort was made to re-evaluate Late Qing literature. Since it stemmed from political consideration, the reappraisal led to a distorted picture of late Qing fiction, leaving some important works neglected. This distortion also resulted in some regrettable shortcomings in the otherwise excellent collections of late Qing literature compiled in the 1950s by the noted scholar A Ying.

[10] Hu Shi 1929: book 1, i. 7.

[11] As a response to Hu Shi, Qian Xuantong tried to trace the Chinese tradition in vernacular literature, and held that there were only 6 novels in traditional Chinese fiction that were 'really worthy': the three classical masterpieces, *Water Margin*, *The Dream of the Red Chamber*, and *The Scholars*, and the three Late Qing novels, *The Bureaucrats*,

No matter what other differences there were, one thing was not in dispute among them: quite a few late Qing works of fiction ranked among the best works of fiction in China.[12]

II

It was Lu Xun who first subjected late Qing fiction to a comprehensive examination, and who, after selecting four novels as the most representative of this period, gave it the name 'Reprimanding fiction' (*Qianze Xiaoshuo*). This label is still accepted by many as it highlights the most salient feature of the important works of late Qing fiction. Late Qing fiction covers a much wider range of subject-matters than the term indicates, though it is true that the few best works are meant to reprimand.

The years 1902 to 1904 were great years for late Qing political fiction. In 1902 Liang Qichao founded the first Chinese fiction magazine *New Fiction* (*Xin Xiaoshuo*) in Yokohama, Japan, which was followed by many others in Shanghai. In the same year Liang Qichao began writing his utopian novel *The Future of New China* (*Xin Zhongguo*

Strange Events Witnessed in Twenty Years, and *A Flower in the Sinful Sea*. (XQN, Feb. 1917). Hu Shi, in his reply, disagreed with Qian's choice of the best Late Qing novels, and insisted that Liu E's *The Travels of Lao Can* should be chosen instead of Zeng Pu's *A Flower in the Sinful Sea*, and that Wu Jianren's *The Sea of Remorse* (*Hen Hai*) and *Nine Murders* were better than his *Strange Events*. He even called *Nine Murders* 'a novel of all the virtues' (Hu Shi 1929: book 1, i. 50). This sounds like an exaggeration, but Hu Shi repeated his opinion later in his critical work 'Chinese Literature in the Last Fifty Years' when he said, 'technically, *Nine Murders* is a most complete novel'. (Hu Shi 1929: book 2, ii. 85).

[12] Later critics, following Hu Shi, give higher praise to *The Travels of Lao Can*. T. C. Hsia, for instance, even holds that *The Travels of Lao Can* is a much better work than anything that the May Fourth writers could produce, because they were too much influenced by Western fiction: 'Lie E turned traditional fiction into something that can express the subtle feeling of the characters. It was a pity that the writers of the next generation only knew to imitate Western fiction that the almost-revolutionary achievement made by Liu E has never been recognized.' (Hsia 1976: 324).

The leftist critics usually praise *A Flower in the Sinful Sea* more than *The Travels of Lao Can*. A Ying, for instance, recommends the novel: 'The reason why this novel was so enthusiastically received at the time was because the progressive ideas expressed in it surpassed all the first-rate works of the time . . . Li Boyuan's and Wu Jianren's works are not comparable.' (A Ying 1937: 89).

His opinion is generally echoed by students of late Qing fiction after 1950. *The History of Chinese Literature* under the general editorship of You Guo'en, for instance, gives *A Flower in the Sinful Sea* much higher praise than *The Travels of Lao Can*, listing the former as 'Literature of Bourgeois Democratic Revolution' and other major late Qing novels under the heading of 'Literature of Bourgeois Reformation'.

Weilai Ji), and Chen Tianhua his *The Lion Roars* (*Shizi Hou*), the most influential of all late Qing political novels. In 1903, Li Boyuan began to serialize his *The Bureaucrats* as did Liu E his *The Travel of Lao Can* (*Lao Can Youji*) and Wu Jianren his *Strange Events Witnessed in the Last Twenty Years* (*Ershi Nian Mudu zhi Guaizhuang*, hereafter shortened to *Strange Events*). In 1904 Zeng Pu began *Flowers in the Sinful Sea* (*Nie Haihua*). All these novels took several years to complete.

The tide of political fiction began to ebb in 1907, with the publication of the magazine *Fiction Forest* (*Xiaoshuo Lin*). The critics associated with this magazine held that Liang Qichao and his followers' assertion of the social benefits of fiction was an exaggeration, and that Western fiction in China had already caused serious damage to society, and it was time to give fiction a sober appraisal and an appropriate position.

Huang Moxi in his publication announcement of *Fiction Forest* performed the first challenge to Liang Qichao's proposition:

Whereas fiction in the past suffered too much contempt, it is now given too much prominence . . . Every novel claims that it is making a great contribution to the progress of the nation, and every review tries to spotlight its purpose of reforming social customs . . . Even the laws of the state, the canons of religion, the textbooks used in school, the code of behaviour in the family and society are all said to depend on fiction. Can this be true? Can this be true?

And he proceeded unequivocally to the conclusion: 'Fiction is an aesthetic use of language.' (XSL 1, no. 1).

Other critics pushed his argument further. Xu Nianci, editor of *Xiaoshuo Lin*, argued: 'It is not fiction that begets society, but society that begets fiction.' He concluded that the entertainment purpose of fiction came before its moral effects or other 'lofty' aims.

Theoretically their stand was more reasonable, but in reality they ushered in something they did not anticipate—a popular entertainment fiction. The publication of *Xiaoshuo Shibao* (*Fiction Times*) in 1908, followed by dozens of other leisure fiction magazines, launched a new wave to meet the public demand for entertainment. The wave of romance fiction occupied the whole fiction market after the fall of the Qing Dynasty in 1911. Most of these romances were so unbearably sentimental that they won the name 'Mandarin Duck and Butterfly'—hackneyed symbols for tragic love (henceforth referred to as the Butterfly school or the Butterfly writers). But this school also produced works on other topics inspired by the new metropolitan life in Shanghai—notably the brothel scandals, and organized crimes of the underworld.

The Butterfly school openly declared that its sole purpose was to help killing time. Xu Zhenya, the major writer of this group, in the publication announcement of *Xiaoshuo Congbao*, made a low-key statement in a hedonist tone which was a striking contrast to Liang Qichao's high-sounding proposition only five years before:

Merely a low-class medium, fiction can hardly be concerned with the running of society. To pass away the after-meal leisure over a cup of tea, fiction only provides topics for gossipers ... Never mentioning politics even if there is no treacherous parrot present, it is only confined to romance or to a bookworm's life.[13]

It seems that late Qing fiction was in a cultural dilemma, swinging from one extreme to the other. The search for the cause of this 'hysteria' would be a fascinating topic for literary scholarship, though no one has yet provided a satisfactory explanation.

Butterfly fiction was a huge commercial success. Some of its novels enjoyed record print runs.[14] The access these Shanghai-based writers enjoyed to other modern mass media—stage performance and, later, moving pictures—greatly helped their popularity.[15]

Perry Link, in his comprehensive study of the Butterfly school, suggests that there were three waves in its development: romances in the decade up to 1910, scandal and detective novels between 1910 and 1920, and martial art novels in the late 1920s. Our discussion of late Qing fiction is only concerned with the first two. Though Butterfly fiction continued to enjoy enormous popularity after the May Fourth Movement almost none of its works are still read.

This school has hardly been mentioned in literary history except with contempt. The negligence is, indeed, probably because modern literary scholarship is the product of the May Fourth Movement, which naturally saw Butterfly fiction as one of its rivals.[16]

[13] Wei Shaochang 1982*a*: 56.

[14] After talking with the surviving Butterfly writers, Perry Link estimates that two novels by Xu Zhenya enjoyed a circulation of over 1 million, including the many reprints since their first publication (Link 1981: 53).

[15] e.g. *Orchid in the Deserted Valley* (*Konggu Lan*)—Bao Tianxiao's adaptation of the popular British novel *Flowers of Wilderness* by the woman writer Henry Holt—was successfully staged as Peking Opera and modern drama, and finally filmed in 1926. It was hugely popular in all these forms. His story 'A Skein of Hemp' ('Yilou Ma') was adapted for Peking Opera by the celebrated female-impersonator actor Mei Lanfang.

[16] Mao Dun, in his memoirs, recalled that for him and other May Fourth critics, there were three main opponents whom they had to combat—the conservatives of the old school, the Babbitt-trained new conservatives, and Butterfly fiction. He described how,

It seems strange that although all Butterfly writers and many May Fourth writers were based in Shanghai, they had almost no connection with each other. Their works almost never appeared in the same magazine. There was a very clear-cut gap between the two groups. Liu Bannong was once a writer and translator of detective fiction in the Butterfly school.[17] After joining the editorial board of *New Youth*, he became one of the leading critics of the May Fourth writers, and denied that what this group produced 'could be called literature at all' (XQN 3, no. 3). In fact it was he who gave his old friends in Shanghai the embarrassing nickname 'Mandarin-Duck and Butterfly'.

Other May Fourth writers, having no contact with the Butterfly writers, did not feel the need to restrain themselves in their use of language to show contempt. There appeared in their criticism of the school such cutting phrases as 'Street Men of Letters', 'Literary Beggars', 'Literary Whores', or even 'Masturbators of Words'.[18]

C. T. Hsia is perhaps the only scholar today who has a very high opinion of the Butterfly writers. He argues:

Though contemptuously dismissed by the partisans of the new literature for its lack of concern for social issues and its unawareness of the Western tradition, this fiction actually boasts of several practitioners who were in narrative skill

after he took over the major Butterfly fiiction magazine *Fiction Monthly* (*Xiaoshuo Yuebao*), he put on ice a huge number of manuscripts by Butterfly writers and translations by Lin Shu which the publisher had bought at a high price. His action greatly angered Butterfly writers and provoked a long-lasting dispute. However, after some years, the Butterfly writers managed to have their manuscripts printed in another magazine by the same publisher, because, after all, they made money (Mao Dun 1981: 245–67).

[17] Liu Bannong came to Shanghai in 1912 as a young man to join a new drama troupe, and made the acquaintance of Xu Banmei, an important Butterfly writer. After that he began to publish in Butterfly magazines until 1917 when he joined the *New Youth circle*. After a careful investigation I found several May Fourth writers who started their writing career, or at least tried their hand at fiction, in Butterfly magazines before joining the ranks of May Fourth writers. Ye Shengtao published almost a dozen stories in these magazines during his apprentice years; the early fiction of Shi Zhecun and Wang Tongzhao had a strong Butterfly flavour, though they might not have published in its magazines. Lu Xun certainly published his first story 'Huaijiu' ('Remembrance of the Past') in *Xiaoshuo Yuebao* in 1913, though, for reasons unknown, he did not write anything else in that mode.

[18] Scant acknowledgement to the Butterfly writers can be found in the works of some May Fourth writers. Zhang Ziping was frank in acknowledging his debt to Butterfly fiction, but this was natural as his work was perhaps the closest to it. Fu Sinian praised Bao Tianxiao's 'Yilou Ma' as 'having something in common with "problem drama"' (Zhao Jiabi 1935: Volume of Theory, 394). Lu Xun once praised Zhou Shoujuan's translation of European stories and, in the name of the Ministry of Education, sent Zhou a certificate of merit. Nevertheless, it is also obvious that the gap between the two groups was too wide to be covered by the occasional courteous exchange of nods.

much superior to their more ideologically enlightened fellow craftsmen. (Hsia 1961: 25)

Hsia's conservatism blinds him towards the achievements of the May Fourth fiction. None of the Butterfly novelists is comparable with the best of May Fourth writers, in narrative technique or other aspects. Most of the criticism by May Fourth critics of Butterfly fiction was directed against its conventional narrative technique and efforts toward pure entertainment. Such criticism is still valid today.[19] Hsia's argument, however, is correct in one sense: the neglect of Butterfly fiction has created a missing link in the study of the development of Chinese fiction.

Though Butterfly writers were generally well versed in Western literature—some were themselves fine translators of Western fiction—the fiction they produced definitely falls into the traditional mode. Butterfly fiction is the last phase of Chinese traditional fiction.

III

As I mentioned before, Lu Xun devides the subject-matter of Chinese vernacular fiction into four categories. The scope of subject-matter expands rapidly in the late Qing. The magazine *New Fiction* divided the fiction it carried into thirteen types according to subject-matter; another magazine, *Fiction Times* (*Xiaoshuo Shibao*), into twenty-four types; and a third, *Fiction Everymonth* (*Yueyue Xiaoshuo*), into forty types.

Today's critics often accuse Lin Shu, the greatest late Qing translator, of failing to be selective since he translated too many second-rate works—works by popular writers like H. Rider Haggard or Conan Doyle.[20] There might have been translators who were more selective (Zeng Pu, for instance, devoted his translation efforts to Victor Hugo, and rendered into Chinese novels like *93* and *L'Homme qui rit.*). But

---

[19] The 'superior craftsman' Hsia had in mind is perhaps Zhang Henshui who carried on much of the Butterfly tradition, but also brought in his own style which made him extremely popular in the 1930s. But he cannot be considered a 'fellow craftsman' contemporary of the May Fourth writers. Another 'superior craftsman' might be Su Manshu, the revolutionist–Buddhist–romanticist, whose fiction works this early century were extremely influential for the Butterfly writers, but he has never been counted by any literary historian as one of the group. I cannot think of any other Butterfly writers whose 'narrative skill' is worthy of Hsia's praise.

[20] This accusation is hardly fair. As Qian Zhongshu points out in his essay on Lin Shu, Haggard was after all not a bad writer (Qian Zhongshu *et al.* 1981: 89).

as is often the case with literary fortunes, the influence of a translation depends on many factors other than the artistic quality of the original work.

The omnivorous approach of the late Qing translators had at least one positive effect: the scope of subject-matter in late Qing fiction was expanded to a range much wider than traditionally conceived. Comparing *The Dream of the Red Chamber* with *The Old Curiosity Shop*, Lin Shu said in his preface to the translation of the latter:

[In society] there is after all more vulgarity than elegance, and people do not like to read the same thing repeatedly. Dickens, brushing aside the dominance of talents and beauties, focused on portraying people of the lower social strata ... I used to say that classical essays were the least capable of describing daily life ... Dickens, however, is especially good in depicting daily life, and at his best with the daily life of the lower classes. This is not a small accomplishment.[21]

This is more a piece of advice for Chinese literature than an evaluation of Dickens's fiction. But, paradoxically, in Chinese literature it was not the classical essay or literary-language fiction, but the vernacular fiction that was 'the least capable' of describing the misery of the lower classes. The suffering of the common people was a topic reserved almost exclusively for literati genres (poetry, essays, etc.). Popular literature has to entertain, and any description of misery in it should be shown to be a temporary one, soon to be replaced by a happy ending.

Lin Shu's call was answered. A number of vernacular novels and short stories devoted to the life of the lower classes appeared—novels like *Bitter Society* (*Ku Shehui*, on the life of the Chinese coolies and other immigrants in Peru and California) were perhaps not imaginable without Western examples such as *The Old Curiosity Shop* or *Les Misérables*.

The most conspicuous new subject-matter to appear in the arena of late Qing fiction was politics. The first attempt at a political novel was made by Liang Qichao with his *The Future of New China* in 1902. However, the novel progressed no further than five chapters before Liang found that what he had produced was 'neither novel, nor history, nor political treatise' and lost the courage to go on.

His failure did not stop other similar attempts. Chen Tianhua began to write *The Lion Roars* which lasted for about twenty chapters and stopped abruptly. Perhaps it was because the author did not know how

---

[21] Preface to *Xiaonu Nai'er Zhuan*, Shanghai: The Commercial Press, 1907, 3.

the revolutionaries in his novel could run the newly formed state. The author committed suicide in Japan during the political protest of December 1905.

Some of the political novels, e.g. *The Sword in the Boudoir* (*Guizhong Jian*) by Peng Yu (using the pen-name of Dongya Pofo), *The Yellow Flowery Globe* (*Huang Xiuqiu*) by Yi Suo, *The Mystery Bond by the Bloom* (*Saozou Qiyuan*) by Zhuang Zhe are actually more in the nature of pamphlets than fiction.

Many late Qing political novels are in fact reportage on recent or current events. *In the Teeth of Death* (*Si Zhong Qi Huo*, 1906–9) by Dui-jing Kuanghu Ke was a report on the Sino-French War of 1885, with a time-lag of about twenty years between the event and the novel. Hong Xinquan's *The War of the East China Sea* (*Zhongdong Dazhan Yanyi*) on the Sino-Japanese War of 1894–5 was published in 1900, after a gap of five years. The few novels on the Boxer Rebellion (1900) appeared about four or five years after the event. But when in 1905 the United States promulgated the Expulsion Law against Chinese immigrants, more than four novels on this topic followed rapidly with hardly a time-lag.[22] After that we find novels appearing right on the heels of the event: Huang Xiaopei's *Wind in Five Days* (*Wuri Fengsheng*) depicting, or rather reporting on, the Guangzhou Armed Uprising on 23 March 1911, was published only one month later (April 1911). What was more surprising was that there were even fiction magazines specially published to cover a certain topic in current events, e.g. *The Guangdong New Fiction Magazine for Combating Opium Addiction* (*Guangdong Jieyan Xin Xiaoshuo*), founded in 1907.[23]

More readily identified as reportage rather than fiction is the so-called Black Curtain fiction (*Heimu Xiaoshuo*), a branch of Butterfly fiction specializing in the activity of the Shanghai underworld—prostitutes, pimps, hooligans, Tong gangsters, and all other kinds of base characters. This was actually a kind of non-fiction, but there was no such concept at the time. Collecting together everything about the colourful Shanghai underworld, which was something dazzlingly new in China, these books were only faintly disguised as fiction. The Black

---

[22] Lin Shu's successful translation of *Uncle Tom's Cabin* was actually done for this special occasion, to remind people that the Chinese were being brought down to the same position as the black slaves.

[23] Vernacular novels about current events appeared as early as the late Ming during the period when the power-struggle between the *Qing Liu* (Clean Party) and the eunuch Wei Zhongxian became critical. But these 'novels' were frank political pamphleteering that did not even bother to pose as fiction.

Curtain novels were a great commercial success but despised by all other writers.

Quasi-science-fiction also made its way into Chinese vernacular fiction. Peng Xunzhi's novel *Double Soul* (*Shuang Linghun*) tells an extraordinary story of how the soul of a dead Indian policeman in the British Settlement in Shanghai sneaks into the head of a Chinese, so that the poor fellow is a Chinese in the morning and an Indian policeman in the afternoon. A Ying said that this was 'an imitation of Western fiction technique'.[24] I myself do not see traces of Western technique in it except for a loaned topos from such short novels as *The Strange Case of Dr Jekyll and Mr Hyde*. Fantasy, though by no means lacking in the history of Chinese fiction, now found a new justification from abroad. When *A Flower in the Sinful Sea* was accused of containing superstitious episodes, Zeng Pu defended his novel by citing examples from Mérimée's story about a bronze statue falling in love with a girl.[25]

By the end of the first decade of this century, detective novels had become best-sellers. According to the sales list of Xiaoshuo Lin Press, detective novels accounted for 70 to 80 per cent of sales.[26] The detective theme also entered other types of novels. In the marginal comments that Wu Jianren himself added to his *Strange Events* the hero is praised as 'almost a private eye'. In the comments to chapters 13 and 14, it is suggested that the book 'should be read as a detective case'. In *The Travels of Lao Can* the protagonist is involved in the solving of a murder case, and he is described in the novel as 'acting like a Sherlock Holmes'. In Wang Yunqing's novel *Viewed with Cold Eyes* (*Leng Yanguan*), the hero, who lodges in a hotel, follows up some mysterious activities in the neighbouring room, and his friend, after hearing his story, congratulates him, saying, 'How wonderful! How wonderful! . . . You acted like a private detective!' (LYG 56). As there were practically no private detectives in China at that time, the role model can only have come from translated fiction.

Nine Murders (*Jiu Ming Qiyuan*) and *The Travels of Lao Can* are the best known of 'serious' novels containing detective episodes, though those in the former have been acclaimed and those in the latter deplored by critics today. In the late Qing, detective novels were regarded by Chinese writers and critics as the best representative of Western fiction

[24] A Ying 1937: 113–14.
[25] Zeng Pu, preface to the new edition of *A Flower in the Sinful Sea*, NHH 4.
[26] Xu Nianci's statistics, *Xiaoshuo Lin*, 9 (1908).

techniques. Liu Bannong in his introduction to the Chinese translation of *The Complete Sherlock Holmes* praised Conan Doyle, saying that 'no other author is capable of such skilful crisscrossing and switching'. Xu Nianci's comment is more to the point: 'Detective novels are stronger in organization than in language; and better in form than in idea.' (XSL 1, no. 1).

Probably stimulated by Western examples, short stories re-emerged in China. Wu Jianren's *Thirteen Stories by Jianren* (*Jianren Shisan Zhong*, 1900) was one of the few short story collections before 1911. After 1911, however, short stories made frequent appearances in Butterfly magazines. Each of the leading writers of this school, Bao Tianxiao, Zhou Shoujuan, Xu Zengya, Li Dingyi, produced at least one collection of short stories.[27]

The plot structure of most of those 'short stories' is not distinctly different from that of novels. They are fiction short in length but not necessarily briefly narrated. Wu Jianren, at the beginning of his short story *The Wronged Souls* (*Heiji Yuanhun*) declares through a narratorial direction: 'The writers of fiction often use a prelude to evoke the main story by another story. This time I am writing a short story, but I would like follow their example and compose a prelude first, in order to win a smile from you gentlemen. The sparrow, though small, has all its intestines.'

In Wu Jianren's short story collection, the only true 'short story' is 'The Supervisor Calls' ('Cha Gongke') which tells how a Manchu Education Supervisor goes at midnight to the students' dormitory and searches for revolutionary newspapers. It resembles the plot structure of modern short stories.

Short stories produced at this time, of no matter what type, failed to impress the readers who were still eager for lengthy works. The authors themselves regarded their short story writings as by-products, and used such words for the titles of their collections as *Ink Splashes* (*Suimo*) or

---

[27] Some scholars hold that it was Bao Tianxiao who invented the term *duanpian xiaoshuo* as the Chinese equivalent for the English 'short story'. But I have discovered that in the founding issue of *Yueyue Xiaoshuo* (1907) under the editorship of Wu Jianren, 44 types of fiction are listed, with *duanpian xiaoshuo* appearing last, after such categories as 'Navigation Fiction' or 'Constitution Fiction', obviously as a rare subgenre of fiction.

The term 'short story', in its modern sense, is relatively new. It apparently did not appear in English until. 1880. The German word *Kursgeschichte* was coined around 1920. In French no term for it exists even now (neither *nouvelle* nor *conte* is the exact equivalent of *duanpian xiaoshuo*, and *récit court* has not yet been accepted by all). In this sense, Chinese writers were not lagging too far behind.

Ink Wasted (*Langmo*). In fact, almost no late Qing short stories are still read by the public today nor reprinted for the convenience of scholarship.[28] This is a pity as some of them contain interesting elements which presage a new direction for Chinese fiction.

---

[28] *Selected Short Stories of Wu Jianren*, edited by Zhong Xianpei, was published by Zhongzhou Guji Chubanshe in 1986.

3

May Fourth Fiction

I

The beginning of the modern age in China is generally considered to be the May Fourth Movement, named after the students' demonstration in Beijing on 4 May 1919. This is a misnomer since it may give the impression that the movement was a political event, and an eruptive one. The movement named after the students' demonstration that day was a gradual process, which had begun to be visible at the end of 1916 or the beginning of 1917, and continued for years after the event. The movement was essentially one of cultural criticism, non-political to a large extent, focusing mainly on such cultural issues as literature, language, education, and social customs, rather than on political issues such as how the constitution should be written, or how the bureaucracy should be organized, which had been the greatest concern of late Qing reformists and revolutionaries.

The movement met with strong hostility from the warlords in power who found the upgrading of the vernacular ideologically dangerous. More than once the government wanted to expel Chen Duxiu, Hu Shi, and Qian Xuantong from Beijing University. Their books were confiscated a couple of times. From the numerous students' magazines at that time we can see that officials in various provinces vehemently opposed the upgraded use of the vernacular too.[1] Fortunately the warlords were so preoccupied with fighting each other for the control of the regime that cultural issues were a low priority for them. All they could do was to issue repeated decrees reaffirming their adherence to Confucianism. Since China was virtually split, and each warlord group could exercise power only in one or two provinces of China, no threat to the new cultural movement was a real one. The enfeebled central government provided a rare opportunity for the greatest cultural re-evaluation movement in Chinese history.

What was special about the May Fourth Movement was that the most

---

[1] Xuanzhu, 'Cries of Opposition from All Sides' ('Simian Bafang de Fandui Sheng'), Zhao Jiabi 1935: Volume of Controversy and Dispute, 151.

influential sector of the new generation of intellectuals became the deviant sector. The movement as it was before some of its activists turned to participate in politics and join the struggle for power was still basically a movement of pure cultural criticism. At least in its early stages, the movement was only a cultural movement, and we have to understand it as such.

The movement was the most serious challenge to Chinese culture from within since the time when that culture had been forced to face the world about half a century before. It was also an effort endeavouring to give Chinese culture shake-up in almost every respect. What made the movement important to literary students was that it started from an argument about literature, and continuously engaged literature as its central issue, a fact deplored by some but praised by others. In all, it certainly presents itself as a good case for our study of the relationship between culture and fiction in modern China.

The evaluation of the May Fourth Movement or of May Fourth literature has always been a highly controversial topic among scholars. But nobody ever denies that it was the most important event in modern Chinese culture. Subsequently the structure of Chinese culture was forced to undergo a series of changes, though *not* in accordance with the ideal of the May Fourth pioneers. It is more than obvious that the May Fourth Movement did not and could not completely shatter the foundations of Chinese culture, which was much more resistant than the May Fourth pioneers had anticipated.

The May Fourth writers comprised a completely new generation. Writers who had dominated literature for the past twenty years—late Qing fiction writers including the Butterfly writers—were completely swept aside from the centre of the literaury arena. Such a 'generation cut-off' has rarely been seen in world literature.[2]

May Fourth literature can be divided into the following phases: the preparatory phase (1917–21), when there was more discussion than creative writing, and when the earliest May Fourth writers already achieved a convincing victory for the movement; the pluralistic phase (1921–5), when many coteries and schools emerged and diverged, though still converging into a movement; and the transforming phase (1925–7), when the 'Revolution of Literature' was gradually replaced by 'Revolutionary Literature'. Toward the end of this period there appeared the early attempts at Proletarian Literature.

---

[2] Shen Yanbing, in taking over *Fiction Monthly* (*Xiaoshuo Yuebao*), decided to ignore all established Butterfly writers.

Fiction is certainly the greatest achievement of May Fourth literature. Fiction writers, as Lu Xun pointed out, did not formally enter the
stage of Chinese literature until the May Fourth period, but once they
were there, they occupied its centre without challenge.[3]

The earliest May Fourth fictional work is Lu Xun's short story 'The
Madman's Diary' ('Kuangren Riji').[4] The maturity of its narrative technique is surprising, more surprising even than its vehemently iconoclastic content, though the latter has been more discussed. For young writers
at that time, the shock they felt most intensely in reading the story came
from the new narrative technique. Wang Tongzhao, then an aspiring
young writer, attests: 'I read Mr Lu Xun's 'Kuangren Riji' and 'Kong
Yiji', and was stunned. I was not by any means able to produce anything like this. I am afraid that even many young intellectuals at that
time were not able to understand it.'[5]

Mao Dun, in his memoirs, also recalls that since the content of the
whole issue of *New Youth*, in which 'The Madman's Diary' appeared,
was breathtakingly stunning from cover to cover, the content of the
story was not immediately striking.[6] Yet he repeatedly expressed his
admiration for Lu Xun as the greatest innovator of narrative forms.
In his important essay 'Reading *Battlecries*' ('Du Nahai', *Wenxue*, 90,
(October 1923)) he explains: 'In new Chinese literary circles, Mr Lu
Xun is often the pioneer in the innovation of forms. Almost every story
in *Battlecries* has a unique form, and each of the new forms exercised
great influence on young authors, inciting a large group of further
experimenters.'

Qian Xingcun (A Ying), one of the few radicalists who relentlessly
criticized Lu Xun for his 'backward ideology', also acknowledged that
'He was an important person in the promotion of new literature. But his
contribution was more in fiction technique than the ideas in his works.'[7]

[3] Prusek was right when he said: 'The literary history of the first twenty years of the
new Chinese literature is, above all, the history of narrative prose, and perhaps even
drama has a greater significance than poesy.' (Prusek 1980: 80).

[4] The first modern short story was 'A Day' ('*Yiri*') by Chen Hengzhe, a girl student
studying in the USA and published in *Quarterly of Chinese Students in U.S.* (*Liumei
Xuesheng Jibao*). By 'modern short story' we mean not only a story written in the
vernacular (as Chinese fiction had been written in the vernacular for a long time) but a
story with distinctive new narratological characteristics. Chen's story certainly qualified,
as it was totally free of any of the conventions of traditional fiction. However, the story
is only a playful recording of impressions of a girl student's life in Chicago University,
and it was published in a magazine with too limited a circulation.

[5] Wang Tongzhao, *Pianyun Ji*, Shanghai: Shenghuo Shudian, 1934, 90.

[6] Mao Dun 1981: 342.

[7] 'The Dead Era of A Q' ('Siquliao de A Q Shidai'), *Taiyang Yuekan* (*Sun Monthly*)
Mar. 1928, 15.

After 'The Madman's Diary' there came another shock—Yu Dafu's long story 'Sinking' ('Chenlun'). It was similarly regarded as non-literature in the first place. Yu Dafu recalls:

I showed 'Sinking' to some friends who were in Tokyo at that time. After reading it, they did not say anything. But behind my back they laughed, saying, 'Will this sort of thing ever be printed in China? How can there be a fiction like this in China?' At that time Chinese literature was a chaotic scene, and the magazine *New Youth* run by Hu Shi and others won sympathy only among a small number of students. Nobody expected that there could come such a drastic change in a few years.[8]

Many May Fourth fiction writers showed their contempt towards the narrative conventions by refusing to pay any attention to form. Guo Moruo declared, 'I am a man who hates form most, and I have never been attentive to form. The things I have written are only random dancing acted out totally on impulse.' (WXZB no. 131 (July 1924)). Yu Dafu also declared that his early stories were all 'playful writing . . . without rethinking or polishing'.[9] These statements are sincere and genuine. But what counted was not the self-statements of the practitioners but the general trend they actually helped to push and the 'language context' in which they had to work. Their *formlessness* was in fact the very condition of new forms.

The actual output of May Fourth fiction is surprisingly small, much smaller than that of late Qing fiction. In the late Qing period, an average of sixty books of fiction were printed every year, while in the May Fourth period, only a little more than ten books of fiction and other genres of the new literature appeared every year.

According to the bibliography compiled by the Commercial Press in 1923,[10] from 1917 to 1923 thirteen volumes of fiction, sixteen of poetry, one of drama, thirty-two of translated fiction, and thirty-nine others were published, making 159 in all. If translations are not counted, there were only two or three volumes of fiction every year in the early May Fourth period!

The output gradually increased. Five years later, Zeng Xubai wrote in his 'An Open Letter to New Writers' ('Zhi Xin Wenxue Jia de Gongkai Xin'):

Recently I looked into the publication of literature, and the result of this thorough investigation is unexpected disillusionment . . . more than ten years' endeavour

---

[8] Yu Dafu 1927: 56.   [9] Ibid. 58.
[10] Quoted in Chen Xiying 1928: 52.

produced only 200-odd literary volumes of translation and 100-odd works of creative writing, totalling a little more than four hundred ... There were no more than ten publishers and two hundred authors, well-known or little-known.[11]

This, of course, does not mean that the market for fiction was shrinking at this time. In fact there were great numbers of works of fiction in the traditional mode published during the ten years, mostly by Butterfly writers. But Butterfly fiction is so distinctively different from May Fourth fiction that there is almost no possibility of confusing the two, and no one has ever counted them together.[12]

In the *Omnibus of Chinese New Literature* (*Zhongguo Xin Wenxue Daxi*) under the editorship of Zhao Jiabi, all the active writers and critics of the May Fourth period are listed, including deadly opponents of the May Fourth movement such as Lin Shu, Mei Guangdi, and Zhang Shizhao, without a single Butterfly writer, critic, or editor. The demarcation line between them is too apparent to be ignored. Until today, there has been no anthology that includes both May Fourth fiction and Butterfly fiction. All historical studies of modern Chinese literature exclude Butterfly fiction in their discussion, and they do so without even offering a justification since Butterfly fiction has never been regarded as part of modern Chinese literature.[13] Yet it was the very small number of May Fourth works of fiction that was to become the mainstream of modern Chinese literature.

Among the little more than one hundred books of 'new literature' fiction published during this whole period, the overwhelming majority were short stories. Novels and short novels long enough to be published in a solo publication, amounted to less than twenty in all.[14] If we count

---

[11] Quoted by Chen Zizhan in 'Movements of Revolutionary Literature' ('Wenxue Geming Yundong'), Zhao Jianbi 1935: Volume of Historical Data, 423.

[12] Perry Link, when discussing Butterfly Fiction, notices the basic difference between the two coexisting literatures: 'The young writers of May Fourth proceed to establish themselves among a better-educated, and more Westernized, but substantially smaller readership than that of Butterfly writers. For the decade of the 1910s it thus becomes easier to identify Butterfly fiction as "popular" and May Fourth literature as "elite" in the modern sense of the terms.' (Link 1981: 11).

[13] It is only recently that some studies (e.g. Yang Yi, 1986) have appeared which give some space to the 'sentimental romance writers of Shanghai'.

[14] If we reduce the generally accepted standard length of 10,000 Chinese characters for novels to about 7,000 characters, there are still very few novels of this period. They are: 1922: Zhang Ziping, *Fossil of the Alluvial Age* (*Chongjiqi Huashi*) and Wang Tongzhao, *A Leaf* (*Yiye*); 1923: Wang Tongzhao, *The Twilight* (*Huanghun*); 1924: Zhang Wentian, *The Travel* (*Lutu*) and Yang Zhensheng, *The Jade Girl* (*Yujun*); 1925: Zhang Ziping, *Flying Catkin* (*Feixu*); 1926: Zhang Ziping, *Daili* and Shu Qingchun (Lao She), *Zhang's Philosophy* (*Lao Zhang de Zhexue*); 1927: Sun Menglei, *Yinglan's Life* (*Yinglan de*

the numerous stories published in magazines but not collected into books, the proportion of short stories is even greater.

The emergence of short stories as the major genre of fiction is itself a phenomenon with cultural implications. It seems to be common to nations at moments of discontinuity of cultural institutions, as can be witnessed in post-Cultural Revolution China, or in post-World War II Germany. According to Hans Bender, the short story is a genre open to various possibilities, and more suitable at a time of cultural transformation: 'If, in German writing after 1945, short stories experienced scepticism about language and the evocation of the real, their evolution tends to become not a form closed upon itself but a text that indicates openness.'[15]

Since the May Fourth Movement caused a rupture in cultural continuity, or a testing of orientations, short stories answered the need as a more appropriate form for cultural reorientation.

II

Wang Tongzhao's remark about 'The Madman's Diary' and other stories by Lu Xun (see above) and Yu Dafu's complaint about his friends' doubts of his works hint at a situation that may sound surprising—not even the young intellectuals at that time were able to understand these fiction works, let alone the general reading public. This might be attributable to the completely new devices employed in the works. Naturally, it always takes time for a new technique to create its audience. But there was another more important reason: May Fourth fiction (as well as poetry and drama) was not meant to be reading material for the broad masses, even though one of the movement's central issues purported to be 'using the language spoken by the common people for the production of literature'.

The central concern of late Qing fiction was popularization—reaching more readers by the most acceptable means. Although both late

---

Yisheng). Unfortunately, almost none of them can be said to be successful enough to win substantial discussion in most literary histories of modern Chinese literature. Lao She's *first novel* was welcomed by many readers at the time for its humour and Beijing local flavour, but was obviously immature in comparison to his later works. It is much discussed now only because it was the beginning of a dazzling writing career.

[15] This passage is my translation from a quotation in French by Prof. Victor Hell. He adds: 'Ni le roman d'éducation, ni *l'Entwicklungsroman* ne pouvait convenir, puisqu'il n'y avait pas eu d'éducation: on est passé brutalement de l'état d'enfance aux responsabilités de l'âge adulte, avoue Heinrich Boll.' (Hell 1976: 391).

Qing fiction and May Fourth fiction used the same means, i.e. the vernacular, what sets the two apart is not only language but something else—the narratological characteristics—which are more important than the language used in the fiction. May Fourth writers sometimes used the vague term 'style' to denote those essential formal features, as Shen Yanbing (who later used the pen-name Mao Dun) said when commenting on Lu Xun: 'For the young people, the greatest impact of "The Madman's Diary" is its style, as it provides the young people with a strong hint that they have to throw away the old wine bottle and use the new form to express themselves.'[16]

The difference between late Qing fiction and May Fourth fiction is also demonstrated by the social status of the protagonists. In the former, the protagonists are mostly literati-officials. The excuse the late Qing writers offer for looking for their characters in the higher social strata is that 'in order to enlighten the masses, we have first to enlighten the officials'. In Butterfly fiction, the protagonists are the marginal people of society—prostitutes, opera-singers, hooligans, or swordsmen, who were alien to the majority of the readers of late Qing fiction—mainly common people in the urban areas. The social composition of these protagonists seems to compensate for what the readers miss in their life. In May Fourth fiction the situation is entirely different: its readers are mostly students and young intellectuals, and its protagonists are mostly the same kind of people. Though Lu Xun started the trend of making peasants the protagonists, which was gradually followed by other writers, the majority of the protagonists in fiction remained young intellectuals until well after 1927. This is in fact a paradox constantly found in Chinese literature: to find their favourite protagonists, the popular mode usually goes up (to the top of society) or out (to the margins of society), while the élite mode tends either to turn back on itself, or condescend to the lowest social strata.

This explains why when modern mass media—local operas on contemporary themes, *huaju* ('talk' plays), and film in the 1920s—first appeared in Shanghai, they were more closely associated with Butterfly writers than with May Fourth writers. May Fourth writers and critics like Shen Yanbing or Fu Sinian kept talking about the necessity of 'reforming traditional Chinese drama'. As late as 1933, Shen Yanbing in his essay 'Literature of the Feudal Petty-Bourgeoisie' ('Fengjian de Xiaoshimin Wenyi') contemptuously denounced the most sensationally

---

[16] 'Reading *Battlecries*' ('Du Nahan'), WXZB 91 (Oct. 1923).

welcomed martial-art film of the time, *Fire in the Red Lotus Temple* (*Huo Shao Honglian Si*), as trash aimed only at arousing the blind emotions of the mob.

The clear-cut distance that the May Fourth writers tried their best to maintain in front of popular literature did not last long. Though the current study will not deal with the post-May Fourth development of Chinese fiction, the Epilogue will describe how Chinese fiction had to return to the popular mode under social and political pressure in the 1930s and 1940s.

PART TWO

The Narratological Development of Chinese Vernacular Fiction

1

Narrator's Position

I

Chinese vernacular fiction boasts a history of more than seven centuries, yet what strikes any Western reader is the surprising homogeneity of its narratological characteristics. It is astonishing that fiction should have adhered to a particular set of formulas for so many centuries.

According to many literary historians, Chinese fiction has its source in oral narrative performance, just as in many other cultures. But, unlike the fiction of many other nations, Chinese vernacular fiction retained a series of narratological and stylistic characteristics of oral narrative performance not only after the initial stage but all through the centuries until the early twentieth century. Indeed it was called tale-book (*pinghua*) or prompt-book (*huaben*) for a long time, and narration-book (*shuobu*) in later years.

These seemingly simple and neat names are, however, problematic. The term *huaben* could refer both to a prompt-book produced mainly for the reference of the story-teller, or to a recording of the performance of the story-teller produced for reading.

Many scholars of traditional Chinese fiction seem to be baffled by the problem. Lu Xun, when discussing *The Three Kingdom Pinghua* (*Sanguo Zhi Pinghua*, one novel in *Five Fully Illustrated Pinghua*), says, 'From the crudity we can see that it was a *huaben* for the use of oral performers'. But he also noted in the same paragraph that the fact that the edition printed during the Yuan dynasty was illustrated indicates that it was meant for reading.[1] Yet he makes the unequivocal statement, '*Huaben* were not [notes of] oral story-telling performance, but retained the style'.[2] It seems that he is unsure as to whether *huaben* were the actual notes for oral performance.[3]

Other scholars are less hesitant on this issue. For instance, the chapter on the *huaben* fiction of the Song period in the standard university textbook *History of Chinese Literature* (*Zhongguo Wenxue Shi*) compiled

[1] Lu Xun 1956: viii. 67.   [2] Ibid. 86.
[3] In Lu Xun (1959) the term huaben is translated as 'prompt-books' and *ni huaben* as 'imitations of prompt-books' wherever they appear.

under the chief editorship of You Guo'en begins with the sentence
'*Huaben* were originally the notes [*diben*] for oral performers', and
throughout the chapter, oral performance and early written vernacular
fiction are discussed together without any distinction made between
them.[4]

Andrew Plaks insists that such a supposition is only an 'idealization
that oral story-telling situation is assumed to present the original, radical,
unadulterated form of the narrative experience'. His argument, however, is based on the fact that oral story performances 'appear relatively
late in the long narrative tradition, and demonstrate considerable inter-
change with sophisticated written forms.'[5] What he meant by 'sophisticated written form' is fiction in the literary language. Like many
Western scholars of Chinese literature, he seems to take such fiction as
the predecessor of vernacular fiction. As I have already mentioned and
shall discuss in more detail below, the two were separated by so wide
a cultural gap that vernacular fiction should be considered an entirely
new genre and can hardly be considered a continuation of the tradition
of literary-language fiction.

The only vernacular narrative texts that can be definitely dated as
early the Tang period are the *Bianwen* found in the Dunhuang caves,
but they are all written in a vulgarized literary language and none of
them is written in a genuine vernacular. Furthermore, they do not have
any of the oral narrative characteristics that became the conventions of
traditional Chinese fiction. Among the extant texts of *Jiangshi fiction*
(historical novels) of the Song and Yuan periods, which is generally
considered to retain many of the features of Song oral narrative, is
Forgotten History of the Xuanhe Reign. Curiously, this is written in a
mixed language: the historical events are in the literary language while
the legendary events are in the vernacular. Many scholars, therefore,
consider it semi-*huaben*. This logic is at fault as the synoptic summary
in the literary language of this work is considered to be a true notation
of vernacular oral performance whereas the passages written in genuine
vernacular are only an imitation.[6]

Nie Gannu discovered that in *huaben* there are actually fewer oral-

---

[4] You Guo'en *et al*. 1979: iii. 144.   [5] Plaks 1977: 70, 327.

[6] Wilt L. Idema divides traditional Chinese vernacular fiction into 2 types: literary
novels by literary men, and the less refined 'chapbooks' by popular writers. What is
interesting are his criteria: literary novels use pure vernacular, while popular chapbooks
use simplified literary language. (Idema 1974: p. xi) His observation is, however, generally correct.

performance characteristics than in *ni huaben* (imitated oral narrative), as those directions of narration are totally unnecessary to the story-teller who knows only too well how and when to insert the convention-alized directions. In written narrative texts, however, such directions become necessary for the purpose of forming a narrative frame simu-lating oral performance.[7]

In literary history nowadays, the two terms—*huaben* and *ni huaben*—are generally loosely used for narrative texts of different periods: those of the Song and Yuan (from the twelfth to mid-fourteenth centuries AD) are called *huaben*, and those short stories (only short stories!) of Ming and Qing are called ni *huaben*.[8]

How can we explain the confusion? If we carefully examine the narratological conventions of traditional Chinese fiction, we can see that the earliest *huaben* fiction of the Song dynasty was considered by some people as more likely to be prompt-books for oral performance, for no other reason than the fact that they are skeleton outlines contain-ing very few oral narrative characteristics. Narratological conventions in later Chinese vernacular fiction became more reminiscent of those of oral performance. The contrast leads us to suspect that the 'oral' char-acteristics (which I shall elaborate in the following chapters) became part of the writing practice because they served some other purposes, the most important of which was to install a stereotyped narrative frame. Any proposition concerning the influence of oral narrative on tradi-tional Chinese fiction must, therefore, be carefully modified.[9]

Why, then, should traditional Chinese fiction adopt this set of narratological characteristics but not others? My suggested answer is that these seemingly 'oral' conventions were the product of the four-century-long Rewriting period of Chinese vernacular fiction and of its

---

[7] Nie Gannu 1981: 141.

[8] Sun Kaidi (1956: 4–5) argues, 'In style the stories written by authors of the late Ming are hardly different from the *huaben* stories of the Song. But their motive for writing is different . . . That was why Lu Xun called it *ni huaben*.' This theory of 'motive' is most risky and seldom reliable in literary study. You Guo'en *et al.* 1979: 146–7 suggest a more complicated set of criteria which could cause more confusion: 'Generally speaking those narrative texts that take Song and Yuan popular legends as their subject matter, and reflect the social life of the Song and Yuan times, with some linguistic details corresponding to the practices of the time such as social *mœurs*, taboo words, and official titles should be considered Song and Yuan *huaben*, even if they are rewritten by later writers.'

[9] Mistakes resulting from that misunderstanding arise frequently in textbooks and in scholarly papers. For instance quite a few scholars hold that the *Cihua* version of *Jin Ping Mei* was 'notes for oral performance', with no other sound proof than the title.

low stratum in the generic hierarchy of Chinese culture. The lack of authorship made it difficult to fix the channel of the message which was necessary for the control of interpretation. When readership instead of authorship became the most important circumstantial context for interpretative guidance, the seemingly oral-narrative conventions were installed to facilitate communication, as the texts then were made most accessible to readers. In a word, it was not the authors of the vernacular fiction but the readers who decided the way of narration.

It was the practice of rewriting that gave rise to the extreme homogeneity of narratological features. This narratological 'mock' orality of Chinese fiction is fundamentally different from the orality of storytelling performance, as it was the result of four centuries of rewriting, not of the oral narrating. Many nations have a much longer and more powerful oral-narrative tradition. Yet their fiction does not show some degrees of orality as Chinese vernacular fiction did.

Many scholars have discussed this simulation of oral-narrative performance as though it were a fairly faithful copy of the actual theatrical performance in the pre-history of Chinese fiction. Jaroslav Prusek, for instance, insists that the extraordinary longevity of this conventionalized narrative frame 'shows the unusual strength of the creative genius of the Chinese professional story-tellers, who had impressed the form of their tales on Chinese fiction so effectively that it lived on without any basic changes for centuries.'[10]

Prusek's affirmation is shared by many. Eugene Ouyang, for instance, maintains, 'If the colloquial fiction fails to please the modern reader, the fault lies in the reader's failure to recreate imaginatively the actual experience of the original audience, for whom the narrative was intended',[11] because Chinese fiction responds to 'the very different requirements of the actual and present audience'.[12]

Because this view is common, let me state my different opinion here though I shall elaborate it in the following chapters in a more systematic way. It cannot be over-emphasized that this narrative frame in Chinese fiction is only a make-believe situation. Written narrative of every nation originates in oral narrative. It is not because the oral performers in those nations are not 'creative genii' that the written narrative does not take over the oral-narrative frame. If it became a narrative convention that the narrator in Chinese vernacular fiction simulated an oral story-teller, there must be some other reason.

---

[10] Prusek 1980: 106, 113.   [11] Plaks 1977: 59.   [12] Ibid. 57.

As for the cause of this simulation, let me repeat my hypothesis: this stereotyped narrative frame simulating oral performance was brought about by the four-centuries-long Rewriting period of vernacular fiction. During this period, fiction writers were unable to claim full authorship of their fictional works, which were both based on previous rewritings and subject to further rewriting. As there was no authoritative source of the narrative message, the narrator assumed a responsibility comparable to that in oral performance; thus, in this simulated oral narrative frame, the authorship could be left out of consideration, as in oral performance in which authorship is almost irrelevant.

By the end of the Rewriting period, around the turn of the sixteenth and seventeenth centuries, the set of narratological characteristics had already become a powerful convention that proved to be highly resistant to changes by individual initiative. That this convention withstood the challenge of some talented authors is mainly ascribable to the fact that the low cultural status of Chinese vernacular fiction remained. This does not mean that Chinese writers did not try to change the convention, nor does it mean that critics of those centuries did not try to argue for a higher cultural estimation of vernacular fiction. Critics like Li Zhi of the late Ming and Jin Shengtan of the early Qing contributed a great deal to the re-evaluation of Chinese vernacular fiction, and the eighteenth century witnessed in a few masterpieces the great climax of this fiction. The narratological homogeneity of Chinese vernacular fiction, however, is not necessarily a narratological rigidity. In this book, I shall demonstrate how adaptable vernacular fiction could be in the hands of its masters as if to prove that conventions can not stifle real genius. Despite these brilliant efforts, the narratological homogeneity of Chinese traditional fiction remained oppressively stable, and radical change in the cultural strata of Chinese fiction did not occur until after the late Qing period, when a narratological revolution finally took place.

II

Theoretically, oral narrative and written narrative should be strictly distinguished from each other. Oral narrative, being essentially a multimedia communication, completely incorporates into the narrative discourse the material presentations (the setting, the sound, the performing, etc.), making the discourse *non-repeatable*. Every performance works out a new version, no matter how faithful the performer is to the 'original story'. As counterweight to the non-repeatability, conventions become important as devices to stabilize reception and interpretation. The situation is very different from written narrative which is basically separable from its material presentations. A novel may come in a number of manuscript versions, or printed into a number of copies, or reprinted as different editions. As long as these versions remain semantically unchanged, they carry the same narrative text. We may say that the text of the written narrative is materially *repeatable* in nature as it is both reprintable and re-readable. Narratological conventions, therefore, are less important in comparison with oral narrative.

Early Chinese vernacular fiction enjoyed re-readability like any written text, but not re-printablity, since almost every new edition was a rewriting. It was precisely this semi-repeatability that made narratological conventionality necessary.[13]

The text of the written narrative is not completely separable from its material form, because certain types of extra-textual material features enter into the composition of the narrative text. One of them is the printing conventions, like the division of chapters and paragraphs, punctuation, capitalization, and so on. These elements can sometimes play a very important role. The rise of May Fourth fiction, for instance, might not have been possible without the adoption of the division of paragraphs and punctuation marks. Some traditional writers in Shanghai (the Butterfly writers) even nicknamed their May Fourth opponents 'New Punctuation Fiction' (*Xinshi Biaodian Xiaoshuo*).

Cyril Birch provides a penetrating insight into the relations between these seemingly unrelated formal characteristics:

It may be worth investigating whether the import of paragraphing from the West did not impose a new discipline on writers ... Where the traditional 'paragraph' (unmarked) was often coterminous with the meandering sentence itself, we now have a carefully contructed unit with a single center of vision.[14]

Those semi-text-bound features play a part in the written narration, and are different from text-free material features such as fonts, illustrations,

---

[13] To use semiotic terms, each performance of oral narration is a sinsign, but every other performance is bound to be a different qualisign and a different legisign. In written narrative, however, each copy is a sinsign, all copies of one edition belong to one qualisign, and all copies of all editions of one book, so long as there is no change in meaning, belong to the same legisign. Chinese vernacular fiction of the Rewriting period, then, lies somewhere in between the two: each copy is a sinsign; all copies of one edition belong to one qualisign; but copies of different editions belong to different legisigns as the text is bound to be significantly altered. For the definition of those terms, see Pharies 1985. His explanations are clearer than Peires' own.

[14] Goldman 1977: 393.

binding, cover design, etc. which, when removed, effect no semantic change on the text itself.

When semi-text-bound features are changed, e.g. when, in modern editions, traditional Chinese fiction is given modern punctuation and sometimes cut into paragraphs, the changes in the narrative texts bring in corresponding, sometimes regrettable, semantic alteration.

III

The discussion on the supposed oral origin of Chinese fiction leads us further into the investigation of the different positions of the narrator in oral narration and in written narration.

In oral narration, the narrator is unmistakably the sender of the narrative message. He exists in flesh and blood and the receiver of the narrative message (the listener) is in positive contact with him. The author (if there is an author for the performed narrative) is only a supposition not indispensable for the narrative frame. The oral narrator is thus a complete realization of the subjectivity in the text.

The position of the narrator in factual narration (say, news report), whether oral or written is hardly different. In written fictional narrative, however, the narrator becomes abstract, reduced to what Roland Barthes called an *être en papier*.[15] In other words, the narrator is only a narratological function. It is the author who puts the narrative text down on paper, not the narrator, as the latter is now a special character, one of the author's creation. When writing the fictional work, the author not only creates the text but also the narrator's relations to the text. The shaping of the narrative text depends on the narrator's ability to perform the following functions: as the teller of the story—the narrative function; as the communicator with the receiver—the communicative function; as the director of the telling—the directing function; as commentator of the story—the commenting function; as more or less a character in the story—the function of characterization.

The list above is my tentative clarification of Gerard Genette's exposition.[16] Genette, however, does not point out that, in performing these

---

[15] Barthes 1977: 65.
[16] Gerard Genette (1980: 255–6) suggests that the narrator performs five functions: narrative function; directing function; forming the narrating situation; function of communication; testimonial function, or function of attestation. The definitions he offers are not always clear in each case. As I understand it, what he means by narrative function is the role of the teller of the story; directing function is the role of the commentator, providing 'stage directions'; to form the narrating situation is to form the narrator-narratee

functions, the abilities of the oral narrator are entirely different from those of the narrator in the written narrative. The oral narrator, being the tangible and positive source of the narrative message and the definite commander of the narration, can perform all the functions assigned to him in an audible or visible way.

The narrator in oral performance speaks, positively sending out the narrative message; he is in physical contact with the receivers of the message—the listeners—perceiving their response, and communicating with them on the spot; he is in actual control of the presentation of the narrative, and can add any explanation to his presentation; he stands aloof above the narrated world, and can impose his value-judgement or moral commentaries on the action and characters so that the listeners can understand the meaning of the story 'correctly'; he can, temporarily suspending his narratorship, impersonate any character in the narrative by feigning the latter's gestures or voice.

In written narrative the narrator performs the five functions in a very different way. The only function he can perform naturally is personalization since he IS a character, and he does not have to suspend his narratorship to become a character. His ability to perform other functions is conditional. Certainly he is not the sender of the message, as he himself is created by the narrative. Narratologically, however, the fictional narrative text is a story told by the narrator but, fictionally, overheard and recorded by the author in some way. No author can speak directly in the narrative as every word in it is supposed to be said by the narrator. Since the narrator himself is a special character, his words are not necessarily those of the author. What makes this distinction more significant is that these two personalities—the author and the narrator—are not necessarily in agreement in tone, in judgement, or in attitude towards the narrated world. That is why the generally accepted term 'authorial intrusion' is, strictly speaking, unacceptable in narrative analysis, though positively 'true'. I prefer the term 'narratorial intrusion', since we can hardly tell how much the author shares in these intrusions, but we can always safely say that they are made by the narrator.[17]

relationship; function of communication is the role of the sender of the message; the last one, in Genette's words, is 'the narrator's orientation toward himself', and is said to be the same as ideological function.

His discussion is rather chaotic. What, for instance, is the difference between the narrative function and the function of communication? Why is only the testimonial function concerned with ideology while the others are not?

[17] In non-fictional narratives this problem generally does not exist. In journalism, for instance, the narrator of oral news reports is not very different from his counterpart in written news reports since in both cases the author and the narrator can be identical.

In oral narrative, as well as in non-fictional written narrative, the narrator, standing aloof from his narration, is a *narrating narrator*. In fictional written narrative, the narrative personality is the result of his narrating, that is to say, he is, paradoxically, a *narrated narrator*, who is begotten by the narrating action supposedly performed by himself.

The characterization of the narrator can be developed to various degrees, and the narrator's position in the narrated/narrating dualism can be varied, thus creating different modes of narrative presentation. Wayne Booth tried to distinguish two types of narrators: explicit and implicit. The two terms should be understood, as I see it, as explicitly narrated narrators and implicitly narrated narrators. The common terms 'first-person narrator' (in lieu of the explicit narrator) and 'third-person narrator' (in lieu of implicit narrator) are convenient but narratologically unsafe as any enunciator has to use the first-person when referring to himself. A 'third-person' narrator is only a narrator who refrains from referring to himself at all in the narrative text. In traditional Chinese fiction, to say that the narrative is in the first or in the third person is oversimplified. But for the convenience of discussion, I shall sometimes use these two terms, when there is no risk of misunderstanding.

Since it is almost impossible for the narrator to remain completely implicit, most of the implicit narrators are only implicit to a certain degree.[18] The idea of 'the degree of implicitness' is especially relevant to traditional Chinese fiction, where the narrator, by convention, refers to himself as 'the Story-Teller' (*Shuoshude or Shuohuade*) which is actually an implicit first-person self-reference. But he never allows himself to participate in the story he tells, so his narration is executed in the third person. Therefore this stereotyped narrator in Chinese vernacular fiction is a non-participant semi-explicit narrator.

In Chinese literary-language fiction the narrator often assumes the name identical with the author. At the end of the well-known *Tang chuanqi* (i.e. literary-language) story Bai Xingjian's 'The Story of Li Wa' ('Li Wa Zhuan'): 'I take up my writing brush and write the story down. This is the autumnal eighth month of the year Yihai. I am Bai Xingjian of Taiyuan.' (TRXX, 36).

The narrator's self-identification with the author is so persistent in Chinese literary-language fiction that literary historians can verify the authorship by finding the narrator's fictional name in the story. There

---

[18] This degree of implicitness is inversely related to his personalization. That is to say, the more explicit the narrator, the more distinct his voice in the narrative. If the narrator is almost completely implicit (in the so-called 'fly-on-the-wall' technique in modern fiction), his voice seems to come from a void.

is a profound cultural motivation behind this which I shall elaborate in the last part of the current study.

This formulaic self-introduction, however, never appears in Chinese vernacular fiction (with the possible exception of *The Dream of the Red Chamber*). The reason seems to be obvious: the position of vernacular fiction was too low in the generic hierarchy of Chinese culture for any author to feel honoured by the authorship. But this is not the reason if we look into the matter more closely. Not until the late Qing did the author begin to let the narrator even borrow his improvised pen-name which could not in the least harm the author's reputation. The main reason was that the narrator's position is generically reserved for that impersonal, non-participant semi-implicit story-teller, who refuses to have a name, and survives by staying nameless and faceless.[19]

IV

The communicative function—one of the narrator's five functions—is to keep the narratee in contact, because any message, by definition, should have a receiver.

The narratee has to perform some functions in correspondence with the functions of the narrator.[20] Without the narratee's co-operation as the communicative partner, it is impossible for the narrator to perform his functions. In other words, to form the narrative frame requires the collaboration of the two.[21]

Depending on the degree of characterization, the narratee can also be either explicit or implicit. Just as the narrator in traditional Chinese fiction is a fixed character of the Story-Teller, the narratee is the Respected

[19] Cyril Birch, in private communication with me, suggests, 'Must there not be some connection with the fact that ONLY China at this time had cheap woodblock printing, widely used for publications for the semi-educated (farmers' almanacs etc.)—so that only in China would the commercial gain from novel-publishing be so great?' This is very possibly the reason for the continuous flow of bookstore recensions.

[20] Corresponding to narrator's narrative function, he plays the role of the listener; corresponding to narrator's communicative function, he plays the role of the receiver of the narrative message; corresponding to narrator's direction function, he plays the role of one who needs the narrator's directions in order to comprehend the narrative technique; corresponding to narrator's commentary function, he plays the role of one who needs the narrator to tell him how to understand the story; he is more or less 'characterized', i.e. he becomes a character in this or that manner in the fiction.

[21] Siegfried Schmidt in *Texttheorie*, when defining what he calls CAG (Communicative Action Game), argues, 'one of its principal features is that it takes the form of role-complementary speech by the communicative partners ... [that] consists of at least one speech act and one further linguistic act'. (Quoted in Watts 1981: 31).

Listener (*Kanguan*) who, as a stereotyped collective personality, is semi-explicit. The conventional narrative frame requires that he plays the role of the listener supposedly sitting in front of the performer in the theatre.

Quite often in Chinese vernacular fiction the narrator imitates what the narratee might say. In the well-known late-Ming short story 'The Oil Pedlar Takes the Top Courtesan' ('Maiyou Lang Du Zhan Huakui Nu') there is an example:

The boy Zhu then changed his name back to Qin. *Story-teller, if a person of higher social stratum wants to change back to his original name, he could write a memorandum to be approved by the court, or notify such institutions as the Ministry of Rites, the Imperial Academy or the State Registry. Who knows that an oil pedlar changes his name?* Well then, he had a way: he wrote on one of the two oil buckets the big character Qin, and on the other the city Bianliang. The oil buckets then became his posters that everybody could see and understand. (XSHY, 105)

The lines italicized in the above quote are the narrator's simulation of what could be a question raised by the listeners during an oral performance. This is the way that the narratee helps in establishing the narrative frame. The position of the narratee in traditional Chinese fiction is even more generically determined than that of the narrator, as the audience in oral performance (which the narratee assumes himself to be) is even less likely to be personalized. He renders great help in stabilizing and perpetuating the conventional narrative frame in traditional Chinese fiction.[22]

At the beginning of *The Dream of the Red Chamber* the narrator identifies himself as Cao Xueqin, the author's name. In the following passage the narrator goes further to call himself 'your faithful servant' (*nupu*) which is a new form of first-person self-reference, so the narrator seems to be breaking away from the narratological conventions.

---

[22] Patrick Hanan, in his article 'The Nature of Ling Meng-ch'u's Fiction' (Plaks 1977: 87), analyses the narrative frame in Chinese vernacular fiction, which he calls 'simulated context': '"Simulated context" means the context of a situation in which a piece of fiction claims to be transmitted. In Chinese vernacular fiction, of course, the simulacrum is that of oral story-teller addressing his audience, a pretence in which the author and reader happily acquiesce in order that the fiction can be communicated.' This, I venture to say, is disputable: the narrative frame, of whatever kind, is not to connect the author and the reader, as none of them directly participates in the narrating instance. What this frame connects is the narrator and the narratee. It is the narrator who assumes the simulacrum of the oral story-teller in Chinese vernacular fiction, not the author, and the narratee poses as the audience, not the reader.

Respected Listeners, you may ask from where this book starts. It may sound strange but it is interesting upon examination. Please let your faithful servant start from the very beginning so that you Respected Listener will not be confused. (HLM, 1)

The narratee, however, remains the conventional 'Respected Listener' (*Kanguan*), thus forcing the narrator to return to the stereotyped Story-Teller, and to put aside the personality he has just taken upon himself.

The discussion gives rise to another narratological problem: the same story can be presented with different narrative texts. This happens beyond question in oral performance where each presentation, by definition, is unique. In written narratives, however, the repeatability of the narrative text obscures the fact that any narrative work can be considered as one of innumerable possible presentations of the story.[23]

Narratologists differ in the names they give to the two elements of the dichotomy.[24] The pair of terms 'story/discourse' suggested by Chatman, though generally acceptable, sound inappropriate in this book, since the two terms shall frequently be used in their ordinary meanings in the current study. The pair of terms *histoire/recit* suggested by Gerard Genette are somehow frowned at by many English readers. Besides,

---

[23] This reminds us of the structuralist *langue-parole* dichotomy. This idea is useful to any serious student of narratology no matter whether he is a structuralist or not. The definition of narration offered by Lotman and Uspensky, for instance, may sound strange: 'Narration is transposition, transposition of the various elements inside.' (Lucid 1977: 237).

[24] The following is a list of the terms used by narratologists denoting the pair of concepts which I call the narrated/the pre-narrated:

Rimmon-Kenan	story	text
Chatman	story	discourse
Russian Formalists	*fabula*	*suzhet*
Ricardou	*fiction*	*narration*
Genette	*histoire*	*récit*
Barthes	*récit*	*discours*
Todorov	*histoire*	*discours*

The dichotomy, however, is not beyond challenge. There are some theoretical as well as practical difficulties: how much 'transposition' can a pre-narrated story allow the the narrated texts to have while still claiming the narrated text as its derivative? How drastic can the narrator's mediation be if the narrated text is to remain one of the narrated texts of the same pre-narrated story? Some critics argue that this dichotomy is groundless since every narrated text is irreducibly unique, and cannot share a common pre-narrated story with other texts. In my discussion, however, I retain this hypothetical dichotomy because, I think, any narrated text is only potentially based on a pre-narrated story, which does not exist a priori but, together with the narrated text, is a product of the narrating instance. Whether it can share a common pre-narrated story with other narrative texts is, then, of secondary importance.

they are not accepted even by French narratologists. I suggest the pair of terms 'pre-narrated story/narrated text', for the simple reason that they cause less ambiguity.

The pre-narrated story can be considered as a continuous flow of events in its unfiltered temporal and spatial state. The amount of detail it contains is beyond observation. Since it is not yet presented in words, it has no narrator, though it is also dependent on the narrating instance in the sense that without its narrated versions it cannot claim to exist at all.

It is impossible for any part of the narrated text to exist without narratorial mediation which is, by definition, omnipresent in narration.[25]

V

At the beginning of the twentieth century, the narratological conventionality of Chinese vernacular fiction finally entered a crisis, when the narrator's position in the conventional narrative frame became problematic.

In the majority of late Qing fiction works, however, the traditional narrative frame fails to take on any substantial change. The earliest restlessness of a narratological transformation can only be found in a very small number of the best of late Qing novels. Nevertheless, we cannot fail to notice, in almost all the novels of that period, a number of modifications, the most apparent of which is the change of the self-reference of the narrator from *Shuoshude* (the story-teller) to *Zuoshude* (the story-writer). This shift could mean the subversion of the conventional narrative frame. Yet the late Qing narrator does not seem to realize the fundamental difference this self-reference could make. The way he asserts his controlling authority remains the same.

---

[25] Chatman argues that in some parts of fiction the narratorial mediation is absent: 'Those that pretend to be constituted by found letters and diaries least presuppose a narrator. If we insist on an agent beyond the implied author, he can only be a mere collector or collator . . . The sole purported change is from handwriting to print.' (Chatman 1978: 67). This is an interesting observation though it is again debatable.

Let us briefly examine the situation in *The Dream of the Red Chamber* as an example. In that novel the narrative is supposed to have been written by the Stone on itself. The Taoist Kongkong then copied down the text and passed it to a person named 'Cao Xueqin' who, 'after ten years of hard work', renders it in its present form. Now here we have three characters, all having a hand in the narrating. Even if we call the Taoist Kongkong a mere collector and 'Cao Xueqin' a mere collator, the Stone is obviously the teller. This is an example of the triple-composite narrator.

In *The Bureaucrats* for instance, the narrator insists on being the moral judge of the events told, or the commander of the narrating action, in the same way as the old story-teller narrator:

You all have to know that these philanthropists ... at least saved a great number of people. This is the unbiased opinion of the Story-Writer. If nothing good is said about those people, it would not be in keeping with the Confucian Credo of Forbearance. (GCXXJ, 507)

The event, so alarming at the beginning, faded into nothing. This is the regular practice with Chinese officialdom. It is not the Story-Writer coming in like a lion but going out like a lamb. (GCXXJ, 489)

The change of self-reference seems to strengthen, not weaken the narrator's controlling authority, as he remains the non-participant semi-implicit narrator.

In a couple of late Qing novels, the narrator goes so far as to change his self-reference to the first-person 'I'. Wu Jianren's *Nine Murders* starts: 'This story took place in Guangdong. *I've heard* that people of all provinces say that Guangdong abounds in burglars. This is true' (JMQY, 1).

However, any hope this change of self-reference raises that the conventional narrative frame may now be removed proves false. For this narrator is still non-participant, and soon shifts back to the more conventional *Zuoshude*. More importantly, the narrator still adheres to his aloof controlling position, never allowing himself to be characterized into the narrative.

I suspect that this self-reference 'I' is borrowed from Western fiction as it had almost never occurred in vernacular fiction before the late Qing. One of the most widely read novels at that time was Lin Shu's translation of *Ivanhoe*. After a brief description of the landscape, the novel starts with a first-person reference: 'Such being *our* chief scene, the date of *our* story refers to a period toward the end of the reign of Richard I, when ...'.[26] In Lin Shu's translation, the self-reference is faithfully retained. Scott's beginning may have given late Qing authors some idea of how the impersonal, non-participant narrator could turn explicit in a localized way, without a radical change in the narrative frame.

What makes the traditional narrative frame safer is that the conventional appellation of the narratee remained the same *Kanguan*, but the meaning could be said to have altered now because of the ambiguity of

---

[26] Walter Scott, *Ivanhoe*. London: Nelson, 1920, 1. Italics mine.

the Chinese character *kan* (to watch or to read)—*Kanguan*, originally meaning the audience for a theatrical performance, now means 'readers', corresponding to the change of the appellation of the narrator. In *Strange Events*: 'When we tried to read the note, Jizhi and I almost split our sides with laughter. You know what was written there? Please let me write down the original so that you can all *have a look*. The text runs like this . . .'. (ESNMDZGXZ, ch. 86, 797). Beside a tricky mixture of the narrated now with the narrating now and the reading now, the reading action of the narratee is spotlighted, an action that the old narratee (*Kanguan* as listener) is unable to achieve.

The ambiguity of the appellation *Kanguan* was convenient for the continuity of the conventions. Often the new narrator–narratee (story-writer vs. reader) communicative pair slipped back into the old pair of story-teller vs. listener. In chapter 12 of *A Flower in the Sinful Sea* there is a passage about a letter which the hero Wenqing writes from Germany to his friend in Beijing: 'There was a postscript recounting how the photo was taken, which was another unprecedented interesting anecdote. You will ask who was in this photo. Please all of you be patient, and let me *tell* [shuo] you in detail. Now it was . . .'. (NHH, 120).

In Wu Jianren's *Strange Events*, one of the novels where the narrator calls himself 'I' from beginning to end and turns himself into a character (in this case, a merchant), the narrative can still slip back into the story-teller vs. listener frame:

This man was none other than a remote uncle of mine whose name was Wang Xianren, alternative name Boshu. Now here I have to tell you about the history of this uncle of mine. Respected Listeners [Kanguanmen], *please lend me your ear!* This Wang Boshu was originally a . . .'. (ESNMDZGXZ, ch. 21, 177). Late Qing fiction abounds in examples like this. It is by no means only sloppy writing.

In the chapter ending-beginning formula, the dilemma faced by the new narratorial personality is revealed in a more telling way. The end of chapter 1 of *Strange Events* runs as follows:

Hearing such words, I was stunned. I had no choice but to find an inn to wait for my uncle to return. Because of this waiting, some incidents were bound to happen:

The family members were to split up though they were of the same flesh and blood;
The poor man in a straw hat was to meet his prosperous friend at the end of the world.

If you want to know what happened after this, please wait for what will be
written in the next chapter [qiedai xiahui zai ji]. (ESNMDZGXZ, ch. 1, 24)

The chapter ending-beginning remained exactly the same, with only
one word changed in the traditional formulaic phrase 'wait for what
will be *told* in the next chapter'. Such was the timid modification of the
narrator's personality in late Qing fiction.

Despite this, the emergence of a real explicit and participant narrator
in some vernacular novels, notably Wu Jianren's *Strange Events* and
Wang Yunqing's *Viewed with Cold Eyes*, is still an event of great
importance for the development of Chinese fiction. First-person narrative is not a tradition of Chinese fiction either in the vernacular or in
the literary language. There are some rare cases of first-person narration, but these had virtually no influence on later fiction. The narrative
ballad 'Mulan Ci' (from the fourth to the fifth centuries AD) is in the
first person, but its suspected 'nomadic' source might be the reason
why it is unique in the history of Chinese poetry. The early Tang
chuanqi tale, Zhang Zu's 'A Visit to the Immortals' Cave' ('You
Xianku', *c*.680 AD), was perhaps the only first-person narrative in Chinese fiction before the late Qing, but the tale was lost for many centuries prior to its rediscovery in Japan in the 1920s, thus precluding the
possibility of its influencing later writers, though it was influential in
Japanese literature. A much more influential narrative, *Six Chapters of
My Floating Life* (*Fusheng Liuji*), is not fiction but memoir, and was
not widely circulated until it was reprinted in the magazine *Amaranth*
(*Yanlaihong*) in 1906. We have no proof that Wu Jianren had any
access to this memoir when he started *Strange Events* in 1904.

If there are only a couple of vernacular novels with explicit participant
narrators, first-person narrative is much more common in the literary-
language fiction by the Butterfly writers. Su Manshu's romantic autobiographical novel *Fragmented Letters* (*Duanhong Lingyan Ji*, 1912) is
a beautiful romantic narrative with the protagonist as the narrator. Xu
Zhenya's *My Wife* (*Yu zhi Qi*, 1916) adroitly shifted back and forth
between the third-person narrative and the first-person narrative. After
epistolary fiction or diary fiction enters into literary-language fiction in
such works as Xu Zhenya's *Tearful History of The Deserted* (*Xuehong
Leishi*), the use of first-person narrative increased rapidly. Lu Xun's
apprentice piece, his only literary-language short story, 'Nostalgia for
the Past' ('Huaijiu', 1913) was also in the first person. I think the first-
person introduction in *La Dame aux camélias* and the explicit narration

in *Sherlock Holmes* must have provided at least some hints to Chinese fiction writers.

In the early twentieth century these works were translated into literary language. However, this was not the only reason why it was fiction in the literary language (which was notoriously inflexible) rather than fiction in the vernacular that showed such remarkable adaptability. There had not been such a rigidly conventionalized narrative frame in literary-language fiction as in the vernacular. By the late Qing period, the cultural gap between the two was still much deeper than most scholars perceive. This is an issue that I shall return to in the last part of this book.

In the very first late Qing political novel—Liang Qichao's *The Future of New China*—we already find the narrator's personality becoming quite complicated. The main body of the novel is supposed to be the speech given by Dr Kong in the year 2016 AD (or 2513 after Confucius's birth), at a meeting to celebrate the success of political reform in China. Kong's speech is said to be recorded in shorthand by the secretaries of the History Society, and cabled word by word to the magazine *New Fiction* in Yokohama to be printed. So the narrator appears in the first person on both narrative levels. But none of them is a participant narrator. That is to say, they are not characters in the event they narrate at all. The remarkable change is that neither of the two narrators calls himself 'story-writer', as they are made characters in the narrative.

The first-person narrator in *Strange Events*, however, is half-participant. Though he still has to perform the routine function which late Qing fiction regularly assigned to the narrator—to string together the many anecdotes and stories—the parts about 'myself' form quite a coherent story and carry more thematic weight than the stories told by various characters in the novel. The beginning chapters recount the attempt by the narrator's uncle to grab the property of a helpless widow and the narrator when he was an inexperienced youth. The narrator's gradual accumulation of worldly experience and his adoption of a contemptuous and cynical attitude towards all the wickedness in the world become the theme running through the whole novel.

Jaroslav Prusek does not have a high opinion of this novel:

It is evident, however, in this case, that the transformation of the traditional narrator into a clearly defined speaker using the first person singular and presenting all the episodes as his own experience, lived through or heard, was not a functional change ... We soon realize, nevertheless, that this is only a pose and that the author had no other aim in mind than to put together a collection of stories and anecdotes to captivate and entertain his readers.[27]

Actually, if we piece together all the passages recounting the personal experience of the narrator, we would have a structurally coherent and beautifully written novel. The whole novel now can be considered to be the blending of two entirely different novels. Prusek's accusation is applicable only to half of it. The narratorial position in the other half can be said to be a significant break in the evolution of traditional Chinese fiction.

The dilemma caused by the double role of the narrator—telling his own story and telling the stories he has heard or seen—is more disastrous in *Viewed with Cold Eyes*. The narrator has his own story to narrate— his ruined relationship with his bride, who was uneducated and pitiably greedy, and his resuscitated romance with the prostitute Sulan. Yet in order to supply as many anecdotes as possible, his passionate lover Sulan has to engage in constantly telling stories at the expense of her own image—she now appears as an extremely gossipy woman.

The narratee in some late Qing novels also acquires a certain explicitness. In chapter 14 of *Viewed with Cold Eyes*, when the treachery of Shanghai prostitutes is discussed, the narratee is called in: 'Those gentlemen who have some experience in the Shanghai whoring circle must know what I am talking about, and I do not have to say too much about it.' (LYG, 122). Though it sounds more natural for an explicit narrator to call the narratee into explicitness, we can find instances when the implicit narrator in late Qing fiction can also play the game. In *The Nine-Tail Tortoise* (*Jiuwei Gui*), after a long explanatory commentary about how irresistibly seductive the celebrated courtesan Lin Daiyu was, the narrator calls upon the narratee as his whoring companion: 'Those of you Respected Readers who are veterans of the whoring circles, and know Lin Daiyu personally, must know that my statement is not groundless.' (JWG, 196). From these two examples we can see that the way to make the narratee explicit is the same in the two novels with different narrators. This shows that the explicitness of the narrator in late Qing fiction could be very superficial.

Nevertheless, encouraged by this opportunity of comparing notes, sometimes the narrator can unwittingly acquire a little characterization, as can be seen in another example from *The Nine-Tail Tortoise*:

[27] Prusek 1980: 115.

Just have a look at how fierce Jin Yuege was! Just think how heartless, how vicious, how totally lacking in conscience these courtesans are, and you understand why it is very ill-advised to marry a courtesan. This advice is derived from *my own* experience, and not loose talk. (JWG, 64. Italics mine.)

That is perhaps the uttermost characterization the traditional non-participant semi-implicit narrator would allow himself, without damaging the narrative frame.

Thus, the narrator-narratee pair in late Qing fiction remains generally unchanged in late Qing fiction. The modifications some novels managed to work up were not sufficient to bring Chinese fiction out of its traditional mode.

VI

A discussion of the narratological characteristics of May Fourth fiction may seem somewhat superfluous as its formal features are not far from the 'normal' modern fiction with which we are familiar. Such an effort is worthwhile only when the discussion is placed against the historical context when compared with traditional Chinese fiction, especially its last phase late Qing fiction, and with post-May Fourth fiction. Because of this, my summary of the narratological characteristics of May Fourth fiction will be more comparative than descriptive.

The conventional narrative frame of traditional Chinese vernacular fiction is completely dismissed in May Fourth Fiction. This dismissal determines all other changes. As Cyril Birch points out: 'The most startling new feature of the fiction published just after the literary revolution of 1917–1919 was not its Westernized syntax nor its tone of gloom but the emergence of a new authorial persona.'[28]

The conventional semi-implicit non-participant story-teller narrator, or the slightly modified late Qing story-writer narrator, disappear, to be replaced by specifically characterized narrators. Every piece of fiction has to design its own unique narrative frame to present the narrator. He can now be a character whose narration is personalized, or almost totally effaced so that his narrative sounds 'objective'. Some general tendencies can still be noticed.

First-person narration becomes the most common form of narratorial characterization in May Fourth fiction. Of Lu Xun's twenty-six stories

[28] Goldman 1977: 390.

written during these ten years, twelve, almost half, are in first-person narration. Since most May Fourth writers are more subjectively inclined than Lu Xun, the percentage of first-person narration could hardly be less than that. In Guo Moruo's stories and short novels, first-person narration amounts to 70 per cent; in Yu Dafu's works, 50 per cent. The percentage of first-person narrative is lowest with Ye Shengtao, in whose stories the number of first-person narratives dwindles from about 40 per cent in the first collection *Estrangement* (*Gemo*, 1922), to 20 per cent in the second collection *Fire* (*Huozai*, 1923), to 9 per cent in the third collection *Under the Fire* (*Xianxia*, 1925), to zero per cent in the fourth collection *In the Town* (*Chengzhong*, 1926). Ye's writing, however, has all along been considered more 'objective' than his contemporaries.

The percentage of first-person narratives is also low in Zhang Ziping's works. Since his writing is the closest to the narrative mode of traditional fiction, there is nothing surprising in this.

Among the first-person narratives, epistolary or diary narrative frames are common, especially epistolary. For example, Feng Yuanjun's 'Traces of Spring' ('Chunhen') comprises forty love-letters with more emphasis on the state of mind of the narrator–protagonist herself than on the events the story describes. Xiang Liangpei's 'Six Letters' ('Liu Feng Shu') is in much the same vein as Lu Xun's 'Hometown' ('Guxiang') but is written in the form of letters to a friend, and the narrator–protagonist's disappointment with his return is more intimately conveyed.

May Fourth writers considered the epistolary-diary form advantageous for establishing the genuineness of the sentiment. Yu Dafu declares in an essay 'Diary Literature' ('Riji Wenxue'): 'Though kept outside orthodox literature, diary is the central genre of literature . . . In comparison with other forms of first-person narratives, diary literature is more firmly grounded and more reliable to establish genuineness.'[29] What Yu Dafu means by this exaggeration ('the central genre') is that the diary form is more self-centred and subjective, thus making the characterization of the narrator more convincing.

Though they were favourite forms for essays, the culturally much higher genre, the diary and epistolary form had never been used in Chinese vernacular literature. The conventional narrative frame precludes their usage. It is true that the epistolary form had been a stock technique in Butterfly fiction which was written in the literary language.

[29] Yu Dafu 1927: 78.

Many novels produced by this Butterfly group read like 'anthologies of model love-letters' (*qingshu chidu*), and, indeed, they sold well on the market as such.

The risk of the diary-epistolary form, or of first-person narrative in general, is that the narrator tends to be characterized into the personality of the author, giving the fictional works an autobiographical slant. Many of the May Fourth writers enjoyed this opportunity for self-identification, although in May Fourth fiction there are also quite a number of successful works of non-autobiographical characterization of the explicit narrator. For instance, the first-person narrator is personalized into a woman in Zhu Ziqing's story 'The History of Laughter' ('Xiao de Lishi'), and into a cowardly philanderer in Li Jinming's 'In a Boat' ('Zhou Zhong').

There are also a few stories of the May Fourth period where the narrative changes hands from one narrator to another—usually with first-person narration shifting to third-person implicit narration. In Pan Xun's story 'Notes about the Mind' ('Xinye Zaji') the first-person narrator gives way to a third-person narrator, turning himself into a non-narrator character, and then takes back the narratorial voice. In Li Jinming's 'In a Boat', the whole story is in first-person narration, but when the story finishes as the narrator-protagonist flees from the woman with whom he had an affair on board the steamer, a paragraph in the third person is added, so that the new narrator can describe the sulkiness of this ex-narrator (now a mere character) and censure his 'irresponsible' action. This change of the narrator might be a reversion to the traditional interpretative control.

Wheres in a few late Qing novels the conventionalized narratee holds back the transformation of the narrative frame, in many May Fourth works of fiction the characterization of the narratee contributes to the individualization of the narrative frame. Feng Yuanjun's 'Secret Mourning' ('Qiandao') is the narrator-protagonist's direct address to his deceased sister-in-law. In Yu Dafu's 'Niaoluo Xing', the narratee—the narrator's wife who does not appear in the story—was repeatedly called up, as the confessionalist narrator-protagonist addresses her in repentance. Both the explicitness of the narratee—in this case the narrator's wife—and the direct appellation of the narratee as 'you' effectively reinforce the explicitness of the narrator.

More frequent is the practice of characterizing the narratee as the narrator's most intimate friend to whom the narrator–protagonist can confide himself. In Guo Moruo's erotic story 'Donna Karmelo'

('Kemeiluo Guniang'), the narrator-protagonist sighs at the beginning of his confession:

In fact I do not have any one whom I can claim to be my genuine friend: if I expose my mind nakedly, I am afraid all my friends will spit in my face in contempt, and I am afraid you will be one of them too. This letter of mine will bring you the sorrow of disappointment. I feel sad about that. But I feel sadder about the fact that we have all along been kissing each other while wearing masks. After much hesitation, I have made up my mind to write to you. (T, 110)

With the narrator-narratee communicative pair thus sufficiently characterized, the narrator in Chinese fiction emerges from his long centuries of impersonality. The narrator thus individually set up does not claim the authority that could control the interpretation. The discursive order that was typical of traditional Chinese fiction is now replaced by a discursive uncertainty.

At the other extreme, the narrator in third-person narratives is more implicit in May Fourth fiction than in traditional Chinese fiction—so implicit that not a trace of narratorial control can be found, and discursive uncertainty is now the result of the apparant lack of any narrative guidance to the interpretation. In Lu Xun's story 'Medicine' ('Yao') and 'A Public Example' ('Shizhong'), the narrator stays completely hidden. 'A Humiliating Demonstration' can be regarded as a fine example of the 'fly-on-the-wall' narrative so highly praised by modern critics. The narrative here becomes 'behaviourist' from beginning to end as the narrator poses as a mere recorder. 'Objective recording' itself is paradoxical. Narrating destroys the independent existence of the narrated world. Yet the narrator's abstention from interpretative control, even if only a gesture, allows the narrative text a broad field of freedom of meaning.

There are, however, some works in May Fourth fiction where the narrator is semi-implicit, that is, implicit but often intruding into the narrative. In Ye Shengtao's best story 'Mr Pan Amid Hardships' ('Pan Xiansheng zai Nanzhong') the narrator exposes himself in a limited way: 'The easy manners of the arriving passengers, the anxiety of the waiting passengers, and the small profiteering of the porters—these are not what *we* are going to talk about, as *we* are only going to tell the story about a certain Mr Pan from the town of Rangli.' (XX, 39). The 'we' in this passage is a more convenient way for the narrator to come out of complete implicitness together with his narratee, and is much less intrusive than the traditional semi-implicit narratorial pair.

In Shen Congwen's story 'Chen' ('Morning'), the narrator began the story by providing another way of calling up the semi-implicit narratee: '*Everybody* knows that this early spring morning was just one of those mornings that sends the love of young couples into full bloom. *Anyone who* has a satisfactory wife, with her hair newly bobbed, would surely know what Mr Lan would do to his wife. I do not have to say more.' (YZ, 63. Italics mine.). This reminds us of the late Qing narrator comparing notes with his whoring companion. Yet in late Qing fiction this evocation of the narratee is in earnest. The narrator needs the help of the narratee to prove his power over meaning control, i.e. the power to control the interpretation of meaning. In May Fourth fiction, however, the evocation of the narratee is mostly satirical in tone. The expected testimony of the narratee does not confirm the intended interpretation, but, on the contrary, helps to vary the meaning.

To facilitate the satire, the narrator has to enlarge the distance between the narrative frame and the narrated world so that he could acquire the power to subject the narrated world to examination. But that is very different from the satire of late Qing fiction, as the narrator's power is not used to exaggerate but to overstate, and the result is not the reaffirmation of the narrator's control of interpretation but indicates his abstinence from it.

Lu Xun's short novel *The True Story of A Q* (*A Q Zhengzhuan*) is the most fortuitous example. Lu Xun's technique is to over-play the game, to let the garrulously intrusive narrator flaunt his privilege to excess so that his manœuvring of the narration itself becomes the target of the satire. At the very beginning of this short novel the narrator, in a series of long intrusions, questions and deliberates on his position and his manner of narrating, to the extent that he not only harbours doubts about his own ability to tell about narrated world but suspects the futility of doing so.[30]

---

[30] In Gogol's story 'The Nose' we find that the narrator appears at the beginning of the story pondering at great length over how to name the protagonist and how to start the narrative. When the story is about to finish, he appears again trying to laugh away his own narrative:

> Only now, on thinking it all over, we perceive that there is a great deal that is improbable in it. Apart from the fact that it is certainly strange for a nose supernaturally to leave its place and to appear in various places in the guise of a civil councillor—how was it that Kovaliov did not grasp that he could advertise about his nose in a newspaper office? I do not mean to say that I should not think it too expensive to advertise: that is nonsense, and I am by no means a mercenary person: but it is improper, awkward, not nice! (*The Collected Tales and Plays of Nikolai Gogol*, New York: Octagon Books, 1978, i. 89)

The only thing that I can comfort myself with is that the syllable A in the name A Q is very exact. There was no groundless supposition that needs to be corrected by more learned men. As for the rest, I can be certain of nothing. My only hope is that one day the disciples of Dr Hu Shi who 'has an obsession with history and textual research' will find new clues. By that time, however, my True Story of A Q will have already vanished. (Lu Hsun 1956: i. 96)

So even in the rare cases in May Fourth fiction where the narrator remains semi-implicit, his manipulation is exaggerated to expose his vulnerability. Thus May Fourth fiction completely destroys the conventional narratorial frame by removing the narrator from the position of controlling meaning.

VII

A narrator has to be concerned with many things other than his job of narrating the story. He can suspend his narration and talk instead about his narrating, or make his own comments on the characters and events in the story. 'Asides' of this kind are natural in oral performance, where the narrator takes care that his listeners will respond properly to his story and understand his intention in telling it. Since the listeners' response is physically perceivable, his intrusions can always be justi- fied by the particular situation.

In written narrative, however, this exchange of messages becomes shadow-boxing, as neither the narrator nor the narratee are physically substantial, and the fictional narrative frame does not justify the nar- rator's departure from the narrating.

In oral narration, the intentional context can be established by a number of extralinguistic and paralinguistic means: tone, gesture, facial expression, etc. In written narrative, the narrator is left with no other means than words, with a little help from paralinguistic devices such as exclamation marks.

The narrator has choice of two detours, by means of which he can express his own opinions: self-characterization and narratorial intrusions. Since in traditional Chinese fiction, the narrator by necessity remains the non-participant semi-implicit story-teller, and self-characterization is out of the question, the only way for self-expression is to intrude into the narrative.

Though literary historians are sure that there existed a fruitful intimacy between the two fiction works, the narrator's over-playing of self-doubt is much more limited in Gogol's story than that in Lu Xun's.

Narrative intrusions can be divided into two types: directions which explain how the story is being told, and commentaries which supply information or explain an attitude to the narrated events.[31]

Most of the abundant directions in traditional Chinese novels are powerfully style-indicative. That is to say, they mark out the narratological characteristics instead of explaining the narrator's way of narrating. When the narrator in written narrative ends a chapter, he does not have to say, 'Please listen to the next chapter if you want to know what happens afterwards', because the text obviously goes on. The direction is used here as a reminder of the conventional narrative frame.

Only a small number of directions are actually used for smoothing out technical difficulties. In *The Dream of the Red Chamber*:

The Rongs' Mansion had altogether more than three hundred persons from the top to the lowest servants. Every day there happened more than a dozen events at least, entangled like hemp fibres, with no event so distinct that it can be used as a starting-point for our narration. I am puzzled as to what event and what character I can use to start the narrative. One day, unexpectedly, someone from a tiny little household hundreds of miles away was coming to the Rongs' Mansion. It is not a bad idea to start with this family. (HLM, 68)

This long-winded direction is justifiable because the way the story starts is unconventional for classical Chinese novels. *The Dream of the Red Chamber* does not mean to impress the readers with its boldness in narratological innovation. A direction explaining the necessity of the new device could alleviate the possible discomfort.

Commentaries can also be used for a series of purposes other than providing the narrator's opinions about the story. Like directions, commentaries which are all but natural in oral performance may reveal the awkwardness of the narrator's position in written narrative. In this example in the Cihua version of *Jin Ping Mei*:

Old Lady Wang said, 'My Master, listen to me. Hanky-panky is by no means an easy thing to do. *Now what is hanky-panky? It's just what we call adultery today.* You have to be capable of five things before you can hope to be successful. . . .' (JPM Cihua, ch. 3. Italics mine.)

---

[31] Sometimes, directions can hardly be distinguished from commentaries. In ch. 103 of *Water Margin*: 'Wang Qing, seeing Lady Peng come out, rushed forward to fight. *You may say that such a strange thing is not believable even if I tell you*: suddenly Wang Qing saw a dozen servants running out, weapons in hand and shouting'. (SHZ, 986). What Wang Qing sees is a hallucination. The narrator's remark is now both a commentary on the story and a direction calling for attention. This is a combined intrusion.

The passage inserted in a passage of reported speech is commentary not said by Old Lady Wang but by the narrator. *Jin Ping Mei's* story is developed from part of the twelfth-century novel *Water Margin*, and this 'teaching of Old Lady Wang' could also be found in many editions of *Water Margin* but none of them has this inserted explanation, as *Water Margin* is 'then' and *Jin Ping Mei* is 'now'. In oral performance, such an insertion is easy, as all the narrator has to do is to switch his tone from that of imitating the character to his tone in narrating. In written narrative, such an insertion sounds awkward. The Chongzhen version of *Jin Ping Mei* deleted the inserted explanation.

What supplementary commentaries supply is not simply background knowledge for understanding a certain event. Sometimes they also supply information about the character's past or future. This is especially common in traditional Chinese fiction in which large-scale flashbacks or flashforwards are rare. In *The Three Kingdoms* and *Water Margin*, most of the characters, upon their first appearance in the narrative, are introduced with a supplementary commentary recounting their past. And most characters are given a supplementary commentary on their future when they leave the story, if the narrative is not going to follow the life of those characters to the end.

Another kind of commentary brings strange characters or events necessary to the social norms, so that the stories are less shocking to the reading public's sense of moderation. In *Jin Ping Mei*, Song Huilian, a servant's wife who had once committed fornication with Ximen Qing, takes her life when she finds it too distasteful:

[The women in the house] were unable to force the door open, and were all panic-stricken. Finally they let a boy servant climb through the window. An *earthen pot can hardly avoid the fate of breaking at the well.* They cut the rope and gave her first-aid but all to no avail. She died soon after. (JPM Cihua, ch. 18)

Such commonplace explanations are abundant in traditional Chinese fiction, though in the best of Chinese fiction, explanations of the *Jin Ping Mei Cihua* kind are reduced to the minimum. In chapter 27 of *Jin Ping Mei*, there is a three-page-long commentary on the unbearable heat of that summer, which states that there are six kinds of lucky people (princes, monks, hermits, etc.) who are spared the heat. Another example is in chapter 8, on the licentiousness of monks, explaining that only monks have the leisure to indulge in lust. This passage, in more or less the same words, can be found in *Water Margin* and other novels too. Such passages have little to do with the narrated events. They seem to be ready-made commentaries copied from novel to novel. In the Chongzhen version of *Jin Ping Mei*, however, those stock commentaries are all deleted.[32]

More important for our study are judgemental commentaries, especially morally judgemental commentaries. They are different from the explanatory commentaries in that the latter aim at helping the receivers understand the apparently strange events or characters, while judgemental ones aim at securing the readers' agreement with the narrator's value-judgements.

We have already mentioned that in oral performance, the narrator can readily switch from narrating into commenting merely by changing the paralinguistic form. In written narration this is difficult. Traditional Chinese fiction, however, tries to simulate it by a stylistic device—inserting poems or rhymed prose. In *Jin Ping Mei*, Ximen Qing has an affair with the wife of a servant, and the narrator offers us a commentary:

> Respected Listener, no head of household should commit adultery with his slave-girls or wives of his servants. Such things will surely confound the hierarchy, give those disposed to evil the chances to take advantage, and cause the social mœurs to deteriorate, until the degeneration is beyond cure. We have a testimonial poem that says:
>
> > Ximen, too lustful, confused the high and the low.
> > The concubines all so beautiful are not enough for him.
> > Why should he, when his wife was not home,
> > Have an affair with a servant, confounding the norms.
> >   (JPM Cihua, ch. 22)

Such poems are, in most cases, not much more than doggerel. Yet they are favourite forms of commentaries to unify the value-judgements in the narrative, and to control the signification of the novel so that the diffusion of interpretations will be limited.

Some scholars hold that using poems as commentaries is another device that the story-teller narrator in Chinese vernacular fiction took over from oral performance, in which the story-teller spiced his narration with singing. This again is a too simple solution to the difficult narratological problems of Chinese vernacular fiction. In fact, there are surprisingly few tunes used for the poem-commentaries in vernacular

---

[32] Some ancient Chinese authors seem to be aware of the banality of those commentaries. *The Scholars*, after the conventional opening verse, acknowledges: 'This poem tells a trite commonplace, nothing more than that, though wealth and honour are all vain, people chase them with too much eagerness, even at the expense of their life.' (RLWS, 5).

fiction, and in early vernacular fiction (supposedly closer to oral performance) there are indeed far fewer poem-commentaries.

I suggest that there is another reason for using poems as commentaries: they were there not only because of their stylistic insulation but also because of their generic superiority in the cultural hierarchy of discourses. The common leading tag of these poems—'We have a *testimonial* poem that says' (*youshi weizheng*)—shows that those poems intrude from a higher cultural level. Because poems are generically endowed with this cultural superiority, the fact that most of those poems were wretched doggerels does not diminish their authority.

Commentaries are, generally speaking, less powerful as style-indicators than directions. While a single direction often suffices to mark a distinct style, only the cumulative effect of the quantity of commentaries may be recognized as such an indication. The most obvious improvement the Chongzhen version of *Jin Ping Mei* made to the Cihua version, as we have mentioned, was to delete a large proportion of the commentaries, thus creating a distinct new style.

The story-teller narrator in traditional Chinese novels seldom refrains from intruding wherever he sees a need, as his conventional semi-implicit position in the narrative situation provides him with unchanged authority over the narrative. However, unlike the self-conscious narrator in some eighteenth-century Western novels, the Chinese narrator holds back from flaunting his power of intrusion. His intrusions are not meant to shock, but are conventionalized, so that he does not have to be so self-conscious in intruding.

A Western reader may feel that both the narrator and the narratee (but not necessarily the characters) in traditional Chinese fiction are always too strait-laced. After the salacious description of Pan Jinlian's sexual encounter with Ximen Qing, a commentary in *Jin Ping Mei* goes:

> Since this woman began her sexual experience with Rich Zhang years ago, whenever did the old man's thing, as soft as snivel, give a brisk performance? After marrying Wu Da, Respectable Listener please imagine, how much prowess could you expect from something three inches long? Today she met Ximen Qing who had long been an honoured soldier in the battlefield of debauchery. How could she not be happy? (JPM Cihua, ch. 4)

This commentary is perhaps the farthest the narrator in Chinese vernacular fiction could allow himself to go. We can hardly imagine Diderot's or Cervantes' narrator letting such a wonderful opportunity go without making the best of it for a good laugh.

The reason why the narrator in Chinese vernacular fiction remains so ethically prudish was not so much due to the rigidity of moral codes in Chinese society but to the cultural function of this fiction. But we shall leave this particular problem to the last part of the present study.

VIII

A salient feature of late Qing fiction is the greater frequency of narrative intrusions than in any previous period of Chinese vernacular fiction. This fact, somehow, has hitherto eluded the attention of students of late Qing fiction.

The increase is more apparent with directions than with commentaries. This, I think, is ascribable to the tension caused by the modifications in the narrative frame within the conventionalized communicative pattern. The huge amount of directions trying to explain the newly adopted techniques betrays the narrator's uneasiness about the instability of his status.

A Flower in the Sinful Sea is a typical case. The author Zeng Pu could be said to be the best informed about Western literature of the major late Qing novelists. He perhaps thought that he was writing a novel drastically distinct from the traditional fiction. Yet he produced a work even more conventional than some of his less-informed contemporary colleagues, partly because the directions, which he abundantly provided for fear that the narrative technique might be too new, actually pull the novel back into conventionality.

At the end of the last chapter, Wenqing, when stepping out of his room, gave out a mad cry and fainted on the ground. I imagine that when you read this, you told yourself that it was just a regular means to arouse your curiosity, and that it is a routine trick played by all novel writers. But this novel *A Flower in the Sinful Sea* of mine is different from any other novel in that it never stops and restarts at will in order to create a situation. There is not a single false line, or a single untrue word. I can only let the text follow the facts, not vice versa. So that day when Wenqing fell to the ground, there must be some reason that made his fall a must. The Story-Writer cannot now tell you everything about the mystery, but only continue narrating to see what happened afterwards. (NHH, 223)

This might not be the longest direction in late Qing fiction, though long directions can be found in *The Bureaucrats* (chapter 11), in Yi Suo's *Yellow Embroidered Ball* (*Huang Xiuqiu*, chapter 6), and in many other novels. It is certainly longer than most directions in traditional vernacular fiction before the late Qing. The lengthy direction apparently defending some new technique is, in fact, offering an apology for a very conventional device, i.e. ending the chapters at a critical moment, with a couplet and a formulaic tail-phrase.

Since many late Qing novels are episodic, comprised of a linked series of stories, and mostly in direct quoted speech uttered by the characters, the continuous and lengthy direct quoting also causes uneasiness, and invites long directions. In chapter 101 of *Strange Events*, there is a peculiar direction:

Halt! I began telling Jin Zi'an and others this story in the middle of chapter 97, and it did not end until the beginning of chapter 101. No need to ask about how much time I took in telling the story: the passage tallies more than 15 thousand characters. How can one have a breath so long? How can one go on talking for so long? You do not know that it took me three or four days to tell the story to my friends. I did not want to mention that I stopped several times, so that the story could appear as one piece. Actually during those four days, another incident happened—Gou Cai fell ill . . .

The uniqueness of the above direction is not only the mixture of narrating action with narrated event but the narrator's attempt to reshape the narrating by means of narratorial intrusion. The story-telling, reported in direct form, is in narratological theory, untampered (otherwise it would not be in direct quoted form), but the narratorial intrusion is so powerful that it recasts the speech.

The number of commentaries is greatly increased too. If the increase in directions is due to the adoption, or the purported adoption, of new techniques, then the no less serious increase in commentaries can only be explained by the fact that the narrator feels the threat of interpretative diversification. The widening of the scope of the subject-matter certainly adds to the pressure, as the more complicated the event is, the greater the need for common-sense commentaries. Moreover, moral commentaries become more tendentious to make the judgements unequivocal.

Since the late Qing narrator always assumes the pose of reprimander of social evils and reformer of society, this moral arrogance makes the usually banal commentaries even more intrusive. An interesting example can be found in chapter 32 of Wu Jianren's *Nine Murders*:

Respected Reader! These are the few superstitious practices in which the Chinese believed, and the Cantonese believed more than the rest of China. That was why Su Peizhi was acting like this to fool them. I think that such a wise man as Su Peizhi could not believe in such things. He only used them to build necessary connections. (JMQY, 245)

This Su Peizhi is the Judicial Envoy specially sent from Beijing to investigate the murder case, and he disguises himself as a fortune-teller in order to infiltrate the criminal gang. But this fact is part of the suspense, not to be revealed until several chapters later when the whole gang is arrested. This narratorial commentary almost ruins the crucial suspense. The narrator takes a risk when he reveals the truth too early only to show that he is morally impeccable.

Sometimes the narrator–commentator in late Qing fiction seems to be over-sensitive about his morally infallible image. In another commentary in *Nine Murders*, also about superstition, the narrator tries to stress that he is above the narrated world:

Respected Reader! Since all these things are absurd, why should I relate them here? Because people at that time believed in them. Since they acted in that way, I have no choice but to tell it as it was. It is not because I who claim to be reforming fiction would follow these people in their superstitions. Please do not misjudge me. (JMQY, 67)

Many explanatory commentaries are provided for the same reason. In *The Nine-Tailed Tortoise*, for instance, the narrator supplies a great deal of information about the rules of the brothels, and adds 'I have to make them clear one by one, lest you Respected Reader should pick fault with me.' (JWG, 89). In Wu Jianren's *Strange Events of the Last Ten Years* (*Jin Shinian zhi Guaixianzhuang*) a character points out to his friends a piece of surprising news in the local newspaper:

Respected Reader! Was it possible that Lu and Li did not read newspapers at all? Was it possible that in such a big inn no one read newspapers? How could those two not see the news until Ziliu pointed it out? You must know that those who read newspapers usually only read the most eye-catching titles. I have to explain this clearly, lest you Respected Reader say that there is a loophole in my novel. (JSNZGXZ, 64)

Never before had the narrator in Chinese fiction felt the need of this kind of desperate self-defence. Never before had the narrator been so worried about the effectiveness of his communication. One feels that the narrator of Chinese fiction now finds himself in a much more vulnerable position.[33]

---

[33] Another interesting example follows of such 'garrulous' explanatory commentary: in ch. 15 of *Strange Events*, the character changes his name, 'and the Story-Writer can only follow him and call him by his new name' (JSNZGXZ, 111). Two ch. later, when that character changes back to his old name, the narrator comments: 'Respected Reader! I, who am writing this novel, have no choice but to call him again by his old name.' (Ibid. 125).

Why should narratorial explicitness lead to an increase in narrative intrusions? The ultimate cause of this uneasiness is the crisis in the relationship between the gradually increasing explicitness of the narrator and the basically unchanged narratee. The narrator is trying to reaffirm this relationship with the narratee with a great number of intrusions so as to ensure an effective communication. In the several centuries of traditional vernacular Chinese fiction when the sharing of the codes was relatively stable, there was no urgent need for increased intrusions.

But the huge number of narratorial intrusions also presupposes the possibility of recovering the shared coding between the partners of the communicative frame.[34] If not, intrusions would become pointless— directions superfluous, and moral-judgement commentaries incomprehensible or unacceptable, which is exactly what today's readers feel when reading these novels.

These two factors—the sense of crisis and the possibility of recovering the coding system—together account for the abnormal increase in narratorial intrusions. They do not indicate a closeness of the communicative pair, but on the contrary, betray a situation in which the communicative frame, previously secure, is now under threat of disintegration in late Qing fiction, though not it has not yet fallen apart.

IX

In May Fourth fiction, the number of narratorial intrusions dropped abruptly to a minimum. The fundamentally different way of installing the narrative frame makes the overdose of narratorial intrusions neither necessary nor possible. In most works of May Fourth fiction, the narrator tries his best to refrain from intrusions, especially from directions, reducing them to virtual non-existence. Even in the earliest May Fourth short-story collection—Yu Dafu's *Sinking* and Ye Shengtao's *Estrangement* (*Gemo*, 1921), there can be found hardly a single direction.

---

[34] Karl Kroeber, when analysing George Eliot, offers an explanation: 'The frequency and importance of George Eliot's authorial comments [my term: narratorial commentaries] testify to how remote she feels her narrative to be from the ready comprehension and sympathy of her audience. Eliot has been accused of being didactic, but the accusers have not always remembered that a teacher-pupil relation is likely to be a remote one.' (Kroeber 1971: 47).

The few directions still to be found in May Fourth fiction generally assumed various disguises to make themselves hard to detect.[35] In Wang Tongzhao's story 'Being Drunk' ('Zuihou'), the direction comes almost like the thought in the drunkard's mind, 'What horror? In this summertime downtown?' In Feng Yuanjun's early story 'Behind the Schedule' ('Wudian'), directions are often combined with commentaries so that they do not reveal too much of the narratorial control of the narrative: 'On one such evening, began the tragedy he had to play.'

In rare cases, directions are intentionally exposed and made conspicuous so as to achieve some special effect. Shen Congwen, a skilful story-teller, sometimes played with directions. The very first sentences of his story 'The Diary of a Woman' ('Yige Furen de Riji') begin: 'The title is "The Diary of a Woman". Now let me continue.' These 'exposed' directions are mostly ironical, purposely overdone so that the narratorial control is made dramatic.

If directions are indeed very rare, commentaries in May Fourth fiction are still common, though much fewer than in Chinese fiction of any other period. But like directions, most commentaries in May Fourth fiction appear less intrusive. Wang Tongzhao's 'A Rainy Spring Night' ('Chunyu zhi Ye') ends with an exclamation, 'Oh! The same rainy spring night, but each had such a different feeling!' It is hard to tell whether these are the words of the narrator or of a certain character, or shared by them.

In Ye Shengtao's stories, though there are hardly any directions, commentaries often turn up. One example from his 'A Heavy Load of Sorrow' ('Bei'ai de Zhongzai') reads: 'The maximum capacity of the boat was forty persons, when there was not much room for the passengers to move. Yet the sorrow of humankind it carried exceeded its capacity by far too much, though it would not sink because of that weight.' (GM, 67). What attenuates the intrusiveness of these commentaries is that most of them appear in first-person narratives where the thoughts of the character are sometimes hardly distinguishable from the narrator's commentaries.

Narratorial intrusions are abundant in the works of some authors who

---

[35] Not all the narratorial intrusions in May Fourth fiction are well-disguised. There are inevitably some 'sloppy' directions, awkwardly introduced. In Guo Moruo's story 'Yueshe' ('Moon Eclipse'):

— I dreamt of Miss Uta last night.
— Oh, you did? How is she now?

When we were exchanging these few words, our scene shifted to Japan.

are more influenced by nineteenth-century Western fiction. Lao She and Xu Dishan, for instance, are writers who use narratorial intrusions extensively. Xu's 'The Spider Weaving Webs Futilely' ('Zhuiwang Laozhu') relies on a great number of intrusions to link up the fast-moving story. Prusek, quoting Z. Slupski, argues that the works by Lao She 'represent an old stage of European realistic prose and at the same time they are closer to the traditions of the old Chinese novel', and he explains: 'Lao She starts from Dickens' novel in which the author–narrator constantly intervenes in the narration in the same way as the Chinese story-tellers.'[36] This is a sharp observation.

Against the background of minimum narratological intrusions, some fiction works can now intentionally employ abundant narratorial intrusions to achieve certain goals. The first examples of such works are deliberate parodies, of which Lu Xun's *The True Story of A Q* is the best illustration. The short novel was widely imitated during the May Fourth period. The narrator in these works is flauntingly intrusive. Sometimes whole chapters, e.g. the first chapter of *The True Story of A Q*, or the sixth chapter of Xu Qinwen's *The Snivelling Second Daughter* (*Biti A Er*) consists of directions and commentaries from beginning to end. But the ironical tone of these narratorial intrusions leaves no doubt that they are installed for self-satire.

Another kind of excessive use of narratorial intrusions is serious experiments with, rather than parodies of, the 'traditional' narratological conventions. Wang Luyan's 'The Cannon from Xinghua' ('Xinghua Dapao'), Li Jianwu's 'The Legend of Zhongtiao Mountains'('Zhongtiao Shan de Chuanshuo'), and Jiang Guangci's 'Olive' ('Ganlan') are good examples. Because of the intrusions, these stories are readily reminiscent of Chinese traditional fiction, with their special stylistic effects. Most of those stories, however, were folktales retold, which was not a favourite sub-genre among May Fourth writers.

During the May Fourth period, however, there are some authors who lapse into the old narrative mode. In their works we can see a resurrection of the narratological conventions of traditional vernacular fiction. Since most May Fourth writers are well read in traditional Chinese fiction (in which they are certainly better informed than in Western fiction, though they may have admired the latter more), the habits formed by reading are bound to turn up unawares in their own writing. Those authors who are more eager to interest the readers, or more concerned

---

[36] Prusek 1980: 61.

with the communicative effect are particularly prone to this. In a word, writers on the popular side of the May Fourth fiction are likely to pick up the traditional techniques.

In Zhang Ziping's stories or novels, for instance, the narrator appears so intrusive that he even tried to appropriate part of the personality of the conventional semi-implicit narrator. In 'Rocking Horse' ('Muma'): 'The owner of the hostel is Lin. We shall call him Old Lin hereafter. His Japanese names are too cumbersome . . . Let's spare ourselves the trouble.' (XDCX, 72).

Even in first-person narratives, the narrator in Zhang Ziping's works an also be so intrusive that he resembles more the conventional narrator. The numerous directions in Zhang Ziping's novel *Fossils of the Alluvial Age* makes frequent use of 'dead time' by means of narrative intrusions: 'I took a train trip of several hours from Mensi to my destination. I remained so gloomy all the way that I do not want to describe the trip any more. As for what happened to Miss Chen afterwards, I will not be able to write about her until the time when I see her or hear about her again.' (CJQHS, 24). Such intrusions can no longer be confused with the character's 'inner voice', as the narrator's time does not overlap with the character's time.

Often in Zhang Ziping's fiction, the narratee is called up to support the intrusions: 'My friendship with Heming was profound. If I do not tell you the history of our friendship, you readers might accuse me of disloyalty to my friend.' (CJQHS, 28). The evocation of the narratee is almost exactly the same as that in late Qing fiction, but rare in May Fourth fiction. The novel even devotes whole sections to judgemental commentaries, e.g. on church philanthropy (section 27), on crime (section 44), and on Sino-Japanese relations (section 47). This reminds us of the pages-long commentaries in traditional novels. Frequent and long intrusions can also be found in Jiang Guangci's short novel *The Sans-Culottes* (*Duanku Dang*), so that some parts of the novel read almost like a political pamphlet. This novel is, regarded as the first piece of proletarian fiction in China.

X

Narrative subjectivity is important in any narrative analysis because it is the source of intentionality that influences the interpretation. It marks the intentional context which, though insufficient to determine the interpretation that also relies on other pragmatic contexts,[37] is, anyway, a context that can be examined by an analysis of the text.

In a written narrative, various personalities—the character, the narrator and the implied author—could all claim to possess narrative subjectivity by participating in the deliverance of the narrative message.[38] This is the integral repartition of the narrative subjectivity.

In a narrative text, however, there can be more than one author (as in the case of *The Dream of the Red Chamber*) or rewriter (as with *The Three Kingdoms*). There can also be several narrators either on the same level or on different levels, and there can be many characters in one narrative text. This then is the distributional repartition of narrative subjectivity.

These subjective elements may or may not agree with each other in their attitude toward the narrative, since each one could assume sufficient personality to take a particular stand. The subjectivity conflict causes dramatic tension in the narrative.

The character's expropriation of the narrator's voice is frequently seen in Chinese fiction. Even in the works of the Rewriting period, with the narrator's stringent control of the discourse after repeated rewriting, the yielding of narrative voice to characters is still a common occurrence.[39]

[37] According to contemporary pragmatics, the following 5 contexts may influence the interpretation of a message: co-textual, existential, situational, intentional, and psychological contexts. Besides the intentional context, perhaps only the situational context can be said to be related to the formal analysis of the narrative text. For the 5 contexts, see Sebeok 1986, *passim*.

[38] Tzvetan Todorov once put forward an interesting argument on the decentring of subjectivity in discourse: 'Dans "Il court", il y a "il", sujet de l'énonce, et moi, sujet de l'énonciation. Dans "Je cours", un sujet de l'énonciation énonce s'intercale entre les deux, en prenant à chacun une partie de son contenu précédent mais sans les faire disparaître entièrement: il ne fait que les immerger. Car le "il" et le "moi" existent toujours: ce "je" qui court n'est pas le même que celui qui énonce. "Je" ne réduit pas deux à un mais de deux fait trois.' (Todorov 1968: 121). Such a decentring does not occur distinctly in oral statement where the 'sujet de l'énonciation énonce' is readily identical with the 'sujet de l'énonciation'. Only in written narration does the subjectivity in the narrative statement split into 3, which can be named in more familiar terms: subject of the narration—author; subject narrated—character; subject of the narration narrated—narrator.

[39] In ch. 16 of *The Three Kingdoms*, Cao Cao is suddenly attacked by Zhang Xiu in Wancheng because he has slept with the latter's sister-in-law. Cao and his army flee hastily. 'Just as Cao Cao had reached the River Yu, the *bandits-soldiers* arrived in hot pursuit.' (SGYY, 39). This word 'bandits-soldiers' (*zeibing*) sounds strange because throughout the novel Cao Cao is said to be the bandit of the nation (*guozei*). To give Cao Cao's enemy this deprecatory epithet, usually associated with Cao Cao himself, is justifiable only under the supposition that Cao Cao's voice takes over in this part of the narration, however short it is.

This usurpation of narrative voice is more frequently seen in novels of the Creative period. In *Jin Ping Mei*, when Pan Jinlian, now a new concubine, succeeds in winning the favour of Wu Yueniang, Ximen Qing's wife: 'Li Jiao'er and the other concubines were all annoyed, seeing that Wu Yueniang favoured her by *mistake*. They all said, "We are good people, but left aside. She came to the house only a few days ago, and yet she is so spoilt. Big Sister really knows nothing."' (JPM *Cihua*, ch. 9). It is not the narrator but the other concubines that would call Wu Yueniang's favouritism toward Pan Jinlian a 'mistake' (*Cuo'ai*).[40]

In *The Dream of the Red Chamber*, the best of the traditional Chinese novels, we find a more subtle takeover of narrative voice. In chapter 21, in Baochai's presence, Xiren complains that her master Baoyu mixes too much with girls. 'Hearing this, Baochai thought to herself, "Why, this girl talks reason." Then Baochai sat on the bed and engaged Xiren in an idle talk, asking her about her age and her family. She examined her carefully. *Her words and her mind were both so respectable.*' (HLM, 376).[41] Here the 'respectable' is Baochai's appreciation of Xiren, not the narrator's. Yet the statement is mixed in with the flow of narrative, not directly attributed to Baochai.

When these takeovers of the narrative voice by characters are allowed to develop, the text becomes somewhat 'polyphonic' in the Bakhtinian sense. Here is an example: in chapter 19 of *The Dream of the Red Chamber*, Xiren's mother and brother came to the Jias' mansion and want to buy her back, but Xiren is not willing to go with them.

Her mother, seeing that her daughter was so insistent, understood that she would not leave with them. Anyway the contract had long ago been signed to have her sold. They came to try because the Jias were known for their generosity. It was not impossible that they would not have even to pay back the money. *What is more, the Jias never maltreated their slaves. There were more kind words than threats. And the chambermaids of the Jia family members received*

[40] Traditional Chinese critics seemed to understand this subtle narrative device. In ch. 8 of *The Scholars*: 'The next year the Prince of Ning defeated the imperial troops in Southern Jiangxi. The people there either opened the city gate or fled. Prefect Wang *resisted* unsuccessfully. He found a small boat and fled on a dark night.' A contemporary commentator had a sharp eye when he pointed out: 'Whence the "resisted"? Only he himself said that he had resisted.' (RLWS Variorum, 196).

[41] The modern editors (e.g. those of the edn. listed in Appendix II of this dissertation) omit any punctuation after 'examined her carefully', leaving the voice of the narrator confused with that of the character. I suggest the insertion of a comma in Chinese or a stop in English.

better treatment than servants of lower grades, even better than poor families
treated their own daughters: so the mother and brother gave up the idea of
buying Xiren back. (HLM, 185. Italics mine.)

Here we have a value-judgement of how generous and amiable the
Jias are, which is definitely not the narrator's opinion. In fact, the
narrator in *The Dream of the Red Chamber* tries his best not to provide
such value-judgements, either in favour or in disfavour of the characters. The only conclusion we can draw is that this must be considered
as a narrative statement with the characters' subjectivity superseding
the narrator's on a large scale.[42]

XI

Since each of the elements of narrative subjectivity—authors, narrators,
and characters—has his own intentions, attitudes, value-judgements,
and his own way of meaning control, when they clash, the tension can
make the fictional narrative both complicated and interesting.

If the elements of the compound subjectivity are on the same level—
different narrators on the same narrating level, or characters on the
same narrated level—they can fall into direct conflict. If, however,
these elements are on different levels (e.g. a narrator and a character),
they cannot clash directly since they dwell in different worlds. They
may clash only when there is an interpretative effort to tidy up their
opinions into a unified 'meaning of the text'.

In trying to find the set of values embodied in the different elements
of subjectivity, we come to the spectral existence of the author. Very
few authors of traditional Chinese novels left us with more than an
alias. In any case, for many of the fictional works of the Rewriting
period, the name of the author does not mean much, as too many hands
have participated in the successive rewritings.

Yet in a narratological analysis the author is a necessary function.
He is, then, regarded as a personality deduced from the narrative text,
an embodiment of the set of moral, psychological, and aesthetic values
which support the whole narrative. Whether this set of values is sin-
cerely cherished by the historically existent author, or only improvised

---

[42] Wong Kam-ming (1974: 103) also comments on this para., and insists that this is
an example of a shift in point of view. I hesitate to agree with him, for, as I see it, shifts
in point of view are always necessitated by the unfolding of the action which can be
experienced or observed by this or that character. Here we find no action but the characters thinking to themselves.

for whatever reason by him when writing the narrative, is beyond narratological concern. The function that embodies that set of values is generally called the implied author.[43]

If the narrator falls into conflict with the implied author, i.e. the narrator's value-judgement is not in agreement with the expected interpretation of the whole text, narratorial unreliability occurs. Since the whole idea of reliability is dependent on interpretation, the whole idea is notoriously elusive, as there are too many contexts that could influence interpretation.

There is, however, another kind of narratorial unreliability. If the narrator, by various means such as self-doubt, abstinence from meaning control, or complete implicitness, induces suspicion of unreliability, this is what I call 'built-in' narratorial unreliability, which is not totally dependent on interpretation, and, in fact, is the only kind of narratorial unreliability that can be subjected to narrative analysis.

But there is another pitfall in the idea of 'built-in' unreliability. Once the narrator is suspected of unreliability, where is the reliable point of reference by which any interpreter can check his interpretation?

To answer this question, we must know that it is in the process of the narrative mediation that the unreliability sets in. In the pre-narrated state the problem of unreliability does not exist as there is no narration yet, and no narratorial subjectivity has touched it. Therefore, if we doubt that the narrative is unreliable, the only way to find the reference is to return to the pre-narrated story.

This seems impossible since the pre-narrated is amorphous. Yet a recapitulation of the pre-narrated is what we naturally (perhaps unconsciously) undertake in order to understand even the basic plot. In our reading we make necessary adjustments as mental reorganizations, e.g. reversing the flashbacks to make the story coherent, expanding the description so that we can see what the focalized character cannot see, etc. After the mental reorganization, the world, now comprehended, is

---

[43] Wayne Booth (1983) made a great contribution to modern narratology when he first expounded the idea of the implied author. But he is ambiguous on some crucial issues concerning this concept. If this implied author is regarded as the so-called 'second self' of the author, he is then 'the executive author', an agent of the actual author at the time of writing. If this implied author is a personality embodying the set of values supporting the text, then he is 'the inferred author' whose identity can only be summed up through reading the narrative text.

We can say that confusion can be avoided since the two may be identical. Nevertheless, the executive implied author (the author's second self) should be identifiable with what the author was at the time of writing, whereas the inferred implied author, on the contrary, is the result of interpretation, and is fixed by the interpretation of the text.

the pre-narrated world rather than the narrated world. Since unreliability can occur only in the narrator's transformation of the former into the latter, reliability could be recovered by turning back the process, i.e. by erasing the narratorial mediation.[44]

Some traditional Chinese critics seem to understand this complex problem of modern criticism. Qi Liaosheng, one of the earliest critics of *The Dream of the Red Chamber*, declares in his preface to the novel: 'But I insist that the author may have two ideas while the reader must have only one opinion. This is like a painting where there is only one most beautiful peak for a mountain with many views; only one elegant tree for the forked creek.'[45] He understands, I think, the mental reorganization in the process of reading.

Is there a narrator who is so completely reliable that his attitude toward every character and every event in the story is exactly in agreement with the implied author? Booth suggested that such a complete reliability can be found in those works where 'the narrator is not dramatized',[46] i.e. as I understand it, not a participant character.

The self-characterization of the narrator, I would like to suggest, has little to do with his reliability, though it is an easy explanation of the general narratorial reliability in traditional Chinese vernacular fiction, as he never participates in the story. The most reliable narrator is the one who successfully unifies the values throughout the narrative text, making the opinion of the implied author the same as his. The narrators of Chinese fiction of the Rewriting period were, almost without exception, highly reliable since the texts were rewritten so many times that the narrator's attitude was almost inevitably reduced to a social average. It is almost impossible to get a succession of rewriters over many centuries to agree in a design of unreliability, as any unreliability is, by nature, highly individual.

Narratorial unreliability in Chinese fiction in fact started with *Jin Ping Mei* and some other late Ming fictional works. Lu Xun found in *Jin Ping Mei*:

The author knows the world so thoroughly that his descriptions are either brisk, or twisted, or satirical as to reveal everything, or concealed as to be

---

[44] See Rimmon-Kenan 1983: 124. Ernst Kris and Abraham Kaplan in their essay 'Aesthetic Ambiguity' (in Kennick, 1964: 419) expound the three criteria in straightening up a narrative: correspondence (as the interpretation should be based on historical knowledge of the subject-matter or the language); author's intention; and coherence (to organize the various parts into a coherent whole).

[45] Huang Lin and Han Tongwen 1982: 492.   [46] Booth 1983: 234.

ironical, or talking about the two sides at the same time so that all aspects are brought out. No novel of that time is comparable with it.[47]

The most subtle narratorial unreliability in Chinese vernacular fiction, however, can be found in some of the best eighteenth-century novels.

As the narrator in the novel *The Scholars* obstinately refuses to provide any judgemental commentaries, the characters, left alone to justify their own actions, come out with a whole spectrum of rationales, leaving enough room for the divergence of subjectivity. 'Negative' characters like Ma Chunshang or Kuang Chaoren show enough virtue to win our sympathy, while 'positive' characters like Du Shaoqing or Yu Youzhong commit follies that make them look stupid. Even Wang Yuhui, the foolish pedant who encourages his daughter to commit suicide after her husband's death, is depicted as one faithful to his beliefs, which distinguishes him from the horde of hypocrites in the novel. Since almost all of the characters are neither positive nor negative, unreliability, then, runs through most parts of the novel.

In chapter 29 of *The Dream of the Red Chamber* the narrator offers some adjectival commentaries:

Baoyu was born with a *reprehensible* disease. That was not all. Now he began to know things, and had read some *depraved* books, he discovered that none of the girls in all his relatives' family could be compared with Daiyu as he grew up in her company. He had long formed some idea in his mind, only unable to speak out. (HLM, 126)

Here the adjectives 'reprehensible' and 'depraved' are the narrator's judgemental commentaries on Jia Baoyu's disposition. But they are obviously not the implied author's opinion (i.e. not the opinion implied by the whole novel). The narratorial unreliability in this passage is pushed to such an extreme that it should be called narratorial irony.

The unreliability in *The Dream of the Red Chamber* is so sophisticated that not many novels of modern times can hope to match it. For instance, the description of Feng Jie and Xue Baochai is remarkably unreliable in that it does not reward any clear-cut understanding of the two characters. The narration of many events limits itself to mere observations that offer no explanation or clue to the causality. Qin Keqing's mysterious death is left unexplained; Feng Jie's flirtation with Jia Rong, as vaguely observed by Granny Liu, is cut short and never

[47] Lu Xun 1956: viii. 147.

picked up again; neither are Baoyu's relations with his sister-in-law
Qin Keqing clearly stated. The narrator in these cases resembles the
taciturn narrator in some twentieth-century modern novels.[48]

XII

While most late Qing fictional works are regarded in literary history as
'satirical fiction' (*fengci xiaoshuo*), they are far from being narratologically ironical. On the contrary, in this period the reliability of traditional Chinese fiction is greatly reinforced.

First, most late Qing fictional works claimed eagerly that they are the
carriers of truth and that their first aim is to impart the truth as faithfully
as possible. In Liang Qichao's *The Future of New China*, after a character recalls the Russian invasion of Manchuria in 1902, there is a note,
which in the original text first printed in the magazine *New Fiction*
were set in smaller fonts, but in brackets in later editions: 'The Author's note: the above were actually events that happened recently, and
have been collected from Japanese newspapers, without my fabricating
even one word.' (XZGWLJ, 55). And after another character talks about
the presence of the Russian fleet in the Pacific, there is also a note: 'The
Author's note: this is the latest report according to Reuters on the
fourteenth of this month.' (XZGWLJ, 59)

Those notes cannot be taken as the explanatory intrusion by the
narrator, since the narrator has to talk at the moment of the narrating
now which, according to the novel, is 2062 AD when China is celebrat-
ing the fiftieth anniversary of the success of the Reformist Movement.
This is the author's direct intervention, as the author talks from the
writing now, when he could cite the news report in 1902 as 'the latest'.
The author's voice strips the text of its narrative casing and destroys the
fictionality of the novel reducing it to a political pamphlet. Such is the
price the late Qing writers were ready to pay for pursuing 'factual
reliability'.

The obsession with narratorial reliability is also demonstrated in the
straightforward moralizing of narrative text. A most conspicuous and
intrusive practice is to give the characters names that indicate what kind
of people they are. In Li Boyuan's *The Bureaucrats*, there is a character

---

[48] Some scholars (e.g. David Hawkes) argue that the novel has been rewritten so many
times by the author, and there exist so many MS versions that there are bound to be
inconsistencies. But obviously some of the 'cut-short' descriptions are intentionally arranged. See Hawkes's introduction to *The Story of the Stone* (1973: i. 39).

with the name Tao Ziyao (the pronunciation resembles The Escapee), and in the novel he indeed flees from his responsibility. There is also a character Diao Maipeng (a playing on Betrayer of Friends), and he lives up to his name in the novel. There are also in the novel names like Jia Xiaozi (Faked Filial Piety), Zhen Shoujiu (Real Old Hat), Wei Qiao, with the alternative name Zhugang (together hinting at Blackmailer), and many others. In another novel by him, *A Short History of Civilization* (*Wenming Xiaoshi*), there are Xin Mingci (Neologism), Kang Bodu (Comprador), and Liu Xuesheng (Returnee Student), who work for a fashionable publisher. When in the novel *A Sea of Remorse*, the boy protagonist meets with someone named Xin Shuhuai (Evil Heart) and befriends him on his way to Shanghai, we know that the boy is in trouble, and he cannot help but be ruined after a few chapters. This practice goes to such an excess that the name Gou Cai (Dog's Stuff) was used in several novels by different authors: in Wei Xiuren's *The Flowers and the Moon* (*Hua Yue Hen*), in Wu Jianren's *Strange Events*, and in Li Boyuan's *The Bureaucrats*.[49] In modern Chinese literature this crude naming-stereotyping was resurrected in the Yan'an literature of the 1940s and in the 'model Peking opera' during the Cultural Revolution of 1966–76.

In this way, characters are turned into stereotypes, and their behaviour morally pre-determined before the action takes place. These names are actually commentaries, more direct than the nicknames in the traditional vernacular novel *Water Margin* or *Three Heroes and Five Gallants* (*Sanxia Wuyi*), because the nicknames in those novels are mostly description of the characters unique 'humour', and generally do not foreshadow the development of the plot.

Because of the moral zeal, exaggerations are almost abusively employed in late Qing fiction, which prompted Lu Xun to the criticism of it 'revealing too much the edge of its language' (*cifeng tailu*).[50] The name he gave to late Qing fiction—Reprimanding fiction instead of Satirical fiction—is quite justifiable in this sense.

Some of the late Qing critics in fact knew what was going wrong:

Today's social fiction, though published in huge quantity, suffers from a common problem—exhaustiveness . . . For social fiction, the more covert it is, the more interesting it appears. When we read *The Scholars* no one can help

---

[49] This is reminiscent of some pre-modern moralist novels in the West, e.g. Bunyan's *Pilgrim's Progress*.

[50] Lu Xun 1956: viii. 245.

being fascinated by the descriptions which are as subtle and miraculous as the celestial tripod made by God Yu . . . Yet the author of *The Scholars* does not provide even one word of praise or blame for the characters.[51]

Narratorial unreliability, nevertheless, is not totally absent from late Qing fiction. In some of the best novels of the period narratorial unreliability takes the form of overstatement. In chapter 2 of *A Flower in the Sinful Sea* there is a commentary on the Zhuangyuan (Number One Winner in the Imperial Examination):

I believe that you, my compatriots, have never read *Records of the Successful Candidates*, and do not know what a great honour it is to be Zhuangyuan. This person is not to be found in any country in the world except in China; and only one in three years. This fortunate person must enjoy the charitable and pious deeds accumulated by three generations of his ancestors; he must never in his life be led to transgress by women; he must not only be able to write properly worded essays but also be well acquainted with the big names in the capital. Once he has won the title, he becomes a leader of the immortals and disciple of the emperor himself. His prosperity and wisdom should scare away Su Dongpo or Li Taibai, let alone Bacon of England or Rousseau of France. (NHH, 5)

This is an overstatement, not an exaggeration. Its intended meaning runs contrary to the surface meaning, while an exaggeration is meant to reinforce the meaning in the same direction. Exaggerations abound in late Qing fiction, on almost every page of every novel: in Wu Jianren's *China Now* (*Zhongguo Xianzao Ji*), the fashionable reformists in Shanghai convene a meeting of suffragettes and make a mess of everything; in Li Boyuan's *The Hell for the Living*, one magistrate after another takes simple-minded pleasure in all kinds of unimaginable tortures. In comparison with these passages, the overstatement in *A Flower in the Sinful Sea*, though not at all subtle, sounds much better.

In a very small number of late Qing novels, or, more exactly, in some parts of these novels, there appears the 'no comments' form of unreliability—a refusal to provide any moral judgement. In *Strange Events*, for instance, the protagonist–narrator Jiusi Yisheng despises an official career, but he buys an official title for himself since 'it does not cost much'. He hates to make money by crooked means, but he helps his friend Wen Shunong to counterfeit antiques and cheat customers. He is never tired of visiting brothels though he obviously enjoys telling ugly stories about prostitutes and their patrons.

The only real hero in the novel, Wu Jizhi, acting as the elder brother

[51] Yuxue Sheng, 'Xiaoshuo Conghua', in A Ying 1960: 80.

of the protagonist and his guardian in this wicked world, proclaims his philosophy that the most important thing in life is just 'to muddle along' (*hun*), and that in the face of evil, the most important thing to do is 'not to lay it bare', because 'to lay it bare means a wet blanket, and a wet blanket means repugnance. With repugnance everywhere, you can no longer muddle along in this world.' Thus, in chapter 14, when everyone in the office accepts a part of a bribe, he does not refuse to take his share.

The same narratorial unreliability can be found more or less in *A Flower in the Sinful Sea* or *The Travels of Lao Can*. After reading the former we really do not know whether the heroine Caiyun should be considered a voluptuous whore with an evil heart, or a bold woman who dares to take her fate in her own hands. This is a more difficult achievement than that in *Strange Events* because the narrator in *A Flower in the Sinful Sea* is not participant, as in the latter, but remains the impersonal semi-implicit story-writer who is in a position designed to comment.

By refusing to let good people be rewarded and bad people be punished, and by refusing to criticize or praise anyone, and more importantly, by making it difficult to judge a character by a consistent code, the anti-heroism tones down the moral urgency of these few novels and makes them unique in late Qing Reprimanding fiction. But what is more important to our analysis is that since the narrator is no longer the executive for the positive values and commonly accepted moral norms, there then appears a certain, though limited, distance between the narrator and the implied author—the basic requirement of an unreliable narrator.

XIII

The relationship between the elements of narrative subjectivity forms a certain narrative scheme. Different schemes are formed by the varying distances between those elements.

In most traditional Chinese vernacular fiction (with the notable exceptions of some eighteenth-century masterpieces), the narrative is fairly reliable and there can be found almost no difference between the values expressed by the impersonal semi-implicit narrator and those embodied by the implied author. In a reliable narrative, the distance between the implied author and the narrator (and that between the implied reader and the narratee as well) is short. When narrative reliability is absolute, the positions of the narrator–narratee pair and the implied author-implied reader pair virtually overlap.

In late Qing Reprimanding fiction the reliability of the narrative is strengthened at the expense of the characters as most of them are objects of ridicule. In this caricature scheme the distance between the narrator and the characters is increased, as he is morally much higher than them.

In Butterfly romance fiction we find an opposite scheme of equal, if not more serious, reliability, where the narrator is not only reliable but refuses to keep a distance from the character. Thus all the participants of the narrative communication collapse into a direct sharing of feelings and values.

Such a scheme, as exemplified by Butterfly fiction, needs a special audience that would unquestioningly identify with the implied reader. If a reader cannot feel completely comfortable in sharing those emotions, this 'squeezed-together' communication pattern becomes repugnant to him.

Such a narrative scheme is rarely seen in May Fourth fiction, where in most cases the narrator maintains a rather great distance from the implied author. In some works, there appear asymmetrical schemes, i.e. the distance between the narrator and the implied author is greater than that between the narratee and the implied reader.

By definition, the narrator knows everything no matter how much he actually reveals, but the narratee is kept in the dark as he is denied sufficient information. This can be observed in the so-called 'open-ended' fictional works where the future of the character is left untold. In traditional vernacular fiction, open-endedness is a rare exception, while in May Fourth fiction, open-endedness becomes the rule as the majority of works pick up only a section of the story with much left untold. For example, we do not know whether the protagonist of Yu Dafu's 'Sinking' really committed suicide in the sea, or, if he did not, how he will survive his hypochondria.

This scheme also applies to those narratives where crucial information is withheld all through the narrative until the very end. Although at the end all the information is supplied in these narratives, the narrative as a temporal process has already benefited from this withholding. Detective stories are the most typical example of this narrative scheme. In May Fourth fiction we can find many other works of fiction playing on this kind of information-withholding. Wang Luyan's story 'Juying's Wedding' ('Juying de Chujia') is an example: the description of a fanfare village wedding goes on until the end of the story, when it is revealed that both the bride and the groom died long ago, and that this is only a 'spiritual wedding' to console the grieved parents and, hopefully, the deceased in another world. In such a narrative scheme, the narratee knows much less than the narrator. The asymmetry remains as the motive force for the development of the plot until the very end, when it is redressed.

The narrative schemes described above are all reliable ones, in which the distance between the narrator and the implied author is relatively short. In unreliable schemes, however, the marked distinction between the narrator's stand and that of the implied author distances the two.

The lack of moral thoroughness seems to be the only type of narrative unreliability in traditional Chinese fiction, including the late Qing fiction. In these few works there appears a greater distance between the implied author (who does not have too good an opinion of, for instance, Feng Jie in *The Dream of the Red Chamber* or the Uncle in *Strange Events*) and the narrator who refuses to make any depreciatory comments about those characters. Yet, even though there is narratorial unreliability, the narrative scheme is still symmetrical, as the narratee-implied reader relationship basically mirrors that between the narrator-implied author.[52]

In many May Fourth fictional works, however, the distance between the character and the narrator (and the narratee) is reduced since what the narrator says and feels does not necessarily carry much more authority than that which the character says or feels. In many of the May Fourth works of fiction the narrator is sufficiently personalized that he is in fact no more authoritative than the characters. In *The True Story of A Q*, for instance, the narrator's intrusions can *never* be taken as the implied author's opinion. The narrator is sarcastic about A Q's tragedy, but the implied author, as the embodiment of the values of the whole text, is more sympathetic toward the protagonist. The unreliability of narration is thus intensified into a narrative irony which brings the narrator into direct conflict with the implied author.

In a totally 'behaviourist' objective narrative such as Lu Xun's

[52] Booth (1983: 278) holds that the position of the implied author and the implied reader can be asymmetrical. This, I think, is against the very definition of implied author-reader. The implied reader can only be regarded as the mirror image of the implied author. He is the *expected* acceptance of the set of values inferred from the narrative. Booth, inventor of this pair of concepts, is here confusing the implied author-reader relationship with the actual author-reader relationship.

'Medicine' or 'A Public Example', the narrator is almost totally effaced, i.e. he definitely refuses to offer any opinion on the events he narrates.[53] Some of Ye Shengtao's stories also adopted this 'callous observer' scheme, as he himself confessed: when writing, he loved to 'watch with cold eyes'.[54] His story 'The Welcome' ('Huanying') relates how in a small town the local celebrities gather to hear John Dewey the American philosopher—which might well be a hilarious episode in late Qing Reprimanding fiction. Yet the narrative in this story is extremely 'unfeeling', so that in the whole story there seems to be mere objective observation with no apparent narrative mediation. The narrative irony, too subtle even for professional readers, has made some literary historians regret that this short story is 'dull' and 'dragging'. Ling Shuhua's story 'The Mid-Autumn Night' ('Zhongqiu Ye'), which won high praise from C. T. Hsia, relates how the happy marriage of a young couple is ruined, starting with a quarrel over the holiday feast. The husband and the wife each hold on to a different explanation of the small incident and its tragic result, but since the narrator remains reticent, refusing to give any judgement, the blind cruelty of fate seems to be more mysterious.

For unreliable narratives, there is also an asymmetrical possibility. When the narrator is a character, and thus morally questionable, his distance from the implied author can be considered greater than that between the implied reader and the narratee not yet turned into a morally fallible character or even remaining completely implicit. In Li Jinming's 'In a Boat', for instance, the narrator–protagonist—a 'cowardly seducer'—is morally low in the eyes of the implied author. We can only infer that the narratee should not be equally lacking in moral sense though he does not appear in the narrative.

But in a few May Fourth fictional works the narratee is often characterized too, and the asymmetry in the communication scheme is no longer a mere conjecture. In Xu Dishan's 'Undeliverable Letters' ('Wufa Toudi de Xin') the narrator–protagonist addresses various people who, for different reasons, refuse to correspond with the narrator—the lonely

---

[53] This reminds us of Zhang Dinghuang's comment on Lu Xun's fiction in 1923: 'We do not know how advanced he was in his study of medicine. We do not know whether he ever practised surgery. But we know that his fiction has three characteristics which belong to an experienced surgeon: *the first is coldness, the second is coldness; the third is again coldness* . . . Has there ever been such a resolute exposer? Has there ever been such a taciturn observer? ('Mr Lu Xun' in Tai Jingnong (ed.), *Guanyu Luxun ji qi Zhuzuo* (Shanghai: Kaiming Shudian, 1933). Italics mine.)

[54] Preface, *Ye Shengtao Xuji*, Shanghai: Kaiming Shudian, 1952, 4.

and mad letter writer. And we can consider that the narratees are nearer
to the implied author-reader pair, as they seem to be more sober in
refusing to receive those letters.

Sometimes a characterized narrator weak in moral or in intellect has
to tell the whole narrative from a lower point of view, as if looking up
to the narrated events at an angle of elevation. This particular unreliable
'angling-up' scheme can be found in many May Fourth fiction works.
In Wang Tongzhao's story 'The Child on the Lake Shore' ('Huban
Eryu'), the narrator, a child wandering aimlessly amid the reeds on the
lake shore, tells how his father does not allow him to go home until
late, and then the truth is gradually revealed that the child's ironsmith
father is unable to feed the family and his mother is working as a
prostitute at home. The narrator, intellectually weak, is unable to understand what he himself relates, but the narratee, an adult who hears his
story, sees the true situation.

A similar unreliable scheme can be found in some fictional works
with the deceptively sentimental narrator. Chen Xianghe's 'Mourning—'
('Dao—') is a very sentimental romance told by a miserable husband
after his young wife's death. But in the end we find that it was the
annoyingly childish wife made 'me' so impatient, and that 'I' cruelly
locked her out in the snow, so that she died because of the cold. The
sentimentalism is subverted by this revelation of stupidity on both sides.
Lu Xun's story 'Lament for the Deceased' ('Shangshi') relating the sad
separation of the young protagonist from his wife is a better example
as the romance turns sour because of the incompetence of both parties
in coping with the pressure of life. The narratorial unreliability now
acquires a thematic profundity as the narratorial unreliability encourages interpretative diversification.

2

Narrator and Character

I

Being a special character, the narrator's relations with the other characters are always problematic, and many narratological characteristics centre around those relations.

In the last chapter I already touched upon them in describing the narrator's position in the narrative scheme, correlating the narrator with the implied author and the characters. There are, however, other important aspects in the narrator–character relationship, such as how the narrator could limit his scope of consciousness to that of the characters, how he should report other characters' speech or thoughts, and how he could let other characters turn themselves into narrators by telling their own stories.

All these things have something to do with the sharing of narrative subjectivity among the narrator and the other characters. We can see that in the development of Chinese vernacular fiction there is an apparent downward movement of narrative subjectivity, in the process of which the control of meaning is decentralized and the narrator gradually hands over authority to other discursive subjects in the narrative, i.e. characters, thus creating more room for interpretative diversification.

II

Modern narratology seems to have grown out of the discussion on the 'point of view'. Yet, after almost a century, even this term itself is not yet settled.[1] For the purpose of this study, I will be using Genette's term

---

[1] Here is the list of the various terms recommended by critics for this concept: Henry James: centre of consciousness. (*The Art of the Novel*, 1915); Percy Lubbock: point of view (*The Craft of Fiction*, 1928); Jean Poullion: vision (*Temps et roman*, 1946); Allen Tate: post of observation (*House of Fiction*, 1940); Cleanth Brooks and Robert Penn Warren: focus of narrative (*Understanding Fiction*, 1948); Tzvetan Todorov: aspect (*Les catégories du récit littéraire*, 1966); Richard J. Watts: filtering (1981). Gerard Genette finds Brooks and Warren's term more acceptable, and renames it 'focalization'. (Genette 1980). This last term seems likely to be more acceptable than the others for the very simple reason that it does not carry serious metaphorical ambiguity. Nevertheless, it is challenged by Seymour Chatman who argues that the term suffers from 'etymological

'focalization', with the proviso that it means nothing more than the narratological meaning of 'point of view', i.e. perception, thus excluding other possible meanings of the phrase.[2]

Focalization is part of narrative mediation,[3] as it takes shape only in the process of the narrator's mediation, in the course of which he limits his privilege and narrates only what his chosen characters can experience.

The character is unable to narrate the story whereas the narrator is unable to experience the events. Thus, this is a joint activity of the narrator and the characters: the 'focalized' character offers an experience of the event, and the narrator offers the voice.[4]

proliferation', and he suggests using two terms 'filter' and 'slant' instead. (Chatman 1986: *passim*).

[2] Chatman presents a hair-splitting argument that there are at least three meanings in the term 'point of view'—interest, opinion, perception. (Chatman 1986: 211). In narratology, I think, perception is the basic meaning.

Some critics, e.g. Scholes and Kellogg insist that there are four kinds of points of view: those of the characters, of the narrator, of the audience, and of the author (1966: 240–1). This, to be frank, piles unnecessary complexities upon this unfortunate term. Wong Kam-ming, in his study of *The Dream of the Red Chamber*, applies the Scholes–Kellogg theory, with surprising results: 'As the point of view of the story-teller, the editor, and the memoirist soon merge into the single perspective of the author after Chapter 1, the gap between the stone and Pao-yu becomes one between the narrator and the author.' (Plaks 1977: 207). As I shall explain, only the narrator has the problem of 'point of view' since only he has to mediate the narration. When he assumes the character's perception as his scope of narration, he moves the narratorial point of view on to the character.

[3] Percy Lubbock's definition of 'point of view', is both an exaggeration and a simplification: 'The whole intricate question of method in the craft of fiction, I take to be governed by the question of point of view—the question of the relation in which the narrator stands to the story.' (Lubbock 1957: 45)

[4] This confuses some literary critics even today. The following is a passage taken from a book on the technique of fiction recently published in the USA: 'The writer who is in control of his material strives to make the point of view consistent. He takes care not to attribute to a character things he couldn't know, think, or feel; nor *does he attribute an unlikely vocabulary to his character.*' (Madden 1980: 112, italics mine.) I would contend that this is wrong. Instead I suggest the following rephrasing: The writer takes care not to attribute to a narrator things the focalized character is not able to experience, but he should let the narrator recast this character's experience into the narrator's vocabulary, unless in reported speech of the direct form.

The confusion arises, I imagine, from the situation of the first-person narrative in which the narrator is simultaneously the focalized character, and the narrator recalls what he once experienced as the character, so that the whole narrative can be taken as a reported speech in the direct form. Still the 'I' as narrator is different from the 'I' as character, since the 'I' cannot be both narrator and character at the same time. The narrator 'I', appearing later, is usually more mature than the focalized character 'I', as we can observe from such novels as *A la recherche du temps perdu*, or memoirs like *Six Chapters in My Floating Life* (Fusheng Liuji). When he is implicit, the narrator may recount the experience of one or several characters, but the narrative voice (and thus, the vocabulary) is still the narrator's.

Apparently, the focalization in traditional Chinese fiction is by no means complicated: the narratorial voice must be that of the Story-Teller, and his scope of consciousness is virtually unlimited. We usually call this kind of focalization 'omniscient'.

This term, however, is sometimes misleading. An omniscient narrator is seldom truly omniscient in the real sense of the word.[5] I agree with Watts when he argues that 'genuine omniscience is represented by the narrator's claim to know what different characters are doing at different places *at the same time*'.[6] Otherwise, when dealing with individual persons, the narrative is almost inevitably character-focalized, with the focus shifting from one character to another and staying on one character only for a while.

III

The narrator in traditional Chinese fiction, supposedly omniscient, often has to limit his power and allow the narratorial consciousness focus on one character, thus forming a partial character-focalization.

Richard Watts argues that in oral narrative, there is little character-focalization (his term: filtering): 'A more plausible explanation is that the minimal amount of filtering in oral narrative is due to the difference in the communicative medium. The narrator in the natural narrative situation is obviously expected by his audience to evaluate the events from his point of view.'[7]

Traditional Chinese vernacular fiction, on the other hand, very often resorts to partial character-focalization. This represents another proof that written narrative in China was not a direct imitation of oral narrative performance.

Jin Shengtan, the prominent seventeenth-century critic, was perhaps the first in the world to point out the advantage of character-focalization in his criticism on chapter 20 of *Water Margin*. He points out that the whole scene of Song Jiang's returning to his mistress is narrated as experienced by Old Lady Yan, who is in the dark as to what happens

---

[5] Chatman holds that only the narrative that shifts from the experience of one character to another at any moment can be called 'omniscient'. (Chatman 1978: 212). Wayne Booth is sharply observant when he calls this kind of narrative perspective 'omniscience with teeth'. (Booth 1983: 161). Genette calls the omniscient point of view 'non-focalizaton' or 'zero focalization' (1980: 224). Chatman (1986: 201) rightly points out that this term 'poses uneasy asymmetry', since 'omniscient' focalization is actually 'all-focalization'.

[6] Watts 1981: 72, italics mine.   [7] Ibid. 71.

that night between the couple, in this way rendering the narrative mysterious and puzzling. Jin Shengtan, when commenting on this chapter, gives this kind of character-focalization an exotic term—'The Moonlight Leaks out of the Shaded Lamp'.[8]

We can find much longer passages of character-focalization in *Water Margin* than those which Jin Shengtan noticed. In the chapters describing how Lin Chong is set up by his powerful enemies—one of the best-known episodes in *Water Margin*—the narrator strictly limits his power and focalizes the narrative on Lin Chong alone. The suspense finally comes to a head when he is almost trapped in the burning barn.

The character-focalization has its pitfalls, as eventually Lin Chong (and the narratee) has to be told the truth, and a coincidence must be engineered whereby his enemies gather at the door of the deserted temple where he takes refuge, revealing everything in their talk so as to allow him to overhear the conspiracy.

But such coincidences for the purpose of explanation are not always necessary. In the best of traditional Chinese fiction, character-focalization could lead to an interesting withholding of information to make the narrative unreliable. In *The Dream of the Red Chamber*, for instance, when Granny Liu visits the Grand View Garden, she sees things that she is unable to understand. She sees, for instance, that Feng Jie swallows her words when she is talking with Jia Rong, and flushes (HLM, 47). No explanation is to be supplied in the whole novel about what has happened between the two.

Sometimes the narrator inserts a direction to call attention to the fact that he is intentionally withholding some information. In chapter 15 of *The Dream of the Red Chamber*, Jia Baoyu teases his favourite the actor Qin Zhong by threatening 'we shall settle our account at night in bed': 'I really do not know how the two settled their account that night. I did not see it by myself. That's why I have to leave it as an unsolved case, with no fabrication on my part.' (HLM, 171) This direction may seem superfluous if the narrator really wants to cover up his withholding of information, but it is actually installed to call attention to a topic both tantalizing and embarrassing. If usually the narrator withholds information on the pretext of the character-focalization, the pretext is the opposite here. For the crucial information is within the character's scope of consciousness, but the 'omniscient' narrator suddenly moves back the focalization upon himself, and claims lack of omniscience.

---

[8] Huang Lin and Han Tongwen 1982: 286.

From this we can see that character-focalization is, after all, only a stratagem for redistributing the narrative subjectivity.

Among the vernacular Chinese novels, perhaps only *More Chapters of the Journey to the West* can be said to be consistent in character-focalization. Many parts of the novel remain enigmatic with the narrative focalized on the protagonist Sun Wukong's experience in his strange long dream. When searching for the First Emperor, Sun Wukong sees many things which, as he does not then understand them, are left unexplained.

What character-focalization really facilitates is a subtle presentation of the observer-subject rather than observed object. For in character-focalization the narrative consciousness is carried by the character, even though the language is still the narrator's.

Jin Shengtan was again the first to notice this subjective self-reflexity caused by character-focalization. In a marginal commentary on chapter 28 of *Water Margin*, where Wu Song promises Shi En to win back the wine tavern with his fists, the narrative goes like this: 'They went together. On the way they drank three bowls of wine at every tavern on the way. After drinking at more than a dozen taverns, Shi En looked at Wu Song and saw that he was not very drunk.' (SHZ, 876) Jin Shengtan shows that he is an astute observer when he comments: 'The purpose of this is not to tell us that Wu Song is apparently all right but to let us know that Shi En is really worried.'[9]

Character-focalization for the sake of subjective self-reflexity becomes very subtle in eighteenth-century Chinese novels. In chapter 4 of *The Scholars*, Zhou Jin the Civil Service Examiner takes the paper handed in by the miserable-looking old candidate Fan Jin:

Examiner Zhou read Fan Jin's paper carefully, and, displeased, told himself, 'What an essay! What language! No wonder he never passed in the first-grade examination', and threw aside the paper. . . . [After reprimanding a too ambitious examinee] he took up Fan Jin's paper again and read carefully once more. When he finished, he sighed, 'The writing is so remarkable that even I, after reading it two times, wasn't able to appreciate it. Only after reading it the third time did I come to understand that this is one of the most perfect essays between heaven and earth!' (RLWS, 95)

Since the narrator refuses obstinately to put in a word of explanation, there is no telling whether Fan Jin's essay is truly good, or whether Zhou the Examiner is deceived by his unconscious sympathy for this

---

[9] Huang Lin and Han Tongwen 1982: 299.

'Old Pupil' whose situation could have reminded him of his own miserable past. Leaving this crucial question unanswered, the narrative goes on to tell Fan Jin's embarrassment of riches, and we wonder whether he deserves this sudden success, or if it is only another absurd joke made by fate.

IV

Most late Qing novelists, even those who seem to be aware of the problem, are far from consistent in their handling of character-focalization. Even in 'travellers' novels, where it is easier to achieve character-focalization, the focalization is still scattered. In *The Travels of Lao Can*, the protagonist who naturally bears the focalization yields it to other characters in about one third of the whole novel. Another such novel *What The Ladies Next Door Say (Lin Nu Yu)* has been praised for its character-focalization,[10] but the focalized character disappears in the middle of the novel and lets the omniscient narrator take over, thus splitting the novel into two distinctly different halves.

Among late Qing writers, the one who seems to be the most conscious about focalization is Lin Shu. His literary-language novel *The Stench of the Sword (Jianxing Lu)*, is fairly consistent in the character-focalization of the protagonist Bing Zhongguang. Every time the narrative has to depart from character-focalization, it supplies a direction to apologize. In chapter 12, after some events that the protagonist could not have seen, the text reads, 'The events mentioned above were all told to Zhongguang by Huiyue'. (JXL, 548) In chapter 12, 'At that time there was no possibility for the families of Bing Zhongguang and Bofu to know anything about each other. All these facts were learned later.' (JXL, 556) The direction in chapter 34 is more interesting. When Zhongguang is fighting with bandits, his fiancée watches, trembling, and there is a long report on what is passing through her mind at this frightening moment. 'All these are the surmise of the author. Mei'er might have been thinking of something else.'

The self-doubt revealed in this direction almost destroys the narrative set-up, as the narrator seems on the verge of ironical narration (that is, negating the authenticity of his own narration). But actually this direction is only a nervous justification by a narrator scared of yielding too much power to the characters.

[10] e.g. A Ying 1937: 84.

This strangeness of the last direction is comparable to another one in Lin Shu's short story 'Xie Lanyan', in which a young lady of a rich merchant family and her fiancé, when crossing the sea, are caught in a shipwreck, but manage to reach a deserted island. The young man wants to 'hold the wedding' with her that night, but the girl solemnly refuses. At the end of the story there is this direction: 'How can a vulgar father have such a virtuous daughter? *I myself cannot believe what I am narrating!*'[11]

No vernacular novel of the late Qing, however, is so attentive to its handling of character-focalization. In many novels there is a limited focalization which shifts among certain main characters. In *The Bitter Society* (*Ku Shehui*), for instance, some Chinese merchants are turned into focalized characters when they arrive in Peru:

> [They saw] . . . the foreigner went to have a close look at those who fell into a fight, and said a few words to the sailors. Jiyuan did not understand what he said, but only saw the sailors all stand without moving. The foreigner became very angry and randomly kicked the sailors. (KSH, 54)

The character-focalization here is necessary, as the scene is made by 'the unreasonable foreign devils' whose language and behaviour are incomprehensible to the Chinese.

Character-focalization is all but natural in novels with first-person narration, or those sub-narratives (which I shall discuss later in this chapter) narrated in the first person, as the protagonist is identical with the explicit narrator, who provides witness to the story he himself told or heard. Nevertheless, this natural character-focalization still caused uneasiness in late Qing fiction, where the limiting of the privilege of the narrator, in whatever way, necessitates justification. In *Strange Events* there is a superfluity of directions. In chapter 87 of the novel, the Old Lady Gou torments her son and daughter-in-law in many strange ways:

> She went on picking fault on her daughter-in-law. Every time she saw her, no matter with a smile or in tears, she would censure her. She also did not allow her daughter-in-law to see her son who was ill in his room. What after all was her intention? *The Story-Writer has not entered her mind, and cannot make a surmise.* The daughter-in-law was really pitiable as she could only wash her face with tears. (ESNMDZGXZ, 385. Italics mine.)

[11] *Weilu Manlu* (*Random Notes in Wei Chamber*) Shanghai: The Commercial Press, 1922, 98.

The traditional narrator would try to explain such strange torments by revealing the character's motives. The late Qing narrator, however, gets away by explaining the narrative technique.

When information beyond the character-focalization is to be provided, the narrator challenges his own narration, so that the trespassing can be explained. In chapter 24 of *Strange Events*, after Wu Jizhi has told the story about the Imperial Academician Liang:

I asked, 'Even if he did cry for a whole night, that was his own business. Who saw it? *Isn't this like fiction—totally fabricated?*' Jizhi said, 'At that time he was living in the Governor's official mansion. When he was crying, two of his assistants were present, trying to console him. Otherwise how could other people know? So you were suspicious!' (ESNMDZGXZ, 134. Italics mine.)

No matter whether the justification is provided by the narrator or by a character, the narrator's discomfort with the situation is more than obvious.

It seems that the late Qing writers knew something of the mechanism of character-focalization but did not understand why it was used. They seemed to see it as a more authentic way to reveal the truth, or to create verisimilitude. Thus character-focalization became a more effective way to reinforce, not to reduce, the controlling authority of the narrator. That is why the narrator would try to keep to character-focalization even at the inconvenience of inserting so many narratorial intrusions.

Since intrusions can relieve the narrator from character-focalization, and the late Qing novelists are not at all scrupulous in using intrusions, the narrator then remains the omniscient one even if he seemingly moves the focalization onto another character.

With so many unnecessary explanations and apologetic remarks, the narrator is virtually pushing Chinese fiction back into its conventionality.

V

In May Fourth fiction character-focalization becomes a natural way of narrating that does not need any apologies or explanatory narratorial intrusions. The stress of character-focalization definitely shifts from the described events to the focalized character. Character-focalization is employed now not because this is a more effective way of convincing the readers of the verisimilitude of the narrative, but because it facilitates the description of the state of mind of the observer.[12] Among Lu Xun's short stories, some first-person narratives (like 'Kong Yiji' or 'New Year Sacrifice') seem to place stress on the events narrated and the character observed, while some third-person narratives, on the contrary, seem to place stress on the character as observer.

Characters of weak morality or intellect bearing the focalization, something very unlikely in traditional Chinese fiction, is quite a vogue in the May Fourth fiction. This angling-up focalization is different from angling-up narration which we discussed in the last chapter, as the former has to do with the personality of the character and the latter the narrator, even though that narrator is bound to be sufficiently characterized.

I was surprised when I counted how many May Fourth works of fiction there are with problematic focalized characters. In Ye Shengtao's 'Horsebell Melon' ('Malin Gua'), the whole story is told from the point of view of a twelve-year-old child; in his 'Pan Xiansheng Amid Hardship', war is described from the point of view of a timid schoolmaster; in Peng Jiahuang's 'Living Ghost' ('Huogui') the adultery is related through the observation of a child. However, the most interesting example is again offered by Lu Xun. His short story 'The Eternal Lamp' ('Chang Ming Deng') puts the focalization on a group of people—the villagers who try their best to thwart a madman's effort to blow out the Eternal Lamp in the village temple. Most space is indeed devoted to the response of the village children who are as ignorant as the clan leaders who are holding a sort of trial of the man. Thus the whole story is distorted by the character-focalization to the extent that it is no longer the character who is being observed but the characters who are observing that becomes the centre of interest.

If in this short story the narrator still makes a couple of commentaries 'A Public Example', one of Lu Xun's least discussed stories, should be considered technically perfect. The narrative consists entirely of the description how curious people in an alley eagerly squeeze up to each other to get a glimpse of a criminal. There is not even one word describing the criminal, since the crowd remains completely callous about his fate. The stress is obviously laid on the lack of sympathy or

---

[12] Booth (1983: 265) insists that the 'point of view' in fiction is not only a choice of the manner of description, but a *moral* choice. His argument seems an unreasonable perversity of the conservatism of the New Aristotelian School. Yet perhaps it can be justified in this sense: the narrated world and the narrating subjectivity are constantly competing for focalization. That is why, in Booth's view, fiction turned more subjective by character-focalization is not morally commendable as it intensifies an individualistic and relativistic attitude toward norms.

feeling on the part of the onlookers. For this is, in Lu Xun's mind, the most abhorrent aspect of the Chinese national character. The focalization is not fixed on a single character, but shifts from one person to another in the group. We can perhaps call it group angling-up character-focalization.[13]

But this does not mean that all May Fourth fictional works are strictly consistent in character-focalization. In Xu Jie's short novel *Gloomy Fog* (*Canwu*) the bloody feud between two villages is observed by a village girl who works in the 'supporting team' and finds out about the battle only through reports by others. The effect of character-focalization is greatly tapered off by too many sub-narratives and narratorial explanatory intrusions in the novel. The same can be seen in Li Jinming's 'Revenge' ('Fuchou') in which villagers inadvertently observe part of a well-planned revenge. Since the most important part of the revenge is not to be witnessed by the villagers, a long sub-narrative is included which moves the narrative out of the original group character-focalization. It is obvious that when the author is too eager to tell a clear story, character-focalization can only add to his difficulty.

In the best of May Fourth works of fiction, unavoidable violation of character-focalization, however frequent, is deftly handled without much perturbation. In some of Lu Xun's short stories such as 'New Year's Sacrifice', where information comes from sources that cannot be observed by the focalized-character narrator, reports by other characters are added (e.g. Xianglin Sao's second marriage and her son's death are related by Granny Wei). Some events are in fact not observed by any one (such as the 'secret talk' between Xianglin Sao and Liu Ma on the splitting of the bodies of remarried women in hell), and are also narrated without explaining the source. Such a violation is quite common in any fictional work with a complicated plot and can be comfortably ignored so long as it is dexterously handled. A direction explaining away the violation, such as those in late Qing fiction, would only make the violation more awkwardly conspicuous. It should be stressed that character-focalization is not a purpose in itself, and that a tacit but tactful reminder of the narrator's adherence to character-focalization is sufficient to compensate any untidiness in focalization, such as this one in Lu Xun's 'New Year Sacrifice': 'But whether she became a beggar

---

[13] There are not many successful examples of the use of this device either in Chinese or in Western fiction. One of Mao Dun's early stories, 'Nining' ('Mud', 1928), can be said to be a successful application of the device. But technically speaking, it is still not satisfactory in comparison with Lu Xun's brilliant performance.

immediately after leaving Fourth Uncle's house, or after staying with
Granny Wei for a short while, is beyond my knowledge.' (PH, 12).

VI

The whole text of fiction, as explained in the last chapter, is to be considered as the author's recording of the narrator's telling of the story.
The narrator's reporting of what a character says or thinks is, then, a
recording embedded within another recording, i.e. a double recording.

Reported speech is controlled by a double subjectivity—the speaking
character and the reporting narrator. Reported speech is both independent of the narrator as it is supposed to be the words of a character, and
dependent on the narrator as it is supposedly reiterated by the narrator,
and remains part of the narrative text. That is why in reported speech,
the problem of the differentiation of subjectivity becomes more complicated as the characters' subjectivity is now thrown together into the
narrator's in the same passage.

Perhaps because there is no sequence of tenses in Chinese, the problem of reported speech has never attracted in China the serious attention paid to it by European rhetoricians. There has never even been any
effort to classify it. Yet even in the West, reported speech is still a
debatable topic with no standardized terminology accepted by all.[14] I
shall adopt a comparatively simple division.

The first: direct form and indirect form. The direct form supposedly
retains the original words of the speaking character who refers to himself as 'I'; the indirect form transposes the words of the speaker into the
words of the reporter, and the speaker refers to himself in the third
person.

The second: quoted form and free form. The quoted form has various
markers, including typographical ones separating reported speech from
the narrative context; the free form does not provide any marker for
reported speech, and thus is not formally separated from the narrative
context. The most common marker of the quoted form is a leading tag
such as 'he said'.

---

[14] Hernadi (1972a: 84), for instance, has a five-item taxonomy: narrated monologue;
substitutionary speech; independent form of indirect discourse; represented speech; narrative mimicry.

Genette (1980: 191–4) suggests dividing reported speech into the following four types:
discours narrativisé; *discours transposé; discours rapporté; discours immédiat.*

The obvious shortcoming of these taxonomic efforts is that they fail to provide a
simple and clear-cut division.

Combining the two divisions, we have a four-item taxonomy—directed quoted form, indirect quoted form, indirect free form, and direct free form. This division applies to both Chinese and English.[15]

Quotation marks are not reliable markers of the quoted form, because, first, there are no quotation marks in Classical Chinese at all, and secondly, in many languages, including modern Chinese, direct quoted form can go without quotation marks. Indeed, direct quoted form can go with no leading tag, or with no quotation marks, or even with neither, as often seen in Chinese literary-language prose. But in vernacular Chinese the leading tag is a more reliable marker than quotation marks.

Theoretically any speech by the character can be conveyed by any of the four types. What is different is the subjective control. It seems that in reported speech the narrator's voice and the character's voice are always wrestling for a bigger share. The presence of the leading tag or quotation marks, and the change of self-reference are all marks of the pressure of the narrative context on the reported speech. We can see in the four types of reported speech the following ways of sharing of subjectivity: in the direct free form, the character is not only in control of his voice, but as it is mingled with the narrator's voice, his voice encroaches upon the narrative context; in the direct quoted form, the character retains almost full control through the insulating effect of the leading tag and/or the quotation marks; in the indirect free form, the reported speech is remoulded by the narrative context, but the omission of the markers of reported speech weakens the narrator's control, rendering the reported speech seemingly independent; and in the indirect quoted form, the character's voice is almost totally assimilated into the narrative context, and the narrator is almost in full control of the reported speech.

VII

Because of the formal linguistic characteristics of Classical Chinese (the absence of quotation marks, of sequence of tenses, and of paragraph-

---

[15] The following simple examples for each form may be of some help: direct quoted form:

He hesitated. He thought, '*I made a mistake.*' Indirect quoted form: He hesitated. He thought that *he had made a mistake*. Indirect free form: He hesitated. *He had made a mistake*. Direct free form: He hesitated. *I have made a mistake*.

For the taxonomy, I am indebted to William Tay's argument in his article 'Wang Meng, Stream of Consciousness and the Controversy over Modernism' (1984: 5).

dividing), and because of powerful narratorial subjectivity, the direct quoted form is by necessity the predominant type of reported speech in vernacular fiction. The leading tag is always used to ensure that reported speech is clearly separated from the narrative context. This is quite different from literary-language fiction where both direct and indirect forms are used, often without markers to separate the reported speech from the narrative background. Since literary language fiction is for the highly educated, professional reader, the practice does not cause too much confusion. Vernacular fiction, on the contrary, is for the less well educated, and the reported speech has to be clearly marked out, so that the text is not too difficult to read. Therefore, direct quoted form is consistently used throughout the text, and it is always preceded by a formulaic leading tag.

Narrative art, however, called for variation. Since direct quote is the only possible form of reported speech for vernacular fiction, direct quoted form varies. Self-reference of the speaker as 'I' could be taken as a marker of direct speech or implied self-reference such as calling the listener 'you' which implies the speaker's first-person self-reference. In some languages, the sequence of tenses renders great help in making the distinction, but not in Chinese. If there are none of these markers, we can only rely on other oblique indicators, such as stylistic features. If the style of the reported speech is in keeping with the narrative context, it is very probably in the indirect form. If it is in keeping with the character's idioms which is different from that of the narrator's, it is supposed to be in the direct form.

This rule, however, is not always applicable to traditional Chinese fiction.

The following is an example taken from chapter 99 of *The Three Kingdoms*: in order to demonstrate the unique situation of reported speech in traditional Chinese fiction where there were no punctuation marks, nor sentence-beginning capital letters, I shall suppress the quotation marks and commas in the English translation of the examples in this chapter, and replaced them by dots which basically correspond to the dots that were used in some Chinese printed matters. The punctuation marks added by editors in modern editions are not always appropriate.

Sima Yi led the army into full battle array, ready to attack . . . he suddenly saw (his generals) Zhang Ge and Dai Ling run back in helter-skelter. they said, *Kongming prepared beforehand in such a way, hence their defeat.* (SGYY, 799. Italics mine.)

The phrase 'in such a way' (*ruci*), short as it is, indicates that the reported speech is already remoulded by the narrator and the speech cannot be considered to be in the direct quoted form. Therefore it must be in the indirect quoted form. The modern editors, adhering too closely to the rule of no indirect form in Chinese vernacular fiction, enclose these sentences between quotation marks and turn them mistakenly into direct reported speech, which reads awkwardly.

To punctuate Classical Chinese has all along been considered a standard test for students of Chinese, as it is indeed difficult. Never has vernacular Chinese been used in such tests. Yet to punctuate Chinese vernacular fiction is by no means an easy matter when it comes to reported speech. In chapter 89 of *The Journey to the West*:

Bajie said. Brother. I have never seen that weird creature. how can I change myself into his appearance. Wukong said. that creature has already been bound there by my Transfixing Incantation and will not wake until this time tomorrow. I remember what he looks like. you stand here and I teach you how to do it. *this way. this way.* and you take on his appearance. (XYJ, 1219)

We cannot enclose all that Wukong said in quotation marks, as the phrase 'this way, this way' (*ruci ruci*) definitely indicates indirect form. Nor can we leave the reported speech without quotation marks since the other sentences are unmistakably in the direct quoted form. It just defies our modern classification. We can only say that this is a unique variation of direct quoted form that could perhaps only be found in vernacular Chinese.

This is not to say that there cannot be any other way of reporting character's speech than direct form. Indeed we often find some interesting passages in vernacular fiction where the direct and the indirect forms are charmingly mixed. In *Jin Ping Mei*:

Jinlian . . . returned to her room in the evening. left unaccompanied except for the lonely pillow and curtain. she could not fall asleep. she rose and took a slow walk into the garden. the moon was on the bottom of the pond. afraid *that Ximen Qing's heart could hardly be harnessed. annoyed at the mating of the cats. teases my heart and makes it disquieted.* (JPM Cihua, ch. 12)

Here again we have a passage of reported speech split into two parts in different forms (which I have indicated by two different fonts), as it suddenly shifts from the third-person self-reference in the first part to the first-person self-reference in the second part. The latter part of the reported speech, detached from the leading tag, is rendered in the direct free form. The rewriter of the *Chongzhen* version of *Jin Ping Mei*, perhaps thinking that it was sloppy, changed 'my heart' in the first example into 'her heart', thus turning the two-part speech into one.

In *The Forgotten Texts of the History of Sui* we find the similar two-part reported speech:

Shiming arrested Deru, and accused him, that *he fooled the Emperor by naming an ordinary bird the phoenix, so as to win a high position. Cut his head. Let his family members go.* (SSYW, 331)

We know that the second part is in direct form because of the style (the imperative).

This unique pattern of reported speech in traditional Chinese fiction can be summed up with the following formula:

leading tag + indirect form + direct form.

This structure could be very effective and is sometimes necessary. There is an example from 'Yu Tangchun in Distress Meets Her Former Lover' ('Yu Tang Chun Luonan Feng Guofu'), a short story in *Jing Shi Tongyan*:

Sister Yu's tears were like rain. thinking where *Wang Shunqing could have gone without a penny. you should let me know before you left. not let me worry all the time. wondering when we can meet again.* (JSTY, 126)

With the indirect quote preparing the background, the direct form, being more intimate, dramatizes the mental frustration of the passionate girl.

In oral performance such an indirect-direct shift is easy as the narrator can change his tone at any time during reporting a character's speech, by merely changing his voice and facial expressions into the character's voice. Sometimes he can even change into chanting or singing to report the character's speech.

In *Jin Ping Mei Cihua*, however, there are some passages where characters' speech is reported in poems:

Ximen Qing became even more angry. and pointing at Old Lady Wang. he scolded her. saying. *there is a testimonial poem to the tune 'Mantingfang'*:
> you old hag with a vicious heart
> always sending away the old to make room for the new,
> and living by forcing pretty girls to be whores
>   (JPM, Cihua, ch. 20)

Here two leading tags head one piece of reported speech. There are more than ten such cases in *Jin Ping Mei Cihua*. The literal meaning of 'We have a testimonial poem that says' (*youshi weizheng*) seems to be neglected in these cases as its sole purpose here is to mark the generic shift from prose into poetry.[16] The *Chongzhen* version deletes all the *youshi weizheng* tags in the first few chapters though it still retains the poems in lieu of reported speech. In later chapters the poems are deleted too.

Since no ordinary character is meant to talk in verse, poetry in lieu of speech as cited above cannot be considered the direct form. Yet calling the listener 'you' means that the passage is in direct form. We can only draw the conclusion that the notion of direct speech in traditional Chinese fiction is much more flexible than our concept of it today.

Both Gerald Genette and Seymour Chatman hold that in direct quoted form there is no narrative mediation, since it is supposed to be recorded just as it is in the pre-narrated state. Judging from the situation in Chinese vernacular fiction, we can see that this is not necessarily so. Indeed the insulation enjoyed by the direct quoted form is only hypothetical. There is not any part of the text that can escape the narratorial mediation.

In the early 1930s Voloshinov, the Russian critic of the Bakhtinian school, made a study of the evolution of reported speech in Russian literature. He found that in Russian, indirect speech remained dominant for long, and he suggested that indirect speech should be divided into two types: referent-analysing and texture-analysing.

Referent-analysing reported speech conveys 'meaning' with the exclusion of tones and other nuances in the speech, letting the narrative context infiltrate the speech reported. Voloshinov insisted that when collectivism gains the upper hand in the intellectual life of the nation, reported speech is likely to be of this type.

Texture-analysing reported speech endeavours to retain the tones and nuances of the speech by keeping its characteristic idioms. But the infiltration and control of the narrative context is greatly weakened. When relativism and individualism gain the upper hand, reported speech is most likely to be of this type.[17]

---

[16] Carlitz (1987) notices the use of songs as reported speech, 'and they are used dramatically, violating the conventions of fiction, at moments when the characters burst into a song to express strong emotion'. However, I hesitate to agree with her on the unconventionality of poems in lieu of reported speech. The author seems to have been using a particular way of installing the leading tag, which is not seen in other extant 17th-cent. vernacular novels.

[17] Matejka and Pomorska 1971: 136.

A comparable situation can be found in Chinese vernacular fiction too, the only difference being that instead of the dominance of indirect speech found in Russian, in Chinese vernacular fiction direct speech is to be exclusively dominant. But both the two types of speech reporting, referent-analysing and texture-analysing, can be found in Chinese vernacular fiction.

In the earliest fictional works of the Rewriting period, there are no distinct stylistic differences between the language of the narrative context and reported speech, as the narrator and almost all the characters speak the same vulgarized literary language. Even 'rude' characters in *The Three Kingdoms* do not retain their characteristic idioms in supposed direct quoted speech. Some humorous characters who had been popular in oral or theatrical performance for a long time, e.g. the 'stammering Deng Ai',[18] lose their characteristic way of talking when they enter the written narrative of *The Three Kingdoms*. This, again, shows how misleading it can be if we consider early Chinese vernacular fiction to be records or notes of oral narrative performance.

The situation improves greatly in *Water Margin* where some of the characters acquire their individual idioms in reported speech. These characters are generally of two kinds: characters with rude temperaments and characters of the lowest social strata. But most of the characters still talk in the same way in direct speech without stylistic difference.

Changes began to set in by the end of the Rewriting period, with *The Journey to the West* and *Jin Ping Mei*. Zhang Zhupo, the seventeenth-century critic, expresses his admiration of *Jin Ping Mei*:

This novel is unique in repeating without redundancy: there is Bojue, and there is also Xida. Yet Bojue remains Bojue while Xida remains Xida. Each has his own personality and his own speech with no confusion.[19]

This was when texture-analysing began to take the place of referent-analysing in reported speech in Chinese vernacular fiction.

We may concede that texture-analysing is not very difficult in these two novels, as most characters in *Jin Ping Mei* are either villains or

---

[18] Li Shangyin, the 9th-cent. poet, wrote in his 'Poem on My Pampered Son': 'Or they laughed at the bearded Zhang Fei, | Or they mimicked the stammering Deng Ai.' Many scholars hold that this is one of the earliest mentions of oral story-telling, though Ren Bantang insists that here children are simulating theatrical performance (*Tang Xi Nong*, Beijing: Zuojia Chubanshe, 1958, 151). No matter which, Deng Ai had been established as a stammerer for centuries.

[19] Huang Lin and Han Tongwen 1982: 384.

voluptuous women, and the reported speech in *The Journey to the West* takes advantage of lampooning.

The real texture-analysing came with *The Dream of the Red Chamber* which dealt with people of various social strata from princes and noble ladies to slaves and city scum. The particular idiom of each person is well preserved, so that most characters maintain control over their own speech and avoid the infiltration of the narrative context.

Nevertheless, the dominance of direct speech remained a distinct feature in Chinese fiction until a narratological revolution finally forced it to make radical changes.

VIII

The dominance of the direct quoted form in Chinese vernacular fiction remained basically unchanged in late Qing fiction, and variations could still take place only within the direct quoted form. In *The Nine-Tailed Tortoise* for instance, the reported speech is reminiscent of novels written centuries earlier:

[Zhang Qiugu] suddenly frowned as he hit upon a stratagem, Overjoyed, he said to himself, *I've got it! I've got it! I should act in such and such a way, and then I shall be in good control of the matter, and fear no more that Shuyu would be arrogant again.* (JWG, 185)

This passage is meant to be in direct quoted form, yet there are some words ('such and such') that should only appear in the indirect form.

Modern editors of late Qing fiction, however, should be sympathized with, as sometimes it is very difficult to decide the forms of reported speech. I do not envy anybody who has to punctuate this passage of *Strange Events*:

My Sister shouted. Damn it. What an ugly scene. She called the maid-servants to drag the two ladies to her own room. She also told Mrs Wu to see to the guests. I shall take care of these things here. She also sent for Jizhi immediately. (ESNMDZGXZ, ch. 44, 400)

However, the increased amount of mental activities reported in the narrative calls for a distinction between the 'thought-out' speech and the 'spoken-out' speech. In some late Qing novels, there is an effort at least to move the characters' thoughts into indirect speech.

In the third-person narrative, the use of indirect speech is a little more difficult as the context is in the third person. But once the shift

to indirect speech is realized, it creates many more discursive possibilities. In Wu Jianren's *A Sea of Remorse*, most of the heroine's mental
activities are still put into the direct quoted form (as the speaker-thinker
referred to herself in the first person), though modern editors of the
novel, for some strange reason, do not put them in quotation marks, e.g.
the text A Ying edited.[20] Perhaps the editor thought (mistakenly!) that
only real speech, not thoughts, should be put between quotation marks.
Another post-May Fourth edition of the novel (published by Guangzhi
Shuju, Hong Kong, 1925), also follows the same rule.

Michael Egan in his article on *A Sea of Remorse* argues that in that
novel the character's speech is no longer so distinctly separated from
the narrative context:

> One important structural change in the evolution of modern literature has
> been the blurring of the clear line between narrator's and character's discourse.
> The opposition between the two lessened or became neutralized, in order to
> give the author more narrative possibilities ... When represented discourse,
> and not direct discourse, is used, the text combines the separate verbal and
> semantic features of the narrator and character's discourse ... In [*A Sea of
> Remorse*] those of represented discourse are not yet fully developed or mas-
> tered, but there are indications of the blurring of lines between the narrator's
> text and the character's text.[21]

What he calls represented discourse is indirect form in my terminology. It seems that he thinks the novel could be taken at least as the
intermediate stage of transformation. But having carefully gone through
the short novel several times, and I found no more than two or three
instances of indirect form. The only thing that makes the novel particular in late Qing fiction is the large amount of mental activity. The long
and detailed recording of the mental process is itself something new in
Chinese fiction. Nevertheless, it is still reported in the direct quoted
form. In the original text neither the spoken-out speeches nor the thought-
out speeches have quotation marks. Only in some modern editions are
they marked differently. So the 'blurring' is brought about by the modern
editor.

The problem of reported speech in the late Qing is complicated as it
is entangled with the problem of the sub-narratives,[22] most of which are
put in the direct quoted form. Since the indirect form is not yet regular

    [20] A Ying 1959: i. 603–70.   [21] Dolezelova-Velingerova 1984: 165–76.
    [22] Sub-narratives are secondary narratives told by a character in the narrative. They
will be discussed in Sections 11–13 of this ch.

practice, the reported speech in the sub-narrative is again put into the direct quoted form. Thus we can find requoted quoted speeches. In *Viewed with Cold Eyes*, for instance, the narrator's prostitute-lover Sulan tells one story after another, mimicking now the incantation of a witch, now the indignant high-ranking mandarin. One only needs to read the following example to see how tiring such a retelling must be. Sulan is now telling the story about a mentally retarded man who is buying an official title with money, and is granted an interview by the Governor:

Sulan continued, 'He *all of a sudden* asked the governor, 'May I ask what is your excellency's hometown?' The Governor was annoyed by this question, but still answered him *slowly*, 'I am of Nanpi of Zhili Province'. Then he asked, 'Could I know your excellency's name?' The Governor at once pulled a long face and *shouted* at him, 'What! You don't even know my name?' ... The Governor, now knowing everything, seized the opportunity to *flare up*, 'You damned scoundrel! I don't want to hear one more word from you. Get out! Such a bastard with not a bit of self-respect, what's the use of talking to him any more!' And then he *turned to the captain*, 'Please show the magistrate of Jianxia in immediately, and let him take the man away ...' (LYG, 152–3. Italics mine.)

Prusek once accused *The Travels of Lao Can* of having a 'too complicated structure of quotations within quotations'.[23] He is apparently referring to the well-known passage of the nun Yiyun's two-chapter-long confession of her love experience in the sequel to the novel. This is a sub-narrative told by the nun to Mrs De. The nun recounts how her lover Third Master Ren told her about his negotiation with his mother on the proposed marriage (i.e. Ren is the sub-sub-narrator). What makes the matter complex is that Third Master Ren quoted what his mother said in the direct form, which is then triply quoted (quoted by Ren, requoted by Yiyun, re-requoted by the narrator of the whole novel). Yet it is still vividly presented in the direct quoted form: 'My Dearest, you are a clever boy. Carefully think over your Mum's words. They can't be wrong for you.' This extreme texture-analysing reporting, after twice direct requoting, sounds really impossible.

What is strange is that this part of *The Travels of Lao Can* has always been appreciated by readers and scholars as one of the most brilliant performances of Chinese vernacular fiction.[24] Why, then, do

[23] Prusek 1980: 106.
[24] It was translated into English by Lin Yutang in the 1930s when the 2nd vol. of the novel was first published.

not the histrionics on the part of this wild-yet-virtuous nun irreparably damage the narrative? The only reason is that when we read these sub-narratives, we usually ignore the fact that they are already in quoted form. When we go on reading the sub-narrative, we again ignore that it is a requote, since the sub-narrative in the direct quoted form is only a conventional device.[25]

Only very occasionally is a sub-sub-narrative told in the indirect form. In *Strange Events*:

Wu Jizhi said, 'There is an interesting joke told by my servant. One day he told me that *when he was unemployed, he went to the tea house every morning, and sat over a cup of tea to kill time for half a day. Often he saw a Manchu come to the tea house too . . .*' (ESNMDZGXZ, ch. 6, 45)

The story goes on, and the Manchu's words are directly quoted. But since this story is told by the servant in the indirect form, the whole retelling sounds more natural, relieved from the frustration of texture-maintaining in re-reported speech. Such a deft handling of the sub-narrative is not very often seen in late Qing fiction.[26]

---

[25] To be fair, this occurs in Western fiction too, especially in 18th-cent. or early 19th-cent. novels. In *Wuthering Heights*, for instance, the first-person narrator Lockwood jots down in his journal what Nelly tells him about Isabella. In ch. 8, Nelly quotes Isabella's long letter in which Isabella, in turn, uses many direct quotations, ' "This is Edgar's legal nephew," I reflected—"mine in a manner; I must shake hands, and—yes—I must kiss him" '. This does not sound unnatural, as long as we readers forget that the episode is now narrated in a letter read by the receiver whose reading is faithfully recorded by a diarist-narrator. Yet when we are reminded of it, we might feel the multi-quoted speech to be overly dramatic.

[26] There are, occasionally, some passages of reported speech in the under-narrative rendered in the indirect quoted form. In ch. 4 of *Strange Events*, for instance, the narrator has a discussion with Wu Jizhi about an official-burglar. Wu tells the narrator that after the fellow is caught and sent to the magistrate, only to be released at once:

The commissars in the offices were all his friends, and felt the case was too difficult to handle. He, on the contrary, was then full of complaints, saying that *it was all his servant's fault who was only a little too greedy so as to steal a pipe, and when the servant was caught red-handed by others, they chased him, and that the comprador on the boat tried to bully him by using the power of the foreign captain, and that it was he who should be worrying about whether his own possessions had been lost after their searches.* (ESNMDZGXZ, 30)

In *Viewed with Cold Eyes*, the narrator sees a pedlar who dares to beat up some soldiers who have refused to pay after eating his doughnuts: 'I felt at once that this was an extraordinary person, and I asked about his name. He was from Hefei, and named Zhang Shuben. He had been a brave officer in the war but . . . *This was the story of that pedlar. After hearing it I admired him strongly.*' (LYG, ch. 4, 23–4). Here the sub-narrative is actually put into the indirect quoted form as the leading tag (in italics) is transformed into a statement after the sub-narrative is ended.

IX

All the varieties of reported speech appear regularly in May Fourth fiction, thus putting a definitive end to the dominance of the direct quoted form in traditional vernacular literature. Apart from some para-textual features such as punctuation and paragraph division, the variation of reported speech seems to be the most visible marker of modern Chinese fiction.

The change in reported speech in May Fourth fiction has hardly attracted much scholarly attention as it merely puts reported speech in its modern form. It appears natural to us modern readers. Nevertheless, the redistribution of the narrative subjectivity brought about by this change is crucial to the development of Chinese fiction.

The direct quoted form in May Fourth fiction is different from that in traditional Chinese fiction in some respects. Very often the leading tag is omitted. Sometimes this technique makes it difficult to tell who is saying what, which, however, is just the intended effect. Lu Xun's story 'Divorce' ('Lihun') begins with a dialogue in direct quoted form with not a single leading tag:

'Ah, ah! Uncle Mu. Happy New Year. Big money in the new year!'
'How are you, Basan. Happy New Year! . . .'
'Er, er! Happy . . . Oh Sis Ai is here too.'
'Ah, ah! Grandpa Mu . . .' (PH, 78)

In this way, the chaotic noise of country folk crowding onto a boat is vividly captured. No passage like this simple one is conceivable in traditional Chinese fiction. The same can be seen in Xu Qinwen's story 'Companions on the Jin-Wei Train' ('Jin Wei Tuzhong de Banlu'); when the tax-collector has boarded the train, his talk with the passengers is recorded without leading tags, making the indistinguishable noise more menacing.

On the occasions when the speakers should be made clear, the omission of leading tags creates a dramatic atmosphere, giving the scene an immediacy. There are often in May Fourth Fiction long passages without a single leading tag, e.g. the first paragraph of Feng Yuanjun's 'The Chaste Woman' ('Zhenfu'), the first two pages of Guo Moruo's 'Datura

In the novel *What the Ladies Next Door Say*, when the hero arrives at Wangjia Ying, a small town in Shandong: 'He took a lot of trouble in finding a horse dealer whose name was Xiong. He was originally a highwayman, and . . . *This whole story was found out by Jin Li the boy servant*, from goodness knows where. Bumo did not care about the fellow's past, and went directly to his house to make the purchase.' (LNY, 69.)

Flower' ('Mantuoluo Hua'), and the third chapter of Tao Jingsun's 'A Concert Melody' ('Yinyue Hui Xiaoqu'). The first section of Xu Zhimo's story 'Li's Story' ('Lao Li de Gushi') is completely composed of reported speech without a leading tag. Not until the beginning of the second section is the speaker revealed, 'These are words said by Li's classmates behind his back'. Thus the form of reported speech causes a structural suspense.

The effect achieved by this device is what traditional vernacular fiction with its fixed leading tag could never hope to achieve. In fact, merely moving the leading tag to the middle or to the end of the speech reported is enough to mark out the modern fiction.[27]

But the most important change in reporting speech in May Fourth fiction is the emergence of a large quantity of the indirect form, though most of the speeches rendered in this form are still reports of the characters' mental activities.[28] Even at an early stage, critics were already aware that it was the indirect reported speech that made May Fourth fiction differ from traditional fiction in appearance. Su Xuelin presents a detailed analysis of the latter's short story 'Tomorrow' ('Mingtian'). She cites a passage:

She felt dizzy, but recovered after a short rest . . . Then she felt another strange thing:—The house suddenly seemed too quiet.

Su emphasizes that a short paragraph like this marks the story as definitely different from any previous fiction in China.[29]

In May Fourth fiction, the indirect free form appears almost as frequently as the indirect quoted form, and the May Fourth writers used the free form adroitly. In Lu Xun's *The True Story of A Q*:

---

[27] It took some time for the May Fourth writers to find a 'Chinese' way to fix the leading tag at the end of reported speech. In Yu Dafu's 'Moving South' ('Nanqian'), the end tags are added in a way that looks strange today:

'You do not look well recently. I advise you to go to the countryside for a few weeks' rest.' The Westerner.
'. . . I do not want to go outside Tokyo.' The young man.

The same can be found in Ni Yide's 'Flower Shadow' ('Huaying'), Chen Weimo's 'Broken Eyes' ('Poyan') and many other stories, sometimes with a dash inserted.

[28] There are some awkward experiments before the May Fourth writers become used to the indirect form. In Zheng Boqi's story 'Zuichu zhi Ke' ('The First Lesson') the character's thoughts are put in brackets (thus still in the direct quoted form) in contrast to the spoken words between quotation marks.

[29] Su Xuelin, 'A Q Zhengzhuan ji Lu Xun Chuangzuo de Yishu' ('*The True Story of A Q* and Lu Xun's Art') in Li Zongyin and Zhang Meng yang 1982: i. 134.

He then sat down at Bearded Wang's side. If this were another idle man, A Q would not have sat down so carelessly. But why should he have any fear of being beside this Bearded Wang? *To be frank, his willingness to sit down was meant to be an honour for the bloke.* (NH, 501)

In many stories, especially those which have long passages describing the mental activity of the characters, there is likely to be a natural mixture of the free and quoted indirect forms. In Ye Shengtao's 'Two Letters in Reply' (*'Liangfeng Huixin'*):

What kind of language should be used in this letter? He was perplexed, without a clear idea in his mind . . . Now the decision is made to write the letter. *But what to write?* (GM, 89)

The first italicized sentence is indirect quoted speech, since the sentence after it can be considered the leading tag. The second is in the indirect free form as no leading tag can be found. The same natural mixture is seen in other May Fourth works, e.g. in Wang Luyan's 'Aunt Li' ('Li Ma'), and Ye Shengtao's 'A Package' ('Yibao Dongxi').

When such indirect free speech appears in first-person narratives, it is naturally transformed into something of the direct free form. In Guo Moruo's 'Moon Eclipse' (*'Yueshi'*):

When all these thoughts went through my mind while I was tying my tie, my wife finished dressing and my two kids were urging me impatiently downstairs. *Oh, it is so difficult even to be a dog, and so hard even to tie a tie!* I was sweating all over as I wasn't able to tie the tie properly.

Guo Moruo seems to be particularly fond of playing with this free shifting of speech, as his fictional works are mostly in the first person. But the varying forms of reported speech can also be seen in the works of other May Fourth fiction writers. Xu Zhimo, for instance, wrote a number of fascinating stories (collected in *The Wheel* (*Lunpan*), 1930) that consist solely of interior monologue.

Naturally, direct free speech is more difficult in third-person narratives, but it emerged there too. This occurred without much strain. In Lu Yin's technically naïve début 'A Young Writer' ('Yige Shaonian Zhuzuo Jia'), when the protagonist is recalling his past, the sub-narrative adroitly shifts from the third person to the first person, and back to the third person, leaving the first-person parts in natural direct free form.

The free direct form is used as an effective stylistic device in *The True Story of A Q*:

Mrs Zhao was afraid that A Q did not dare to come because of the incident that Spring. But Master Zhao did not think it was possible: *because it is I who have sent for him.* (NH, 512. Italics mine.)

But in less than ten minutes, Ah Q walked away contented. He felt that he was the first one who was able to despise himself. Forget the 'despise', what was left was the 'first'. Even Zhuangyuan was just a first. *What are you, after all?* (NH, 500. Italics mine.)

In Guo Moruo's few stories in the third person, the characters' long interior monologues shift back and forth between the indirect free form and the direct free form:

What did *he* do today? Stealing! Stealing! Pick-pocketing! What a degenerate! . . . Degenerate! Degenerate! Degenerate! How could *I* have so easily committed an unpardonable crime like this! *He* thought that he should throw away the stolen thing he was carrying, but was the crime redeemed once the thing was thrown away? ('Manbiki' (Wanying), T, 45. Italics mine.)

In this short passage we can see three forms mixed and interwoven to create the monologue—first the indirect free form, then the direct free form, and finally the indirect quoted form.

The examples cited above are enough to conclude that the elimination of the dominance of the direct quoted form in traditional Chinese fiction effectively facilitates the subtle mingling of the subjectivity of narrator and the characters.[30]

From the beginning of the May Fourth period, the form of reported speech had already become a touchstone of the new narrative form. Guo Moruo's first piece of fiction writing, 'The Tragic Story of the Shepherds' ('Muyang Aihua') is, according to Guo's own criticism, 'full of conceptual descriptions and operatic dialogue (*kebai*)'. What he meant by 'operatic dialogue' is actually conventional reported speech— the direct quoted form with the preceding leading tag. The form is used in the story from beginning to end without any variation. This simple device is enough to mark the whole narrative as conventional in style.

---

[30] Prusek argued that in May Fourth fiction there are passages of interior monologue that can be considered stream of consciousness: 'An analogy to the recording of the stream of spontaneously generated emotions, eminently attempted by J. Joyce and his various successors, is to be found in the early works of Yu Dafu, Guo Moruo and others.' (Prusek 1980: 124).

But beside being in the direct free form, the most important requirement for stream of consciousness is free association, which is not to be found in May Fourth fiction. Stream of consciousness in the strict sense of the term did not occur in Chinese fiction until the mid-1980s.

Guo Moruo pardons himself on the ground that the story was written as early as 1918 and could hardly be technically satisfactory. This apology shows that the variation of forms of reported speech was not a simple imitation of Western fiction. May Fourth writers had to find the basic tool-kit suitable for modern Chinese fiction.

X

When the character's speech being reported tells a story and becomes a narrative of its own, we have a narrative within a narrative. Narrative stratification occurs when a character on one level becomes the narrator on another level. In other words, when one narrative level provides a narrator for another narrative level. The level providing the narrator can be said to be higher than the level it provides for. If there are three levels in one work, we may call the level above the main narrative the over-narrative, and the one below it the sub-narrative.[31] Though these terms are relative, and one can give a narrative level any name so long as the other levels are named in relation to it, the main narrative is generally the level that takes up the most space in the text.

It is strange that specially installed super-narrative almost never appears in Chinese vernacular fiction. The frame structure binding short-story collections[32] is not to be found, with probably only one exception— the seventeenth-century story collection *Idle Chats Under the Bean Trellis* (*Doupeng Xianhua*), where a group of villagers gather in the heat of summer night to hear each other's stories.[33]

As for Chinese vernacular novels, there is absolutely no over-narrative except the conventional arrangement to simulate oral performance and let the character Story-Teller come out to enunciate the whole narrative text. Since this is omnipresent in almost every fiction work, I do not regard it as an over-narrative scheme.

[31] Genette names them (1980: *passim*) extra-diegesis, intra-diegesis, and meta-diegesis. These terms are neither easy to understand nor clearly related. Moreover, they are insufficient when there are more than three levels in the narrative text.

[32] This seems strange because the frame story (an over-narrative that provides the narrator or narrators for a group of stories that form the main narrative level, a device which can be seen in e.g. *The Arabian Nights, The Decameron*, and *The Canterbury Tales*) is almost a formulaic structure for collections of Buddhist tales. It does not, however, appear in Chinese vernacular fiction, or in its supposed predecessor, the *Bianwen* texts unearthed in the Dunhuang Caves.

[33] Zhao Jingshen (1980: 400) states, 'The beginning of every chapter on the Bean-Trellis scene is better than the narrative proper.'

Many of the early Chinese vernacular novels have a thematic enveloping structure. In *Water Margin*, for instance, General Hong arrogantly opens the sacred seal, thus releasing one hundred and eight imprisoned spirits, who turn into the partisans of Mount Liang. In *The Three Kingdoms Pinghua*, the first emperor of the Han Dynasty wrongly executes the three generals who made the greatest contribution to the founding of the new dynasty, and the three spirits are reincarnated as the three rival warlords who finally split the Empire. But what this kind of prelude (*xiezi*) provides is an aetiological framework, not a narrative stratification, as it does not provide a new narrator.

There is a touchstone for determining the stratification in the narrative text. Since any narrative must tell a story of the past, an event on the narrator-provided (lower) level must take place earlier than an event on the narrator-provided (higher) level. Thus the sub-narrative can be regarded as a flashback in disguise. The narrative levels from higher to lower, then, follow a regressive temporal order. Since the aetiological prelude in Chinese vernacular fiction, e.g. the story of General Hong releasing sealed spirits in *Water Margin*, takes place in earlier time than the main body of the novel, the former cannot be on a higher narrative level than the latter.

In Chinese *Fu* verse which flourished in the Han dynasty, an over-narrative frame-story is the regular technique to tie up the sections of the verse. In literary-language short stories, we often find that an over-narrative supplies a character as the teller-narrator and another character, bearing the author's name, as the editor– or scriber–narrator, and together these form a composite narrator. For example, Shen Yazi's 'Notes of a Strange Dream' ('Yimeng Lu') starts with such a passage:

> In the tenth year of the Yuanhe Reign, Shen Yazhi followed Duke Longxi to be stationed in Jingzhou. Many celebrities of Chang'an came to visit. On the eighteenth of the fifth month, Duke Longxi entertained the guests at the Villa of the West Pool. When all had sat down, the Duke said, 'When I was young, I followed Xing Feng in travelling and remember many strange incidents. I shall be glad to tell them.' The guests all said, 'We'd like to hear them.' And the Duke said ... (TRXX, 89)

So the Duke is the teller of the main narrative. But at the end of the short story all the guests persuade Shen Yazhi (the character who bears the author's name) to write down the story the Duke had told, and the latter duly does so. Thus the over-narrative provides both the teller–narrator and the scriber–narrator.

The purpose of this over-narrative is to give the short story more authority and authenticity by dragging into the over-narrative the author's name as well as the names of many celebrities of the time.

Vernacular fiction, on the contrary, does not hope to claim such an authority or authenticity because of its low social status, and such a specially designed over-narrative seems to be too much a luxury.

The only Chinese vernacular novel with successful narrative stratification in traditional Chinese fiction is *The Dream of the Red Chamber*, which, I venture to say, is one of the world's most complicated premodern stratified novels. Its stratification exercised a great influence on late Qing novels.

The Dream of the Red Chamber has at least four narrative levels. At the beginning of chapter 1, the narrator comes out to claim himself to be 'the author'.

This is the first chapter to start the novel. *The author says*, 'Since I have experienced a long dream, I have to suppress the actual facts, and borrowing words from the Inspired Stone to write this novel' . . .

We know that only in literary-language fiction would the narrator introduce himself as 'the author'. This unconventional beginning of *The Dream of the Red Chamber*, though not yet freeing the entire novel from the conventional narrative frame, was of great significance for the development of Chinese fiction.

After that, the novel enters into another story of how a stone is left by Goddess Nu Wa after patching up the sky, how Buddhist Monk Mang Mang and Taoist Miao Miao bring the stone to 'a state of prosperity, a family of noble lineage, a country of pleasure, a land of richness', how 'after nobody knows how many Kalpas', the Taoist Kong Kong happened to walk by the foot of the hill where the stone lies, and sees on the stone 'a clearly written text recounting what it had once experienced', and how, upon the request of the Stone, Kong Kong copies the text to show to the world.

Kong Kong's manuscript is passed to a man bearing the author's name 'Cao Xueqin' who 'worked on it for ten years, rewrote it five times, divided it into chapters with titles, and added the song "Twelve Hairpins of Jinling" together with a *Jueju* poem. This was how the novel came into being.' (HLM, 3).

Thus, on the second over-narrative level, we have a composite narrator with the Stone as the teller, Kong Kong as the scriber, and 'Cao Xueqin' as the editor. They are all characters in the over-narrative turned into partners of the composite main narrator. This over-narrative is so important that the last third of the novel (believed to be written by another author Gao E after Cao Xueqin died leaving the novel unfinished)[34] has to resume the over-narrative while continuing the main narrative:

> That day, Kong Kong passed by the foot of Mount Blue Swelling, and saw the stone still lying there with the text on it. But when he read it again, he saw many words about the ending of the story which he had not read before. So he copied the ending and brought it again to the land of prosperity and the madding crowds ... (HLM, 1545)

In Gao E's mind, only the addition of such a sequel of over-narrative could justify his sequel to the novel. Yet the two sequels could not be so easily matched.

After the over-narrative, in *The Dream of the Red Chamber* there comes the story of Zhen Shiyin and Jia Yucun, and their story merges into the story of Lin Ruhai and his daughter Lin Daiyu whose coming to the Jias' Mansion launches the main body of the novel. This part sounds very much like a prelude, which, although containing in the speech of some characters hints of what will happen in the main body of the novel, is in fact narrated by the same composite narrator, and is anterior in time. So it cannot be considered another over-narrative.[35]

The main narrative contains, as is often seen in a long novel with many plot-lines, a number of sub-narratives. These include the incident of the Fan Murder told by Ping'er in chapter 48, and the story about Lin Siniang told by Jia Zheng and set to verse by Jia Baoyu in chapter 78.

To sum up, *The Dream of the Red Chamber* is stratified into four levels:

Over-over-narrative	'the author says'.
Over-narrative	Brother Stone was brought to the world;
	Kong Kong copied the text on the stone;
	Cao Xueqin rewrote it in ten years.

[34] The current study does not intend to be involved in the controversy over the authorship of the novel. Whether Gao E is the author of the last 40 chapters is contentious. There are even scholars who argue that the whole novel was written by one author. Chen Bing C. (1986) suggests that a computer-based study of statistic stylistics proves that the last 40 chs. were written by the same author as the first 80 chs. I hesitate to agree with this, for a number of reasons. One of them is that there is no need to resume the over-narrative if the whole novel is written by one person.

[35] Huhua Zhuren, an 18th-cent. critic of *The Dream of the Red Chamber*, wrote in his General Commentary, 'Zhen Shiyin and Jia Yucun are the narrators of the whole book'. He was evidently not well trained in narratology.

| Main-narrative | story about Zhen Shiyin and Jia Yucun; main body of the novel. |
| Sub-narratives | case of the Fan Murder; story about Lin Siniang, etc. |

The main purpose of narrative stratification is to substantiate the personality of the narrator.[36] In written narrative the narrator, as discussed previously in this part, finds himself in the embarrassing situation of being reduced to an abstraction while he still has to perform the various functions assigned to a story-teller. Now, with stratification, the narrator is made into a character on a higher level, thus creating at least the impression that the narrator has resumed his corporeal reality.

Of course this is only an impression, and, in any case, the narrator of the highest level is still a shadow without flesh and blood. I am glad to find that Zhiyan Zhai, the first critic of *The Dream of the Red Chamber* and a faithful friend to the author understood this problem when he said in his marginal comments on the novel: 'If we have to believe that it was Cao Xueqin himself who rewrote the novel, then who wrote this prelude? This is actually a trick played by the author . . . Please, Dear Readers, do not be taken in by our author's trick.'[37]

Sub-narratives are often used as a less intrusive method of introducing a flashback, especially as traditional Chinese fiction does not favour temporal dislocation. Ping'er's recounting of the case of the Fan Murder sounds more natural in Chinese fiction than the main narrator telling it in a flashback. Mao Zonggang, the celebrated Qing commentator of *The Three Kingdoms*, found that sub-narrative had a 'distancing' effect, and he suggests the term 'Light Touches for Remote Trees'.[38]

Narrative stratification can also have a thematic implication. Roland Barthes insists that 'discovering lost diaries, receiving letters, or finding manuscripts' are 'efforts made by the bourgeois to naturalize narrative'.[39]

---

[36] Genette has offered the most detailed discussion on stratification among all major narratologists, but he does not seem to understand its function. He suggests that the lower narratives take place, 'as if to answer the curiosity of the characters, but actually to answer the curiosity of the readers.' (Genette 1980: 182). This is not a good defence for stratification since all narratological devices can be said to serve the same purpose.

[37] Yu Pingbo 1960: 6.

[38] Huang Lin and Han Tongwen 1982: 337. Among the examples Mao Zonggang listed are 'Zhao Yun's seizure of Nanqun and Zhang Fei's occupation of the other two prefectures were presented by what Zhou Yu heard'; 'Liu Bei's killing of Yang Feng and Han Xian was only narrated in Liu Bei's own words'; 'Zhang Fei's capture of Gucheng was only told through what Lord Guan heard', etc.

[39] Barthes 1977: 251.

Bourgeois or not, stratification can indeed give some apparent authentication to the narrating action.

The Dream of the Red Chamber is outstanding in the development of vernacular fiction, since the over-narrative, so frequent in literary-language fiction, is virtually absent in vernacular fiction. On the one hand, the stereotyped narrator in vernacular fiction refrains from identifying himself with the author as the cultural hierarchy does not allow him to do so. On the other hand, it is not feasible to put this conventional narrator into an over-narrative and substantiate him as a character as he would then lose his impersonality. Despite the immense success of *The Dream of the Red Chamber*, stratification nevertheless remained rare in vernacular fiction before the late Qing period.

Sub-narrative is not very common in literary-language fiction since most pieces are too short to contain stories told by the characters.[40] In early vernacular fiction, sub-narratives are used occasionally when characters introduce themselves upon their first appearance in the main narrative, or when incidents that have happened in another plot-line have to be related by a character, but they are generally quite short. The only work that conscientiously makes use of sub-narratives is *More Chapters of The Journey to the West*. A contemporary critic of the novel (most probably the author himself) tells us that in the novel there was 'story-telling within story-telling, and balladry within story-telling'. (XYB, 89)

XI

A careful reading of *The Dream of the Red Chamber* reveals many events that seem to be smuggled from one narrative level to another.

The character Jia Yucun is a shrewd careerist on the main narrative level. But by the end of the novel, Kong Kong, one of the members of the composite narrator, carrying the new manuscript, meets Jia Yucun in a hut at the Awakening Ferry, and the latter tells him how to find the editor Cao Xueqin. Thus, Jia Yucun appears in the over-narrative and interferes with the action of narration.

The Buddhist monk Mang Mang and the Taoist Miao Miao who belong to the over-narrative, enter the main narrative eight times to interfere in the mundane life of the characters. Since the two come from

---

[40] One of the earliest *Chuanqi* short stories of the Tang period, 'The Story of the Old Mirror' ('Gujing Ji'), is unusual in structure as it contains as many as four sub-narratives.

an upper narrative world, it is not strange that they have supernatural powers to save the characters from insanity or deadly disease, or to drop hints about their future.

Jia Baoyu's dream of the Supreme Empty Land in chapter 5 of the novel is a passage in the main narrative, thus narratologically the Supreme Empty Land belongs to the main narrative level. But in chapter 12 when Jia Rui is on his deathbed, Taoist Maio Miao brings to him the Magic Mirror of Sex, and tells him that the mirror comes from the Supreme Empty Land. In chapter 117, when Mang Mang comes to ask for the jade, Baoyu asks, 'Are you from the Supreme Empty Land?' All these hint that the Supreme Empty Land of which Baoyu dreams is situated in the world of the over-narrative. Thus Baoyu's wet dream is a breaking into the higher narrative level.

What I suggest calling 'trespass of stratification' occurs when what should take place on one level breaks through the boundary between two levels to be relocated on another level.[41] God does not live in the world he creates, neither does the narrator.

Trespass of stratification was a stock technique in Chinese drama for many centuries,[42] and is still frequently used in popular theatrical performance today such as in *Xiangsheng* (Comic Dialogue), where the actor often jumps out of his role and comments 'from outside'.[43]

Such trespassing, however, almost never occurs in Chinese vernacular fiction. The main reason for this, I think, is that the 'oral storytelling' formulaic over-narrative does not encourage variation. Only the individually installed over-narrative could allow its boundary to be trespassed.

The complicated trespassing in *The Dream of the Red Chamber* reinforces the over-narrative by letting some characters and events from the main narrative (e.g. Zhen Shiyin and Jia Yucun, and the Supreme Empty Land) enter into the over-narrative level, thus forming a huge

[41] Genette (1980: 162) calls this breaking of boundaries 'metalepsis', which could cause confusion since this word was used in European classical rhetoric with the meaning of 'transumption'.

[42] In act 3 of Guan Hanqing's *The Butterfly Dream* (*Hudie Meng*), for instance, the *Fu* character Wang Er who is not allowed to sing (because only one character is allowed to sing in Yuan Drama) suddenly sings. When he is asked why he dares to sing, he answers, 'Isn't it the end of the Act?' Here he justifies his singing by stepping out onto the dramatizing level, thus avoiding the rules governing the dramatized world.

[43] Genette insists that the purpose of such trespasses is to produce the impression of absurdity or buffoonery (Genette 1980: 212). This is not always true as trespasses can often be used for serious reasons. I have the impression that trespasses in fiction are more 'serious' than in drama or other theatrical performances.

'over-narrative group', embracing virtually all the chapters before chapter 5. This is why in chapter 6 the narrator has to use a long direction to justify his restarting of the narrative, using Granny Liu's first visit to the Jias' Mansion.

We can further conclude that any narration is multi-stratified, since any narrating instance is by definition executed on the higher level, and all the narrator's intrusions can be considered *de facto* trespasses of stratification since the narrator's intrusion is a breaking-out of the narrating level onto the narrated level.

One of the best-known eighteenth-century Chinese novels, *Flowers in the Mirror* (*Jing Hua Yuan*), offers an extraordinary example of trespassing of narrative levels. In the first chapter of the novel, at the gathering of fairies, Hundred Herb Fairy mentions a mysterious jade stele on Little Penglai Island, the text of which contains some celestial secret that will not be revealed until hundreds of years later. Her companion Hundred Flower Fairy becomes curious about it but fails to find it. In chapter 48 the girl Tang Xiaoshan does in fact come to the island, sees the stele, and copies the text. The white monkey kept by her friend picks up the copy and studies it carefully. At the sight Tang Xiaoshan jokingly tells it to pass the text to 'the person destined to make it public'. At the end of the novel, when the main narrative has finished, there is a passage:

> The white monkey was actually an immortal monkey of the cave of Hundred Flower Fairy. He followed his mistress when she was exiled to the mundane world. He thought that he could return to their cave together with her when their mundane life was ended. But she ordered him to pass the text to a man of letters to turn it into fiction . . . The immortal monkey searched for the man for centuries, until at last in this Sacred Peaceful Dynasty he met with a descendant of Lao Zi who enjoyed a little reputation for his writing. Already impatient, he handed the text to the man and returned to his cave. This man, considering the text to be too eventful and difficult to narrate . . . worked many years on it until finally the hundred chapters of *Flowers in the Mirror* was compiled. (JHY, 617)

Here we have a quadruple composite narrator formed by the scriber (Tang Xiaoshan), the messenger (the white monkey), and the editor (the descendant of Lao Zi—apparently hinting at the author Li Shizhen). No teller (the one who wrote on the stele) is mentioned, but he is not indispensable. What is strange is that the over-narrative is not above the main narrative but mixed in it as all elements of the composite narrator are characters of the main narrative, not of an over-narrative. Thus the main narrator is, paradoxically, provided by the main narrative itself. The trespassing of the stratification, then, seems to be the pre-condition of the stratification itself.[44] This is a very intriguing way of introducing an over-narrative, which as I shall show was to become a favoured device in late Qing fiction.

If the stratification itself has complex thematic implications, its trespassing pushes them further. If characters can pass from one level into another, then none of the narrated worlds is 'real' as the characters of another world above or below can enter and exit freely. This, perhaps, was just the purpose of the complicated trespassing of stratification in novels like *The Dream of the Red Chamber*.

XII

If the over-narrative is a rare device in traditional Chinese fiction, its fortunes took a surprisingly turn in late Qing fiction. It seems that the narrator, still basically traditional but under the pressure of becoming explicit, found a relatively easier escape.

The Dream of the Red Chamber must have been influential in encouraging the huge amount of over-narrative in late Qing fiction, while interest in over-narrative could have been fuelled by the translations of Western fiction. A careful examination, however, shows that perhaps the only Western novel translated at that time that has over-narrative structures was *La Dame aux camélias*.[45] This novel was the most widely read translated novel of the time, and became known as 'The Foreign *Dream of the Red Chamber*'. It is safe to say that Chinese and Western sources must have reinforced each other for the successful promotion of over-narrative in the late Qing.

The most common formula for over-narrative in late Qing fiction is the chance discovery of manuscripts. This probably follows the example of *The Dream of the Red Chamber*, where Kong Kong discovers the Stone's confession. Among the novels using this formula are Wu Jianren's *Strange Events* and *Wronged Ghosts* (*Heiji Yuanhun*), Chen Tianhua's *The Lion Roars*, Suran Yusheng's *A Trip to Utopia*

---

[44] Zhou Ruchang (1976: 177) argues that since *Flowers in the Mirror* was produced almost half a century later than *The Dream of the Red Chamber*, its over-narrative structure might be an imitation of the latter. This is of course very possible. But, as my analysis shows, the two novels are very different in their handling of the over-narrative.

[45] Of course *The Cases of Sherlock Holmes* has a clear over-narrative. But its influence came much later, and was felt more in the popular entertaining novels.

(*Wutuobang Youji*), Xuelei Yusheng's *A Dream of the Goddess of Flowers* (*Huashen Meng*), and Tenggu Guxiang's *The Thunder that Hits the Sky* (*Hongtian Lei*).

Another formula is for the over-narrator to hear the character telling a story and turning himself into the main narrator. This, however, seems to have been followed more in literary-language fiction of the late Qing, as we can see in He Zou's *The House of the Broken Zither* (*Suiqin Lou*), Lin Shu's *The Monk Who Floats on Water* (*Fushui Seng*), and Zhou Shoujuan's *The Shadow of Cloud* (*Yunying*). It is possible that they were inspired more by *La Dame aux camélias* than by *The Dream of the Red Chamber*, since Lin Shu's translation of the former is in literary language. In fact, Xu Zhenya's *Jade-Pear Soul* (*Yuli Hun*) is very similar to *La Dame aux camélias* in its beginning with an over-narrative, and ending with quotations from the deceased heroine's diary. The novel ends with 'Principal Shi Ci knew that the author had won the name of the Dumas of the Orient, and asked him to write this novel *Jade-Pear Soul*'. This must have sounded very boastful at the time.

This difference in over-narrative schemes shows that the gap between literary-language fiction (despite the fact that these novels were popular in late Qing) and vernacular fiction (despite the fact that *The Dream of the Red Chamber* was the most élitist among vernacular novels) was still wide.

Another possible source for inspiration seems to be the Japanese political novels, which were eagerly read by late Qing political novelists. Liang Qichao began writing *The Future of New China* after reading and translating Shiba Shiro's *The Strange Adventure of the Beauty* (*Kajin No Kigu*), which tells how a Japanese man meets a Spanish young lady and her maid on his visit to the Bell of Freedom in Philadelphia, and overhears their emotional talk. He asks about their past. After some hesitation the lady tells him how the turmoil in Spain in 1867 led to the invasion of Napoleon III, and how patriots died to defend their country. This structure of using stratification to provide a retrospective narrative was adopted by Liang Qichao in his own political novel.

A cyclical over-narrative structure similar to that in *Flowers in the Mirror* can be observed in *The Bureaucrats*, *The Thunder That Hits the Sky*, and other novels. At the end of *The Bureaucrats*, the character Zhen Xuege hears his severely ill brother recount a strange dream he has had:

In a while, people inside sent out a loud cry. Everybody was shouting, 'Fire! Fire! Fire!' Then many people rushed out carrying volumes of books. . . .

[After the fire] these people came back to carefully check the salvaged volumes, and said that only the first half of the book they had been proof-reading
was there. (GCXXJ, 456)

This over-narrative does not provide a clear narrator. Zhen's brother
is only a witness to this scene in his dream. The proof-readers are
mentioned too briefly to be considered as editors. No matter who is the
narrator, the narrating instance of the main narrative (the introducing of
the manuscripts) is embedded in the main narrative itself.

A similar but clearer example can be seen in *The Thunder that Hits
the Sky*. The last chapter of this novel recounts how a group of the
protagonist's friends have a dinner, during which one character, Jianzhai,
says, 'I bought from a bookstore a book with the title *The Thunder that
Hits the Sky*.' After the dinner another character, Jingfu, borrows this
book and opens it, 'and saw the Preface, which is now copied here as
the post-script to the novel'. (HTL, 418) Again we have an over-
narrative supplied by the main narrative[46] even though this cyclical
over-narrative is, logically or narratologically, impossible.

Thus we can see that in late Qing fiction, there are at least three types
of over-narrative: the *Red Chamber* type (discovery of manuscripts),
the *Camélias* type (listening to a story), and the *Flowers in the Mirror*
type (over-narrative embedded in the main narrative).

Oddly, there is no mention on the part of the late Qing authors and
critics to show that they ever noticed the structure of narrative stratification in either *The Dream of the Red Chamber* or *La Dame aux
camélias*, or that in their own works. It seems that those authors themselves were not aware that their narrative stratification had been pushed
into such a complicated pattern. They just followed the trend.

Nevertheless, the presence of an over-narrative does not always guar-
antee that the narrator's personality can be sufficiently substantiated. In
A Flower in the Sinful Sea for instance, there is a specially designed
over-narrative:

Freedom-Lover was writing. Suddenly he threw down his writing brush and
said, 'Bah! What a fool I am! Now my friend Sickman-of-the-East is widely

---

[46] The novel *The Thunder That Hits the Sky* has a over-over-narrative on top of this
cyclical over-narrative: Someone named A Yuan receives a package from the post office
which contains a novel in Japanese and a letter from a Chinese friend of his to the effect
that he is dying, and that before his death he would like to send to his best friend A Yuan
the manuscript of a novel the Chinese original of which had been lost. Since A Yuan does
not know Japanese, he has to co-operate with a friend in translating it back into Chinese,
which becomes, then, the main narrative.

acknowledged to be the King of Fiction, and specialized in compiling this kind
of new fiction. If I tell him the story in all its details, can't he write it out
chapter by chapter?' He at once left his home, carrying the manuscripts, to the
publisher's office of *Xiaoshuo Lin*, found his friend Sickman-of-the-East, and
told him this interesting story. While Freedom-Lover was talking, Sickman-of-
the-East wrote down the whole thing. (NHH, 4)

But this over-narrative structure, having supplied a particular narrative frame, does not stop the narrator (now the combined voice of a
teller and a scribe) from referring to himself in the main narrative as the
conventionalized 'Story-Writer' (*Zuoshude*) and the narratee 'Respected
Reader' (*Kanguan*).

There are several other examples of this obsession with over-narrative
which almost becomes an abuse. The novel *The Lion Roars*, for example, makes its over-narrative unnecessarily prolonged: an 'I' finds an
unfinished novel. After reading it 'I' falls into a dream, in which 'I'
witnesses the British warships invading the Yangtze and massacring the
Chinese people. Then 'I' watches a play, and visits a library where 'I'
finds a book on the history of the Republic. 'I' steals it but is caught.
After waking up 'I' finds the book in 'my' hand bearing the title *The
Lion Roars*. So this 'I' is made the editor of the main narrative. This
over-narrative, though long enough, does not render much help in sub-
stantiating a narrator.

So what is the purpose of late Qing fiction turning to over-narrative?
The most obvious reason for the increased number of over-narratives,
it seems, is the uncertain position in which the narrator now finds
himself. He is no longer that firmly stabilized story-teller narrator of
earlier vernacular fiction. He needs to find a way to substantiate himself, to increase his explicitness while not damaging the narratorial
control. But a 'sufficient' characterization does not seem necessary as
he is not yet ready to become an explicit and participant narrator. That
is why in late Qing fiction we find narrative stratification so abundantly
applied, yet so inefficiently used, which is again one of the symptoms
of the narrator's uneasiness on finding himself in a demanding new
situation where the conventional narrative frame cannot go on unchanged,
but the change has not yet found a direction.

XIII

Narrative stratification dropped drastically in May Fourth fiction.
Since the narrator's self-characterization in May Fourth fiction is quite

sophisticated, there is hardly any narratological necessity for the higher-level substantiation. Stratification is still frequently used, however, although its purpose now may be different. Narratorial commentaries, generally frowned upon in May Fourth period, could sound less obtrusive if made by a character-turned narrator. Xu Dishan's long story 'A Merchant's Wife' ('Shangren Fu') tells of the vicissitudes of a Chinese country-woman's life in Malaysia and India, and the first-person narrator-protagonist comments:

> Dear sir, nothing in this world can be distinctly said to be sweet or bitter. When you suffer, it is bitter. When you hope, it is sweet. When something happens, it is bitter, though it could be sweet in retrospect. (ZWLZ, 67)

This commentary sounds too admonitory in May Fourth fiction, no matter what philosophy underlies it. What saves the story is that the above narratorial intrusion is made in the form of a reported speech uttered by the narrator in her other capacity—the character of the merchant's woman in the over-narrative.

The subtle shift of narratorial mediation by stratification can be demonstrated by comparing Lu Xun's 'The Happy Family' ('Xingfu de Jiating') with its acknowledged model 'The Ideal Spouse' ('Lixiang de Banlu') by Xu Qinwen. In the latter there is a over-narrative: 'A friend of mine' comes to chat. 'I' records his reverie about what kind of girl he hopes to find, which becomes the text of the main narrative. Zhao is described in the over-narrative as a man 'with the style of Dongfang Shuo, the famous Han courtier with quick wit'. This is actually a commentary, and a pre-determining one at that, to alert readers to the unreliability of the main narrative. In Lu Xun's story, however, this cross-level commentary is transformed into a more substantiated scheme: a writer is writing an essay with the title 'The Happy Family', but he is constantly interrupted by his busybody wife with the petty mundane affairs of the impoverished family. His reverie thus becomes an indirect commentary in ironic conflict with the main narrative.

Both of the two schemes of stratification try to contrast reality with fantasy, but in Lu Xun's case the irony is less predetermined, as the unreliability of the sub-narrative is revealed only gradually through the whole text. Moreover, if Xu Qinwen's stratification provides an 'agreeing' hetero-stratification commentary, Lu Xun's, then, is a 'conflicting' cross-level commentary, thus turning the stratification itself into a vehicle for irony.

More interestingly, sentimentalism hardly avoidable in first-person monologue, could be offset in a more subtle manner by 'conflicting' stratification than by direct satire.

Lu Yin's long story 'Father' ('Fuqin')[47] is a tragedy of the intense platonic love between a young man and his stepmother. This main narrative is almost intolerably sentimental but the over-narrative counterbalances it: 'I' and 'my' cousins are bored and ask 'my' brother to read a story, which is the main narrative. After Brother finishes reading, the youngsters make jokes about the text, 'though I felt sad at heart'. Then the text stops short with a cold and ironical twist—'A new guest came. That put an end to their joking.'

Xiao Ming's 'The Story Told by My Wife' ('Qi de Gushi')[48] has a more strongly ironical over-narrative: 'I', a young writer, is obsessed with writing romances, which displeases 'my' wife. Thereupon she offers to tell him 'a true story of her own life' about her calf-love-affair with an adolescent monk. Her story is finally cut short as 'I', after experiencing a myriad of different emotions, grows more and more disquieted. The mingling of the two levels demonstrates a deft handling of the hetero-stratification contrast and mutual comment.

Nevertheless, today's critics might feel that stratification is, in general, still used too frequently in May Fourth fiction. The May Fourth writers seemed to feel this too, and many then tried to install a less meddlesome stratification. A simple method often used was to move the over-narrative to the end, making it something of a postscript. Bai Cai's story 'The Jilted' ('Bei Binqi Zhe') is a woman's confession, with the over-narrative added at the end which explains that it is a manuscript 'I' picked up by chance. The over-narrative is banal, declaring that the woman might have been saved by God. If it did not trail at the end, it could have ruined the whole story.

In Feng Yuanjun's twin stories 'Custody' ('Gejue') and 'After Custody' ('Gejue Zhihou') a character in the first story becomes the narrator in the second story, and both stories are in the first person. The two stories, when read together (which was quite possible at that time, since not many stories were published every year) form a *de facto* stratified pair.

The over-narrative most adroitly hidden seems to be Xu Dishan's

---

[47] The story is included in Lu Yin's 1930 collection *Tides in the Sea of Mind* (*Linhai Xichao*) but was written in 1925.

[48] The story was printed in Yusi in 1925 and selected by Lu Xun for the second volume of fiction of the *Omnibus of Chinese New Literature*. The author (Xiao Ming is obviously a pen-name) regrettably remains unknown.

'Undeliverable Letters' where the over-narrative appears only as short notes in brackets under each letter explaining why the letter was undelivered—'To Xiaolan. Reason for failure of delivery: the man is now in an asylum'; 'To Danguang. Reason for failure of delivery: she has gone south to marry and requests that all the letters from her former boy friends be returned without opening.' This over-narrative scheme facilitates intense irony, but leaves almost no trace of intrusiveness.

If over-narratives are less used in May Fourth fiction than in late Qing fiction, there are even fewer sub-narratives. It should also be noted that many of the sub-narratives in May Fourth fiction are in indirect reported speech whereas most sub-narratives in late Qing fiction are in directly reported speech. This difference makes the former more natural. For instance, in Lu Xun's 'New Year Sacrifice' ('Zhufu') the narrator 'I' meets Xianglin Sao and is perplexed by the few words they exchanged. When 'I' hears about her death on a snowy night, 'I' recollects her life, recalling reports by different characters about her life which 'I' could not have witnessed. These passages in indirect form merge into a sub-narrative in third-person narration. Thus May Fourth fiction generally avoids the histrionics of reported speech in sub-narrative formed in the late Qing period.

Lu Xun, as the greatest craftsman of the May Fourth writers , successfully explored almost all the possibilities of stratification in his works, and all manner of character-narrator transformations. In 'In the Wine Tavern' ('Zai Jiulou Shang') the narrator 'I' meets an old friend Lu Weifu who tells his own story which is quoted in direct speech, turning himself into the second first-person narrator. This is the double explicit scheme.

The short story 'The Happy Family' tells of a character trying to write a narrative in which he appears as the first-person narrator. This is the implicit-explicit scheme.

And finally the double-implicit—this scheme of stratification seems to be more natural with sub-narratives, i.e. in a third-person narrative a character relates a story about some other people. In the main narrative of 'New Year Sacrifice', for instance, the character Old Lady Wei tells the story of Xianglin Sao's second marriage.

As a contrast, the explicit-implicit scheme often seen in late Qing novels—such as in *The Strange Events* or *Viewed with Cold Eyes* where the narrator 'I' jots down the anecdotes told by all kinds of people he meets—is no longer seen, since May Fourth writers do not need that scheme to string a number of stories into a novel.

All these aspects of narrator–character relationship—focalization, reported speech, stratification—are, essentially, a matter of the division of narrative subjectivity. We can see an obvious downward movement of subjectivity, from that of the narrator to that of the character, until the pressure becomes almost unbearable in late Qing fiction. The apparent technical problems then become part of the driving force for the further development of Chinese fiction.

3

Narrative Time

I

There are two kinds of temporal distortion in the narrative text: the deformation of temporal duration, and the dislocation of the sequence. No narrative is possible without distorting the pre-narrated time.

Indeed, written narrative actually does not have a temporal dimension. The printed or written space can only be measured by the number of words, or of pages. To indicate time, written narrative has to resort to relative spatial proportion. Then the space allocated to the narrating of a certain event acquires a temporal implication. This is signifier time.[1]

Narrative has another time-indicating system—the signified time. The phrase 'after three days' or 'in a moment' indicates time duration not by the space the phrase occupies but by its meaning. Obviously, signified time is clearer than the spatio-proportional signifier time.

However, there is a third time-indicator in written narrative: since the events narrated form a relatively complete line or network of events, when there are some parts missing, we know that a period of time passes without being mentioned. In this way, the duration of time is indicated by the zero-sign—the absence of narration of time.

The three time-indicators (signifier time, signified time, and absence time) join to form the time-duration scheme of written narrative, for which Chatman provides a clear-cut chart.[2] I have only replaced some of his terms with mine for the sake of consistency:

ellipsis	*narrated* time = 0, and < *pre-narrated* time
summary	*narrated* time < *pre-narrated* time
scene	*narrated* time = *pre-narrated* time
stretch	*narrated* time > *pre-narrated* time
pause	*narrated* time > *pre-narrated* time, which = 0

[1] Christian Metz (1974) first used these two terms in his discussion of cinematic semiotics. He holds that narrative is a doubly temporal sequence: 'There is the time of the thing told and the time of the narrative (the time of the signified and of the signifier). This duality not only renders possible all the temporal distortion ... more basically, it invites us to consider that one of the functions of narrative is to invent one time scheme in terms of another time scheme.'

[2] Chatman 1978: 123.

Zero-sign time can only mark ellipsis, while signifier time and signified time are both used as indicators of other types of durations of narrative time.

Yet some difficulties still remain in this chart, since almost the whole scheme depends on the comparison between the spatio-proportional *narrated* time and the natural time duration in the *pre-narrated*. Is there a way to recognize a scene (*narrated* time = *pre-narrated* time)? My suggestion is that, when there is direct reported speech in the narrative, the space devoted to the speech can be said to represent the time duration in the *pre-narrated*. Passages that can be considered faster than this then should be called summary, and those slower, stretch. These are, of course, only imprecise proportions. The actual measuring of either the pre-narrated time or the narrated time is impossible, and in fact of little significance to narratological study.

The few stretches in traditional Chinese fiction are mostly descriptions of martial arts, usually with directions supporting the time stretched. In chapter 74 of *Water Margin*, for instance, a stretch is preceded by such a direction:

Every move in this kind of wrestling must be narrated clearly. My telling is slow now but the actions at the time were as fast as meteors or lightning in the sky. They did not allow any slowing down. (SHZ, 635)

Directions have to be used to justify the stretches since they are so rare in traditional Chinese fiction.

Direct reported speech can be said to be the slowest part in Chinese fiction, since there are few scenes in traditional Chinese fiction, and even fewer stretches and pauses. The texts of traditional Chinese fiction are almost completely composed of summaries, and the narrative appears speedy and sketchy.

Almost all traditional Chinese fictional works start with a summary. Most novels of the Rewriting period start with a sweeping summary reaching back to the very beginning of the world and of Chinese civilization. Short stories or novels of limited length would often start with an introduction of the family background and the past experience of the protagonist, with definite place and date. We may call such a far-reaching summary beginning an *ab ovo* beginning, which is by necessity very speedy.

It can be further noted that in Chinese vernacular fiction of the Rewriting period, those events derived from history tend to be narrated speedily, while the events passed down through legend and oral literature are generally related at leisure in more detail. This is visible in *The Three Kingdoms*. Its first few chapters sketchily recount the chaotic civil wars from about AD 170 to about AD 194. When it reaches the more personal experience of Cao Cao (exactly the point when the character changes from a man of destiny in history into the cold-blooded coward that folk literature made him) the narration slows down markedly.

Quasi-historical novels like *Water Margin* display a similar pattern: the speed is much greater when narrating the battles of the rebels' troops against large government armies than when narrating the personal wrongs the individual rebels suffer before they went to Mount Liang one by one.

This pattern of speed variation is first mentioned by Lu Xun in his discussion on *Newly Compiled Five Dynasties Pinghua* (*Xinbian Wudai Shi Pinghua*):

The narrative is sometimes very fast, but slow at other times. Generally speaking when historical events are told, there are not many digressions. But when it comes to small things, many details are added, with descriptions in verse, and poems mixed with doggerels, cited as testimonial poems, so as to win laughter.[3]

C. T. Hsia found the same when he discussed *Forgotten Texts of Sui History*:

The first forty-five chapters of the novel are actually a biographical novel of Qin Shubao, and unfold in no haste ... After chapter 46, the novel centres around the emperor-to-be Li Shimin, and the narration proceeds at a much faster pace since it has to report so many important historical events. (Hsia 1977, 6)

Though neither of these two scholars tried to generalize from their observations, I think it is safe to say that this is a rule in Chinese vernacular fiction.[4]

---

[3] Lu Xun 1956: viii. 90.

[4] There are some misunderstandings among scholars. Meng Yao insists: 'For quite a long period, many of the best novels were unable to get out of the limitation of oral story-telling (*Shuohua*) whose characteristic style was the sketchiness with which the narrative unfolded fast and full of action.' (Meng Yao 1966: 387). Is speediness a characteristic of oral story-telling? The various kinds of oral narrative performance (*Pingshu* in North China, or *Pingtan* in South China) are all notoriously slow, much slower than written narrative of any sort. The Wu Song episode told in *Yangzhou Pinghua* is renowned for its lingering description of the moves in martial art; and *The Pearl Pagoda* (*Zhenzhu Ta*) in Suzhou Pingtan is believed to set the world record for slow narration in spending 18 days (sessions) in describing how the heroine descends 18 steps of the staircase.

We do not know exactly how slow story-telling in former periods could be, but at least we know that during the Qing the pace of oral story-telling could be extremely slow. An

Traditional Chinese fiction regularly begins with a summary and proceeds through a series of summaries, slowing down only in dialogue.[5] Speediness is less apparent with novels topically more distant from the historical mode. Quasi-historical novels like *Water Margin*, or fantasy novels like *The Journey to the West* have more scenes than historical novels, thus acquiring much-needed retardation. But it was not until Chinese fiction outgrew the Rewriting period with fiction on family relations like *Jin Ping Mei* that the speed of narration slowed down markedly.

The Chongzhen version of *Jin Ping Mei* makes an important improvement on the *Cihua* version by replacing the *ab ovo* summary beginning with a scene beginning. The new version starts almost directly (only preceded by a very brief summary of Ximen Qing's past) with Ximen Qing waiting on the second floor of the wine tavern to see Wu Song parade into the town with the tiger he has killed. This is a completely new way of starting a novel for Chinese fiction. Because of this opening scene, the Chongzhen version sets an entirely different tone for the whole novel.

After that, quite a number of novels seem to have picked up this beginning scheme. *The Scholars* starts with a similar scene: after a brief summary—a few words about how a little village obtained its name—there then appears a long scene with the villagers gathering to discuss an important issue concerning the whole community. *The Dream of the Red Chamber*, after the group over-narrative extending as long as six chapters, restarts with a scene describing Granny Liu approaching the Jia's Mansion, preceded only by a very brief introductory summary of Granny Liu's family.

observer of Qing oral performance reported, 'Old people told me how good story-tellers narrated Wu Song Fights in the Inn. After Wu Song had put his foot on a mound, they took more than one month before letting him take his foot off.' (Xu Ke: *Qingbi Leichao* Shanghai: The Commercial Press, 1957, 67)

The earliest Chinese vernacular fiction—the so-called *Huaben* fiction—is really fast in its narrative speed, and sketchy. This is not the heritage of oral performance.

[5] This is different from the Western tradition of narrative. Neither Homeric epics nor medieval romances comprise such a large number of highly speedy summaries as found in traditional Chinese fiction. Western epics and novels proceed at a much more measured pace with more scenes. If we can call traditional European fiction 'scenario' narrative, then traditional Chinese fiction is 'synopsis' narrative.

The most important reason for this speedy narration, I think, is the influence of historiography in Chinese fiction. Novels on historical subject-matters have the aim of popularizing rather than fictionalizing history, and the number of events contained in these novels usually exceeds by far the number in Western historical novels from *Morte d'Arthur* to *Ivanhoe*.

Nevertheless, even these few great novels do not try to shake off the introductory summary preceding the scene beginning. What is more, most other Chinese vernacular novels and short stories still stick to the conventionalized *ab ovo* summary beginning.

II

Repetition takes place when the event is recounted or the same information provided more than once. Repetition seems to be superfluous and omissible, but is in fact a regular feature in all types of narrative. There are two kinds of repetition in traditional Chinese fiction: generic and technical.

Generic repetitions are repetitions indicative of style or genre. The most conspicuous repetitions in traditional Chinese fiction appear in the chapter-beginning, which recounts what has been told in the previous chapter, and the chapter-ending, which is a cryptic flashforward of what is to happen in the next chapter.

These are supposed to be simulations of oral performance—at the beginning of each session the story-teller had to remind the audience of what had already been told the last time, and at the end of the session he had to drop some hints on what would happen next to arouse the curiosity of the audience so that they would pay to listen once again. The reason that this repetitive device survived in traditional Chinese fiction for so long was solely because it reminds the readers of the conventional narrative frame.[6]

But when repetitions take on different focalizations or other different ways of narrating, they may become necessary repetitions. Patrick Hanan has suggested that there was at least one good example in traditional Chinese fiction of repetition with different character-focalization—the short story 'Lord Xiangmin Lost His Son on the Evening of Yuanxiao, and the Thirteenth Young Master of Five Years Old Was Received by His Majesty' in *The Second Collection of Amazing Stories* (*Erke Pai' an Jingqi*), edited by Ling Mengchu.[7] In the story a child is stolen but returned because of his own wit. His adventure is described first from the focalization of the servant taking care of him, then from the child's focalization, and then from the kidnappers. Part of their experiences overlap which makes the narrative more interesting. But generally

---

[6] In the late Qing, however, there emerged another practical reason for this type of formulaic beginning and ending—serialization in newspapers or magazines.

[7] Plaks 1977: 242.

speaking, this kind of necessary repetition did not occur in Chinese fiction until the May Fourth period.

Another type of repetition, however, abounds in Chinese vernacular fiction in the form of repeated reported speech. We can pluck a huge bouquet of such examples by leafing through any Chinese novels of the Rewriting period. In chapter 3 of *The Journey to the West*, the Monkey extorts a magic weapon from the Dragon King of the East Sea, and finds the weapon can change size at his wish. When he returns to his cave in Mount Flower-and-Fruit, he shows the magic to his monkey subjects, which is a repetition of previously told events, only this time in reported speech. Later in the novel he has to explain the magic of the weapon to other people using more or less the same words.

In chapters 45 and 46 of *Water Margin*, Monk Hai Sheli has an affair with Pan Qiaoyun. The two arrange a signalling scheme to ensure safety: when Pan's slave girl lays out the incense table, it is to be interpreted as her husband's absence from home; when the Turkish monk beats the wooden fish in the lane, it is to signal that there is no one around, and he can come out of Pan's house. This scheme is repeated seven times in seven pages: Monk Hai Sheli tells the Turkish monk about his scheme; the Turkish monk does as agreed and finds the scheme safe; Shi Xiu sees this series of strange events and tries to make out what is going on; Shi Xiu tells his sworn brother Yang Xiong about the whole scheme; since Yang Xiong does not believe him, Shi Xiu waylays the Turkish monk and forces him to confess the whole scheme; Yang Xiong kidnaps his wife and the slave girl, and asks the latter about the whole scheme; at the point of a dagger, the slave girl has to tell everything about the scheme.

We can see that five out of the above seven passages are in the direct quoted form, which is virtually the only form for reporting the character's speech. Since direct speech is not supposed to be abridged or recast by narratorial mediation, repetition is then unavoidable. Such repetitive quotes persisted into the Creative period.[8] In *Jin Ping Mei*, there are even longer repetitive quotes. In chapter 9, Liu Er comes to Wang Liu'er's home and beats her. Immediately after that passage, Chen Jingli comes to ask what has happened, and he hears a report from Butler Lu who repeats the whole event. In chapter 20, Ximen

---

[8] Both Jin Shengtan and Mao Zonggang praise the repetition or duplication in Chinese vernacular fiction. But what they are discussing is actually repetition of the topic—two similar murders in the same novel, for instance. (Huang Lin and Han Tongwen 1982: 213, 229. Also see Rolston 1990: 143, 170).

Qing gets into trouble in a brothel. In the next chapter, when his concubines ask the slave boy Dai An about what happened the previous
day, Dai An's report repeats the event related in the last chapter. These
repetitions in the *Cihua* version are not rephrased in the *Chongzhen*
version. The author obviously did not consider them omissible.

In later novels we no longer find so many repetitive quotes. In the
best of Chinese novels of the eighteenth century, repetitive quotes disappear almost completely, and are never resurrected in late Qing fiction.
This disappearance coincided with the emergence of indirect speech.

The problem of ellipses is even more complex than that of repetition.
Ellipses can be marked either by signified time or by absence time,
which corresponds neatly to the terms Genette suggests—explicit and
implicit ellipses. We may say that if a narrative is symbolized by a line,
implicit ellipsis is then a blank with the line disappearing but still
understood, while explicit ellipsis is a line of dots marking the omission
of some events with a summary continuing the line, only making it
thinner. The number of ellipses and the kind of ellipses the narrative
uses will determine the shape of the narrative—it may be seriously
fragmented or apparently lineal.

No narrative can be formed without ellipses since selectivity is the
most essential aspect of narrative mediation. But traditional Chinese
fiction seems to endeavour to maintain its narrative linearity to the
maximum. Within a time scheme every event, it seems, is told, with
nothing left out. In chapter 74 of *Water Margin* for instance, Yan Qing
wants to go to Tai'an for the wrestling championship, to which Song
Jiang reluctantly agrees:

*Nothing else happened that day. The next day Song Jiang gave a farewell
banquet in his honour.* After that he took the road to Tai'an. (SHZ, 342)

The first sentence is a cliché ellipsis but the absence of event is stated
in an emphatic form that makes it sound almost like a summary.[9] The
second sentence provides some unnecessary information as such ban-
quets are routine among Mount Liang partisans, not just for special
occasions.

These 'fillers' in lieu of ellipses are frequently seen in Chinese vernacular fiction. In chapter 46 of the same novel, when Yang Xiong cuts
his wife Pan Qiaoyun to pieces on the hill slope and flees, and the
whole town is shocked:

---

[9] Genette argues (1980: 145) that 'after three months' is ellipsis, while 'three months
passed' is a summary.

Father Pan bought a coffin to bury his daughter, but this we do not have to mention. Yang Xiong and Shi Xiu left Zhaozhou and spent the day walking and the night sleeping. *This went on for more than one day.* (SHZ, 234)

Both of these statements are meant to skip certain events. Yet they assume the form of summaries instead of ellipses.

Even in the best Chinese vernacular novel, *The Dream of the Red Chamber*, this summary in lieu of ellipsis is not infrequent. After trivial 'filling-ins' there is always the short direction *buti* ('this is not worth mentioning'). In chapter 26:

At the time of lighting lamps that day, *Jia Yun had his supper, and made his bed to sleep. Nothing happened that night. The next morning he rose, washed,* and went to the South Gate Avenue. (HLM, 280)

The italicized part consists totally of 'filling-ins' of insignificant information. In traditional Chinese fiction there is a constant effort to maintain linearity by using explicit ellipses rather than implicit ellipses, by using summaries rather than explicit ellipses, and by insignificant filling-ins instead of ellipses. What makes the situation more interesting is that reported speech, as I have discussed above, is often directly quoted in full rather than summarized in the direct form. Thus the impression could be created that all events are told without any omission. I suggest naming this temporal treatment 'time-brimming'.[10] This is, of course, only an impression, since no narrative can report all the events in the pre-narrated without selectivity.

In such novels, it seems, the only thing which can cut the sequence of events is another plot-line of narrative. But even at such moments traditional Chinese fiction still makes an effort to maintain the impression of linearity. Often such a line-crossing is handled painstakingly with the help of directions. In chapter 49 of *Water Margin*, Song Jiang is ready to launch a third attack on Zhujia Zhuang, and Wu Yong offers a stratagem:

Upon hearing this, Song Jiang said enthusiastically, 'Won-derful,' and broke into a smile. *Story-teller, what stratagem was it? You will hear about it soon. Respected listener, please keep this line in your mind. Certain incidents were taking place at the same time as Song Jiang was engaged in his first attack on*

---

[10] Hanan points out (1967: 176), 'The vernacular fiction shows great concern for spatial and temporal setting. Elaborate calendars of events can be extracted from long works like *Water Margin* and the *Jin Ping Mei*; with their constant reckoning of time, they can even become wearisome.' I do not know why Hanan spares *The Dream of the Red Chamber*, which suffers no less from this tendency.

Zhujia Zhuang. Since I cannot give one sentence to this plot-line and one
sentence to that plot-line, I have to put aside the line of the attacks on Zhujia
Zhuang and recount the line of how some people who wanted to join the rebels
of Mount Liang tried to seize the opportunity, and, finally, I shall connect the
two. (SHZ, 326)

The direction seems too lengthy to be necessary, but the narrator in
Chinese traditional fiction appears to be very conscious of the linearity
of his narrative. Here the breaking of the strict linearity is seized as an
opportunity to reinforce the time-brimming impression. It seems safe to
say that a direction, though not necessarily such a long one, is indispensable when the plot-line shifts.[11]

Time-brimming naturally goes hand in hand with detail-brimming.
Passages like the following two are often seen in vernacular Chinese
fiction:

Among those who tried to sail abroad to trade, there were some leaders whose
names were unexceptionally [*wu fei shi*] Zhang Da or Li Er. (CKPAJQ, ch. 1)

Upon the order came out two *yamen* runners whose names were unexceptionally
Zhang Qian or Li Wan. (EKPAJQ, ch. 23)

The mention of those 'everyman' names (similar to John Smith in
English) is obviously not meant to be providing any information about
those people, as there is no need to give their names at all. Such passages are to create the impression that every bit of information is provided in the narrative.

---

[11] In *The Journey to the West*, some passages relating events of a pseudo-historical
dimension are singularly time-brimming, with almost no ellipsis.

The next day the Jade Emperor ascended the throne and presided over the court
session. Zhang the Celestial Master led the Head and Deputy Head of the Imperial
Stable to kneel below the scarlet platform, and made his report . . . Upon hearing this,
the Jade Emperor gave his imperial order . . . From among the cabinet members the
Tower-in-Hand Heavenly Duke Li and the Third Young Master No Zuo came forward
to report . . . The Jade Emperor was overjoyed . . . and gave them the mandate to
conduct the expedition. Heavenly Duke Li and No Zuo kowtowed in gratitude before
taking leave. Back at their own palace, they mustered the whole army with all the
officers, and ordered the Giant General as the vanguard, the Fish-Belly General as the
rear guard and Herb-Fork General as the supervisor of the reinforcements. In a moment
they were out of the South Heavenly Gate, and, arriving at Huaguo Shan, they chose
a piece of open and flat land to set up the camps, and ordered the Giant General to go
ahead to provoke a battle. Receiving the order, the Giant General put on proper armour
and . . . (XYJ, 97)

This unnecessarily detailed report is possibly meant to be a mockery of the grandeur
of the Heavenly court and the style of historiography.

It was Hu Shi who first noticed the meagreness of narrative selectivity in Chinese historical novels. He was rather harsh in his comments: '*The Three Kingdoms* is very capable of gathering, but unable to sift. All rubbish and scraps have been collected with nothing left out. Due to the reluctance to tailor itself, this novel cannot be called a literary work at all.'[12]

He arrived at this conclusion through comparing *The Three Kingdoms* with *Water Margin*. Apparently historical novels are more likely to be trapped in time-brimming. But the difference between historical novels and non-historical novels in time-brimming is only a matter of degree. Ellipses are never mentioned by traditional Chinese fiction critics.[13] Luo Yi's *The Notes of a Drunken Man* (*Zuiweng Tanlu*), now acclaimed as the earliest Chinese critical work on vernacular fiction (*c.* fourteenth century),[14] offers a typical exposition on the temporal scheme in narratorial mediation: 'Arguments should not be dragged out or verbose; presentations should be of a magnitude and well-rounded. *When uneventful, mentioning should be well-arranged*; when more eventful, narration should be more prolonged.'[15]

Here we have a fairly comprehensive scheme for the temporal treatment in fiction, but the absence of ellipses is conspicuous, as even when there is no event, 'mentioning' (*tiduo*) has to be carefully made.

In other genres of traditional Chinese literature, such as Ming and Qing opera, time-brimming is also a salient characteristic. The reluctance to omit any link in the line of events could protract a play to forty acts. No drama critics, who outnumbered fiction critics by far, ever mentioned ellipsis, although they repeatedly emphasized 'close knitting' and 'dense stitching'.[16] The cause of this negligence cannot be purely technical since very elliptic plays of only four acts had been the standard practice in the Yuan Dynasty. Chinese playwrights and audiences must have preferred the time-brimming type of plays and fiction for some other reasons, a topic to which I shall return later.

[12] Hu Shi 1929: book 2, iv. 134.

[13] Indeed the great Chinese commentator-critic Jin Shengtan discussed 'frugality'. What he means is a kind of coincidence that could make the narrative 'economical'. He cited two examples from *Water Margin*. Neither of them is an ellipsis. Please see Huang Lin and Han Tongwen 1982: 229.

[14] Both Zheng Zhenduo and Zhou Yibai hold that *Notes of the Drunken Man* was produced in the Yuan Dynasty, but Zhao Jingshen argued that it could be as early as the end of the Song Dynasty and the beginning of the Yuan Dynasty (Zhao Jingshen 1980: 82).

[15] Luo Yi 1957: 4. Italics mine.

[16] Some modern critics, e.g. Yang Jiang, find the Ming plays 'more novelistic than dramatic' (Yang Jiang, *Chun Ni Ji*, Beijing: Renmin Wenxue Chubanshe, 1978, 87).

III

The high narrative speed of traditional Chinese fiction does not slow down significantly in the late Qing period. Political novels like *The Lion Roars*, historical novels like *A Flower in the Sinful Sea*, and social novels like *The Bureaucrats*, all maintain the sketchy-speedy characteristic of traditional Chinese vernacular fiction. In Butterfly romances, the speed slows down markedly, but the slow parts are mostly sentimental long letters exchanged between lovers. Just as in traditional vernacular fiction, the slowest part is still the direct quoted speech.

In some late Qing novels, retardation of the narrative tempo appears in when recounting the characters' mental activities or providing scene descriptions. There are not many such novels, and the best known among them are Wu Jianren's *A Sea of Remorse*, Han Bangqing's *Lives of Shanghai Flowers*, and Liu E's *The Travels of Lao Can*.

The narrative technique of *The Travels of Lao Can* has been praised by many. But precisely what specific quality in it makes this novel so outstanding among late Qing novels has never been clearly brought out. A Ying holds that the specific quality is 'scientific' description,[17] and Prusek suggests that it is 'analytical' description.[18]

It is in fact retarded description—slow, detailed scene description—that makes this novel excel in technique. When Hsia praises Liu E for creating 'the longest night in traditional Chinese fiction', thereby proposing that Liu E far surpasses the author of *The Dream of the Red Chamber* in scene description, he puts his finger on the matter.[19]

[17] A Ying holds (1937, 176): 'Liu E believed in science ... this spirit was reflected in his writing, assuring the unique artistic value of *The Travels of Lao Can*. What I call "scientific descriptions" are such passages as Wang Mian's painting of a lotus flower, the breaking of the ice on the Yellow River, Wang Xiaoyu's singing of *Dagu* balladry, and the trip to Daming Lake etc'.

[18] Prusek, when comparing Liu E with Mao Dun, says (1980: 128): 'Already in the *œuvre* of Liu E we find exceedingly well worked up and complicated descriptions, in which the author seeks to present the most diverse aspects of reality. Liu E's descriptions are, without doubt, one of the milestones of Chinese literature's road to modern realism, to the analytical rendering of many-faceted reality.'

[19] Hsia argues in his study of *The Travels of Lao Can* (1976: 276): 'The author of *Honglou Meng* is a skillful reporter of the seemingly irrelevant talk among the characters, but he is not to be compared with Liu E in the description of scenes. From Chapter 12 when Lao Can meets Huang Renrui in the evening, to their falling asleep at dawn next morning, we have almost forty pages of long narration, vividly conveying to us their talk in the company of the two prostitutes Cuihua and Cuihuan. Continuously unfolding, this scene must be the longest night in traditional Chinese fiction, and, so far as narrative technique is concerned, the most vividly described night. All four characters are as clear as life, especially Huan Renrui who can be said to be the most lovable opium-addict in Chinese fiction.'

The Travels of Lao Can is quite exceptional among late Qing novels
as far as narrative tempo is concerned, as no other fiction work of that
time enjoys such retardation. Yet one feature does become relatively
common among many novels of the time—retarded scene description
at the beginning. What makes *Nine Murders* a surprise to late Qing
readers is not only its flashforward beginning but also its scene beginning. The French model for *Nine Murders*, a short novel translated by
Wu Jianren's friend Zhou Guisheng and serialized in *Xin Xiaoshuo*,[20]
the same magazine where *Nine Murders* was serialized, was—and the
following translator's note brought this out clearly—a narrative with a
scene beginning instead of the conventional *ab ovo* beginning:

Chinese novels usually start with the name and the family background of the
hero. There could well be a prologue, an introduction, a poem or a statement
preceding the story. This used to be the only way to start a novel, and authors
all followed this pattern familiar to the readers. The present story is written by
a master of French fiction. The beginning is the dialogue between father and
daughter which comes all of a sudden like the Flying Mount coming from
nowhere, or like the the the dazzling explosion of a firecracker. Upon careful
examination, it is well-structured by a master's hand. This has gradually become the regular practice in Western fiction. (XXS, August 1906)

Scene beginnings are frequently seen in the translated novels of the
time. Lin Shu's translation of *Uncle Tom's Cabin*, influential among
many authors, starts with a scene and dialogue between two men whose
names are not revealed until much later. This is a behaviourist beginning, in which the narrator limits his privilege to be a mere recordist
who knows nothing about these characters, whereas in the *ab ovo* beginning of traditional vernacular Chinese fiction the narrator flaunts his
complete knowledge of everything.
   It seems that the beginning scheme of a brief summary plus scene
description used in such novels as *Jin Ping Mei Chongzhen* version or
The Scholars was reversed in late Qing fiction, where the format was
scene description followed by another *ab ovo* beginning. *Nine Murders*,
for instance, added an *ab ovo* beginning recalling past things after its
much praised scene beginning, thus dampening its effect. That is, I
believe, why Prusek complains about the novel:

[20] Judging from the Chinese translation, the author's name sounds something like
[bjufo], and the title should be something like *Le Circle de serpent venimeux* (*Dushe
Quan*). I have not been able to identify the original, nor has anyone else, to the best of
my knowledge.

The opening chapter is nothing else than the traditional prologue and in its further course the novel does not differ in any way from all earlier criminal stories ... A mere formal change left the essential character of the work unaffected.[21]

The scene beginning, however, was not a 'mere' formal change. It is a very fundamental change. The reason that the change left the essential temporal treatment of the work unaffected is because late Qing writers found it advantageous to adopt the scene beginning but failed to get rid of the conventional *ab ovo* beginning. Therefore they kept both of them.

On some occasions, it seems, late Qing writers were beginning to see the need for a radical change. *A Flower in the Sinful Sea* for instance, has a long *ab ovo* beginning which is sarcastic in tone, making it almost a mockery of this convention.[22] Late Qing critics even try to defend the conventionalized beginning of Chinese fiction. Xiaren, an important critic of the time, writes:

The Chinese novel always has a flat beginning, but as the novel gradually unfolds, it becomes more and more unexpectedly absorbing. The Western novel tends to have unexpected beginning but gradually goes flat. In most cases, the Chinese novel does not benefit from suspense. Their significance lies in the well-told story itself, in the glamour of the characters and in the style of the language. Western novels pick up what Chinese novels discard. Though they may be a curiosity, they are lower in status. (XXS, i., n. 4, 1904)

He does not realize that these two statements are contradictory. If the Chinese novel needs no suspense (which, by the way, is not true), it does not have to unfold through unexpectedness. But from this kind of argument we can see that the beginning scene was now understood as one of the most essential features separating Chinese fiction and Western fiction since, to a certain degree, the tone of the whole novel is established by it.

The temporal complications make it more difficult for late Qing fiction to maintain the time-brimming scheme of traditional Chinese fiction. Yet there seems to be no relaxation in the preservation of the narrative

[21] Prusek 1980: 76.
[22] Twenty years later, in the 1930s, when he tried to write his second novel *Lu Nanzi*, Zeng Pu, the author of *A Flower in the Sinful Sea* chose a 'behaviourist' scene beginning lasting as long as one whole chapter. However, the second chapter starts again with a flashback *ab ovo* beginning. It seems that Late Qing authors were hardly able to reform themselves even when eager to keep up with the changing times.

linearity. In *Strange Events* there is a direction which reveals quite a lot about this issue:

Generally all narratives should quicken when not eventful, and slow down when eventful. Seven or eight days passed without my realizing it, and finally my uncle's letter arrived. (ESNMDZGXZ, ch. 9, 32)

The direction reaffirms the same pattern of time-brimming as expounded by *Notes of the Drunken Man* seven centuries before. Interesting enough, this direction itself is a 'filler' to facilitate the time-brimming of the novel. In chapter 18 of *A Short History of Civilization*:

Those few people, not in the mood to enjoy the night scene in the street, hurried back to the inn, exchanged a few words and went to bed. *A night was easy to pass, and another dawn soon came.*' (WMXS, 144)

This filling-in is so handy that after a few pages exactly the same sentence is used again.

The time-brimming would sometimes take the form of detail-brimming. In *Nine Murders*:

The persons around the table had to introduce themselves to each other. *Several of them had nothing to do with this novel, and we shall pass them over.* But one of the people, a man with the name Su ... (JMQY, ch. 30, 134).

There are many similar examples in late Qing fiction. Even in more sophisticated novels like *The Travels of Lao Can*, time-brimming is also carefully preserved. In chapter 17 of the novel:

Each one of them, needless to say, enjoyed the banquet in his or her own way. *There is no need to recount that after the banquet each went to his bedroom and slept.* (LCYJ, 178)

The most extreme effort is to be seen in *A Flower in the Sinful Sea*, where because of the criss-crossed plot-lines, the narrative time is less linear than that in other novels. And the only way to preserve time-brimming in this situation seems to be the use of so-called 'dead time'. In chapter 6 of the novel:

I shall take the opportunity when Wenqing and Caiyun are less busy in Germany to put them on one side, and recount how some celebrities in the capital tried to advance scholarship. (NHH, 101)

This is an intentional mixture of the narrating now (in which the narrator can choose to narrate only one plot-line), and the narrated now (in which many plot-lines proceed simultaneously). The use of 'dead time', a new technique learned from Western fiction,[23] is used here only to preserve the time-brimming.

IV

A narrative is by definition retrospective, recounting events that have already taken place.[24] Oral narration is an action that extends in time, while written narrative is to be read as text already written. I prefer to see the narration of written narrative as a momentary action that does not extend in time. That, I believe, was what Zhang Zhupo the seventeenth-century critic of *Jin Ping Mei*, meant when he said 'The one hundred chapters of *Jin Ping Mei* were not composed in one day but created in one day.'[25]

The lagging-behind of the narrating now after the narrated now is a principle important for the analysis of narrative time, since in traditional Chinese fiction the narration is expressedly anchored to the narrative frame of 'oral story telling' and the commentaries and directions have to be riveted onto the narrating now to get a foothold. In *The Journey to the West*, for instance, constant references are made to the narrating now to support the narrated now. In chapter 63, Sun Wukong defeats a monster in a fierce fight and cuts off nine of its ten heads:

The wounded monster fled to the North Sea to save his skin ... *The worm which we call Nine-Headed-Bleeding worm today is the offspring of this monster.* (XYJ, 456)

[23] The use of 'dead time' was common in 19th-century. Western fiction. Chatman cites many examples in novels ranging from Balzac to Proust (Chatman 1978: 215–18). We may find occasional instances in May Fourth fiction too, but by that time, it was already regarded as artificial by Chinese writers.

[24] Genette argued (1980, 212) that there could be four different positions for the narrating time: subsequent (the story is narrated in the past tense, as in most fiction); prior (the story is narrated in the future tense, or occasionally in the present tense); simultaneous (in the present tense, as in *Nouveau Roman*, esp. some early works by Alain Robbe-Grillet); and interpolated (between moments of action, as can be seen in epistolary novels). I suggest that narration is basically analeptical, no matter what tense is used. Utopian fiction or science fiction that describes the future generally supposes that the narration take place after the events, in the further future.

[25] Huang Lin and Han Tongwen 1982: 178. The narrative is completed at a fictional moment in the imagined timetable of the narrative. Sometimes, the narrated now can be fictionally dated later than the writing now, such as in science fiction. With regard to the narrating now, the only thing we can be sure of is that it must occur at a fictional moment *after* the narrated now. But if there are several levels of narrative, we may see several narrating nows interpolated with narrated nows. The writing now occurs at a definite time which can be positively confirmed by biographical studies, but is not necessarily after the narrating now since the latter is fictional and can be placed at any point on the time axis.

In chapter 99, Tang Seng and his disciples are thrown into the water together with their luggage when crossing the river on their way back home. On the shore, they dry the soaked sutras in the sun:

They had not expected that some pages of the Benxin Sutra should get stuck on the stone, and when they picked up the sutras, it tore. *This is why today the Benxin Sutra is incomplete, and on the Drying Sutra Stone there are some characters still discernible.* (XYJ, 682)

Sometimes this zeal to anchor the narrative to the narrating now causes structural disorder. In *The Dream of the Red Chamber*, for instance, the narrating now for the main narrative is dated 'who knows how many Kalpas after' the main narrative, when Kong Kong happens to pass by the stone and copied the story. As I mentioned in Chapter I of this Part, Gao E, who is credited with writing the last forty chapters of the 120-chapter-long novel, had to make an additional sequel to the over-narrative. In the added part, Kong Kong is made to pass by that stone again, sees a sequel, and copies it down.

However, obviously between the first narrated now and the second narrated now there could not be a gap of 'several Kalpas' as the story did not allow this. What is more important is that since Gao E's job was to complete the novel left unfinished by Cao Xueqin, his was not a sequel in the strict sense, the whole main narrative was one piece and should have only one narrating now. The confusion comes from the conflict between the need to substantiate the narrator and the justification for the sequel.

As for the dislocations of the temporal sequence of the narrative, there can be only two types—flashbacks and flashforwards. These two terms are related to a temporarily more or less stable main line of the narrative.[26]

Temporal dislocations are reduced to the minimum in traditional Chinese fiction. The flashbacks there are mostly technical ones, dealing with events that can be told in no other way than in a flashback. Most of the flashbacks serve to recall some incident of a character's past upon his first appearance in the narrative. Few exceed several lines. As I suggested in Chapter 2 of this part, such flashbacks are actually

---

[26] But the amount, the extent (temporal duration), and the time gap (the temporal gap between the flashes and the main line) of the flashes may distort the main narrative to such a point that its temporal linearity is not reconstructable. Such a situation, however, does not occur in traditional Chinese fiction. When there is no longer a stable main plot-line, the whole text comprises a continuous temporal shuttling without the disinction of the main line and the dislocations.

supplementary commentaries. In *Water Margin*, however, there is a flashback as long as three chapters beginning from chapter 101 which recounts how Wang Qing grew up from a rough village boy into a gangster chief. This is perhaps the longest flashback we can find in traditional Chinese fiction, but it is still a technical flashback, as it is the only possible way to handle the temporal sequence. Flashbacks are used in order to maintain the linearity of the narrative, not to confuse it.

Another kind of linearity-maintaining flashback occurs when two plot-lines cross, and some event that occurs in the other line has to be told. This type of flashback can extend to many chapters in length.

If flashbacks are to be used as a narrative device, the narrator of Chinese fiction would prefer to put it in directly quoted reported speech to avoid temporal disorder. In chapter 45 of *The Three Kingdoms*, Cao Cao, when chatting with Liu Bei, tells him how, on an expedition the year before, he successfully quenched the soldiers' thirst by lying to them that there were plum trees ahead. The story sounds more interesting in Cao Cao's own boastful words than in the narrator's voice.[27]

The number of flashforwards in traditional Chinese fiction, opposite to that of flashbacks, is very numerous. In flashforwards, events which should happen later are narrated. Narratologically, only the narrator can know these events as he narrates at a certain moment after all the events have ended. Since no character is to know an event in flashforwards, flashforwards can never appear in reported speech, they must be provided directly by the narrator in the form of narratorial commentary.

Like flashbacks, flashforwards are often preceded or followed by directions. The wording of some of them, however, may be misleading. In chapter 106 of *The Dream of the Red Chamber*:

The slaves, seeing their masters on the decline, seized the chance to be naughty. They even borrowed money from the rent of the East Farm. *As this should be told sometime later, I will not talk about it here.* (HLM, 754)

But the event is never mentioned again in the novel. The direction (*ci shi houhua*) is so formulaic that it serves only as a marker of a flashforward which is not to be echoed.[28]

---

[27] Mao Zonggang, when discussing flashbacks in *The Three Kingdoms*, insists that they are used mainly for the balance of the narrative. 'The method of narrative requires that what is lacking in this part should be borrowed from another part; what is superfluous in the first half can lend itself to the second half.' And he calls this 'Moving the Needle to Make an Even Embroidery' (Huang Lin and Han Tongwen 1982: 160).

[28] But sometimes the event recounted in the flashforward marked by the phrase *ci shi houhua* is actually narrated later:

In traditional Chinese fiction, flashforwards play more important roles than just varying the sequence order. As a matter of fact, in the prelude to almost all early Chinese novels, the end is told before the story begins, thus making the story more the exposition of a process than the solution of an enigma. In *Forgotten Texts of the Sui History*, for instance, the whole story is foretold:

Since Heaven wanted to let the Tang Dynasty rise to replace the Sui, it prepared a group of killers who would liquidate Yang Guang and his ministers, a group of capable generals to help Li Yuan who would not only wield their swords in the battlefield to lay the foundation for the new empire, but also save him on every occasion. (SSYW, 16)

In the last section we mentioned that at the end of each chapter in traditional Chinese novels, there is a passage supposed to imitate the device used in oral performance for attracting the audience. Examples are abundant even in novels of the Creative period.

At the end of chapter 2 of *The Scholars* when Zhou Jin fainted in the examination hall:

Because of his fainting, some events will happen:
    After years of misfortune, success suddenly would come;
    Miserable all his life, his name was to be greatly honoured.
If you want to know whether Zhou Jin would recover from his faint, please listen to the next chapter. (RLWS, 34)

This flashforward chapter-ending scheme is almost omnipresent in all Chinese vernacular novels, though there are some exceptions. In *The Dream of the Red Chamber* the chapter-ending lines are sometimes omitted, and the ending couplets, if still kept, only summarize and comment on what has been told, throwing no light whatsoever on what is to happen.

Another type of flashforward, a sort of 'destined' flashforward, often appears at critical moments in the narrative. In *The Journey to the West*, for instance, often when Tang Seng is about to be cut up and cooked by a monster, there is the intrusion, 'But because of fate this time Tang Seng was not to die' (*ming bu gai si*), and the narrative goes on to tell

Baoyu . . . had no alternative but to rest for his convalescence. Seeing that Baochai was so gentle, he gradually transferred some of his passion for Daiyu to Baochai. *This should be spoken of later.* (HLM, 765)

Later in the novel his new love is narrated in detail in its proper temporal position. These echoed flashforwards cause less sequential disorder than the unechoed ones.

how he is saved. Such 'destined' flashforwards are frequently seen in novels of the Rewriting period, as well as the early Creative period. In *Jin Ping Mei*, for instance, almost every crisis seems to be preceded by a direction 'Anyhow this was the time when a certain incident should happen' (*yeshi hedang youshi*) or 'This was exactly the way the disaster was supposed to happen' (*hedang huo zheban qilai*).

Nevertheless, the number of 'destined' flashforwards declined drastically in eighteenth-century Chinese novels, and disappeared completely in the best novels of that period—*The Dream of the Red Chamber* and *The Scholars*.

Finally, we have to compare flashbacks and flashforwards in terms of the important function they are supposed to perform—that of creating suspense. Suspense is the potential to arouse curiosity about some unsolved puzzle in the narrative. Flashbacks may cause suspense since partial information about an event is given in its proper position, and the narratee has to wait for the rest of the information to be supplied later in a flashback.

Genette holds that flashforwards are less common in Western fiction because they destroy suspenses.[29] This is not necessarily so, as flashforwards may also create suspense of another type by giving a little information before the proper position of the event, thus arousing curiosity. In other words, flashback suspense benefits the narrative by postponing the revelation of the solution to an enigma, whereas flashforward suspense creates a similar effect by disclosing the result before the exposition of the process. In the latter case, curiosity is expected to be aroused as to the way the result can be brought about.

The dominance of flashforwards in Chinese fiction, as we have shown, greatly helped to maintain narrative linearity while providing the necessary temporal variation. Nevertheless, localized flashbacks, especially those reported in characters' speech, are not likely to damage the narrative linearity, as the eighteenth-century Chinese critic Mao Zonggang said in his comments on the flashbacks of *The Three Kingdoms*, 'It makes one feel that the whole novel is like one sentence'.[30]

---

[29] Genette 1980: 52.

[30] Huang Lin and Han Tongwen 1982: 345. What is more, larger-scale flashforwards appear in the earliest novels of the Rewriting Period, and develop into a complex structure in the Creative Period. The aetiological prelude in *The Three Kingdoms Pinghua, Tales about Yue Fei* (*Shuo Yue*), *Water Margin*, and other early novels are all examples. Prophecies are common in fictional narrative in many nations, but in traditional Chinese fiction, the prophetic scheme presents a structural framework that embraces the whole narrative.

V

The narrative dislocation of the sequential order of events is perhaps the most outstanding impression late Qing writers received when they read or translated Western fiction. At first, they tried to tidy up the sequence of the events back into their pre-narrated order. When such tidying was not feasible during translation, an apologetic note would be inserted to facilitate the readers' reconstruction of the story. In Lin Shu's translation of *David Copperfield*, the following note is inserted:

The foreign method of writing is often to choose some event which should happen in the future and to tell it beforehand, so as to surprise the readers. But this is only a different habit of writing. In my translation I usually slightly rearrange those parts for the convenience of the readers. But as it is not convenient to rearrange this section, I cannot but follow the original.[31]

Paradoxically, when he alters rather than follows the original, the translator does not feel it necessary to add an apologetic note. These kinds of notes, inserted between brackets, are too numerous in Lin Shu's translations. In chapter 7 of *La Dame aux camélias* we have: 'The following will be words said by Armand'; in chapter 8 of *Joan Haste*: 'These are words recapturing the past'; in *Dombey and Son* there are added many notes such as 'This is how the story is narrated in the original, and I can only follow it'.

However, these repeated notes could have drawn the attention of late Qing authors to sequential dislocation in Western fiction. Naturally, the next step was to transplant the device into their own writing. They did, with varying success. Some critics even hold that flashbacks become dominant in late Qing fiction.[32] Yet a careful examination shows that the treatment of narrative time in late Qing fiction remains flashforward-dominant. The seeming increase in flashbacks is attributable largely to the increased criss-crossing of plot-lines (which calls for technical

---

In most from the novels from the Creative period, this prophetic scheme, if any, is removed from the beginning part of the novel, and turned into a localized passage in the reported speech of the characters. In *Jin Ping Mei*, for instance, the prophecy is placed in the mouth of a wandering diviner whose advice is solicited by the concubines, half jokingly (ch. 29). In *The Dream of the Red Chamber*, the prophetic scheme is located in a wet dream of Baoyu in ch. 5. As the prophetic foreshadowing is now mingled with other events, it loses its controlling authority.

[31] *Kuairou Yusheng Shu*, Shanghai: The Commercial Press, 1908, 3.
[32] Dolezelova-Velingerova 1984: *passim*; Chen Pingyuan 1988: *passim*.

flashbacks), and sub-narratives (which, strictly speaking, are not temporal dislocations).

Gilbert Fong declares in his article 'Time in *Nine Murders*' that the novel has four flashbacks, but he also notices that every one of the four is introduced by the phrase 'originally' (*yuanlai*), and he discovers: 'the formula phrase makes the later time inversions of *Nine Murders* less conspicuous as new technique.'[33]

True, this kind of flashback is nothing new in the Chinese tradition, as there is actually no other way of arranging the criss-crossed event-lines. In chapter 31 of *Nine Murders*, for instance,

Peizhi . . . dragged Zhu Yifu to a two-storeyed building behind, to see someone. Respected Readers! Who do you think this person could be? The person was none other than Liang Tianlai, whose nine family members or friends had been murdered. *He had been* (*yuanlai*) . . . trying a direct appeal to the Emperor, but he had exhausted all his property in the lawsuit . . . (JMQY, 122. Italics mine.)

The same can be seen in some other late Qing novels with more complicated plot-line criss-crossings than *Nine Murders*. In *A Flower in the Sinful Sea*, for instance, there are many narratorial directions, unconventional in wording but leading to the same conventional type of flashback:

Though we do not have to follow them to the court, I have to tell you how Shalia came into this situation. (NHH, 160).

At this moment what everyone of you wants to know is, first . . . and second . . . But now I have to beg you *Kanguan* (there *is* the entry) to forgive me that I should lay beside all these important issues and tell you about a farmer's family in a remote hilly island. (NHH, 287)

On the other hand, the 'predetermining' flashforward, characteristic of traditional Chinese vernacular fiction, abounds in most late Qing novels. In *The Nine-Tailed Tortoise*, for instance, there are many predictive flashforwards about the result of a conflict between the customers and the courtesans.

How could those celebrated courtesans in Shanghai favour that kind of rural wealthy man? It was certain that they were to spend big money only to get frustration. (JWG, 33)

---

[33] Dolezelova-Velingerova 1984: 125.

She did not expect that this man was a miser, and she would meet only great disappointment and an unhappy parting. (JWG, 43)[34]

The traditional chapter-ending and chapter-beginning formula with flashforward recapture is well preserved in most late Qing works of fiction, even in the best ones such as *The Bureaucrats, A Short History of Civilization*, and *The Nine-Tailed Tortoise*. Liang Qichao's *The Future of New China*, with its compound narrator, changes its chapter-ending into something like

Please wait until Saturday when a new session for Dr Kong's speech will be held. (XZGWLJ, 44)

But chapter 5, the last chapter of the unfinished novel, slips back into a perfectly conventional formulaic ending with the couplet and the ready-made flashforwarding scheme:

Giving no thought to all this, he ran up in one breath. As a result:
    The blue-eyed Westerner was to bow to our law expert;
    The pale-skinned scholar to join the secret society.
If you want to *hear* what was to happen later, wait until the next chapter. (XZGWLJ, 56)

The author Liang Qichao seems to have forgotten that his narrator is no longer the conventional Story-Teller. Is this an indication that the author has exhausted his courage to pursue formal originality? We do not know, as the novel is left uncompleted. The author seems to be tired of resisting conventionality.

Some modern critics have hailed *Nine Murders* as 'a novel of all the virtues' in narrative technique because of the flashback beginning.[35] This, I think, is a confusion between flashbacks and flashforwards. If some information about an event is provided before the proper position on the main narrative line, it is a flashforward. If after, it is a flashback. Whether an 'out-of-sequence' event is a flashback or a flashforward

---

[34] In *The Bitter Society*: 'That day some incident was predetermined to happen. This was the causality decided by one's former life. Otherwise how could the Old Immortal in the Moon make such a long trip to send the person here?' (KSH, ch. 7, 22).

In *What the Ladies Next Door Say*: 'He took on a servant boy whose name was Jin Li . . . The boy would give him much help but this should be told later.' (LNY, ch. 1, 262)

In *The Yellow Embroidered Ball*, 'This bad fellow later had a good son named Huang Fu who co-operated well with Huang Xiuqiu on many things. But this should be told later.' (HXQ, ch. 5, 38)

[35] Hu Shi 1929: book 2, ii. 127.

depends on what should be taken as the main narrative line. This may be difficult for some modern or post-modern fiction works, but certainly not for late Qing fiction where the temporal dislocation is minimum.

Temporal dislocations in late Qing fiction generally followed the pattern that Lin Shu explained in the preface to his translation of *A Study in Scarlet*: 'The story begins with the exposure of the killer, and then proceeds to the start of the events. This beginning can surprise the readers so that they will be interested in what follows.'[36] This is by no means a 'flashback structure', as the exposure of the killer can only be taken as the flashforward to the main sequence, which is the whole story that leads gradually to this exposure.[37]

This is exactly the flashforwarding pattern of *Nine Murders*: it begins with a scene where a group of gangsters are setting fire to a house, which should take place in chapter 16. Accordingly, in chapter 16 there appears an echo to the foreshadow, 'The scene of plunder outside the house was told in chapter 1, and here I shall refrain from writing about it again.'

In a number of late Qing works of fiction, especially those by the Butterfly writers, this scheme almost becomes a new formula, sometimes called by them 'Dragon with Head Unseen' (*qianlong wushou fa*). Take Xu Zhenya's short story 'The Poison Bottle' ('Duyao Ping') as an example. The story starts with the bride taking poison in the wedding chamber, and then proceeds to the beginning of the romance: how the couple met and fell in love. The story ends with the due punishment of the perpetrator of the evil. This temporal dislocation, typical of late Qing fiction, has been called by some critics, perhaps oddly, a 'flashback scheme'.[38]

Genuine flashbacks—not flashbacks in the form of sub-narratives— began to appear much later in late Qing fiction. The novel *Frost in July* (*Liuyue Shuang*) offered a complex time-scheme: it starts with Wu

[36] *Xieloke Qi'an Kaichang* (Shanghai: Shangwu Yinshu Guan, 1908), 2.

[37] Nevertheless, Lin Shu's description is not true to the pattern followed by most Western detective novels, which usually start with the discovery of the dead body and proceed to the search for the killer. This is actually neither flashback nor flashforward as the discovery of the body is narrated at the chronological position of the main line, which is the process of searching for the killer. The discovery of the dead body is only a foreshadowing. In other words, it is narrated at its proper position, with its potential meaning revealed later. Of course, when everything is found out, there will be a flashback to reconstruct how the murder happened in the first place.

[38] In the advertisement for the story 'The Phoenix That Changes Nests' ('Huanchao Luanfeng') in *Xiaoshuo Congbao*, no. 16 (1915): 'The whole story uses a purely flashback scheme. This unusual structure definitely provides something new for the New Fiction.'

Zhiying reading in a Shanghai newspaper the news about the death of
her friend, the revolutionary martyr Qiu Jin, and then proceeds to the
previous events of Qiu Jin's arrest, trial, and execution, and then goes
even further back to Qiu Jin's life from her childhood days. The novel
finally ends with the mass protest provoked by Qiu Jin's death. Thus,
the part about Qiu Jin's life (almost half of the novel) is definitely a
flashback. Such a complex sequential dislocation, however, is rare in
the late Qing.

VI

Some critics hold that the change of narrative time in May Fourth fiction
is insignificant as compared with the changes that have already taken
place in late Qing fiction, especially in Butterfly fiction.[39] As I argued
in the previous chapter, narrative time in late Qing fiction basically
retained the conventional characteristics of traditional Chinese vernacular fiction, including time-brimming, *ab ovo* beginning, linearity in
temporal order, and flashforward dominance. In May Fourth fiction
none of those characteristics is found any more.[40]

In Lu Xun's short story 'The Lonely Man' the protagonist's life is
told in several separate passages, sometimes as the narrator's recollection (flashbacks), and sometimes in the characters' sub-narratives (flashbacks in disguise). In Yu Dafu's short story 'The Past', the narrator
meets his former girl friend in Macao, and his recollection of their past
romance in Shanghai is cut into several parts, interwoven with their
present encounter. This 'parallel' structure, interpolating the present

[39] Chen Pingyuan argues (1988: 55–6), 'On the one hand, the flashback of detective
stories is so simple that May Fourth writers were not eager to use it. On the other hand,
the narrative time of Laurence Sterne and Fyodor Dostoevsky was so complex that May
Fourth writers were unable to learn it. The rest is silence.'
[40] Occasionally in some May Fourth works of fiction, temporal treatment reminiscent
of Late Qing fiction can be found. Ye Shengtao's short story 'Food' ('*Fan*') starts with
a quoted speech (which has a similar effect as a scene beginning): 'Time for class now.
Where is your teacher?' The story then goes back to the very beginning of the pre-
narrated sequence, and in the middle of the narrative we find a narratorial directory to
provide the 'echo': 'This man entered the classroom, cast a casual look, and suddenly
frowned. He then looked around intensely as if examining the situation angrily. After that
he asked the students with contempt the question which appeared at the beginning of this
story.' This at once reminds us of the flashforward structure of *Nine Murders*. Such a
structure can also be found in Zhang Wentian's novel *The Road* (*Lutu*) where a scene that
should take place in the middle of the novel is narrated at the beginning as a flashforward,
and then the novel proceeds along the pre-narrated sequence, with an 'echo' at the proper
place.

with the past (or, occasionally, with the future), can be found in many May Fourth works, with interesting variations. Among them, Feng Zhi's 'Cicada and Evening Prayer' ('Chan yu Wandao') and Wang Tongzhao's 'Separated Only by a Barred Window' make good use of the time contrast, infusing it with a symbolic meaning. Though sometimes leitmotifs are installed at the returning points which make the time-scheme more or less mechanical, as can be observed in Ye Shengtao's 'A Hour of Class' ('Yike') or Tai Jingnong's 'A New Grave' ('Xinfen'), the use of temporal dislocation in most May Fourth works is admirably sophisticated.

Withholding of information is generally deftly handled in May Fourth fiction to create suspense. In Ye Shengtao's 'The Speech' ('Yanjiang') the protagonist ponders long over the topic of the speech he is asked to give until he hits upon a good idea and says, 'I've got it!' But what he has got is not revealed until he actually gives the speech. In Zhang Ziping's long story 'Spring on the Plum Hill' ('Meiling zhi Chun') the affair between Baoying and her uncle is not revealed until very late in the story, thus making the result of the affair—Baoying's giving birth to an illegitimate child and her humiliation—more despairing as it remains mysterious.

In some works by May Fourth writers the narrative time became complicated beyond reconstruction. Chen Xianghe's 'Eyes' ('Yanjing') and Lin Ruji's 'It Will Soon Be Past' ('Jiang Guoqu') have such complex criss-crossing between the past time and the present time that it is difficult to determine the main line, and the stories seem to take place in neither time.

But what is more significant is that temporal mediation in May Fourth fiction is treated as something natural and necessary, not something which needs apology or explanation.[41] Since the conventional narrative speed characteristic of traditional Chinese fiction has been almost completely retained in late Qing fiction, the retardation in May Fourth fiction is then more notable. This is mainly due to the drastic increase of ellipses and scene description.

First, almost no trace of *ab ovo* beginning is left in May Fourth fiction unless to achieve a stylistic purpose. Scene beginnings become an established practice. Leafing through any collection of May Fourth short stories, we find very few pieces starting with an introduction

---

[41] Yu Dafu (1978: 85), when discussing narrative technique, declares carelessly, 'It does not matter whether you go along the normal sequence, or use flashbacks, or adopt both, so long as the development of the events is unfolded, and consistence is maintained.'

either of the protagonist's past or the previous events that led up to the beginning moment. Most of the stories start with what state the protagonist finds himself in at the time when the story begins. 'Recently he had been feeling more lonely', is the opening sentence of Yu Dafu's celebrated short novel 'Sinking'. But until the very end of the story only little of the protagonist's past life is told. Even his name remains unknown. This special treatment of narrative time was highly recommended by contemporary critics. Chen Xiying, when recommending 'Sinking' as the best fictional work of the ten years of the May Fourth period, comments:

When a story starts, we do not know why it should start at that moment. When it closes, we do not know why it should close at that moment. . . . This is where the power of the story lies.[42]

This 'no past nor future' sectional scheme greatly reduced the narrative speed of May Fourth fiction. Soon the scheme became normalized so that we no longer feel its originality. At the time of the May Fourth, however, it marks the distinction between entirely different narrative styles. Zhang Ziping's *Fossils of the Alluvial Age*—a novel, similar to 'Sinking' in subject-matter, and by an author who was a close friend of Yu's, and a fellow student in Japan—reads rather conventionally. One of the main reasons for this is its lack of sectional selectivity.[43]

'Sectional' narrative becomes almost the principle for fiction. Shen Yanbing (Mao Dun) emphasizes this in an essay in 1922:

The aim of the short story is to draw a section of life so as to hint at the entirety. An event can be described without mentioning what precedes or follows;

---

[42] Chen Xiying 1928: 338.

[43] Occasionally a story starts in a way which seems to be a twist of the conventional beginning in traditional Chinese fiction, e.g. Yu Dafu's 'Niaoluo Xing', which begins: 'I, who am sitting in the calm afternoon air when all the housemates have gone out, appear as quiet as the sea in spring'. (NLX, 3). Another story, 'Shadow of Smoke' ('Yanying') begins with an even longer sentence: 'Wen Pu, who wanted and wanted to go home everyday, but finally settled down in a shattered house because, on the one hand, he had been spitting blood and was afraid of emergencies, and, on the other, the few pennies of his royalties were far from enough, was again taking his sulky walk this afternoon.' (NLX, 89) This kind of beginning has some imitators. Luo Heizhi's 'Zai Dan'ai Li' ('In the Thin Fog') begins with: 'Mr Qin, who was scheduled to leave the hospital yesterday but delayed there until half past nine this morning, is not lying on the narrow bed in his home.' These sentences might be frowned upon by today's Chinese-language purists, as the long attributive is really too Europeanized. But they are experiments by the May Fourth writers who wanted to begin their story with something different from the conventional introductory beginning.

a character can appear without mentioning his past or his family background; there can be only one character in the story, the plot can be reduced to only a passage of recollection.[44]

The argument neatly delineates the basic requirements of the short story in the modern sense of the term: a short story is not only a story sufficiently short in length but a story economically told. This understanding sets May Fourth short stories apart from traditional Chinese short stories in which a sense of wholeness is maintained in spite of the limited number of words.[45]

Among Lu Xun's twenty-six stories of the May Fourth period, two-thirds are 'sectional', with only selected scenes presented, leaving out most of the events behind the narrative. His most extreme experiment (and also the most successful) in ellipsis is the short story 'Medicine' which selects only four isolated scenes, without mentioning the events before, in between, or after. What is left out, e.g. the child's death, seems to be hinted at only vaguely. The sectional selectivity is the essential part of the story. Any reconstruction is both difficult and unnecessary, as the tragic sense of confusion involved is vividly shown in this elliptical narrative.[46]

One of the many reasons that make Lu Xun's 'A Madman's Diary' a much more satisfactory short story than Gogol's story of the same title is the former's extreme ellipsis. Gogol's story maintains the wholeness, with the Madman's illogical thoughts presented in a logical progression, while Lu Xun's story is presented in fragmented thought and scattered events. The narrative form itself acquires a symbolic dimension. Gogol's madman is, then, mad in reason since the narrative form is still logically constructed, while Lu Xun's madman is mad not only in reason but in rhyme, thus elevating himself above the tyranny of formal norms.

[44] 'Naturalism and Modern Chinese Fiction' ('Ziran Zhuyi yu Zhongguo Xiandai Xiaoshuo'), XSYB 13, no. 7 (1922).

[45] Hu Shi made a speech on the short story at Beijing University in 1918, in which he offered the following definition for the short story: 'A short story is a sufficiently satisfactory work which selects the most interesting passage or aspect to describe, with the most economical literary means.' (Hu Shi 1929: Book I, i. 176) This is a fairly adequate definition. However, he went on to declare that works in all the 3 major genres—poetry, fiction, drama—had been becoming shorter all over the world, and that longer items (including novels) would not be favoured any more. (Ibid. 191–93)

[46] Some critics (e.g. Wang Furen 1983: 89) suggest that Lu Xun's 'Medicine' is comparable with Chekhov's 'Dowry'. The latter selects two sections to present, with a time lapse of seven years in between.

VII

Closely related to narrative time is the problem of motifs which are bricks constructing the plot of a narrative.

In modern narratology the plot structure is perhaps the area most discussed but least agreed upon. The few studies that have been acclaimed as successful mostly limit themselves to the literary genres which allow distinctly repeatable plot schemes such as folktales, detective stories, romances, or other popular sub-genres, as their plot scheme is easier to summarize.[47]

There are two approaches to the study of plot: the macroscopic and the microscopic. The former concentrates on constructing a feasible plot taxonomy to describe the basic plot patterns for all fictional narratives. The latter devotes itself to the atomic composition of plot. I shall start with the latter.

The smallest unit of text still significant to the plot is usually called motif.[48] For a typology of motifs, Tomashesky suggests two basic divisions—dynamic vs. static, and bound vs. free.[49] Dynamic motifs push forward the unfolding of plot, while static motifs do not, as they are more descriptive. Bound motifs are those which cannot be removed from the narrative without changing the plot whereas free motifs can. Combining the two, we have a four-item division.[50]

Dynamic motifs are consecutive, forming a chain of causality. Among

[47] Interesting but not necessarily successful efforts can be found in Vladimir Propp's *The Morphology of the Folklore* (1930); George Forster-Harris's *The Basic Formulas of Fiction* (1944); Ronald Crane's *The Concept of Plot and the Plot of Tom Jones* (1957); Norman Friedman's *Form and Meaning* in Fiction (1975), and others.

[48] How small can motifs be? Tomashevsky seems to suggest that motifs can be as small as sentences or clauses (Lemon and Reis 1965: 62). Propp holds that motifs can be as small as a few words (ibid: 23). Greimas seems to go further than Propp when he says that motifs can be as small as 'any semantically significant unit' that is to say, as small as morphemes (Greimas 1987: 185).

[49] Lemon and Reis (1965): 61–5, and *passim*.

[50] Barthes also suggests a 4-item classification: functions (nuclei and catalysers) and indexes (indices and informants) (Barthes (1977): 78).

After a careful comparison of the two, we can see that they correspond more or less to each other:

Tomashevsky	Barthes	
dynamic bound motif	nucleus	function
dynamic free motif	catalyser	
static bound motif	indice	index
static free motif	informant	

them, dynamic bound motifs push the plot forward by raising questions that are to be answered by later events in the narrative,[51] while dynamic free motifs supplement and expand this chain of causality. Static motifs provide relevant information about the characters or events. Among them, static bound motifs indicate some particularities of characters or situations, providing 'pure data' that may not have anything to do with the characters or situations in the narrative.

A classification of motifs is worthwhile not merely because it enables us to tell what motif a certain phrase or word in the narrative should be. Since a narrative text contains a huge number of motifs, such an analysis is of little benefit to critical practice, except for studies in computational stylistics. The classification of motifs, however, can be used to determine basic plot types, that is to say, to extend the microscopic analysis into a macroscopic study of plot that eventually leads to a plot taxonomy. With the dominance[52] of a certain type of motif, a narrative text acquires a certain quality that gives rise to a series of characteristics in the plot structure and other respects. Correspondingly, we can see four types of plots.

1. Dynamic bound narratives: with the dominance of this type of motif, the narrative knitted into chains of causality proceeds at a fast speed, as it is full of events and action with flimsy detailed description. Folktales are the most typical as they unfold with a strict causality. Detective stories or science fiction are their modern variations. Chinese vernacular historical novels (*Jiangshi*), and fiction of detection (*Gong'an*) of the seventeenth and eighteenth centuries basically fall into this category. The following passage, taken from *The Three Kingdoms*, proves how swiftly the narrative moves:

In the meanwhile Dong Zhuo missed the Marquis and doubt filled his heart. Hastily taking leave of the Emperor, he mounted his chariot and returned to his palace. He saw at the gate Lu Bu's well-known steed, riderless. He questioned the doorkeepers and they told him that the Marquis was within. He sent away his attendants and went alone to the private apartments. Lu Bu was not there. He called Cicada, but she did not reply. He asked where she was and the

[51] This seems similar to what Barthes later calls 'hermeneutical codes' (Barthes 1975: *passim*).
[52] The concept of dominance was first expounded by Roman Jakobson in 1935 in his remarkable essay 'The Dominant' (English transl. in Matejka and Pomorska 1971: 82–90) which is a development of the Russian Formalist idea of the evolution of literature. The dominant is not necessarily the element of the greatest amount but the element which carries the greatest weight, so deciding the generic nature of the text.

waiting maids told him she was in the garden among the flowers. So he went
into the garden and there he saw the lovers in the pavillion in most tender talk.
(SGYY, 45)[53]

The above passage is full of dynamic bound motifs (with only a
couple of dynamic free motifs such as 'sent away his attendants') that
link to each other closely, and the events come fast and thick.

2. Dynamic free narratives: the narrative is still full of action, though
its chain of causality is more or less broken down and its continuity not
sufficient. Epics of many nations that are full of highly interesting but
not well-connected episodes can be regarded as dynamic free narratives.

It is difficult for this type of narrative plot to be realized in short-
story form, since the free motifs can more easily form a chain of causality, thus binding themselves into a plot. Many traditional Chinese
vernacular novels, however, build themselves on episodicity so that the
only plot structure is some non-causal connection. In *The Journey to
the West* and *Water Margin* the episodicity is balanced with a causal
framework which strings the episodes together. In *The Scholars*, however, the only thing grouping the episodes is a common theme. A
protagonist in one episode becomes the main character in the following
episode, and the narrative seems to continue like a relay. The connection between the episodes displays a certain degree of randomness.

The following passage is taken from chapter 21 of *The Water Margin*:

Yan Poxi was upstairs lying on the bed, and was just idly thinking and
gazing at the lamp. When she however heard her mother say that her lover had
arrived she at once thought it was Zhang, and got up in a hurry. She put her
hair in order while muttering to herself. 'The damned fool! I am tired of
waiting for him. Let me box his ears first.' She rushed downstairs, and looked
through the door screen. The glass lamp gave a good light in the room. It was
no one but Song Jiang. She immediately turned round and going upstairs again
lay down on the bed. (SHZ, 226)[54]

The chain of causality remains quite visible. But most of the motifs
describe actions that are related to certain links on the chain. Though
removable, they greatly enrich the narrative. In comparison with the
passage from *The Three Kingdoms*, the situation is presented in fuller
details.

[53] Transl. C. H. Brewitt-Taylor (*Romance of the Three Kingdoms*, Rutland, Vermont:
Charles and Tuttle Co., 1959, 81). I made a few tiny changes to retain the dynamic
motifs.
[54] Transl. J. H. Jackson (*Water Margin*, Shanghai: Commecial Press, 1937, 270). I
made some changes to retain the dynamic free motifs.

3. Static bound narratives: the chain of causality is not only broken but often neglected, while digressions become almost the main body of the narrative. Such fictional works often have a vivid characterization, and are impossible to paraphrase. In traditional Chinese fiction, the best examples are *Jin Ping Mei* and *The Dream of the Red Chamber*.

As soon as it was light the next morning, Bao-yu was off again to the girls' room, shuffling along in his slippers, and with a gown thrown loosely round his shoulders. The maids were not yet about, and the two young mistresses still lay fast asleep under the cover. Dai-yu was tightly cocooned in a quilt of apricot-coloured damask, the picture of tranquil repose. Xiang-yun, by contrast, lay with her hank of jet-black hair tumbled untidily beside the pillow, a white arm with its two gold bracelets thrown carelessly outside the bedding and two white shoulders exposed above the peach-pink coverlet, which barely reached her armpits. 'Not quiet even in her sleep!' Bao-yu muttered ruefully as he gently drew the bedding up to cover her. (HLM, ch. 21, 238)[55]

Most of the motifs are not related to the links on the chain of causality but only provide information about some situations which do not have a clear relation with the chain of causality. They are still bound motifs as the information is related to the characters. This type of narrative proceeds rather slowly.

4. Static free narratives: both the chain of causality and the characterization are neglected. The main effort seems to be in the creating of an atmosphere. Such works, generally, did not appear either in the West or in China until the twentieth century.

From the examples I have cited above, it can be seen that traditional Chinese fiction seems to follow a progressive order along the dominant types of motifs from the dynamic type to the static type, and from the bound type to the free type.

VIII

The events in any narrative must have a certain 'followability'[56] in order to form a sequence. Temporality, spatiality, and causality are generally

---

[55] Transl. David Hawkes (*The Story of the Stone*, Harmondsworth: Penguin, 1980, 415). I made one or two tiny changes.

[56] It was W. B. Gallie (1964) who first suggested the term 'followability'. He explains that in some narrative texts the relationship between events becomes so tenuous that the only reason the reader would want to go on may simply be because the events or happenings are related to a person or a historical period he happens to be interested in. The important thing, however, is that even in a loosely constructed plot, there remains a certain degree of followability about its structure, *without which it would cease to be a plot.*

regarded as the three basic types of followability. But it seems that in any narrative the three mingle, and the temporal sequence is generally the main sequence we can find in narrative.

Spatial followability is the chain of spatial positions of the individual events in the narrative, and is not in close connection with the temporal form of the narrative.[57]

The 'spatial form of narrative', however, a popular term among scholars, is only a metaphorical explanation for narrative temporality. Traditional Chinese commentators-critics of vernacular novels suggest such spatial metaphors as 'Grey Traces Left by the Grass Snake' and 'Fog Cross-cutting the Cloudy Mountain' (Jin Shengtan), or 'Bridge Locking the Creek' and 'Two Peaks Confronting Each Other' (Mao Zonggang). The term for spatial scenes in Chinese landscape painting are borrowed here metaphorically to indicate the temporal arrangement in written narrative.[58]

In narrative, temporal order is always mixed with, and often overpowered by, the causal order. Logically speaking, what comes after is not necessarily the result of what goes before (which was refuted long ago as the fallacy of *post hoc, ergo propter hoc*). Fictional narrative texts, however, are selective in nature and the reception of narrative, either oral or written, has long been conventionalized into perceiving the causal order implied in temporal order. Thus, temporal order in written narrative is always associated implicitly with the causal order.[59]

---

[57] The definition Oswald Ducrot and Tzvetan Todorov offered for narrative is 'a referential text with represented temporality' (Ducrot and Todorov 1972: 378).

[58] I feel that most of the 'spatial form' proponents are just using this concept to dodge the complex problem of the temporal deformation. What they mean by spatial form is merely the new quality that narrative acquires with a high degree of temporal deformation.

It was Joseph Frank who first suggested the idea of 'spatial form' in *Sewanee Review* 1948. His argument seems to be less attractive than the term he invented. In 1977 Princeton University Press published a collection of articles, *Spatial Form in Narrative*, trying to sum up the 30 years of discussion on this topic. But, reading the articles, one feels that the critics differ too widely among themselves. The editors of the collection, however, declare, 'Spatial form, in its simplest sense, designates the techniques by which novelists *subvert the chronological sequence inherent in narrative*.' (Smitten and Daghistan 1977: 13. Italics mine.)

[59] Only in some non-narrative genres like chronologies or yearbooks does temporal order have no direct causal implications.

I think that Todorov is correct in his argument that the difference between 'Jean jette une pierre. La fenêtre se brise' and in 'Jean jette une pierre pour briser la fenêtre' is only the difference between explicit causality and implicit causality, though the difference can be a distinction between good style and bad style. (Todorov 1968: 126). Roland Barthes affirms this in stronger words, 'Everything suggests, indeed, that the mainspring of narrative is precisely the confusion of consecution and consequence, with what comes *after* being read in narrative as what is *caused by*'. (Barthes 1977: 89).

If the narrative wants to shake off causality, it has no other choice but to throw away temporal order. The time-brimming scheme which I described in the previous Section made earlier Chinese novels so tidy in their temporal order that a complete time-table can be reconstructed with precise dates. This conventionalized temporal-causal followability began to change when Chinese vernacular fiction entered the Creative period. Zhang Zhupo discovered that there were some mistakes in the dates of the important events in *Jin Ping Mei* and he tried to defend the novel: '*Jin Ping Mei* is different from other novels . . . in that it *intentionally* confused the time sequences, so that each day in the three to five years of high prosperity can be presented in a more lively fashion.' (Huang Lin and Han Tongwen 1982: 375) Zhang Zhupo seemed to be defending sequential confusion but he is actually confirming the time-brimming in *Jin Ping Mei*, though, as he says, the novel shows almost as strict an adherence to the proper time sequence as historical writing.

Only in some eighteenth-century masterpieces did Chinese vernacular fiction achieve a certain degree of dislocation of the strict causal-temporal order. The narrative of *The Scholars* is so fragmented by a non-retrievable temporal deformation that reading the novel, we have no reason to believe that what happens after is the result of what has happened before. Moreover, not only is the whole novel left open-ended, but every section is actually unfinished with an open end. There is no finality in the fate of any main character as it is merged into the seemingly endless waves of episodes that offer many possibilities of end-results. The fate of the characters is mentioned only in passing after other stories have long since taken over. For instance in chapter 5, the scholar Yan Zhihe plays foul to grab the property of his widowed sister-in-law. No result is given for the fight in which he and other characters are involved at the time they quit the novel for good. It is not until thirteen chapters later that the result of this fight is casually mentioned in another character's passing remark, and the end-result, which is morally important as evil should be punished, then carries no longer any weight.[60]

Ernst Cassirer finds this causal misinterpretation common to all mythic thoughts: 'every simultaneity, every spatial coexistence and contact, proves a real causal 'sequence'. It has been called a principle of mythic causality and of the physics based on it that one takes every contact in time and space as an immediate relation of cause and effect.' (1946: 45).

[60] There seems a deliberate neglect of time in the novel, which some of its contemporary critics noticed. In ch. 38, the same magistrate 'took office last year', but somewhere else the magistrate is said to have been there 'for almost a year'. A contemporary commentator criticized this as negligence—'the plot line is really too attenuated' (RLWS Variorum, 1984, 56).

In fact, because of the seemingly random order of events, no character's life is told from beginning to end (except a couple of morally perfect characters). This is completely different from the Chinese narrative tradition where even minor characters enjoy an account of their life from birth to death with virtue rewarded and evil punished.

In *The Scholars* time sequence is so seriously neglected that it is not only impossible but meaningless to reconstruct the temporal order, thus leaving causal order in a shattered state.

IX

Episodicity is the most conspicuous feature of almost all late Qing fiction. Starting from Hu Shi, all scholars discussing late Qing fiction seem to agree that its episodicity is due largely to the influence of *The Scholars*.[61] But strangely enough, late Qing writers or critics seldom mention *The Scholars*.[62] The adoption of a plot structure vaguely resembling that of *The Scholars* is more or less coincidental, as commercialism forced the authors to write speedily. When they started a novel, they had only an idea of the subject-matter plus something of a framework to string the separate stories together, without the whole plot in mind.

In Bao Tianxiao's *Memoirs of the Hairpin House*, there is a passage:

I became acquainted with Wu Woyao [Wu Jianren's another name] on the editorial board of *Yueyue Xiaoshuo*. He was writing *Strange Events*. I asked him to teach me how to write. He showed me a notebook in which were many newspaper clippings, and notes of stories told by friends. He said that all these were material. The only thing you have to conjure up is how to connect them into a novel.[63]

[61] In his long essay 'Chinese Literature in the Last Fifty Years' ('Wushi Nian lai di Zhongguo Wenxue') Hu Shi acknowledged that *The Scholars*, among all major Chinese vernacular novels, enjoyed the smallest circulation in the Late Qing period. But he jumped to a different conclusion, 'This novel enchanted the circle of literati! . . . Its composition is the most easy to learn, and most convenient at that. Thus its structure became the regular practice of recent satirical novels.' (Hu Shi 1929: Book 2, ii. 124)

[62] Perhaps the only definite witness is to be provided by Bao Tianxiao the leader of Butterfly fiction, who said in his *Memoirs of the Hairpin House* (*Chuanyinglou Huiyilu*), 'The writers of social fiction at that time all adored *The Scholars* and everybody imitated it.' (XSYB No. 19, 1942). But if we search through the 647-pages-long vol. of *Late Qing Literature—Studies on Fiction and Drama* (*Wanqing Wenxue Congchao—Xiaoshuo Xiqu Yanjiu Juan*) compiled by A Ying, we can see that *The Scholars* is seldom mentioned, while lots of second-rate 18th-century novels are repeatedly discussed.

[63] Bao Tianxiao 1971: 40.

What is more, serialization and rapid publication encourage the author to write in this disconnected way, whereas before the late Qing,
Chinese authors spent their lifetime writing only one novel, to have it
published posthumously. Liu E's son writes in his memoirs about his
father:

The novel *The Travels of Lao Can* was my father's playful leisure-time. *There
was no overall plan or organizational structure beforehand.* He wrote several
pages a day and showed it to friends as a pastime. He did not expect that the
novel would become such a sensation ... My father often sighed that it was
only through playful writing that he won this reputation, which were against his
intention. So he did not want readers to know his real name. (LCYJ, 342. Italics
mine.)

Serialization, however, is not the decisive factor for the episodicity
in late Qing fiction. There are indeed 'one-piece' novels that first appeared in serialization form. I think an important factor is that novels
were still the dominant genre at the time as short stories were unable
to satisfy the readers. Yet because the narrative remains speedy-sketchy,
a certain number of episodes have to be piled up to make the work as
long as a novel. That is why most of the late Qing social novels have
a very interesting story running through the first ten or twenty chapters,
but after that a prolonged anticlimax of loosely connected episodes. In
The Bureaucrats, the first fifteen chapters, which form a more or less
closely knit section (about General Hu's campaign against 'bandits'),
are much more readable than the remaining chapters. The first ten
chapters of *A Short History of Civilization*, about the two magistrates
and their different ways of dealing with the conflict between the ignorant local people and the foreigners, form the most interesting part of the
novel. These are in fact two seperate short novels, different even in
narrative style from the rest of the novel.

In late Qing fiction there are at least three different ways of stringing
the episodes into a novel:

1. Pure juxtaposition: there is indeed no formal connection in these
novels. The episodes come together only because they can be said to
belong to the same category of subject-matter. There is no connection
between one story and another except for the episode, sitting astride the
chapters. Li Boyuan's novel *The Hell for the Living* is an example.

2. Character-switching after the model of *The Scholars*: Li Boyuan's
The Bureaucrats and *A Short History of Civilization* are examples where
one secondary character in the former episode becomes the protagonist

of the next episode. However both of these two novels lack the hidden interlocking of *The Scholars*.

3. Story linking: this is the most common type of connection in late Qing novels. The connecting story could be some personal experience (as in *What the Ladies Next Door Say, Viewed with Cold Eyes, The Bitter Society*, or *Strange Events*), or the romance of a couple (as *A Flower in the Sinful Sea*).[64] Obviously narrative stratification is frequently used in this kind of plot structure.

However, none of these methods is successful in turning the connection between the episodes into a whole. Many scholars have tried to discover the 'design' or the 'organizational principle' of late Qing novels,[65] but I doubt the feasibility of such efforts, as the authors themselves acknowledged that they did not have such a design in mind.[66]

Unlike *The Scholars*, most episodes in late Qing novels are well-ended. In chapter 29 of *The Nine-Tailed Tortoise*, the prostitute Shuanglin is hired to set a trap for Zhang Qiugu, but the plan is foiled because the latter is too experienced to be taken in. Since Shuanglin is said to be a young lady 'of good heart', the novel adds:

After that Shuanglin returned to Suzhou, and, upon Qiugu's advice, married the owner of a fabric store. She was fortunate to give birth to a boy, and she lived happily with them until old age. (JWG, 29)

[64] Lin Shu revealed his connecting principle in a directory in *The Stench of the Sword*: 'If works of fiction are not loyal to historical reality, they are only gossip useless for providing supplementary information for the official history. If they are loyal to historical reality in every detail, then why not go to the official history directly? In writing about such an extraordinary world, if we do not use one character as a link, there will only be separate chapters with no novel. This is not the proper style of fiction.' (JXL ch. 32)

Bao Tianxiao provided a similar statement: 'My intention was to choose a character to be the protagonist who had nothing to do with politics so as to string together all the events.' (Bao Tianxiao 1971: 45)

[65] V. I. Semanov discovered that in the *Strange Events* there is 'a chain reinforced by interlacing wire'. (*Evoljucia Kitajskogo Romana*, Moscow: 1970, 238) Milena Dolezelova-Verlingerova, in her essay 'Typology of Plot Structure in Late Qing Novels', finds that the string-like plot of Late Qing fiction can be developed to form 'the novel of cycles' (e.g. *The Bureaucrats* has ten cycles in succession), and the unitary plot novels. (Dolezelova-Velingerova 1984: 38–56)

[66] Bao Tianxiao's *Memoirs of the Hairpin House* has two versions. The version serialized in *Xiaoshuo Yuebao* (1942) was slightly different from that published in Hong Kong (Dahua Chubanshe, 1971), which I quoted in n. 63. In the original version there are a few more sentences:

Showing me this huge and disorderly notebook of newspaper clippings, he said, laughingly: 'What I mean by 'witness' [*mudu*—referring to the title of his best-known novel *Strange Events Witnessed in the Last Twenty Years*] is just these things.' I asked, 'How can these materials be put into order?' Mr Wu said, 'A running-through thread is important. Writers of social novels generally use the same method.'

The narrator in *The Hell for the Living* provided a moralistic commentary in defence of neatly winding-up the episodes. When the cruel
magistrate Shan is dying of skin ulcers, he is horrified to see a horde
of ghosts attacking him:

The Story-Writer is by no means one of those old fogeys who try to persuade
people to worship Buddhas. Yet if I allow such people as Magistrate Shan to
enjoy prosperity and long life, and have sons and grandsons all around him, I
am then inducing readers to evil. (HDY, ch. 22, 132)

So the ending not only of the whole novel but also of each episode
is of extreme importance. In the postscript to *Lives of Shanghai Flowers*,
there is a statement on the technique of the novel: as its author Li
Boyuan said, the difficulty in combining the stories into one novel is
that,

There should be nothing missing [*gualou*]. If there is no mention of the final
fate of a character, this is an error. If a story has no end, this is an error too.
(HSHLZ, 5)

Despite this statement, *Lives of Shanghai Flowers* seems to be the
only novel in late Qing fiction with an open ending. The novel finishes
before the future of the main characters is decided. But the postscript
indicates, 'Some will be surrounded by sons. Some will suffer misery
and poverty ... Everything will be duly displayed in the sequel.' As the
plan to write a sequel was later abandoned, the novel's preface, added
later, could boast of having 'an ending with no end'. (HSHLZ, 349)

In summary, we can say that late Qing fiction returns forcefully to
dynamic plots with definite causality, withdrawing from the heights
achieved by eighteenth-century Chinese novel. Even the episodicity in
the late Qing novel does not smash but reinforces the dominance of
dynamic motifs.

X

What May Fourth fiction writers are concientiously trying to achieve is
the disintegration of the conventional plot composition. Cheng Fangwu,
in his criticism of Lu Xun in 1923, declares that direct description
should be considered 'the last resort for writers', and stories with a
discernible plot are 'not what we call modern fiction'.[67] Mao Dun (Shen
Yanbing) seems to have a different opinion as he criticizes the Creation
Society writers for ignoring the proper form in plot: 'It is too rigid a

[67] '*Nahan* de Pinglun' CZJK 2, no. 1.

rule that fiction should be written as poetry: nowadays almost nine out of ten writers claim that if they work had to construct a story, it is bound to be a failure, and only those written on momentary inspiration can be successful.'[68]

His criticism triggered a debate on the principles of fiction composition. However different the attitudes of the individual writers may be, the general trend of May Fourth fiction is to create a new followability by shifting from the more dynamic plot type to the more static type. Temporal dislocation that further destroys the causal chain reinforces this tendency. Sometimes the predominance of static motifs leaves the story without a plot in the strict sense of the word.

We can perhaps get an idea of how few dynamic motifs there are in May Fourth fiction from this incident: Tai Jingnong's first story 'The Wounded Bird' ('Fushang de Niao') was originally more than ten thousand characters long when first published in a magazine. When it appeared in his first collection *Son of the Earth* (*Di zhi Zi*) it was compressed to two thousand characters, one fifth of the original length. Obviously many of the motifs were 'removable', thus free.

Even before any May Fourth fiction works appeared, in May 1917 Liu Bannong had already stated that he preconceived of the new fiction as 'half-told tales'.[69] True to his expectations, most May Fourth fiction works, even the very earliest ones, are open-ended. Lu Yin's well-known short novel *Old Friends on the Beach* (*Haibin Guren*) ends with the protagonist Lu Sha's friends revisiting her on the beach at the appointed time, where they find only an empty house:

They recalled that they had not been in touch with her for almost a year, and had no idea how she was getting along. The hostess of the house was far away, and they were missing her so much. It would be really too unbearable if she could never return, leaving only the house to carry her memory.

The ending leaves things open, echoing the sense of perplexity that permeates the whole short novel.

This refusal to provide a resolution-ending seemed to be the favourite device of another woman writer, Feng Yuanjun, whose story 'Tenderhearted Mother' ('Cimu'), tells about a 'rebellious' girl student returning to her mother who wants her to stay at home. She wants to leave and be reunited with her lover in Beijing but cannot make up her

---

[68] WXXK, no. 33 (Dec. 1922).

[69] 'My View of the Reform of Literature' ('Wo zhi Wenxue Gailiang Guan'), XQN 3, no. 3 (May 1917).

mind to tear herself away from her mother. The story ends with her unresolved hesitation.

A more interesting 'hesitating ending' is found in Feng Yuanjun's most daring story 'A Trip' ('Luxing') which recounts the affair between a girl student and a married man. They take a trip to a seaside resort for a few days, and then come back to school to their normal lives. 'It was Beijing again. Naturally our life returned to its old track of the days before the trip as if nothing had happened . . . Three days later he made a phone call to me and said, "It is so hard to recall it!"' The story closes with no resolution proffered. We get no hint at all of how the life of these two could go on.

Other authors come up with other kinds of unsettled endings. Guo Moruo's 'Hard Is the Journey' ('Xinglu Nan') tells a story about the difficult life of a couple in Shanghai. After an unresolved quarrel between the man and his wife the story suddenly turns into emotional prose verse on how the great Yangtze purges everything, while the story itself is left as it is.

Xu Dishan's 'Undelivered Letters' comprises ten letters that have only a vague connection with each other. No hint is given as to who writes these letters, for what purpose they are written, nor what results from them. We may say that the story is composed entirely of static motifs, especially static free, since there is no causal chain at all.

Though such a radically static plot is not frequently seen, many May Fourth fiction works resemble traditional fiction so little that they might rather be called poetic fiction in the structuring of the plot. Yu Dafu comments on Cheng Fangwu's story 'The New Year of a Wanderer' ('Yige Liulangren de Xinnian'), 'This is really a prose-verse, a beautiful essay.' (CZJK, i. n. 1). This comment can be applied to many other stories, such as Lu Yin's 'My Landlord' ('Fangdong'), Bing Xin's 'Laughter' ('Xiao'), Lu Xun's 'The Comedy of the Duck' ('Ya de Xiju'), and Xu Qinwen's 'My Father's Garden' ('Fuqing de Huayuan'). We can say that the whole story comprises static motif.

There are also impressionistic stories like Wei Jingzhi's 'The Dusk at the Town of Liuxia' ('Liuxia Zheng shangde Huanghun'), Jian Xian'ai's 'Morning Fog' ('Zhaowu'), Wang Tongzhao's 'The Evening of Spring Rain' ('Chunyu zhi Ye'). They read like skeches in silhouette, without any temporal extension, and without a proper plot.

Many May Fourth writers are fond of writing 'Fiction of Personal Triviality' (*Shengbian Xiaoshuo*), e.g. Yu Dafu's 'A Night that Does Not End' ('Mangmang Ye'), Guo Moruo's 'Trilogy of Wandering'

('Piaoliu Sanbu Qu'). They appear as random notes on passages of their own lives, containing no narratorial selectivity. Their temporal sequence is flattened into pure temporality with no causality.

Thus we can see that in May Fourth fiction, motifs have become freer and more static. Eventually there appears fiction with static free plots, such as the works by Fei Ming, author of the celebrated story collection *The Stories of the Bamboo Grove* (*Zhulin de Gushe*).

There is no water in the river. Only a stretch of sand. The dike now looks like a coiled snake, and the people standing on it black dots. Viewed from here, the crescent-shape gate tilts so much to the ground that it almost touches it. The bridge can be seen only in paintings . . . You have a clear view when you are on the dike. But once you are on the sand, you lose the marks which you thought you remembered. You only feel that the bushes are like woods on distant hills. As for the noise, you could hear better when standing afar. Birds are singing their evening songs in bamboo groves as usual. But for the ear that is used to it the sound only adds to the silence.

The one who finally broke the silence was Mother.

Motifs that push the plot forward are perhaps only to be found in the last two sentences. The rest are all static free motifs. Fei Ming's pastoralist stories have so many of these motifs that there is hardly any plot. Or rather, the flimsy plot-line is installed only as a pretext for atmospheric descriptions.

Such fiction can be said to be the modern and fictional variation of the Classical Chinese *belles lettres*, which are never seen in Chinese vernacular fiction.

4

A Summary

A careful examination of traditional Chinese vernacular fiction through its early Rewriting period to the Creative period and its last stage, the late Qing period, reveals that its narratological characteristics remained surprisingly stable. Despite the fact that important changes did take place and many new devices were introduced in late Qing fiction, the basic narrative mode of Chinese vernacular fiction stayed unchanged, and some conventions were even reinforced.

May Fourth fiction created a rupture in the history of Chinese fiction and changed its course. Before that, Chinese fiction had all along presented itself as a socially stabilizing discursive practice, with its narrator unwaveringly in control of the narration. The challenge launched by some eighteenth-century masterpieces of Chinese fiction hardly changed this general stability, as the majority of the vernacular fiction output did not follow suit. Some new elements, such as narrative stratification, had been absorbed into the convention without causing radical changes, as the backlash into conventionality of the Chinese vernacular fiction in the nineteenth century proves. At the beginning of the twentieth century, when Chinese culture encountered the most serious crisis it had ever had to face, changes forced their way into Chinese fiction. Though modified in this or that minor aspect, the narratological conventions remained fundamentally unchanged, until May Fourth fiction turned this slow and half-hearted change into a revolution.

The narrator in traditional Chinese vernacular fiction was a non-participant semi-implicit narrator, self-referred to, by convention, as 'the Story-Teller', and firmly embedded in a narrative frame supposedly imitating the situation of oral story-telling performance. Thus the narrator, free to intrude at any time, was the virtually monopolized source of subjectivity that firmly controlled the narrative, and, by doing so, discouraged any interpretative diversification.

In late Qing fiction, the narrator slightly changed the wording of his self-reference. As a result, the narrative situation of oral story-telling performance is made dubious, but the narratorial control still holds ground. The participant narrator made his first appearance. The narrator, however, felt uneasy about his threatened authority, and tried hard to

pull the narrative together by excessive intrusions. Thus the general
narrative reliability of traditional Chinese fiction was apparently even
more strengthened. The preservation of narratorial domination was a
strained effort. Sometimes the narrator, garrulous with too many intrusions, appeared nervous and unnecessarily apologetic in his attempts
to maintain control, thus betraying the great pressure to which he was
subjected.

What happened to the narrator in May Fourth fiction, generally, tre-
mendously reduced his dominating position, as he either went into an
almost complete implicitness or personalized into a character participant
in the narrative. The self-sufficiency of the narrated world, now under-
mined, was not shored up by judgemental or explanatory commentaries.
With this general tendency of disintegration of narratorial control, the
whole narrative text was then opened to interpretative diversification.

Thus, in the development of Chinese vernacular fiction we can notice
a continuous 'downward' movement of narrative subjectivity, from the
implied author to the narrator, from the narrator to the characters. For instance, only localized character-focalization is seen in traditional Chinese
vernacular fiction. In late Qing fiction, the shift toward character-
focalization was started, but single-character-focalization existed mostly
in first-person narrative, while in other texts it was still inconsistent.
Not until the May Fourth period did character-focalization become a
regular practice as the narrator now felt comfortable in yielding control
over the narrative.

The reported speech, which was dominated by the direct quoted form
in traditional Chinese vernacular fiction, began to vary in late Qing
fiction, and the indirect form emerged to some extent, due to the increase in descriptions of the characters' mental activity. Only in May
Fourth fiction did variation of reported speech forms contribute to the
loosening of narratorial control, as it facilitated the exchange of subjectivity between the narrator and the characters.

The extensive increase in narrative stratification is another effort on
the part of the narrator in late Qing fiction to reconsider his position.
But generally this device caused more confusion than stability.

The change in narrative time is most conspicuous in late Qing fiction, but the narrative linearity of Chinese traditional vernacular fiction
with its flashforward dominance persisted. Despite a variation in the
opening scene in some novels, the overall scheme for handling time in
the narrative stayed. Abundant ellipses in May Fourth fiction led to
sectional description that not only enabled the narrative tempo to slow

down, but broke up the integration of the narrated world in traditional fiction glued by the time-brimming. With static motifs taking over, the temporal dislocation went so far that it irretrievably fragmentized the causal chain.

So in late Qing fiction, with all these changes and preservations, the narrative remained in the shadow of monolithic narratorial subjectivity. In order to cope with more complicated subject-matters and new narrative devices, narratorial intrusions increased drastically, making the narrative more strained than in previous vernacular fiction. The narrator's effort to incorporate various modifications made his position vulnerable so that, paradoxically, he resorted increasingly to some conventional devices in order to stabilize his position. Thus, late Qing fiction can only be regarded as the last phase of Chinese vernacular fiction, more a continuation than a transformation of the tradition.

In May Fourth fiction, the narrated world turned out to be the realm of relativity, with no centripetal structure to control interpretation. The interpretative codes were then forced to become polyvalent, leaving the fiction free from attachment to definite cultural values. By giving up the saturated rendering of the narrated world, May Fourth fiction was answered the crying need of Chinese culture to open up to new possibilities.

Yet, in order to find an answer to why the change in formal features could mean so much, we have to go much deeper into the complex relationship between Chinese fiction and Chinese culture.

PART THREE

A Cultural Study
of Chinese Vernacular Fiction

1

The Cultural Status of Vernacular Fiction

I

Chinese culture has all along displayed a pyramidic structure which presents itself as a rigid generic hierarchy of discourses.[1] The Confucianist scriptures and official dynastic historiography at the top of the hierarchy enjoyed almost absolute authority, and were never seriously challenged after the canonization of Confucianism around the second century BC, and re-canonization by the Neo-Confucianists in the twelfth century AD.

In accord with Confucianist social philosophy, a 'scale of meaning-power' is spread over the generic hierarchy of cultural discourses, fading off towards the end of the range, leaving the lower strata of social activities very similar to what modern Western sociologists call the subcultural discourses. Chinese vernacular fiction, being one of the genres at the very bottom of the generic pyramid, possesses a series of strongly subcultural characteristics.

No problem concerning Chinese vernacular fiction can be understood without taking into consideration its particular cultural position. We can have a look at C. T. Hsia's accusation against *Jin Ping Mei*:

> I gave a very careful reading to *Jin Ping Mei Cihua* version years ago, but since then I have never had the appetite to read it again. The artistic crudity is not the main reason for my objection. The whole novel does not represent in any way the true spirit of Chinese culture.[2]

---

[1] Jurii Lotman and A. M. Pjatigorskij in their essay 'Text and Function' suggest that there are two types of culture: the syntagmatic and the paradigmatic:

> Paradigmatic cultures create a single hierarchy of texts with a constant intensification of textual semiotics such that at the summit is found a culture's Text, which has the greatest indices of value and truth. Syntagmatic cultures create a set of various types of texts that comprise various aspects of reality and are thought to be equal in value. These principles are complexly interwoven in the majority of actual human cultures. (Lucid 1977: 130–1)

The two terms are unnecessarily difficult as their definitions here are obviously different from those in semiotics. The two kinds of relationships of cultural discourses in different societies can perhaps be better termed as parallel and pyramidic.

[2] Hsia 1975: 5. English translation mine.

In the same article he also makes a similar charge against *Water Margin*, though in less severe terms.[3] Thereupon he suggests excluding the two novels from the list of masterpieces of Chinese vernacular fiction.

I am not here to argue for the merit of *Jin Ping Mei* or other novels. My question is rather: should, or could, a vernacular novel, especially those of the Rewriting period, hope to be an embodiment of the 'true spirit of Chinese culture' of traditional Chinese society?

If the generic structure of traditional Chinese culture had not been a pyramidic but a 'parallel' one, any text could at least hope to embody part of the 'true spirit' of that culture. For instance, both avant-garde art and pulp magazine literature in modern society can be taken as the embodiments of different aspects of the 'true spirit' of that culture, as they function more or less independently of each other. Chinese vernacular fiction, however, is generically too subordinate to the culturally dominant discourses—historiography, poetry, *guwen* essays, and others—to function independently in cultural signification. It serves as their popularized illustrations. Therefore, vernacular fiction could not be representative but diluted expositions of Chinese culture. If in some vernacular fiction works the social unconscious, usually silenced, is let loose, it is still not the 'true spirit of Chinese culture' that is expected to show up. Hsia's accusation is the result of a misguided approach to Chinese vernacular fiction.

This is not to deny that Chinese vernacular fiction is also a product of Chinese culture. Subcultural discourses, even in a pyramidic culture, are coded with the same ideological system. Therefore, we are bound to be disappointed with Chinese vernacular fiction if what we seek is not the subculturally distorted signification but a direct embodiment of the acknowledged values of Chinese culture.

Apart from the subordinated, there exists another possible group of non-mainstream discourses—the counter-cultural. This group of texts moves itself out of the discursive hierachy, and refuses to be measured on the generic scale. It asserts its own values in defiance of the norms.

Though cultural deviations repeatedly showed up in Chinese history, they were only recognizable in a limited scope and in an ambiguous manner in some Chinese vernacular novels, and never developed into a fully fledged discursive mode until the May Fourth period.

---

[3] Hsia continues, 'The errantry extolled in *Water Margin* is anything but moderate. The whole novel is stuffed with cruel and sadistic scenes which represent the unrestrained side of Chinese culture.'

Since subcultural and counter-cultural are two essential concepts to my analysis in this part, a brief description of the two is perhaps not inappropriate here.[4]

I understand that any theoretical framework is dangerous in a cultural study since it could impose the observer's intention upon the observed. No one, however, can approach his object of study without a tentative, ready to be corrected, methodological framework. And what is more, what I shall describe below is not actually a preconception but a conclusion after years of research and study of the cultural functions of Chinese vernacular fiction. By exposing it before the actual discussion, I am merely trying to highlight the crucial issues so that they will not be neglected.

If, as I suggested in the introduction to this book, we consider all cultural activities as various types of discourse for signification, the subcultural discourses and counter-cultural discourses differ in the following respects: their practitioners are different. Subcultural discourses are likely to be produced for the culturally and educationally underprivileged section of society, who incline to a more readily comprehensible form of signification; counter-cultural discourses are more likely to be produced for professional or semi-professional reception by the educationally privileged sections of society.

Their expected mode of consumption is different: subcultural discourses are unequivocally produced for leisure; counter-cultural discourses tend to blur the distinction between 'work' and 'pastimes', and are seemingly more serious.

Their duration is different: the subculture is a more stable institution, though subject to a gradual change of style; the counter-culture is more likely to be linked to a crisis of the cultural discursive structure, thus presenting itself as a rupture in the normal evolutionary process of the culture.

Their ways of deviating from mainstream culture are different: subcultural discourses, even when frowned upon by the establishment as

[4] On this issue I have greatly benefited from recent sociological studies on youth delinquency, and on the Hippy movement that spread in the West two decades ago. The two terms—sub-culture and counterculture—began to be widely used only after the social disturbances of the 1960s. I hesitated for a long time over the question of whether it was advisable to apply these conceptions, which are derived entirely from modern sociological study of contemporary Western society. After much thought, however, I came to believe that, given the necessary modifications, these terms can be appropriated in a more or less satisfactory manner to describe two diametrically different phases in the development of Chinese fiction.

aberrant, do not challenge the basic interpretative system; the counter-cultural discourses take a more overtly ideological stand, consistently articulating their challenge to the established discursive norms.

In subculture, a series of apparent characteristics manifest themselves as specific styles,[5] which look deviant only superficially. Such a deviance actually defuses the possible threat of subcultural discourses against the dominant cultural discourses. The counter-culture, on the contrary, is constructed on an intentional confusion of codes, thus posing a more serious challenge to the discursive structure.

Finally, they are different in the way they resolve their conflict with the cultural norms: the subcultural discourses passed from generation to generation, thus forcing the cultural establishment to tolerate them. They institutionalize their particularity in style, in appearance, in attitudes, and in other aspects, making themselves a necessary complementary element, even a safety valve, in the culture so that the norms of the latter could effectively cover society; counter-cultural discourses emerge only at the moment of crisis and, though antagonistic to the dominant culture, play a very important role in the service of the whole culture by testing possible reorientations. Though never able to push the culture exactly in their desired direction, the counter-cultural discourses give the cultural structure some flexibility in handling the crisis.

Therefore, although both the subcultural and the counter-cultural are deviant to the norms, there is a great difference between them. At the risk of simplification, we can say that subculture is generally conservative as it helps to maintain the ideology of the culture, whereas counter-culture is subversive by nature as it aims at changing this ideological system.

II

Chinese historians and bibliographers have always had difficulty in categorizing fiction. It seems that the very idea of fictionality baffled the Chinese cultural establishment. The first categorizing attempt was made by the renowned historian Ban Gu in the first century BC who defined *xiaoshuo* (literally 'small talk') as 'gossip and hearsay in the streets'. Although *xiaoshuo* writers were listed as the last of the ten categories of writers, Ban Gu warned that 'only the former nine are

---

[5] Hebridge insisted that the sub-cultural is demonstrated more on the signifier level than on the signified level (1980: *passim*).

worth reading'.[6] The fifteen books he listed under the heading *xiaoshuo*
were all lost as early as the Sui Dynasty (sixth century AD), but we
can see from the titles that they were works of various types that Ban
Gu was unable to place under the other nine headings. At that time,
and for centuries after that, *xiaoshuo* was generically defined by its
indefinability.[7]

No matter how chaotic the categorization of *xiaoshuo* was, it rarely
included vernacular fiction. Hu Yinglin in his *Notes of Shaoshi Shanfang*
(*Shaoshi Shanfang Bicong*) divided *xiaoshuo* into six types, and Ji Yun
in his weighty *Digests of Siku Collectanea* (*Siku Quanshu Tiyao*) discussed three types of fiction. Neither of them mentioned vernacular
fiction at all. Actually the term *xiaoshuo* had hardly been applied to
vernacular fiction before the late Qing, and even then the old term
shuobu (*story-telling books*) remained the formal literary-language term
for vernacular fiction.

Strictly speaking, Chinese vernacular fiction was not a culturally
well-defined genre or sub-genre until the beginning of this century.
Even as late as the late Qing, vernacular fiction was still mixed with
other popular narrative genres such as drama or balladry. Liang Qichao's
essay 'Scattered Notes about Fiction' ('Xiaoshuo Lingjian') covered
three *chuanqi* plays; Tian Liaosheng's 'On the History of Chinese Fiction' ('Zhongguo Lidai Xiaoshuo Lun') included in its discussion *biji*
prose of the Tang Dynasty, *zaji* prose of the Song, drama of the Yuan
and *tanci* ballads of the Qing. Similar generic confusion was common
before May Fourth.

Official dynastic histories almost never stooped to mention vernacular fiction, as if it were a disgrace to the culture. The compilers of the
local histories (*fangzhi*) shared the same attitude. They would mention
all the folk rituals and festivities, but hardly anything about vernacular

---

[6] Huang Lin and Han Tongwen, 1982: 2.
[7] Before literary-language short stories emerged in the 7th century, there had been at
least two kinds of works which could be called *xiaoshuo* in the modern sense (i.e.
fiction)—fantasies like *The Book of Mountains and Seas* (*Shan Hai Jing*) and *The Book
of Supernatural Things* (*Shengyi Jing*), and legends such as *The Private Life of the
Hanwu Emperor* (*Hanwu Di Neizhuan*) and *The Life of Dongfang Shuo* (*Dongfang Shuo
Zhuan*). Yet in the Bibliography attached to each official dynastic history such books are
placed under *Shibu Dilei* (History—Geograpical Books), or under *Shibu Zalei* (History—
Miscellaneous). In *The New History of the Tang* (*Xin Tang Shu*), under the general editorship of Ouyang Xiu in the 11th century, however, the books listed under *Xiaoshuo* are
more or less in agreement with its modern meaning: fiction. However, the inclusion of
such non-fiction books as Lu Yu's *The Book of Tea* (*Cha Jing*) indicates that the term
still covers a much wider area than what is considered fiction today.

writing or publishing, which obviously were tolerated in practice but were not to be recognized in the record of culture. In the local history of Anhui, for instance, the editions before the founding of the Republic in 1911 mention Wu Jingzi briefly in less than forty characters and nothing about his life-work, the vernacular novel *The Scholars*. The early twentieth-century editions of the local history give him a longer entry, but *The Scholars* is still mentioned only in passing, after his other long-lost poetry and prose collections. *The Scholars* is one of the most 'literati' works of Chinese vernacular fiction. Other writers had even less hope of being mentioned in local histories.

The cultural position of vernacular fiction was not far from such cultural 'discourses' as prostitution. The comparison sounds strange, but is unequivocally documented. There were many government decrees after the founding of the Ming Dynasty in the fourteenth century, imposing a ban with severe punishment on the practice of all kinds of sub-cultural 'discourses'—fiction, drama, balladry, together with popular cults, paranormal communication, prostitution, etc. Emperor Kang Xi's decree of the fourth month of 1709 promulgated 'a strict and perpetual prohibition against omen-rites, drawing magic figures, obscene balladry, or fiction.' Another decree five years later stated:

I rule the country on the basis of proper *mœurs*. In order to rectify social *mœurs*, it is imperative to favour the study of the Scriptures and strictly ban blasphemous books. This is an unalterable rule. Recently there have been seen in book markets numerous fictional works that abound in nonsense and vulgarity far from proper reason. Not only the foolish common people are seduced, even gentry and scholars who browse through them are tempted. This is no small matter in regard to social *mœurs*. Those books should be banned strictly without exception.[8]

Like other subcultural activities, vernacular fiction could hope to enjoy some tolerance on the part of the dominant culture, despite the repeated decrees of suppression. Except for some short periods, there was not much effective suppression of the subculture in China so long as these discursive activities stayed in subordination, and not even much complaint if it remained in the oral sphere.

Nevertheless, the generic hierarchy of Chinese culture could not stand any confusion. In Chinese historical documents we can see constant efforts to preclude the danger. The Wanli Emperor of the Ming issued a decree in 1602 forbidding using 'words taken from fiction' in official

[8] Wang Chuanxiao 1958: 35.

memorandums. In 1728, the Yongzheng Emperor of the Qing severely punished a high-ranking official by removing him from office and making him stand in the pillory in public for three months simply for a brief allusion to *The Three Kingdoms* in his memorandum presented to the court.[9]

It was not only the Imperial Court that was excessively strict in applying generic distinctions. The literati seemed to be even more finicky about them. In Yuan Mei's *Suiyuan Shihua* there are recorded several anecdotes about how some fine poets used historical allusions drawn from the novel *The Three Kingdoms*, and they 'spent the rest of their life in remorse after being singled out as ridiculous'. Similar accusations can be found in Hu Yinglin's *Notes of Shaoshi Shanfang* which argues that self-respecting literati 'must spit' on poems using allusions to 'nonsensical' fiction.

This does not mean that all Chinese men of letters colluded in the discrimination against vernacular fiction. The first serious challenge to the hierarchy of discourses occurred in the late Ming and the early Qing. Represented by Li Zhi and Jin Shengtan, several generations of literati, in the more liberal-minded south, tried to re-evaluate vernacular literature. They carefully edited vernacular literature, and invented the 'marginal notes' criticism suitable for vernacular fiction. They made a great contribution to the development of Chinese fiction. But they hardly ever challenged the generic hierarchy of Chinese culture. There were indeed a few critics who tried to raise the cultural position of some of the best vernacular novels. Their witty remarks, though appreciated by readers of vernacular fiction, were generally regarded by mainstream literati as the crazy remarks of eccentrics.

Late Qing critics tried to justify the resurgence of vernacular fiction by extolling it in high-sounding words, claiming it to be the most important genre in literature. Exaggerations of the function of Chinese fiction did not come only from editors who wanted to boost the sale of fiction magazines, but also from political leaders of the reformist movements.[10]

[9] Ibid. 287.

[10] Liang Qichao made the following groundless claim: 'Reading the history of Western civilization, we can always find that in no matter which nation and or period, writers of literature are always the greatest contributors to civilization. The people worship these masters.' (Liang Qichao 1941: x. 56).

Kang Youwei, the foremost leader of the reformists, urged his disciple Liang in a poem in 1900 to adopt this stand toward popular fiction:

> I want to save the nation but have no means,
> I frown in hesitation when the sky is overcast.

Each wave of effort at the promotion of vernacular fiction yielded a good harvest in fiction writing: the late-Ming-early-Qing re-evaluation heralded the great achievements of eighteenth-century fiction; the late Qing re-evaluation brought about the flourishing of late Qing fiction. Despite all these efforts, however, vernacular fiction was not able to break away from its subcultural position.

The re-evaluation efforts during the sixteenth to the seventeenth centuries were isolated ones, limited to some deviant members of the literati. The failure in late Qing re-evaluation was ascribable to the overly practical aim of using vernacular fiction for political education.

Liang Qichao, the leading reformist who was also the most influential promoter of vernacular fiction, revealed his true intention in his well-known apology for vernacular fiction in 'Scattered Notes About Fiction':

> The barely literate may not be able to read the Confucian Scriptures but they definitely read fiction. That is why when it is impossible to teach them the Canons, teach them with fiction; when it is impossible to teach them history, teach them with fiction; when it is impossible to teach them philosophical analects, teach them with fiction; when it is impossible to teach them the laws, teach them with fiction.[11]

Here, the traditional generic hierarchy was well preserved, with the position of fiction not altered at all.

Since the whole idea was simply to create some 'improved' reading material for the 'barely literate', it was only natural that when the political aim disappeared, these enthusiastic apologists lost interest in vernacular fiction. This explains why, a decade later after his hyperbolic praise of fiction, Liang Qichao turned around to accuse vernacular fiction of debasing the Chinese people, and, when asked to recommend Chinese classics (*guoxue*) to young readers, he refused to include any vernacular fiction in his list, cautioning young people 'not to read fiction at all unless you want to become fiction writers.'[12] In his mind, fiction

> . . . Common people are all fond of this,
> Good reading accessible to both the upper and the low.
> When I visit bookstores in Shanghai
> What books enjoy the best sales?
> Historiography cannot compete with eight-legged essays
> Which in turn have to yield to fiction . . .
> In our land today this school is prevalent
> Turning the Six Arts into Seven Peaks.
>   (Kang Youwei 1900: 232)

[11] Liang Qichao 1941: i. 34.   [12] Ibid. iii. 287.

had never had a high position, and his endorsement of fiction was for no other purpose than reformist propaganda.

Perhaps the greatest contribution of late Qing fiction to the changing of the cultural status of vernacular fiction was that it encouraged a generic mixture: the same magazines could carry vernacular fiction as well as literary-language fiction; the same foreign novel was translated into literary language and the vernacular; the same author could write in both vernacular and in the literary language. This mixture greatly helped the final subversion of the generic hierarchy of cultural discourses in the May Fourth period.

The May Fourth Movement shattered this hierarchy by completely eliminating the demarcation line between literary-language fiction and vernacular fiction. The vernacular was refined by the May Fourth writers to such a degree and used so effectively for all genres that the literary language finally became obsolete and was pushed into disuse, thus removing the linguistic obstacle for vernacular fiction to rise above the subcultural level.

Hu Shi in his famous essay 'Wenxue Gailiang Chuyi' ('A Modest Proposal for the Improvement of Literature') in the January 1917 issue of *New Youth*, which ushered in the May Fourth 'Literature Revolution', talked mainly about the reform of the Chinese vernacular as a tool for producing decent literature. He summed up his opinions in an eight-point proposal, in mild words with no revolutionary fanfare at all.

Those who try to belittle Hu Shi's contribution argue that he was by no means the first one to advocate the use of the vernacular.[13] This is true, but the previous advocates of the vernacular had the same attitude as the late Qing fiction apologists—they wanted to use the vernacular only to serve the barely literate. That was why even their articles advocating the vernacular and the magazines carrying those articles were, paradoxically, in literary language. Their proposal, then, amounted to a mere readjustment within the traditional generic hierarchy.

The paradox is dramatized in Liang Qichao's novel *The Future of New China*, in which the protagonist Dr Kong gives a speech in the year 2050, at the centenary celebration of the successful modernization of China. In his speech Dr Kong retells a debate between two reformists:

[13] It was not Hu Shi but Qiu Tingliang who first suggested replacing the literary language with the vernacular. His essay 'On the Vernacular as the Starting Point for Reform' ('Lun Baihua wei Weixin zhi Ben') was published in 1898 in *Su Bao*, the well-known anti-Manchu paper, and put forward the proposal of 'abolishing the literary language'. His essay, like the whole newspaper, was written in the literary language.

When Mr Huang and Mr Li were debating this issue, Dr Kong was of course not present. How could he know it? How could he recite the whole text without leaving out a word? Because when he was studying abroad, he wrote a *biji* book with the title *Sailing with the Wind*, in chapter 4 of which the whole text of this debate was all recorded. During his speech, Dr Kong was reading the text verbatim. All he did was to turn its literary language into vernacular. *I, the scribe, saw all this with my own eyes.* (XZGWLJ, 43–4. Italics mine.)

The arch-reformist Liang Qichao, himself enthusiastically advocating and seriously writing a vernacular novel, believed that more than one hundred years later the vernacular would be merely the language to address the common people, and that the literary language would still be used for books!

Before Hu Shi's proposal, in 1914, the Butterfly magazine *Fiction Pictorial* (*Xiaoshuo Huabao*) had begun to use vernacular exclusively. Since it was a fiction magazine, and fiction had long been written in the vernacular, the magazine was declared to be dedicated to vernacular fiction exclusively, which was claimed to be 'suitable for everyone: housewives, students, merchants, and workers'.[14] Against such a background, Hu Shi's seemingly modest proposal to adopt the vernacular, till then a tool for subcultural discourses, for use in élite genres, was indeed launching a fundamental challenge to Chinese culture.

Many writers at this time began to remould the Chinese vernacular to make it a medium applicable for élite genres. Hu Shi praised Zhou Zuoren's 'literal' translation of Western fiction as 'the starting-point for the Europeanization of Chinese'. Fu Sinian, the most active among Hu Shi's disciples, argued that 'people's speech' alone was not enough for the remoulding of the Chinese vernacular, and that only in the European languages could there be found a 'more superior model'. (Zhao Jiabi 1935, i., 249). Starting from 1917 Qian Xuantong began his controversial campaign for Europeanizing the Chinese vernacular by adopting Western punctuation marks, the printing and writing conventions, and the romanized transcription of Chinese characters. Europeanization was avidly put into practice and brought great changes to the modern Chinese language though it did not necessarily always result in good style. Even Bing Xin, the most refined stylist of the time, acknowledged that her language was 'vernacular-turned-literary' and 'Chinese-turned-Western'. As a result of the massive effort of the May Fourth generation of writers, the vernacular was eventually raised from its

[14] Wei Shaochang, 1982*a*: 134.

subcultural vulgarity to élite refinement. When vernacular fiction became *the* fiction, vernacular became *the* language.

Lu Xun's first short story 'The Madman's Diary', the first piece of May Fourth fiction, is a powerful symbol of this transformation. The story has an introductory over-narrative which is written in the literary language, whereas the main narrative—the madman's notes—is written in the vernacular, without following any stylistic conventions. The tone of the literary-language over-narrative is sober, rational, and elegant, while that of the vernacular main narrative is chaotic and disconnected, 'with many mistakes'. In the literary-language part, the madman, already recovered, has returned to mainstream culture by taking up an official post, while in the vernacular part, totally isolated by society, he is deranged, his stand denied any understanding. Nevertheless, it is in the vernacular part of this first piece of modern Chinese literature that the verdict on traditional Chinese culture is proclaimed: 'This is a history of thousands of man-eating years.' Only those who are free from this culture are still innocent enough to see through the evil. In this way, the normality/insanity opposition is made ironical, and the vernacular has been endowed with a moral power and cultural meaning infinitely superior to that of the literary language. In a sense, 'The Madman's Diary' is a manifesto for the reconstruction of the cultural hierarchy of Chinese culture.

2

The Fortune of Vernacular Fiction Writers

I

In traditional Chinese society, vernacular fiction writers almost never let their names be known to the public, leaving much game for scholarly hunting today. In the works of the rewriting Period, paradoxically, the name of the author was often clearly printed on the cover of most editions, no matter how drastically the novel was rewritten. Yet resounding names like Luo Guanzhong or Shi Nai'an are more likely to be figureheads than real persons. Zhou Lianggong, the early Qing scholar, completely rejected the assertion that Luo Guanzhong and Shi Nai'an could be the authors of *The Three Kingdoms* and *Water Margin*, with a well-grounded argument. 'No one who wrote such books would have dared to have their names revealed. Such purported authorship is really suspicious.'[1]

On the rare occasions when they were mentioned in literati works, vernacular fiction writers were mentioned with contempt. Hu Yinglin, one of those literati writers who condescended to talk about vernacular fiction, did not fail to pick on these anonymous authors, calling them 'vulgar scholars in the backwoods' or 'petty village pedants', as he saw their works 'totally lacking any knowledge of history'. He showed a remarkable appreciation of *Water Margin*, but after praising the novel he comments on its alleged author: 'I often regret that this person should have spent so much effort on such a low craft. But the skill is only a sideline gift [piancai]. Should he be asked to engage in real learning and essay-writing, he might not be able to produce anything good.'[2] Zhang Xuecheng's well-known criticism of *The Three Kingdoms* was also representative of the traditional literati: 'These fiction writers are not to blame since they do not possess enough knowledge,

---

[1] Zhou Lianggong 1958: 67.

[2] Hu Yinglin 1958: ii. 18. This statement sounds like a university president today deploring a top-notch scientist turning to the writing of science fiction. This is not only a problem of evaluation but also of a distinction between 'work' and 'leisure', which, as I mentioned in Ch. 1 of this Part, is one of the criteria to judge the sub-cultural discourses.

and can hardly be rid of the habit of fabricating.'[3] What he was sternly against was their encroaching on the sphere of historiography by mixing fictionality with history and their confounding of the generic hierarchy.[4]

The social status of vernacular fiction writers changed a little in the seventeenth and eighteenth centuries. Lu Xun was the first to point out that some members of the literati moved into vernacular fiction writing at that time, and he suggested that four novels should be regarded as Literati Fiction (*wenren xiaoshuo*)—Li Ruzhen's *Flowers in the Mirror*, Xia Jingqu's *Unworthy Words of a Country Man* (*Yesou Puyan*), Tu Sheng's *The Story of the Bookworm* (*Yin Shi*), and Chen Qiu's *A Tale of Yanshan* (*Yanshan Waishi*)—because these works also demonstrated their authors' erudition in terms of the literature in the élite and canonized genres.

Hsia reconsidered this list and suggested that the 'scholar-novelists' should include some of the more important writers of the time, including Wu Cheng'en (author of *The Journey to the West*), Dong Yue (author of *More Chapters in the Journey to the West*), Wu Jingzi (author of *The Scholars*), and Cao Xueqin (author of *The Dream of the Red Chamber*). Actually all the major vernacular fiction writers in the seventeenth and eighteenth centuries are on the list.[5]

What these authors had in common was that they were all from well-off family backgrounds, and well-educated in the classics. They all seemed to have had an opportunity to join the power élite as they were candidates (unsuccessfully) for the *Keju* (civil service) examination, the accepted route for a government career. By some twist of fate, not only was the door to power closed to them, but their family could no longer retain their wealth. Cao Xueqin and Wu Jingzi suffered from extreme poverty after their family fortunes were exhausted, Wu Cheng'en was forced to quit his post and return to his home town, and Dong Yue went into a Buddhist monastery after the Manchu occupation. They differed from the professional vernacular fiction writers (mostly hack-writers employed by publishers), but at the same time, they also withdrew from the establishment, and were no longer bound to the mainstream culture.

[3] Huang Lin and Han Tongwen 1982: 23.

[4] There was, however, an even sterner view: 'I feel sorry for the man, who made his name by writing fiction'. These are lines by Cheng Jinfang. (*Mianxing Tang Ji*, ii. Quoted in *Kong Lingjing Zhongguo Xiaoshuo Shiliao* (Shanghai: Shanghai Guji Chubanshe, 1982), 260.)

[5] Hsia 1977: 228–321.

The first few Chinese fiction critics at the end of the Ming and beginning of the Qing—Li Zhi, Jin Shengtan, Mao Zonggang, Ye Zhou, Zhang Zhupo, and others—can be listed together with those authors. We may call them 'scholar–commentators'. Although among the most intelligent men of their time, none of them held any office, or had a conventionally fulfilled life. Li Zhi committed suicide in jail; Jin Shengtan was executed for joining in a protest; Zhang Zhupo died young in poverty.

Naturally, the majority of students of the classics were not able to pass the *Keju* examination, but not many had the courage to free themselves from cultural prejudice. Those authors and critics we have mentioned, who did condescend to such low genres as vernacular fiction, became the very few who dared to exile themselves from the centre of the culture to its margins.[6] From the scanty biographical data we can now gather from various sources, we find that almost all of them were described as 'eccentric though excellent in essay-writing' (Wu Jingzi), 'with intentionally strange behaviour' (Ye Zhou), etc.

None of them took to writing vernacular fiction before he gave up his effort to pass the civil service examination. For a member of the literati to go so far as writing in the subcultural genre was itself a deliberate offence against the cultural norms.[7]

What makes these literati writers particularly important to Chinese fiction is that when they descended the cultural ladder down to the subcultural rung and invaded the formerly secluded subcultural discursive domain, they brought with them some new qualities which the subcultural discursive community did not possess.

It was precisely through this process that Chinese vernacular fiction rose from the Rewriting period into the Creative period. As Hsia points out:

The scholar-novelists would appear far less content with plain story-telling in the exercise of their role as scholars and literary men ... They would take a more playful attitude towards their medium but at the same time more innovative

[6] Robert E. Park in 'Human Migration and the Marginal Man' (*American Journal of Sociology*, 33: 881–93) defines the marginal men as 'those who emigrate from one culture to another'. I prefer to see marginal men in a broader sense—people who try to migrate from one cultural milieu to another, but end up in between the two.

[7] Drama was an exception as only part of the dialogue was in the vernacular while all the lyrics were in literary language. We find among the playwrights leading scholars, high-ranking officials, or even princes. Among vernacular fiction writers, the one who had the highest social position was perhaps Wen Kang (author of *Ernu Yingxiong Zhuan*) who was a Manchu aristocrat.

and experimental because they were not writing to please a large public and could indulge their every creative whim.[8]

This group of strangers to vernacular fiction produced the best novels of Chinese vernacular fiction, though some of their works were unbearably pedantic. Zhao Jingsheng once commented on *The Flowers and the Moon* (*Huayue Hen*) and *The Dream of the Blue Chamber* (*Qinglou Meng*) that 'it would have been probably more appropriate if those works had been written in literary language'.[9] However, despite their participation, vernacular fiction remained a subcultural genre, something decided by the social status of the readers rather than the authors.

By the late Qing, vernacular fiction writers were still socially despised. Li Boyuan was once recommended for a position by an important official, who was then impeached for recommending a vernacular fiction writer for office. Hu Jichen told us about his contemporary Wu Jianren:

> Jianren was a man much greater than a mere novelist. Yet the world sees him only as a novelist. Alas! Jianren once wrote a biography for Li Boyuan which says, 'With such a talent you should not be remembered only as a novelist. This is a great misfortune for you but a great fortune for Chinese fiction'. I would deplore the misfortune of Jianren in the same words.[10]

The exaggeration of the role played by fiction did not bring about any actual improvement in the social status of the fiction writers in the late Qing.[11] It was only the abolition of the *Keju* civil service examination, the royal road to the power élite, that gave rise to the change. Aspiring scholars, not knowing where to go for a career, blundered into the field of fiction writing. Yin Bansheng wrote in 1906, the year of the abolition of the *Keju* examination system: 'Ten years ago the world was one of eight-legged examination essays, today it is one of fiction writing.

---

[8] Hsia 1977: 270–1. English transl. mine.
[9] Zhao Jingshen 1980: 68.   [10] Wei Shaochang 1982b: 18.
[11] Li Boyuan revealed the essential sub-cultural position of the Late Qing authors and readers in the Prelude to his novel *China Today* (*Zhongguo Xianzai Ji*): 'But I am only a poor person at the bottom of society, with no power at all. Even though I have an earnest wish to rectify society and sufficient learning to put my plan into realization, my words remain empty talk as nobody will listen to me. Then why not put aside all these cares and spare myself the trouble. When, after wine-drinking, I can enjoy my leisure, and go to the melon-watcher's tent, to chat with village folks about everything on earth, and all kinds of people in history' (ZGXZJ, 17).

The title seems to indicate that this novel was meant to be a contrast to Liang Qichao's utopian novel *The Future of New China*. The emphasis on sub-culturality was also meant to be a contrast to Liang Qichao's exaggeration of the social function of fiction.

For those people who once devoted themselves to eight-legged essays are now trying every trick today to vie with each other, all claiming to be fiction writers.'[12] There were even people who seriously suggested replacing the 'Eight-Legged' examination essays with fiction, and 'establishing a Civil Service Examination system on fiction writing so that the writers could have a career'.[13] Zhou Guisheng, the well-known translator and colleague of Wu Jianren, even claimed that Mark Twain once won '*Juren*'—the title of honour for successful *Keju* candidates—in the United States. These interesting anecdotes were probably due to fiction writers' dreams when the possibility of moving out of the sub-cultural status began to be discussed.

The social composition of fiction writers of the late Qing was different from before. Instead of professional compilers or alienated scholars, there now appeared several new groups of people engaged in fiction writing. The first group consisted of activists of the political opposition: revolutionaries and reformists. It was surprising to see so many leading anti-Manchu political figures dabbling in vernacular fiction writing: Liang Qichao (author of *The Future of New China*), Chen Tianhua (author of *The Lion Roars*), Qiu Jin (author of some popular ballads), Huang Xiaopei (author of *Twenty Years in a Dream of Prosperity* (*Niannian Fanhua Meng*)), and others. Among the members of the Southern Society (Nan She), which was the rallying point of anti-Manchu 'dissident' poets and was regarded as the *de facto* Propaganda Department for the revolutionaries, many moved to fiction writing after the 1911 Republican Revolution. In fact most leading Butterfly writers had been Southern Society members, and the People's Rights Press (*Minquan Chuban Bu*) run by the Southern Society later became one of the publishing centres of the popular entertainment Butterfly fiction.

The second group of fiction writers were members of the newly emerging comprador-technocrat class. Liu E was a notorious 'traitor' in his life, because he wrote a memorandum in support of borrowing foreign funds for the Tianjin–Zhenjiang railroad and because he once held the office of Director of the German-owned Shanxi coal mines. *The Travels of Lao Can* mentioned many things which interested him—railways, Western medicine, patents, newspapers, upholstered armchairs, etc. Wu Jianren once served in the Southern Machinery Works where

---

[12] 'Xiaoshuo Xianping Xu', *Youxi Shijie*, 1, no. 1 (1906).
[13] Yiming, 'Method of Reading New Fiction' ('Du Xin Xiaoshuo Fa'), *Xin Shijie Xiaoshuo She Bao*, no. 6.

he was said to have invented a remote-control steamboat model.[14] Zeng Pu was originally an entrepreneur in the silk industry and in publishing, and later, after the 1911 Revolution, served in the Jiangsu Provincial Government, and was even Governor of Jiangsu for a short period. During his life he was regarded as 'not a typical politician, nor a typical novelist, nor a typical scholar'.[15]

The third group, and the largest one, was made up of professional writers. Never before had there been in China a group of writers of any genre of literature who could make a living by selling their fiction to magazines. It was the first time in Chinese history that fiction writing had become a profitable profession that could provide the authors with a reasonably comfortable life. One of Wu Jianren's numerous short novels *The Returning of the Soul* (*Huan Wo Linghun Ji*) was written as 'advertising fiction' for a medicine-producer on payment of 300 *yuan*. That was why late Qing writers like Li Boyuan and Wu Jianren could afford to stay away from a *Keju* career and made fun of it in their works.

Thus the social composition of late Qing fiction writers was very different from that of the previous centuries: they were neither the 'country pedants' nor the professional compilers of the Rewriting period, nor the impoverished failed scholars of the Creative period. The composition of writers determined some salient features of late Qing fiction which is either politically or commercially inclined. This can be seen from their attitude towards the *Keju* examination. The authors of *The Scholars* and *The Dream of the Red Chamber*, although condemning the *Keju* examination, seemed to be constantly preoccupied with the idea, as they almost paranoically kept talking about their contempt for the examination in their novels. In late Qing fiction, however, the *Keju* was no longer the central issue.

In chapter 4 of *A Flower in the Sinful Sea*, for instance, the protagonist, a *Zhuangyuan* (Number One Successful Candidate in the Highest Imperial Examination), discovers after meeting some top intellectuals of the time:

Though I am a *Zhuangyuan* renowned nation-wide, I never knew that there is so much knowledge to learn about foreign countries. It looks as if the success of the *Keju* examination is insufficient. What is more important is to learn about the West and know more of current affairs, and go to serve in the Foreign Ministry. Only thus can I be called an outstanding scholar. (NHH, 12)

[14] Wei Shaochang 1982*b*: 19.   [15] Wei Shaochang 1962*b*: 23.

II

In the vernacular fiction of the Rewriting period, the personality of the writer becomes too diluted due to the repeated rewritings. The weight of the author's personality began to increase in the Creative period in some scholar-novelist novels, as Prusek points out when discussing Xia Jingqu's *The Humble Words of a Country Man* (*Yesou Puyan*) and Li Ruzhen's *Flowers in the Mirror*: 'In these cases, the authors looked upon their novels as a kind of compensation for their lack of success in life, as a means of satisfying their longing for fame and immortality.'[16] Yet since the narrator remained the conventional impersonal Story-Teller, the personal quality can be found only through a biographical study of the author. For instance many students of Chinese fiction find that the character Du Shaoqing in *The Scholars* carries much of the personality of the author Wu Jingzi. However, if we knew nothing about Wu Jingzi's life we would not be able to detect that. The two heroes of *The Flower and the Moon* are now held as being imbued with the two sides of the personality of the author Wei Zi'an—one of the protagonists, a pitiable failure though extremely gifted, is regarded as his real self, while the other, who is fortunate enough to become a meritorious general, was the author's aspirant self. This was detected, however, only after the author's identity was revealed and his scattered biographical data gathered.

Chinese vernacular fiction was basically non-autobiographical as its narratological conventions reduced the individuality of the narrative to insignificance. Even in the late Qing, vernacular fiction writers would still just sign their pen-names, which generally were so oddly made as to attract public attention. The author of *A Flower in the Sinful Sea* was called 'Sickman of the East' (Dongya Bingfu); *Strange Events* was signed 'I Who Come From Foshan' (*Wo Foshan Ren*). Yet since they were not reluctant to reveal their authorship to the public, they were actually no longer so eager to remain anonymous. Their insistence on signing their pen-names on their novels was more due to a respect to the convention of vernacular fiction.[17]

---

[16] Prusek 1980: 12.

[17] There is an example for the convention of anonymity in fiction works: the novel *The Mirror of Flowers* (*Pinghua Baojian*) bore the author's name as Shihan Shi, which was apparently a pseudonym. The author Chen Sen signed his real name on his *Chuanqi* play *Dream of Plum Flowers* (*Meihua Meng*). This was only natural as Chuanqi plays were considered a prestigious genre. What was strange was that in the preface to the novel *Mirror of Flowers*, the author, under his pseudonym, identified himself by saying, 'I am

In the May Fourth period, the situation changed completely. Authorship of fiction works could not be publicized more explicitly. By that time the author's name not only appeared below the title but within the text—it was often given to the narrator and the protagonist, as if only in this way could the writer's desire for self-exhibition be satisfied. Guo Moruo often names his protagonist 'M'. The protagonist in Chen Xianghe's many stories is 'Mr C'. Zhou Quanping writes a series of stories about a 'fool in the City' whose name is 'C' (initial for the Wade-Giles romanization of his name); Yu Dafu's heroes receive names such as 'Yu' or 'Y', or 'Da', or 'Yu Zhifu'; Tao Jingsun's protagonist in many of his stories is given his own name 'Jingsun'. Most of Liu Dajie's stories are so professedly autobiographical that the hero adopts the full name of the author. The most extreme case is perhaps Hu Shanyuan, leader of the Muse Society, whose short novel *Three Years* (*San Nian*) is a faithful record of his three-year intense romance with his wife, and the couple in it are given his and his wife's full names.

This strong, almost compulsive self-exhibition is obvious not only with the autobiographically inclined writers but is apparent with almost every author. The first-person narrator in Lu Xun's stories like 'New Year Sacrifice', 'In the Tavern' ('Zai Jiulou Shang'), and 'My Old Home' ('Gu Xiang') so much indulges in contemplation of the weakness in his own character that the illustrators of these stories, since Lu Xun's lifetime, have given the narrator Lu Xun's appearance. Lu Xun never objected to such a confusion in his lifetime.

As a by-product of May Fourth fiction, there were published great numbers of letters and diaries, either fictional or genuine. Indeed the two were intentionally confused. Lu Xun published his love-letters with his student girlfriend in *Letters Between Two Places* (*Liangdi Shu*), which are genuine, and a diary called 'Immediate Diary' ('Ma Shang Riji'), which is not genuine. Feng Yuanjun's short novel *Trace of Spring* (*Chun Hen*) is composed of fifty letters written by a young woman to her fiancé, and it looks as if these are excerpts from the author's own love-letters to her fiancé Lu Kanru.

Guo Moruo's words in a letter to Zhong Baohua in 1920 can serve as witness to this compulsory self-exhibition:

also the author of the *Chuanqi* play *Dream of Plum Flowers*.' So actually he did not mind whether people found out his real name. It was only because of the convention that he had to sign his novel with a pen-name.

You made public my last letter to you. This was exactly what I wanted. How can I 'blame you' for that? I often hate myself for not having the talent of a St Augustine, Rousseau, or Tolstoy for making a naked confession. But if I do not pour out everything from my past, my future will forever be wrapped in shadow, with no hope of being revealed. If I do not unload my feelings as early as possible, my pitiful soul will eventually be bogged down in a sea of tears, with no chance for redemption.[18]

It was definitely not the habit of the Chinese literati to examine their own guilty conscience in any genre except poetry, where such self-examination could be ambiguously covered. Some literary-language stories, like Yuan Zhen's 'Yingying Zhuan' were confessional, but they are rare exceptions. In vernacular fiction, this self-exhibition was almost impossible as the impersonal Story-Teller narrator and a conventional oral performance narrative set-up excludes any possibility of confession. Only in some of the best novels, where the narratological convention is more or less set aside, and the subjectivity of the narration has an opportunity to be diffused, as in *The Dream of the Red Chamber*, *The Travels of Lao Can*, or *Strange Events*,[19] could the personality of the writer hope to assert itself to a certain degree. It was only after the conventional narrative set-up was completely removed that confession and self-exhibition could hope to strike a major chord in Chinese fiction.

Being only a paratextual feature, a signature seems to be a matter of little real significance. Yet when we compare the situation of vernacular fiction with that of literary-language fiction, we can see that only the authors of the culturally acknowledged genres would sign their real names, or even let their names enter the text, so that their individuality could merge into the cultural order of meaning power. It is in this context that we should understand why such highly individual genres as diaries and letters never entered traditional vernacular fiction.

Indeed, in literary-language fiction, the rule that the name of the narrator can be no other than the author's name is so reliable that many literary historians have used it to reconstruct the authorship. The early Tang *chuanqi* short story 'Gu Jing Ji' ('The Story of the Ancient Mirror') was always anonymous. But Wang Pijiang holds that the author is

---

[18] Three Leaves (*Sanye Ji*) 1921: 56.
[19] Few have noticed the autobiographical nature of *Strange Events*. Wu Xiaoru checked the first edition of the novel (Shanghai: Guangzhi Shuju 1907), and found printed on that edn. many marginal notes, obviously written by the author himself. In ch. 108, there is a note: 'The discovery of the brother in the last chapter is the happiest thing in the author's life. An artist painted a picture for this occasion . . . The funeral in this chapter is the most rueful thing in the author's life.' (Wu Xiaoru 1982: 163–5).

Wang Du, as the name is given to the narrator. Another story 'The Old Man of the East Town' ('Dong Cheng Fulao Zhuan') had always had the name of the author as Chen Hong. Yet the narrator in the story is named Chen Hongzu, and Wang Pijiang insists that the author's name should be changed accordingly.[20]

The author of vernacular fiction could never hope to achieve this kind of self-confidence, not even by the end of the late Qing. Liu E's attitude toward his own great novel *The Travels of Lao Can* is quite interesting. According to his son, he was often very depressed that his pastime writing won him fame, and, therefore, reluctant to let the public know that he was the author.[21] Yet at the end of every chapter of the novel there is attached a 'Comment by Liu E'. If it was his strong intention to hide his name, he did not have to reveal it in the comments. Actually the type of signature and accrediting was decided by the generic requirements. The author of vernacular fiction should sign a pseudonym as it was a subcultural discourse, while the author of comments should sign his real name, just as the official historians did when commenting on historical events, or commentator-critics did in commenting on fiction.

That is why the signature of the May Fourth fiction is a powerful indication of the fundamental change of the cultural status of Chinese fiction. May Fourth writers were no longer on the margins of the society: they definitely belonged to the élite, and soon became the core of the new generation of intellectuals. On the other hand, they were still deviants from the cultural norms. One thing they had in common was a sense of a lack of belonging. A great number of them were returnees from abroad. As Zheng Boqi—himself a returnee author—tells us: 'They lived abroad for a long time, and often had a strong nostalgia for the Fatherland. Nevertheless, the many disappointments they received at home gave them a feeling of emptiness. The more they longed for home when abroad, the more they feel angry once they are home.'[22] And he insisted that works by these authors 'had a strong resemblance to immigrants' literature' (*yimin wenxue*). They were, indeed, marginal people in their society.

This coincides with the description Lu Xun gave to another group of authors—the young intellectuals in Beijing or Shanghai who came from

[20] Wang Pijiang 1958: 116.

[21] Liu Dashen, 'Guanyu Lao Can Youji', in *Lao Can Youji* (Taipei: Lianjing Chubanshe, 1976), 251.

[22] Zhao Jiabi 1935: Volume 3 of Fiction, p. xii.

provincial towns. Both the authors and their protagonists in May Fourth fiction were constantly and nervously on the move from one place to another. As Yu Dafu confessed in one letter, 'Hermits enjoy a better name, but a wandering life is more to my taste'.[23] These estranged young intellectuals formed an estranged sector of the élite, whose attachment the culture failed to win.

[23] Yu Dafu 1927: 207–8.

3

Cultural Paradigms for Vernacular Fiction

I

Any act of signification has to be executed through a certain medium. However, medium (in our case, the Chinese vernacular language) is neither neutral nor passive. It moulds the formal features of the message into a culturally acknowledged pattern habitually called genre. Genre facilitates the interpretation, but, on the other hand, restricts the scope of signification.

For literature, this restriction is not always desirable. Often we find in any type of discourse an inclination to break away from the boundary of its own communicative pattern in an effort to achieve the effects of other genres. This extra-generic emulation may take place at an early stage of new genres. Early photography emulated painting, and early film emulated theatrical performance. One of the main reasons for this emulation of other discursive genres, apart from technical reasons, is that the 'lower' genres have to prove that they can function in a similar fashion to more prestigious genres. They grow out of this premature extra-generic emulation when their own cultural position is established and culturally recognized.

In a pyramidic culture like that of China, however, extra-generic emulation can become a constant aspiration for the culturally lower genres, as they do not hope to enjoy a cultural mobility to move out of the lower strata. Chinese vernacular fiction, for centuries situated so low in the cultural discursive hierarchy, had to continue to emulate certain prestigious genres in order to justify itself. In this way, the extra-generic emulation finally turned into the cultural paradigm of the genre,[1] to be its basic principle of signification.

Historiography used to be the supreme narrative model in China, and, in the light of the long-standing proposition that all the Six Scriptures mentioned by Confucius (*li*, ritual; *yue*, musical; *shu*, documental; *shi*, poetical; *yi*, divinatory; and *chunqiu*, chronological) are *de facto*

---

[1] Paradigm is a pattern that recurs in a certain type of discourse, and helps formulate its meaning. According to Kuhn (1970: 113), a paradigm has little to do with the subject-matter, but much to do with the groups of participants.

histories (*liujing jieshi*), historiography is indeed regarded as the paramount paradigm to all cultural discourses, occupying the supreme position resembling religious canonized texts in other cultures. This almost absolute domination of historiography exercises great pressure on all genres of discourses, élite genres included. In poetry, for instance, historical allusions are so extensive that they take on an over-coding,[2] making it interpretable only to professional readers.

The pressure from historiography was strongly felt even in literary-language fiction, the only narrative genre other than history among all the culturally privileged genres. Writers of literary-language stories prided themselves on being capable of 'supplementing the official histories'. Most of the salient narratological characteristics of literary-language stories are ascribable to this emulation of historiography. Always supposed to be recounting anecdotes of real persons, the literary-language story starts with a formulaic short summary of the protagonist: his home town, and the date of the incident. At the end (or less often, at the beginning) of the story, a super-narrative is installed where the narrator, inevitably adopting the name of the author, can come out with comments in the same manner as historians commenting on the historical character at the end of his biography.

If élite genres feel the pressure so strongly, for a discourse in as low a position as vernacular fiction, the emulation of historiography is virtually compulsory.

To praise fiction works as being 'history-like' became the regular commendatory term among Chinese fiction writers and critics. Ge Hong of the fourth century, one of the earliest Chinese fiction writers, claimed that his collection of stories, *Miscellaneous Notes from the West Capital* (*Xijing Zaji*) was compiled from the data left over by the well-known historian Liu Xin, and his book should now be read as a supplement to Liu Xin's history. And indeed *Miscellaneous Notes from the West Capital* was listed under the heading of 'history' in the bibliography of the ensuing official dynastic history. Almost 1,500 years later, in the eighteenth century, Ji Yun, editor of the *Siku Quanshu Zongmu*, praised Ge Hong's book for exactly the same reason as the writer expected:

The contents, although fictional, are gathered from a wide range of material. Li Shan used them to annotate *Selection of Refined Literature* (*Wen Xuan*). Xu Jian alluded to them in his *Textbook for Children* (*Chu Xue Ji*). Even Du Fu,

---

[2] Over-coding occurs when 'on the basis of a pre-established rule, a new rule is proposed which governed a rarer application of the previous rule'. (Eco 1976: 133).

who was very strict in verifying his allusions, referred to this book repeatedly. After so many hundreds of years of usefulness we can say that these notes have proved to be well-grounded historical facts, and cannot be easily ignored.[3]

If we remember those unfortunate poets who mistakenly used allusions to vernacular fiction and had to spend the rest of their life in repentance, we can see that the same fabrications in literary-language fiction could be taken as historical facts, at least in poetry. Such is the difference between the two genres of fiction!

Being more subordinate to historiography, the best that vernacular fiction could hope for was actually not to supplement official history (*bu shi*) but to illustrate it (*yuyi xin shi*).[4] Its restriction and its freedom all stem from this role of illustrating history. Xiaohua Zhuren in his preface to the vernacular short-story selection *Marvels Ancient and Modern* (*Jingu Qiguan*) holds, 'Fiction is codicillary to history'. (JGQG, 5) For this claim, the well-known vernacular fiction writer Zhu Renhuo offers an interesting explanation: 'It is very true for our ancestors to think of *The Grand Chronicle* (*Tongjian*) as the great ledger of the past. But there should be both the general ledger and the small items account books. That is why romances about the past dynasties have kept coming up.' (Preface, STYY, 4) Here the cultural subordination of fiction is held up as something of which to be proud. With this sense of subordination critics adopted a strange standard for the appreciation of good novels.[5]

Since the emulation of historiography was imperative, studying history was regarded as fundamental training for fiction writers. Luo Ye advised in his *Zuiweng Tanlu*: 'Although a lesser scholarship, fiction requires a wider range of learning. [Fiction writers] are not those with scanty knowledge, but should, by necessity, be erudite. When young, they have to study *Taiping Guangji*, and when grown up, they must master histories of all dynasties'.[6] This emulation of historiography continued well into the late Qing. Liu E did not care much about his *The Travels of Lao Can* but he declared in a comment made in his own

[3] Ji Yun 1965: 1182.

[4] Plaks points out with acumen that the titles of almost all literary-language stories are bound to sound as if they should be read as historiography, e.g. *Zhuan, Zhi, Ji*. (Plaks 1977: 312) Most vernacular fiction works, though not all, followed this practice.

[5] As late as 1897, Qiu Weihuan in his *Shuyuan Zuitan* still held: 'The best fiction is those works which record facts and can stand verification. Fiction works dealing with foxes or ghosts, or relating folklore, are like chess, only for time-killing. They can never hope to compare with those recording facts and discussing reasonable matters.'

[6] Luo Ye 1957: 3.

name at the end of chapter 4: '[These facts] are not known to many
people. Fortunately they are recorded in this book, thus providing
material for an official historiography to be compiled in the future. So
how can we despise fiction?' (LCYJ, 38)[7]

In the late Qing to use a love-story to frame historical events became
common practice. The best-known example is *A Flower in the Sinful
Sea*, of which the design was 'to borrow a character as the thread to
knit in *as much as possible* the history of the recent thirty years' (NHH,
56. Italics mine). Other writers soon followed: Lin Shu's *The Stench of
the Sword*, Fu Ling's *The Bird that Carries Stone to the Sea* (*Qin Hai
Shi*), Zhong Xinqing's *New Dame aux camélias* (*Xin Chahua*), and
others. Wu Jianren's *The Sea of Remorse* is a tragic romance of two
couples, but A Ying included it in his collection *Literature on the
Boxer Rebellion*. It is amazing to see how A Ying neatly collects almost
all major late Qing fiction works into volumes on historical topics such
as 'Opium War', 'Boxer Rebellion', 'Movement Against the US Exclusion Bill', '1911 Revolution', 'Constitutional Movement', etc.

Indeed, in late Qing fiction, the emulation of historiography becomes
something of an *infatuation* with historiography. In Chen Tianhua's
The Lion Roars, which recounts the imaginary history of an island
Utopia, there are some very strange passages:

Wen Mingzhong . . . made up another song and taught his students to sing it
every day, it runs: (The lyric of the song is missing in the manuscripts, so we
have to leave it out).

Suddenly there came a lumberman who was singing while walking (The lyric
of the song is missing). (SZH 597, 612)

The brackets are added by the modern editors. However, it is very
difficult to find an explanation for those statements with or without
brackets. Chen Tianhua could well have left out those lyrics, as the
narrative selectivity enables him not to cite the lyric in the first place.
If he did not have the time or patience to make these two lyrics (he did
compose some lyrics in the novel), his pretext could only make things
worse.

---

[7] Another interesting case was Lin Shu, who repeatedly expressed a similar hope of
contributing to official history. In his preface to *Jiewai Tanhua* he hoped that 'Probably
these things can serve as materials when an official history is compiled'. But when he
was invited to be an Honorary Compiler of *The History of the Qing*, he declined, acknowledging that he was only good at 'unofficial history' (*yeshi*).

What he seems to me to be trying to achieve is to create an impression that everything about this island is faithfully recorded, so that if there is something missing, its absence should still be mentioned, just as in a history.

The reason why such an infatuation with historiography culminates in the late Qing is not hard to find: the social significance imposed upon fiction by Liang Qichao and other champions of 'New Fiction' was more than fiction could bear, and forced fiction to draw support by means of the emulation of historiography.[8]

II

Imaginative discourses are unprivileged in Chinese discursive hierarchy because Confucius declared in *The Analects* (*Lun Yu*) that he 'refrains from talking about the abnormal, the supernatural, the magic, or the weird'. In order to make possible the necessary fictionality, it is necessary to find a justification within the dominance of the historical paradigm. Feng Menglong, in his preface to *Stories Ancient and Modern* (*Gujin Xiaoshuo*),[9] makes this interesting statement, 'When historicity dwindles, fiction arises' (*Shitong san er xiaoshuo xing*). And he goes on to point out the true lineage of Chinese fiction: 'It started in the time of Zhou but flourished in the Tang period. In the Song, it went into full blossom. Han Fei, Lie Yukou and others should be considered the

---

[8] Some authors by the late Qing apprehended the basic contradiction between historicity and fictionality. In the historical novel *A Romance for the Leisure Time* (*Xiaoxian Yanyi*), which was written around 1920 but is still justifiably included by A Ying in his collections of late Qing fiction, there are a great many contradictory narratorial directions about historicity and fictionality. Let me select only a few:

Fictionality is most misleading. In this novel of mine no groundless fictionality would be tolerated, and no libel allowed to appear. If you do not believe me, you can examine it carefully and see that every word I say is true to facts. (A Ying 1959: 337)

My dear readers, don't you think that the passage above is really interesting? But people all say that historical novels are composed of events taken from historical documents. Then from where did I copy that passage? Haha! Let me tell you: this is sheer fabrication made by me. (Ibid. 437)

Some people would ask how could I say that this minister was killed by the Boxers as he was actually executed by an imperial order? Here is my answer: the proper method of fiction writing is that so long as it does not go far off the track, let it be as interesting as possible. We should not be too fussy over facts. The purpose of romance is to let you readers know that evil would never go unpunished. (Ibid. 405)

[9] This preface was written by Lutianguan Zhuren, which, according to Sun Kaidi, was Feng Menglong's pen-name. (Sun Kaidi 1931: 45).

ancestors of fiction.'[10] Feng Menglong shows acumen in tracing the source of the imaginative paradigm to texts regarded as heretical by the orthodox Confucianists.

Another way to justify fiction is to prove that fictionality is a mode of signification entirely different from historiography. Nevertheless, there has never been in Chinese thinking a proposition distinguishing historiocity from fictionality like that put forward by Aristotle which became the starting-point of Western literary philosophy. The Aristotelian proposition, though simple in wording, produced a series of significant philosophical and aesthetic conclusions: the proposition leads to the superiority of poetry over historiography. This is not only because history is related to what has happened and literature with what could have happened, and not only because history deals with the particular and poetry with the universal, but more importantly, because literature is closer to truth than the narrated historical events.[11]

The absence of an Aristotelian-like proposition in Chinese philosophy reveals some important aspects of Chinese discursive structure: actuality is stored only in history, which, although managed by Heaven, is also in keeping with the basic structural rules of society (i.e. the celebrated credo *Tian Ren Heyi*, Heaven and Men are one). The singular (i.e. the 'actual facts') is thus imbued with the absolutism of truth, and is by definition superior to fiction based on probability whose agreement with the universal truth has yet to be proved. What has happened, as recorded in historiography, is always superior to what might have

---

[10] Han Fei was one of the leading rivals of the Confucian school in the pre-Qin era, and his philosophical writings, collected together as the *Han Fei Zi*, are full of imaginative fables. Lie Yukou, the alleged author of the collection of stories and fables in *Lie Zi*, was probably the earliest Chinese fiction writer. Those two authors can be said to represent the non-Confucian non-historiographical discourses in early Chinese culture, though we may suggest that the Taoist writings by Zhuang Zi provided more food for Chinese imaginative thought, and Buddhist discourses, which came into China in the first or second centuries AD, greatly reinforced Chinese imaginative power.

[11] Louis Mackey in 'Poetry, History, Truth and Redemption' (in Schulze and Weltzels 1978: 66–7) tries to draw a logical inference from the Aristotelian proposition. What Aristotle really meant, he suggests, was that 'the difference between history and poetry is a difference between the modalities of their discourses. History is written in the indicative mode, the mode of assertion and matter of fact. But poetry, at its most philosophical, is in the mode of necessity, and, at its least philosophical, in the mode of probability and possibility.' And his conclusion is this: 'Poetry is more philosophical than history only on the condition that possibility (fiction in the "what if" sense of imaginative hypothesis: likelihood poised in stable equilibrium between probability and dissimilarity) is closer to necessity than actuality is.' Therefore, the Aristotelian conception serves as the basis on which later critics developed the idea of poetic truth. Allen Tate, for instance, developed his cognitive poetics along this line. (1955: 24–45)

happened (as depicted by fiction), and the generic priority of historiography is unquestionable.

Meng Liang Lu, one of the first *biji* collections that mentions oral fiction narratives, vaguely suggests a comparison by saying, 'Stories (*xiaoshuo*) can tell the history of a dynasty or an era, and in a moment bring them to an end (*niehe*)'.[12] Although this is a comparison between two sub-genres of oral narratives, not exactly an Aristotelian comparison between fictionality and historicity, it already touches upon the possible way to argue for the superiority of fictionality over historiography. Jin Shengtan was one of the first to put forward a proposition in this direction: 'The creativity [*xu*] of the historian is to handle events by means of narrative [*yi wen yun shi*]; whereas the creativity of the fiction writers is to fabricate events for the sake of narrative [*yin wen sheng shi*].'[13]

This comparison, after all, only reveals differences in the scope of the two genres, emphasizing that fiction enjoys a much greater freedom. But freedom is not truth value. Zhang Zhupo tried another argument for fiction's alleged superiority:

> *Jin Ping Mei* is another *Grand History* (*Shi Ji*). But in the *Grand History* there are separate biographies and treatises for each person and each important subject-matter, while in *Jin Ping Mei* the one hundred chapters comprise a single biography of hundreds of characters, who share the one biography, while each one has his own story. That is why the author of *Jin Ping Mei* was definitely able to write a *Grand History*. How can I be so sure? Since he was capable of the more difficult he was naturally capable of the easier. (JPM, p. vi)

Although boldly in favour of fiction, his enthusiasm for fiction is based on the difficulty of technique alone, and is hardly a philosophical argument.[14]

---

[12] Wu Zimu, 1980, 196. *Ducheng Jisheng*, another early *biji* book that discusses oral fiction narrative has almost exactly the same words with the last word *niehe* changed to *tipo*, which can be roughly translated as 'breaking suddenly onto the truth'.

[13] Huang Lin and Han Tongwen 1982: 254.

[14] One of Feng Menglong's arguments more or less in the same vein is seen in his preface to *Jingshi Tongyan* which dared not declare the superiority of fiction: 'Should fiction be all real? I say, "Not necessarily". Should it be all false? I say, "Not necessarily". Then should we delete the false and retain only the real? I say, "Not necessarily" ... Real events with truth in them, are the same as unreal events with some truth in them, doing no harm to morality, giving no opposition to the sages, posing no contradiction to the canons and histories. Why should such books be abandoned?' Such arguments do not uphold the superiority of fiction over historiography, and in fact the conformity with historiography is listed as one condition of the *raisons d'être* for fiction.

Perhaps Yuan Yuling's argument is the only one in Chinese theoretical thinking that approaches an Aristotelian proposition:

Literature without imagination (*huan*) is not literature. Imagination without going to extremes is not imagination. So we know that the most extreme imagined thing in the world is also the truest thing; and the *most imaginative argument is the truest argument*. That is why talking about reality is less worthy than talking about imagination, just as talking about Buddha is less worthy than talking about a demon. The demon is no one else than myself.[15]

Yuan Yuling does not launch a challenge to the dominance of historiography, and his words read like a statement instead of a theoretical argument. Yet this seems to be the highest understanding ancient Chinese fiction critics reached on the nature of fiction, although a little vague in argument, as perhaps an argument deviant to the norms had to be. It is regrettable that no modern scholar seems to have paid attention to Yuan Yuling's highly interesting argument on the paradox of the truth value of imagination in literature, and his penetrating insight in an almost heretical presentation.

Late Qing fiction criticism, to our great regret, does not even arrive at Jin Shengtan's understanding, let alone Yuan Yuling's. Yan Fu and Xia Zengyou in their well-known 1897 essay first touch the topic: 'A book recording people and events is history; a book recording people and events that might not actually have happened is fiction.'[16] Five years later, Xia Zengyou published another article 'Principles of Fiction' and reiterates the same proposition, but with a much more feeble explanation, which shows that he fails to come close to an Aristotelian understanding: 'Fiction is the writing about the already-known truth in detail, thus it is superior. History is the writing about the already-known truth in succinct terms, and therefore is inferior to fiction.' (XXXS, 1903) Again this is a comparison of some specific technical device, not a philosophical contemplation on the truth value of the different genres.

The difficulty that Chinese critics faced in this debate is ascribable to the fact that the cultural value of historiography was considered so superior that fictionality could never hope to match it in any way. Any speculation on the comparison was simply groundless, and so far as the cultural structure is concerned, irrelevant. The above-mentioned debate

---

[15] Introduction by Yuan Yuling under the pen-name Manting Guoke to the edn. of *The Journey to the West* annotated by Li Zhuowu. Quoted in Sun Kaidi 1931: iv. 77. Italics mine.

[16] 'Guowen Bao Fuying Shuobu Yuanqi', repr. in A Ying 1960: i. 13.

arose only in the discussion of how to handle historical facts (as recorded in official history) in historical novels. It could hardly be serious contemplation upon the truth value of the two genres. In a word, Chinese vernacular fiction can only try to win a limited amount of freedom for imagination.

As a result of this emulation of the historical paradigm traditional vernacular assumes the following narratological characteristics:

Emulating the historiographer, the status of the narrator in traditional vernacular fiction must be impersonal, never personalized so that his narration can pose as the objective record of actual facts.

Since he is responsible for the factuality of what he relates, the narrator, above the narrated world, intrudes abundantly. His narration is almost always reliable as his task is purportedly to record what has already taken place in history (or, narratologically, in *histoire*—the pre-narrated state), and narratorial mediation is apparently reduced to the minimum.

Emulating the historiographer, he generally adopts zero-focalization (the omniscient perspective), and avoids character-focalization, since his main purpose is supposedly to tell as objectively as possible what has really happened. The direct quoted form of reported speech reinforces the impression of being absolutely factual.

Emulating the historiographer, he pays great attention to time in the narrative, and appears punctilious in indicating the moment of the occurrence of an event, and meticulous in filling in every link in the temporal chain, making it 'time-brimming'. He seldom feels the need to use flashbacks in his narration unless two plot-lines cross. In order to maintain fundamental suspense, he frequently uses flashforwards, a habitual narrative device in historiography, as flashforwards reinforce the temporal linearity. Also, *ab ovo* beginnings are favoured, so that the narrative can be safely anchored in historical context. Emulating historiography, the dominating type of motif tends to be more functional, making the narrative sketchy and speedy.

Although this emulation of historiography in vernacular fiction is similar to that in literary-language fiction in many respects, there are some basic differences. Since literary-language fiction is much higher in the cultural hierarchy, the pressure to emulate historiography is less. The narrator makes fewer commentaries, and in a less intrusive way. Since the narrative frame is not conventionalized, there is more room for verifying the distribution of subjectivity.

It was in the May Fourth period that Chinese fiction was finally relieved from the unbearable pressure of historiography. Anti-historiography became a favourite game among May Fourth writers and critics. Hu Shi, for instance, accused Jin Shengtan of 'reading fiction in the same way as reading history, trying to find non-existent hidden meanings'.

Lu Xun, in his iconoclastic satire *The True Story of A Q*, dealt this emulation a shattering blow, as the narrator, ironically posing as a historiographer, tries in this short novel to subjugate fictionality with historicity. The short novel starts with a long-winded straight-faced direction discussing what category in the rigid system of Chinese official or unofficial historiography this story of A Q, the homeless farm labourer, should belong to, but finally helplessly gives up.

Then Lu Xun tries to start the story in the conventional *ab ovo* manner—name, birthplace, lineage, etc.—and ends up in despair again that these conventions do not fit A Q's life at all. Historiography is therefore found to be not only useless but also stupid. And the narrator does not let a chance go by without poking fun at the solemnity of historiography:

Whenever they met, women in the village were bound to talk about how Zhou the Seventh Aunt bought a blue silk skirt from A Q which, though used, cost only ninety cents, and how Zhao-the-White-Eye's mother—*Another version says that it was Zhao Sichen's mother, which remains to be verified by future scholarship*—also bought a child's crimson silk shirt which was 70% new and cost only 392 coins in cash. (NH, 509. Italics mine.)

Zhou Zuoren recalled in his memoirs that the 'interweaving of arguments' in *The True Story of A Q* was meant to be a mockery of 'the infatuation with history' (*lishi pi*).[17]

However, another story by Lu Xun 'The Madman's Diary' can be considered a more devastating blow to the emulation of historiography, not because it condemns the whole history of Chinese civilization as a history of cannibalism, but because of the participant narrator's—the Madman's—particular way of reading historiography:

I opened the history book to have a careful reading. The history has no chronology. Scrawling on every page are written the four characters 'Benevolence and Morality'. I couldn't fall asleep anyway, so I kept on reading until the small hours before I found out from in between the lines that on every page there was written the word 'man-eating'! (NH, 15)

---

[17] Zhou Zuoren 1980: 207.

So the truth is not to be found within history but without, where the language of history could hardly reach, that is, the opposite side of what is recorded. In this way Lu Xun drives home a total negation of the history-cult in Chinese culture and a complete refutation of the truth value of this supreme genre in the Chinese discursive hierarchy.[18]

On the whole, the narrator in May Fourth fiction resembled a memoirist or autobiographer more than a historiographer. The truth value of fiction did not lie in its correspondence to facts, or to the probability of facts. Cyril Birch points out that 'norm-sharing and communal celebration' is the dominant attitude of Chinese traditional fiction, in contrast to the 'individual, relatively alienated' attitude in May Fourth fiction.[19] Since the historiographical paradigm is the supreme embodiment of the discursive norms of Chinese culture, its emulation would necessarily result in a conformity with the norms. Thus, this narrative mode of Chinese traditional fiction should be a *conformable* mode. On the other hand, this norm-sharing forced the narrator to stabilize his conventions, to ensure that the readers join the norm-sharing. That is why his narrative was also in a *communal* mode.

By emulating the prestigious generic paradigms, by complying with the scale of meaning-power, narrative texts under the control of this narrative mode aligned themselves with the cultural norms, thus reinforcing the cultural structure. Moreover, they reinforced the structure 'from below' as they were subcultural narrative discourses, and were essentially communal to the broad masses of the lower social strata, thus ensuring a collectivized interpretation. In this way, the narrator of traditional Chinese fiction succeeded in bringing the subculturalness of Chinese vernacular fiction into conformity with the cultural metalingual system.

III

The norms for individual behaviour in Chinese society used to be culturally coded in an explicit and unequivocal way. For a fictional narrative text, then, there appears to be little leeway for different moral judgements on the narrated world. Since the moral coding is publicly imposed inclusively on all cultural discourses, fiction was by no means an exception. Nevertheless, because of the particular social position of vernacular fiction, this control could work in a very complicated manner.

---

[18] It was not until half a century later that Louis Althusser made a similar statement on the relation between texts and history: 'On the reverse side of what is written will be history itself' (quoted in Macherey 1966: 28).

[19] Goldman 1977: 391.

If before the twelfth century, there was still a certain degree of ambiguity in the coding for individual behaviour as well as that of the characters in the narrated world, after the emergence of Neo-Confucianism in the Song and Ming dynasties, moral coding became almost absolute in controlling the cultural discourses in China. This was exactly the time, perhaps not coincidently, of the emergence of Chinese vernacular fiction.[20]

It was Zhou Dunyi, one of the leading Neo-Confucianists, who first put forward the ethical principle for all discourses—'Letters are vehicles for morals' (*wen yi zai dao*).[21] His celebrated statement does not conceal that this doctrine is directed against *belles lettres*—the aesthetic use of literary discourses:

> Letters are to serve as the vehicle for morals. If the wheels and shafts are beautifully ornamented but one cannot drive the chariot, it remains only decoration. Words can be art, but morality [*daode*] is the fruit. It is only because of their love of the fruit that the artists put the words down on paper. As they are beautiful, they are loved. As they are loved, they spread. Thus the wise can learn from them and put them into practice. This is the way of teaching.[22]

This is an extremely pragmatic and teleological doctrine. Artistic merit is regarded as only sugar-coating for morality, making the latter easier to accept. This doctrine became so prevalent after the rise of Neo-Confucianism in China that few discourses in Chinese culture were able to escape it.

The pressure of moral codification on Chinese vernacular fiction is extremely stringent, more stringent than on literary-language fiction, as subcultural discourses are more remote from the moral norms. The more vernacular fiction wants to entertain the masses, the heavier is the normalizing pressure it undergoes. The emergence of the Novels of Manners (*Shiqing Xiaoshuo*), on daily life and sexual relations, resulted

---

[20] The stories purged in modern eds. of some late Ming fiction collections such as *Amazing Stories* (*Pai'an Jingqi*) were not considered pornographic according to late Ming standards. The notorious obscene story 'The Lustful Life of King Hailing' (Hailing Wang Huayin) was anthologized repeatedly from the late Song to the late Ming (story 21 of *Jingben Tongsu Xiaoshuo*, story 23 of *Xingshi Hengyuan*, and possibly other collections) but was purged from all reprints after the early Qing. This shows how the pressure of moral control over sub-cultural discourses had gradually built up in China over the last few centuries.

[21] The *Dao* here used to be translated as 'way', the mystic centre of Chinese philosophical thinking. But it can also be understood as *daode* (morality), and I think in this case, morality is what Zhou Dunyi had in mind. Indeed he used the word *Daode* in his exposition of the motto.

[22] Zhou Dunyi, 'Tongshu Wenci', in Zhang Shengyi and Liu Jiuzhou 1985: 6.

in a more stringent implementation of moral codes as seen in Talent and Beauty fiction in the seventeenth and eighteenth centuries, and in Butterfly fiction on the eve of the May Fourth Movement.

We can also find some strange phenomena in Chinese popular literature: the narratives written by women (especially the large number of *tanci* ballads produced in the nineteenth century), while letting their heroines compete with men in all fields, also make them paradoxically ultra-conservative with regard to the feminine virtues, as if to show that women can outdo men in stereotyping women. Most ancient Chinese scholars who cared about popular literature justified their interest in these subcultural discourses by emphasizing their moral-admonitory power.

What is perhaps more thought-provoking is that the novels on licentious sex, considered highly entertaining in the late Ming, are all highly moralistic. In those novels, the lustful heroes and heroines are bound to be punished for their wild sexual escapades. And those novels usually have a very defensive introduction and almost censorious narratorial intrusions to show that the texts are within the boundaries of morality. Hanhan Zi, author of *The Unofficial History of the Embroidered Bed* (*Xiuta Yeshi*), one of the 'most obscene' late Ming novels extant, provides a typical apology for this kind of novel in the preface:

A friend who dropped by asked, 'Aren't you, sir, teaching sexual indulgence?' I said, 'No! I am only showing my worry about this world'. He asked, 'How is that?' I said, 'I want to stop the whole world from sexual excess, but as it is already too far gone in that direction, nobody will listen to my advice. If I show them what result may come out of it, and lead them gradually on in the right direction, people can be saved.'

The self-justification sounds hypocritical. Yet we can hardly blame the author for being fraudulent. The subcultural discourses, as mentioned in the last chapter, do not have a separate set of cultural values to go by. They have no choice but to accept the dominating morality of society, even though that morality appears to be coded for the interests of the continuous domination of mainstream culture.[23] In Chinese vernacular

[23] We can find some interesting passages in Lu Xun's *The True Story of A Q*:

A Q had some opinions that came from who knows where. He held that to be a revolutionary meant to rebel, and to rebel meant to harm him. Therefore he hated the revolutionaries. (NH, 476)

A Q was an upright person. Though we do not know which wise man was his mentor, he maintained a very strict attitude toward the segregation of men and women, and displayed sufficient rectitude toward heretical people like little nuns or phoney foreign devils. (Ibid. 477)

fiction there is often a paradoxical warning. Ling Mengchu, in the preface to his collection of short stories which contained quite a few licentious descriptions that gave later publishers much headache in purging them, condemned pornographic authors and earnestly suggested to the government a ban on their books. A great many of the narratological conventions in Chinese vernacular fiction are actually inserted and maintained to meet the high moralistic pressure.

In the various documents banning fiction collected by Wang Chuanxiao, we find an interesting document—'Notice of Prohibition in All Villages'—which can be said to be a spontaneous manifestation of the common people (at least local gentry) concerning the popular literature on sexual relations.

Adultery is the ugliest of all crimes, and licentiousness the foremost of all evils. Yet the opera troupes in our country are fond of staging these ugly sexual stories, in which there is neither a worthy plot, *nor retribution to make them acceptable*. Only the ignorant masses would go for such enjoyment . . . Now, in accordance with the official decree, the staging of opera is to be strictly prohibited everywhere.[24]

Such was the Chinese attitude toward fiction: so long as there was some proper retribution in plot and a moral ending to serve as a safety valve, the undesirable subject-matter could be tolerated.

In the flashforward scheme of vernacular Chinese fiction, one thing particularly noteworthy is the formulaic prelude of moral admonition attached to almost all stories and novels to provide some moralizing message before the actual story starts. It is interesting to note that the placing of the moral admonition reverses that in some Western admonitory literary works such as Aesop's fables, which do not try to sum up the moral message until the story is finished. In Chinese culture, the moral is rigidly predetermined disregarding the particular situation, and the story serves only as an illustration.

IV

Thus in vernacular fiction we find two kinds of beginning schemes: to emulate the historiographical paradigm, the *ab ovo* beginning was well installed, so that the historical continuity could be preserved; to facilitate the adherence to the moralistic paradigm, the end-result was carefully stated in the prelude. Indeed the two beginnings often appear

---

[24] Wang Chuanxiao 1958: 119. Italics mine.

CULTURAL PARADIGMS 213

together in a fiction work, and we can see that these two paradigms co-operate in determining the narratological features of Chinese vernacular fiction. Most of the conventionalized narratological characteristics are in the service of both of these modes.

The morals preached in the prelude are, like judgemental comment-aries, bound to be hackneyed common truths, as vernacular fiction is in no position to be original in moral judgement. The first section of *Zuiweng Tanlu*, entitled 'Preludes (Universally Applicable for Either Historical or Moral Fiction)' is meant to be a model that can be readily adapted to any story:

Since ancient times, people have been divided into grades. The wise are clean and intelligent; the foolish are unclean and muddle-headed. The intelli-gent know about the Three Credos and the Five Morals [*San GangWu Chang*], the muddle-headed commit Five Felonies and take to the Ten Evils [*Wu Nie Shi E*]. Good or evil is decided by temperament, and the wise and the foolish are distinct as to be respectable or despicable. Good people are like rice; evil people distress their relatives, as weeds disgust the farmers. Such people are not worth talking to. (Luo Ye 1957, 1)

What calls for attention in this paragraph is not only the crude vulgariza-tion of Confucian ethics, but also the metaphors and the wording it uses to appeal to the common people. The fact that this passage was de-signed for stories on any subject-matter shows that moralist principle did not have to adapt to the particular story. Rather the story had to adapt itself to the moral principle.

The didactic pressure is much lighter on literary-language fiction. In literary-language literature, there are not so many apparent efforts at moral apology. Description of sexual encounter in plays like *The West Chamber* (*Xixiang Ji*) and in literary-language short stories like *Stories from Liaozhai* (*Liaozhai Zhiyi*), no matter how direct, still remain elegant.

The moral apology, sincere or hypocritical, exists only in subcultural texts which have a double cultural function to perform: they must con-form visibly to the dominant norms to avoid self-expulsion from the culture; they must provide entertainment to the popular audience so they could not afford to be prudish. This dilemma is finally demon-strated in the narratological characteristics of vernacular Chinese fiction, especially in the large amount of moral judgemental intrusions.

This ethical subordination was even more obvious in late Qing fic-tion. *Lives of Shanghai Flowers* for instance, opens with an unabashed statement:

Since Shanghai was opened to international trading, prostitution has run more and more rampant. Huge numbers of young people meet disastrous ends in bordellos. The warning from their fathers and brothers does not stop them; the advice of their teachers and friends is unheeded. Are they really so obstinate? It is only because there has not been one who could show them his own experience. When these people fall in love passionately, they of course see only the bright side. Once all these scenes are described in detail here, they will be disgusted, and realize that it is a waste of life. Then they will return to normal life. (HSHLZ, 1)

Almost all the late Qing novelists were outspoken moralizers. Wu Jianren declared repeatedly that he was 'all for the restoration of the old morality'. In his best novel *Strange Events*, there are some stories about evil-doers receiving retribution by fate. Those stories are so nonsensical that we almost suspect tongue-in-cheek. But we find in his *biji* collection *Wo Foshan Ren Biji*, that those stories were recorded as 'real events that I myself witnessed, and rewrote into my novel with only the names changed so as to be lenient to those evil persons already punished in life'.[25]

Moralizing is the first and foremost proclaimed aim within a typical 'Reprimanding Novel' of the late Qing. Ouyang Juyuan in his preface to Li Boyuan's *The Bureaucrats* states:

Filial Piety, brotherhood, loyalty, and sincerity are all destroyed at the hand of the officials; rites, honour, decency and uncorruptibility are all ruined by the officials ... The author heaved a sigh, 'I have no personal relations with the officials. To achieve my goal, all I can do is to be lenient in my description, while throwing out hints on the hidden evils.' (GCXXJ, p. iv)

As can be observed from late Qing novels, romance fiction has to try harder to harp on the same moralist string in order to justify its subject-matter and prove that it has no intention to challenge the Chinese ethical codes. Every leisure magazine run by that group spares no effort in emphasizing that its aim is to denounce the degeneration of social *mœurs*, and that for this purpose interesting stories are more effective than direct admonition. The Black Curtain fiction, generally considered as the most degenerate type in late Qing fiction, is also the most markedly moralistic. There are, after every few pages, statements to the effect that the sole purpose of those novels is to reveal the seamy side of

[25] Wei Shaochang 1980: 56.

society 'so that those inside the curtain would fear, and those outside the curtain could be on their guard'.[26]

This general reiteration of moralization greatly reinforced the continuity of the narratological characteristics of Chinese traditional fiction. Many of the late Qing novels pin great importance on the moralizing prelude, and judgemental commentaries. Even one of the best late Qing works of fiction, Li Boyuan's *The Bureaucrats* has a prelude introducing, through a character's words, the admonitional purpose of the novel; *Flowers in the Sinful Sea* has more than one prelude, deleted only in the revised editions after 1927.

Posing as the moralizer, the narrator stands in a controlling position aloof from the narrated world. Thus he has to remain neither explicit nor implicit. If he is too implicit, his judgemental voice, seemingly coming out of a void, would carry no weight, whereas his judgement would be too personal if he is explicit. As a moralizer, he is justifiably intrusive, inserting judgemental commentaries at every possible moment of the narrative, to preclude a diffusion in interpretation.

Posing as the moralizer, he is straightforward, not allowing his narrative to become unreliable, since any irony encourages diversified interpretation; he must make the best use of his omniscience, so that his complete knowledge of the narrated world may be displayed, and the authority of his moral judgement assured.

Posing as the moralizer, the narrator has to ensure that the temporal-causal chain in the plot is clearly maintained, so that good and evil may be developed to their completion to justify the reward or retribution.[27] He favours flashforwards in his temporal mediation, since in flashforward the suspense hangs more on the process leading up to the retribution or reward rather than on whether retribution will eventually come.

V

I mentioned above that the emergence of Chinese vernacular fiction was almost simultaneous with the rise and growing dominance of Neo-

---

[26] Introduction to the *Omnibus of Chinese Black Curtain Stories* (*Zhongguo Heimu Daguan*) (Shanghai: Zhongguo Tushu Jicheng Gongsi, 1920), p. ii.

[27] Macauley and Lanning (1964: 181) provided a clear-cut argument the moral importance of ending: 'One of the things that plot leads most powerfully toward is a moral judgment on the people it has dealt with. Even if the judgment is implicit, it is nevertheless there. The very idea of denouement demands a sorting-out of life; a plot cannot end without the assigning of values, without the identification of right and wrong. This, in an abstract way, is what the denouement really is.'

Confucianism (*Li Xue*). No scholar has ever paid attention to this concurrence and its meaning to Chinese culture. In fact, it was not Neo-Confucianism alone but the combined force of it with the rise of vernacular fiction that turned China into what we now usually call 'ritual-moralist society' (*Lijiao Shehui*).

Of course Confucianism had all along been an ethics-centred social philosophy, and early Confucianists laid down strict rules for social and family manners. But early Confucianists emphasize that high moral sense is to be expected only from the upper class—the gentlemen (*junzi*), whereas the common people (*xiaoren*) are only encouraged to follow the example set by the upper class. The *Scripture of Rites* (*Li Jing*) and other books stipulating moral behaviour, compiled into its present shape around the first century BC, are obviously meant for the members of upper class, as the the stringent rules (e.g. the in-laws of different sex are not allowed to talk to each other directly even when dwelling in one household) cannot be followed by common people at all.

So the generic hierarchy of Chinese cultural discourses matched the hierarchy of moral requirements, with the literati to be held as moral examples. That was the price the literati had to pay in order to keep the mandate to rule. The lower classes enjoyed exemptions to different degrees. So long as the exemptions were not expressed in significant discourses, e.g. not in written text, they were generally tolerated by the mainstream culture, or even recorded as 'exotic local customs'.

The Neo-Confucianism that gradually gained control of Chinese spiritual and social life in the Song and the Ming dynasties was basically a fundamentalist movement supported by an exquisite idealist philosophy inspired by Buddhism. It went all out to make Confucian ethics cover lower social strata which had used to be more or less exempt from the restrictions. We may call it a downward extension of moral codes. The rise of Chinese vernacular fiction in the Southern Song period was a part of this movement. The subcultural discourses, now iterated in written form, had to rely heavily on the established moral codes in order to justify themselves. Indeed, vernacular fiction showed a slavishly submissive attitude toward the mainstream moral codes, as discussed above. On the other hand, the downward moral extension movement needed popular genres like vernacular fiction and drama to educate the common people.

During the early years of this fiction, some members of the literati already noticed and highly recommended the moralist fervour of vernacular literature. Yang Weizhen, one of the leaders of the literati in the last years of the Yuan dynasty, pointed out that the zeal of popular dramatists to propagate morality 'could make the literati ashamed of themselves'.[28] In his preface to the short story collection *Shuo Fu*, he proposed a general scheme for the relationship between various genres:

All things in this world come together as the city, and the five Scriptures and other texts form the city wall. That is to say the Five Scriptures walls in all discourses in the world. If a discourse does not refer to the *Five Scriptures* [*wu jing*], only recording a myriad things happening day and night, what use can it be to Confucian ethics?[29]

Such was the the moral hegemonic structure formulated by Neo-Confucianism where discourses of lower social status have one justification for its existence—their subordination to the canonized texts. It is interesting to note that the high recommendation of the moral usage of subcultural discourses went hand in hand with the warning against any confusion of the generic hierarchy.

Enclosed in the wall of the *Five Scriptures*, nevertheless, the exemptions of subcultural discourses were now greatly reduced. Being placed in the newly acquired semi-literacy, vernacular fiction now no longer enjoyed the freedom of discourses conveyed in orality.

If in the Southern Song this moral extension movement was, generally speaking, not yet an officially endorsed movement, and was anyway cut short by the century of Mongolian rule (1271–1368), the Ming Dynasty, founded by the peasant uprising that toppled the 'Barbarians' returned to Confucian social ethics with a vengeance. It laid down an imperial policy to push Confucianist moral codes down to the lowest rung of the social ladder. Starting from the earliest years of the Ming Dynasty, the government-awarded titles for filial sons or chaste women were only granted to common people, not to literati families, since to behave morally was considered the undeniable duty of the literati and did not need commendation.

The downward moral extension movement, now officially promoted, was so successful that the number of 'awarded chaste women' soon became overwhelming, and local histories had to devote many pages to brief accounts of their glorious deaths. So eagerly did common people crave for moral commendation that the government had to make the bureaucratic procedure difficult so as to discourage the applicants. As

---

[28] Yang Weizhen, 'Song Zhu Nushi Guiying Yanshi Xu', in *Donglai Zi Wenji*, *Sibi Congkan* edn. (Shanghai: Hanfeng Lou, 1929), vi. 12.

[29] Ibid. v. 45.

a result, women tried harder to die for moral principles in all imaginable ways, and the male members of the family would spend their
whole fortune and time in fighting through the procedure.[30]

The immensely successful extension of the coverage of moral codes
inevitably attenuated morality and made it hypocritical. More importantly, the literati whose class-privilege moral adherence used to be,
now found morality distasteful and vulgar. That was at least part of the
reason why some deviant members of the literati took to vernacular
fiction writing. Some of the most notoriously licentious novels, e.g. *Jin
Ping Mei* and *Flesh Prayer Mat* (*Rou Putuan*), were said to be, and
indeed read like, works authored by scholars. No matter whether the
novels the scholar-authors produced were sexually explicit or not, their
engagement in vernacular fiction writing itself was an act that con-
founded the social norms, even if it did not alter the subculturalness of
Chinese vernacular fiction, as I have discussed in previous chapters.

So while the vogue of dying for morality ran rampant in villages and
small towns, the bookshops in cities exhibited a large number of novels
that indulged in explicit sexual descriptions. This paradox was but natural
as the pyramid of moral strictness was now turned almost upside down.

This might not be a bad thing, as when part of the élite was trying
to reconsider the established norms, the cultural structure could then
acquire the flexibility necessary for a cultural reorientation. Regrettably,
the hurricane of peasant uprising of the mid-seventeenth century swept
away the Ming Empire together with any social order. The Manchus took
the opportunity to fill in the power vacuum and, largely for the purpose
of justifying a non-Chinese regime, tried fervently to re-establish the
Confucian ideology and social order. In this way, the Qing continued
the downward moral extension movement while successfully disciplin-
ing the élite. Due to severe legal punishment, sexually explicit literature
virtually disappeared from bookshops by the end of the seventeenth
century.

The present book does not intend to go deeply into the complicated
problem of Chinese licentious literature (either in the literary language
or in the vernacular) of the seventeenth century. To handle that problem
would require a book-length study. I will here only point out that the
Neo-Confucianist effort to make the whole of Chinese society moral
played an important role in the rise and development of Chinese vernacular fiction in the following two ways: the necessity of educating the

---

[30] For a detailed description of the situation, please see T'ien Ju-k'ang 1988.

common people facilitated the prosperity of vernacular fiction during the Rewriting period; the excess of the movement could have prompted some deviant sections of the literati class into the subcultural discourses, thus pushing Chinese vernacular fiction into its Creative period.

VI

The only choice left for subcultural discourses, if they were to win some leeway from the dominant value-system of mainstream culture, was to emphasize their purpose of entertaining the masses. The first critic who openly praised the ludic elements in popular literature was Xie Zhaozhi, the late Ming critic and connoisseur of vernacular fiction. He holds in his *Five Miscellanies* (*Wu Zazu*): 'All fiction works or *Zaju* plays should mix fictionality with reality to achieve a style of playful enjoyment. The descriptions should go as far as their own worth carries them, without caring whether they are real or not.'[31]

After him, a more competent critic Ye Zhou proposes an advocation of playfulness (*xi*) and amusement (*qu*). One of his comments on *Water Margin* runs:

There was a village pedant who said that Li Kui was too fierce in killing Luo the Taoist, while Luo was too un-Taoist in lacerating Li Kui. This kind of comment is no more than farting. No part in *Water Margin* can be compared with this chapter, since every part and indeed every sentence of it is full of playfulness. Amusement is the first and foremost criterion for discourses all over the world. So long as there is amusement, what does it matter if the events and persons are real or not? Those who try to find out whether they are real or not are simply idiots![32]

This advocacy of playfulness is an escape from the frustrating problem of the truth value of fiction, as this problem is insoluble within the discursive structure of Chinese culture, where truth values were pre-determinately assigned to the specific genre according to their status in the generic hierarchy.

Ye Zhou's stand—insisting on the 'subculturalness' of the communal discourses while at the same time refusing to emulate the culturally superior genres—is self-contradictory, and not feasible in traditional Chinese culture. This is because in Chinese society, the pyramidic structure produces more intense pressure on discourses at the lower levels. So long as vernacular fiction is still regarded as one of the lowest

---

[31] Huang Lin and Han Tongwen 1982: 78.   [32] Ibid. p. ix.

communal discourses, the practitioners (both writers and readers) will not feel safe with the entertainment without the support of the established value systems. No wonder this argument on amusement did not win much support during the three centuries of the Qing Dynasty.

But weariness with the indigestible didacticism of late Qing Political or Reprimanding fiction meant that amusement became the key note in Butterfly fiction. The leading magazines of Butterfly fiction flaunt their playfulness. Their titles, *Playful Magazine* (*Youxi Zazhi*), *Saturday* (*Libai Liu*), etc. blatantly claim themselves as no more than diversions. The Publication Note of the most important of the Butterfly magazines, *Saturday*, is a rather revealing statement:

People say, 'There are so many enjoyable things to do on Saturday afternoons. Why not go to the theatre for opera, or to the wine-tavern to get drunk, or to a bordello for a smile? Why should we come instead to buy your fiction?' My answer is 'The bordello costs more; drunkenness harms the health; opera is noisy. Reading fiction is then the most economical and enjoyable pastime.'[33]

This is a frank admission of the subculturalness of vernacular fiction, as it unequivocally puts itself on a par with other subcultural discourses.

Soon there appeared in *Saturday* the ill-fated advertising motto invented by a few Butterfly writers: 'You'd rather give up your concubine than give up *Saturday*', which was seized on by their May Fourth opponents as clear evidence of the degenerate nature of old-type fiction.

The first cry of protest of the May Fourth writers against traditional literature, nevertheless, is against its moralist paradigm. Chen Duxiu says in 'On Literary Revolution' ('Wenxue Geming Lun'): 'Literature is definitely not the vehicle for morality.'[34] Liu Bannong echoes him and emphasizes, 'they [literature and morality] can never be mentioned in the same breath'.[35] Their principle of separatism was enthusiastically responded to by many May Fourth writers. We need mention only the statement made by Yu Dafu who argued that, 'The artistic value of fiction is entirely determined by truth and beauty . . . As for social or ethical values, no author should care about them when writing.'[36] Naturally it was not these statements (which might be shared by all May

[33] *Libai Liu*, 1, no. 1 (1914) 2. Shen Yanbing, as one of the most serious attackers of Butterfly fiction, insisted that Mandarin Duck and Butterfly (*Yuanyang Hudie Pai*) was a misnomer, and the group should be called the *Saturday School* (*Libai Liu Pai*), for, as he observed, some of its writers wrote on themes other than love stories. They tried to widen the scope of their subject-matter, esp. after 1919, but their guide-lines remained the same. (Mao Dun, 1981: 172)
[34] XQN, Feb. 1917.   [35] Ibid. Apr. 1917.   [36] Yu Dafu 1927: 78.

Fourth writers) but the writing practice of May Fourth fiction that transformed the cultural paradigm of the narrative texts.

VII

Self-expression has always been an important element in Chinese classical literary theory and practice. The problem is that it is reserved only
for some literati genres (e.g. poetry and *belles lettres*). It does not even
reach the literati narrative genres (*chuanqi* drama and literary-language
fiction). The *Gong'an* school of poets in the late Ming and the *Xingling*
school of the early *Qing* who upheld self-expression in poetry as the
criterion for good literary works, never applied this doctrine to popular
fiction, though some of the members (e.g. the Yuan brothers) showed
a keen interest in vernacular fiction.

For Chinese vernacular fiction, there was never a proposal for a self-
expressive paradigm, because it was virtually never free from communal
subculturalness. Self-expression is hardly compatible with a whole set
of narratological conventions of Chinese traditional fiction apart from
some eighteenth-century masterpieces. It is not until the May Fourth
period that self-expression becomes the most important guiding principle
for fiction writing.

Most literary historians hold that realism is the mainstream in May
Fourth fiction, and that individualistic self-expression, if any, is mainly
to be found in May Fourth poetry. It is, however, the self-expressive
paradigm that makes May Fourth fiction unique in the history of Chinese fiction.

There are, to be sure, realistic elements in May Fourth fiction, but
they are of lesser importance in this period than the self-expressive
elements. A fully fledged realism did not appear until after the May
Fourth period, in the early 1930s. The majority of May Fourth writers,
especially in the early years, are eager for self-expression, giving barely
enough thought as to how to reflect reality. Yu Dafu sums up the
situation: 'One of the greatest achievements of the May Fourth Movement is the discovery of individualism. Before that time, to be a man
is to live for the Heavenly Truth (*Dao*), for the emperor, or for one's
parents. From now on one is determined to live for himself'.[37] And Lu
Yin, when she took up her pen to write fiction, found that 'I did not
know what to write, apart from writing about myself myself',[38] and felt
that fiction was only 'a symbol of my own personality'.

[37] Zhao Jiabi 1935: Volume 2 of Essays, p. iii.   [38] Lu Yin 1934: 80.

It might be said that such statements are made by some writers known for their distinct individualistic stand, but Chen Duxiu, the leading thinker of the period, emphasizes that individualism is the primary principle of the new era: 'As individuals, we live in this world to create happiness, and to enjoy happiness, and endeavour to preserve this happiness in society so that the future generations may enjoy it and pass it on to others.' (XQN, iv., n. 2) Lu Xun with his strong sense of social responsibility, also asserted this self-expressive principle. As early as 1907, he said that literature 'has nothing to do with the survival of individuals or nations',[39] which is an extremely bold declaration in the late Qing. He thinks that in writing, one should 'cry like nightingales if you are nightingales; cry like owls if you are owls'.[40] He acknowledged that he began writing fiction only because 'these memories . . . torment me and I am unable to forget them completely'.[41] In the 1927 heat of revolutionizing the Chinese nation, he insists: 'Good works of art never obey orders from others, as they come out naturally from the heart. If you first give yourself a theme before writing, what you produce will not be far from the Civil Service Examination papers.'[42] Not long before his death, in the thick of the Left-Wing literature in 1935, he still told one of his young disciples that so long as an artist 'expresses what he has experienced, his works would be good . . . if you try to be purposeful, what you produce cannot be genuine and profound, and cannot be art at all.'[43] Again, emotionally self-restrained writers like Bing Xin also declared, 'Literature that expresses the self is good literature.'[44]

The motto 'all literature is autobiographical in nature' successively endorsed by Saint-Beuve, Georg Brandes, and Anatole France won an enthusiastic response from many May Fourth writers. In fact the majority of the fictional works produced in this period by writers of all coteries or inclinations are autobiographical to some degree. The fact that many works of May Fourth fiction were apparently auto-biographical can be verified not only through the biographical data of the authors but through the style, the tone of the fiction etc. But the most important intrinsic feature that points to this tendency is the narratological transformation,

---

[39] 'Defending the Poetry of the Moloch' ('Moluo Shi Lishuo'), in Lu Xun 1956: i. 71.

[40] *Wild Grass* (*Yecao*), in Lu Xun 1956: ii. 285.

[41] 'Preface to *Battlercries*' ('Nahan zi Xu'), in Lu Xun 1956: i. 89.

[42] 'Literature in the Era of Revolution' ('Geming Shidai de Wenxue'), in Lu Xun 1956: iii. 418.

[43] Letter to Li Hua on 4 Feb. 1935. Lu Xun 1956: x. 256.

[44] Bing Xin, 'Wenyi Congtan' ('Talking about Art and Literature'), XSYB 12, no. 4.

which replaces the conventional non-participant narrator with the individually characterized narrator. The social position of fiction was, then, completely changed, as the personalities of the authors were now pretentiously exhibited, as a matter of pride, as a daring gesture to challenge the cultural norms. Yu Dafu's relentless self-exposure in his fiction won him a large following at the time, and writers vied with each other in writing themselves into their fiction. The absence of any structure in Guo Moruo's short novel *The Trilogy of Wandering* (*Piaoliu Sanbuqu*) hints that it is a hardly fictionalized record of a passage of his own life turned directly into fiction. Zhou Quanping turned his own love and hatred into an epistolary short novel, *The Interflow Between Love and Blood* (*Ai yu Xue de Jiaoliu*); Ni Yide, a painter-writer, subtitled his best story 'Autumn on Xuanwu Lake' (*'Xuanwu Hu zhi Qiu'*) as 'The Diary of a Painter'. This trend finally became known as 'Fiction of One's Own Life' (*Shenbian Xiaoshuo*).[45]

Thus, the basic discursive mode of Chinese fiction changes from the communal to the personal. Individual experience becomes the focus of attention. As Yu Dafu argues, the shift of attention in fiction from the crowded streets and alleys to people's mental state is an indication of 'the real beginning of modern fiction'.[46]

VIII

Perhaps as a symbol, perhaps as an essential element for self-expression, sexual relations become almost the central theme of the literature of the May Fourth period. According to an article by Shen Yanbing which cites statistics on fictional works appearing in three months of 1921, 98 per cent are on sexual relations, and he draws the following conclusion: 'Most authors are distant from the life of the labouring masses in the city and the countryside, and pay little attention to social events. What interests them most is love, and the tendency of *individualistic* epicurism is more than apparent.' (XSYB 12, no. 8).

Yu Dafu is undeniably the best representative of the theme in the May Fourth period. His works touch on almost every 'deviant' aspect of sex: voyeurism in 'Sinking', homosexuality in 'A Night Too Long' ('Man Man Ye') and 'The Sunset' (Luori); fetishism and masochism in 'The Past' ('Guoqu'); and confessional impulse in 'The Late Osmanthus' ('Chi Guihua').

[45] Zhao Jiabi 1935: Volume 3 of Fiction, p. v.   [46] Yu Dafu 1978: 189.

Addictive whoring appear in Lin Ruji's 'All Will Be Past' ('Jiang Guoqu'), Yu Dafu's 'The Cold Night' ('Han Ye') and 'The Street Lamp' ('Jiedeng'), lesbianism in Ye Shengtao's 'The One Forgotten' ('Bei Wangque de'), incestuous love between sister and brother in Ye Lingfeng's 'The Night When Sister Married' ('Zi Jia zhi Ye'), love between brother and sister-in-law in Xiang Liangpei's 'Vague Dream' ('Piaomiao de Meng'), and suppressed infant sexuality in Guo Moruo's 'Late Spring' ('Can Chun') and 'The Grave of Ye Luoti' ('Ye Luoti zhi Mu').

The masochistic tendency is most romantically demonstrated in Teng Gu's 'The Mural' (Bihua): a Chinese student in Japan is in love with a Japanese woman but too introverted to take any action. Finally, before his death, with the blood he spits out, he paints upon the wall a dead body on which a woman is dancing.

This concern about every aspect of sexual relations in May Fourth fiction is very different from the themes of sexual relations in traditional Chinese vernacular fiction—notably the *Xiaxie* (prostitution) fiction of the eighteenth and nineteenth centuries and Butterfly fiction of the early twentieth century. Both *Xiaxie* fiction and Butterfly fiction indulge in the 'lofty sentiment' and chastity of both sides, with much emphasis on how the lovers are tormented by their attachments to each other, and how they restrain themselves within the Confucian moral code. The actual description of a sexual encounter is avoided so that the lovers seem to be doing nothing much more than exchanging elegant poems or shedding tears. In the eyes of the May Fourth writers, such treatment is shamelessly timid and hypocritical. The traditional code controlling the behaviour of the lovers—the motto 'Start with desire but halt in accordance with the Rites', which all Talent and Beauty fiction and Butterfly fiction never violate—is contemptuously discarded in most works of the May Fourth period.[47] Sex, which used to be the testing-ground for the subcultural manœuvring—to be entertaining while staying conformable to norms—of traditional fiction now seems to be the breakthrough point for the self-exhibitive challenge launched by May Fourth fiction.

The new openness is by no means without expense. May Fourth fiction on the sex-theme seems to suffer from a overwhelming sense of

---

[47] In some May Fourth stories, this 'rule of decency' is still adhered to. In Feng Yuanjun's best story 'Luxing', a college girl-student goes on a trip to a hotel with a married man. The two, it is said, embrace on the bed every night without 'going over the boundary'.

guilt. The subjective persona (writers, narrators, and characters) are members of the élite class who had been brought up in due respect to the traditional norms which they now find incompatible with the self-expressive impulse. Since these young intellectuals have been uprooted from their native soil, their sense of traditional morality is sufficiently loosened. Their moral responsibilities, which as élite members of society they are unable to ignore, add to their guilty conscience, as can be clearly seen in Yu Dafu's 'Niaoluo Xing' which tells how the narrator-protagonist sends away his wife whom he does not love, only to suffer more severe remorse.

Thus, psychological impediments in dealing with sex become the central theme instead of sex itself, while in Talent and Beauty novels and Butterfly novels, the impediment to love is always social. This accounts for the fact that in May Fourth fiction the openness does not lead to a hedonistic attitude toward sex,[48] and is partly why the tragic and the melancholic becomes the major tone in May Fourth fiction. The tragic tone used to be found only in literati genres of Chinese literature like poetry or prose but was rare in subcultural genres.

The protagonist in Yu Dafu's celebrated long story 'Sinking' is a typical victim of this moral conflict. Each time after masturbating, he recalls the Confucian teaching of 'not harming any part of your body

[48] The May Fourth writers were drawn to the newly developed Western psychological approaches to literature. Freud's theories were known and put into practice by authors like Lu Xun and Guo Moruo who had studied medicine abroad. Lu Xun stated clearly that in writing the story 'The Buzhou Mountain' ('Buzhou Shan') he was 'using Freud to explain and create the beginning of humankind and literature'. In another essay ('After the Setback' ('Pengbi Zhiyu'), in Lu Xun 1956: iv. 67) he celebrated the victory of Freud: 'After the paranoid Mr Freud propagated his psychoanalytic theory, the cloaks of many gentlemen were torn to pieces.'

Guo Moruo, in an article 'Piping yu Meng' ('Criticism and Dream') tries to defend the sexual perversities in his fiction by saying, 'The psychology I describe is a flowing of subconsciousness'. (Guo Moruo 1979: 68). In the same article he used more explicit Freudian terms of phallic fantasy to explain his own story 'Late Spring' ('Can Chun'): 'In a dream M and S met on Mount Pen-Upright, which was a dream-manifestation of the desire he had not been able to satisfy during the day.' (Ibid. 89).

But most May Fourth writers were more familiar with Havelock Ellis than Freud who, after all, was by that time not yet widely accepted even in psychological circles in the West. The abridged version of Ellis's gigantic Studies in the Psychology of Sex had at least three translations in China. Zhou Zuoren said that after reading Ellis's book in its 7-vol. original he suddenly felt that he had been awakened: 'This was my revelation. I felt that the scales covering my eyes all dropped away, and I came to a good understanding of society and life.' (Zhou Zuoren 1980: 108).

If we remember that Ellis's great book was banned by the British courts at the time, and accessible only to medical professionals, we can understand how closely the May Fourth writers were following the developments in the West.

since it is given to you by your parents'. Self-reproach makes his
hypochondria more serious, and leads to his final collapse. Commenting on this type of theory, Shen Yanbing picked a phrase from another
story of Yu's—'the anxiety for good and the agony resulting from
desire for evil', and held that this was the 'common sentiment of all
modern youth.' (WXXK, Aug. 1, 1922). This feeling of norms lost, of
being caught in the conflict between the old and the new results in an
overwhelming sentiment of melancholy.

Feng Zhi in an article recalled that it was the melancholic note in Lu
Xun's stories that struck him and other young people of the time:

The fiction works that we [members of The Sunk Bell Society] discussed most
were not *The True Story of A Q* or 'New Year's Sacrifice' though they may be
the most profound of Lu Xun's works. We sympathized more with Lu Weipu
of 'In the Tavern', Wei Lianyu of 'The Misanthrope', and Juansheng in 'Regret
for the Past'.[49]

This can be confirmed by Lu Xun's own admission: 'Excessive melancholic sentiment is common to intellectuals, I have too much of it, and
perhaps shall not be able to free myself from it in the rest of my life.'[50]

Melancholy permeated May Fourth fiction. The first line of Yu Dafu's
celebrated 'Chenlun' runs 'Lately, he had been feeling lonely, pitiably
lonely.' In Yu's another story 'A Night Too Long', the protagonist
(with the name Zhifu reminiscent of Yu's own name) finds everything
saturated with sorrow: 'the Fatherland on the verge of collapse, mankind
on the verge of extinction, the night that seems unending, the autumnal
star that is so far away, are all seeds of sorrow.' (CL, 121) And in an
essay entitled 'A Feeble Sound in the Northern Country' ('Beiguo de
Weiying') Yu offered a curiously modern, even existentialist explanation
for this almost self-destructive melancholy: 'The desperate loneliness is
the only solid sensation we mankind can feel from birth to death.'
(CZZK, no. 46)

Almost all the May Fourth writers were given to sorrowfulness, though
writers of different temperaments offered different explanations. Chen
Fangwu, the outspoken apologist for romanticism, for instance, replied
to his friend Yu Dafu in an article 'The Spring News from the Southern
Country' ('Jiangnan de Chunxun'), 'You said that all actions are motivated by this feeling of "loneliness". I would rather say that revolt

---

[49] Feng Zhi, 'Preface' to *Chen Xianghe Xuanji* (*Selected Works of Chen Xianghe*),
Chengdu: Sichuan Renmin Chubanshe, 1980, 3.
[50] Lu Xun 1976: i. 533.

against this feeling of "loneliness" is the main motive force.' (CZZB, n. 48) Rebels or not, both of them are right in the sense that the tragic is part of the definition of the counter-culturality, as the deviant sector of the élite is alienated from the conventional social structure. The writers are left alone in the world, stripped of all normal or communal protection.

Thus, the self-expressive narrative mode finally enabled Chinese fiction to break away from the subcultural conformable and communal modes. The narrator no longer acts as a historiographer, nor poses as moralizer, but becomes something of a memoirist and autobiographer. This makes not only possible but necessary the following narratological characteristics:

No longer conventionally semi-implicit impersonal, he ceases to be aloof above the narrated world but either sufficiently self-characterized to give himself a self to express, or sufficiently implicit so as to allow his characters to be self-expressive. As the conventional narrative set-up is dismantled, the narrator's commentaries, having lost authority over the characters and events narrated, are reduced to the minimum.

The varying forms of reported speech, the infrequent but never stereotyped stratification, and the effective use of character-focalization, facilitate the dissolving of rigid conventionality, so that the distribution of subjectivity could be arranged with greater freedom.

The well-preserved linearity of temporal mediation in traditional fiction is now replaced by highly elliptical, sectional and retarded narrative time. The dominance of dynamic motifs gives way to static motifs. As a result, the temporal-causal chain is likely to be shattered.

All these new narratological characteristics make May Fourth fiction a discourse fundamentally different from Chinese traditional fiction and can be said to be an answer to the need for the emulation of the self-expressive paradigm, which élitizes Chinese fiction, and even turns it into a serious challenge to the overall structure of Chinese culture.

When the narrator was dislodged from the controlling position in the narrative, taking a centrifugal move towards the isolated personalities, and when the dominance narratorial subjectivity yielded to the freer play of character subjectivity, the position of fiction in the Chinese discursive hierarchy moved out of its communal subculturalness. As this movement was not permitted by the signification system of Chinese culture, Chinese fiction turned itself into an essential part of May Fourth counterculture.

4

Western Influence on Chinese Fiction

I

One difficult issue for any serious study of late Qing fiction is foreign influence. At first glance this seems to be no problem at all as this influence is virtually omnipresent and undeniable. Yet since late Qing fiction is such a unique mixture of the old and the new, and since the traditional narrative features remained basically unchanged despite foreign influence, there has been much scholarly dispute over the extent and manner of the reception of this influence.

In the late Qing, the authors of the numerous essays calling for a revival of Chinese fiction all emphasized that fiction should play a major role in the development of society, since, as they saw it, it had successfully done so in Western countries and Japan. Liang Qichao said in his first influential essay on fiction 'Yiying Zhengzhi Xiaoshuo Xu' ('An Introduction to the Translation of Political Novels'): 'At the beginning of reform in every Western country, leading scholars and enthusiastic reformers often wrote fiction out of their own experience and their political opinions . . . Often when a novel came out, public opinion within the whole nation completely changed.'[1] Liang, however, did not mention the names of those 'leading scholars' who had so miraculously changed the fate of the nations with their novels.[2]

Although Western literature began to appear in Chinese translation much earlier,[3] it did not attract any serious attention until around 1900 when it began to be published in astonishing quantities. According to A Ying's statistics, among the 1,107 books of fiction published between 1882 and 1913, 628—almost two thirds of the total—were translations.[4]

[1] Liang Qichao 1941: Book 2, iii. 34–5.
[2] C. T. Hsia once suggested that one of Liang's role models might be Jean-Jacques Rousseau. In another essay he expanded the list to include Bulwer-Lytton, Disraeli, Voltaire, and some Japanese novelists-politicians, well-known at that time. (Hsia 1977: 78)
[3] Biblical stories were translated by Western missionaries into Chinese around 1740. In 1871 Wang Tao translated 'La Marseillaise', the first Chinese effort at literary translation. In 1872, part of *Gulliver's Travels* was translated, but it was in fact a sinicized retelling of the story. In 1888, Aesop's *Fables* appeared in a more or less faithful translation.
[4] A Ying 1937: 84.

This wave was ushered in by Lin Shu, the greatest translator of the late Qing, with his remarkable rendition of *La Dame aux Camélias* in 1889. Chen Xiying tells us 'a well-noted scholar said that the Chinese Revolution was brought about by two Western novels *La Dame aux Camélias*, and *Joan Haste*.'[5] Lin Shu's translations certainly gave these two novels a disproportionate influence.

In 1903 the first great year of literary output, forty-five translations were published, including Charles and Mary Lamb's *Tales from Shakespeare*, and Pushkin's *The Captain's Daughter*. But the most influential translated novels in the late Qing period were the following five: Harriet Beecher Stowe's *Uncle Tom's Cabin*, Walter Scott's *Ivanhoe*, Charles Dicken's *David Copperfield*, and the two we have mentioned, all translated by Lin Shu.

Nevertheless, as the translations were almost without exception tampered with in various ways, they became a problematic source of knowledge about Western fiction. The most serious way of tampering was to paraphrase the whole novel to make it a story with Chinese characters and Chinese background. The translator who most resorted to sinicized retelling was Bao Tianxiao, the leading Butterfly translator and writer, who continued to rewrite Western novels as late as the 1930s.

The purpose of this adaptation was to increase the readability so as to boost sales. Since in the late Qing period Chinese readers were not accustomed to reading Western drama, most translated Western plays were adapted into prose, e.g. Lin Shu's 'translation' of Shakespeare's *Henry IV* and Ibsen's *Ghosts*.[6] The predominance of direct reported speech in traditional Chinese fiction certainly made it easier to turn Western drama into Chinese fiction.

Almost all of these translations suffered from abridgement to a great extent. As in any abridgement, the dynamic motifs or passages were more likely to be retained (since the plot must be clearly told) while the static motifs were left out. With the dynamic motifs thus made dominant, Western novels became sketchy and speedy, and look more like Chinese traditional fiction. For example, the two volumes of *Don Quixote* were condensed to one slim volume in Lin Shu's translation. This led

---

[5] Chen Xiying 1928: 57.

[6] Sinicized Western drama not adapted into fiction, but adapted into plays with Chinese characters, played an important role in the initial development of modern Chinese drama in the early 1920s. Apart from Bao Tianxiao's numerous sinicized plays, Hong Shen's slightly sinicized version of *Lady Windermere's Fan* provided a great impetus to China's budding modern drama and film.

to a serious misunderstanding even among critics of fiction of the time. The following argument made by Xia Ren was obviously based on the impression he received from reading these translations:

Chinese novels are all voluminous. The more you read, the deeper you are engrossed. Western novels, even the best-known novels like *Robinson Crusoe* or *La Dame aux Camélias* are only booklets, less than one tenth the length of Chinese fiction. That is why readers are likely to be disappointed no matter how interesting these novels are.[7]

Another reason why abridgement was favoured during this period was that more than half of the translations used literary language rather than the vernacular. As a dead language burdened with cultural associations, the literary language was not flexible or 'innocent' enough to recast foreign narrative without colouring it with Chinese culture.[8]

The two trend-setters in late Qing translation, Yan Fu and Lin Shu, were also the last representatives of elegant prose writing in literary Chinese. They perhaps thought that turning foreign fiction into elegant literary language would strengthen the claim that these works of fiction were refined enough to be considered literature of high status.[9] Since most late Qing fiction writers wrote in the vernacular, Western fiction rendered in the literary language could hardly serve as a model, because vernacular fiction followed a set of narrative conventions entirely different from those of literary-language fiction. This is actually an important reason why the formal characteristics of late Qing vernacular fiction remained resistant to foreign influence.

As for the extra-textual conventions of Western fiction, punctuation was generally turned into simple dots in translation. Paragraph divisions

[7] A Ying 1960: 328–9. Italics mine.

[8] There are many jokes about literature translation at this time: the first Chinese translation (1903) of Pushkin's *The Captain's Daughter*, opens with a landscape description of Siberia: 'Those who have read Bao Zhao's *Verse on the Deserted City* could imagine the scene' and Mao Dun in his memoirs recalled that after he was recruited by the Translation Board of the Commercial Press in Shanghai, his superior added to his first translation—an English juvenile story—such things as tea-pot, ink-stone, incense-burner etc., to make the stationery on the young gentleman's desk more impressive. (Mao Dun 1981: 112–23)

[9] A Ying tells us that translation at that time was generally handled in the following way: the publishers hired both translators and 'polishers' for a translation project; the translators made draft translations, and let the 'polishers' who did not have to know foreign languages turn the drafts into elegant literary Chinese. (A Ying 1981: 234). Such a practice obviously followed Lin Shu's successful example, as Lin Shu did not know any foreign language. The literary gift that served as compensation in Lin Shu's case was lacking in other 'polishers'. Translations thus produced were unquestionably traitorous.

were generally ignored, making the texts resemble traditional Chinese fiction. Su Manshu was perhaps the first to preserve paragraph division in translation, and then used it extensively in his own fiction. Both his translations and his own fiction were in literary language, and his example was hardly followed by writers of vernacular fiction.

Sinicization in translation was not limited only to formal features. Zhou Zuoren in a speech made on 1918 bitterly criticized the late Qing attitude toward Western literature:

Western works did not attract much imitation, since translations were made not because the translators admired these works but because these works reminded them of Chinese classics. Walter Scott's novels were translated and recommended to readers because they resembled Shiji; T. H. Huxley's *Evolution and Ethics* was translated and admired because it was reminiscent of the pre-Qin philosophers ... They did not want to learn from foreigners, so they busied themselves in making foreign works resemble the Chinese. Such was the result of the motto 'Chinese Learning the Fundamental, Western Learning the Utilizable'.[10]

True to his observation, many translators in the late Qing tried to bring out the advantages of Western fiction by comparing them with the Chinese privileged genres: Lin Shu, for instance, declares in his marginal notes to *Ivanhoe* that its narrative techniques 'are similar to those of our classical essays (*guwen*) masters', or 'reminiscent of Neo-Confucianists of the Song'; while the plot composition in Haggard's *Allen Quatermain* was 'the same as that used by the great historian Sima Qian'.

Such strained form of comparisons became quite a vogue at the time. In the novel *Flowers in the Sinful Sea*, Saint-Simonism was compared to the Gongyang School of Confucianism, and Francis Bacon and Jean-Jacques Rousseau were compared to the Tang poet Li Bai and the Song poet-essayist Su Shi.[11]

Though such sinicization might make these foreign works more accessible to Chinese readers, it certainly emasculated their potential to blow the wind of change into Chinese fiction. It also had a sinister side:

[10] Zhou Zuoren 1980: 373.

[11] A comparatively minor but no less harmful practice in translations at that time was the sinicization of Western novel titles. Among Lin Shu's translations: *Dombey and Son* was retitled *Romance of Ice and Snow* (*Bingxue Yinyuan*); *She—The Charming Dead Body of Three Thousand Years* (*Sanqian Nian Yanshi Ji*); *Pêcheur d'islande* (by Pierre Loti)—*Waves of Tears in the Fishermen's Sea* (*Yuhai Leibo*); *Antonine* (by Dumas fils)—*Lovely Eyes as Fragrant Hooks* (*Xianggou Qingyan*). If most of those changes were obviously made for commercial reasons, changing *The Old Curiosity Shop* into *The Filial Daughter Nell* (*Xiaonu Nai'er Zhuan*) was definitely an effort 'to civilize the barbarians'.

if there was something in the Western novel which could not be justified by a reference to Chinese classics, or was morally offensive to the
Chinese ethical code or narratologically impalatable, a surgical opera-
tion was then called for. A typical case was the two translations of
Haggard's novel *Joan Haste*. The novel was first translated in 1901 by
Bao Tianxiao and Yang Zilin who, after praising the novel's great
merit, said that the second part of the novel was, to their great regret,
'nowhere to be found'. The translation was quite a success as a romance of idealized pure love. In 1905 Lin Shu translated the whole
novel, but he was soon vehemently attacked by many because in the
second part the titular heroine gives birth to an illegitimate son. Jin
Songcen, an important fiction critic of the period, criticized Lin Shu's
translation as a threat to the morality of Chinese society:

Now those young men who go whoring can declare, 'I am Armand' [hero in
La Dame aux Camélias] and dare to defy their father's prohibitions; those girls
who are degenerated could declare, 'I am Joan Haste,' and readily give up their
virginity . . . For the benefit of Chinese society, only Mr Bao's translation is to
be welcomed.[12]

Another critic, Yin Bansheng, was so carried away by his indignation
that his language became quite abusive: 'Since what the first translator
of *Joan Haste* wants to transmit is virtue, everything violating virtue is
dropped. What Mr Lin wants to transmit in his translation is nothing
but licentiousness, cheapness, and shamelessness.'[13]
   It is not accidental that the translators of the 'purged' edition and the
critics lashing out at Lin Shu belonged to the Butterfly group and specialized in sentimental romances or romances about prostitutes. They
were the natural inheritors of the basic moral paradox of Chinese subcultural literature.

II

How much does late Qing fiction owe to Western influence? This has
been a controversial topic since the beginning of this century. A Ying,
after a thorough study of late Qing literature, concludes: 'No matter
in what form, the majority of literary works of the time were directly

---

[12] 'On the Relations between Romance and the New Society' ('Lun Xieqing Xiaoshuo
yu Xin Shehui zhi Guanxi'), XXS no. 17 (June 1905).
[13] 'After Reading the Two Translations of *Joan Haste*' ('Du Jiayin Xiaoshuo Liang
Yiben Shuhou') *Youxi Shijie*, no. 11 (1907).

or indirectly influenced by Western literature. This was more than apparent.'[14]

Indeed many late Qing political novel writers and critics acknowledged that they were indebted to Western fiction, because they had to cite 'Western examples' on the capability of fiction to bring about economic and military reform. Their attention focused mainly on the propagandist effects of fiction. The artistic merit of Western fiction was always viewed with doubt by the Chinese literati, even by the late Qing translators. Lin Shu, for instance, undertook translation only as an opportunity to test his ability in elegant prose (*guwen*).[15]

Even this kind of moderate admiration for Western fiction subsided in 1907. It was no coincidence that at the same time a 'sober' estimation of the social function of fiction replaced the exaggerated promotion of the 'New Fiction'. Some critics began to complain that Western influence was excessive and harmful. In its publication note, the magazine *Chinese Fiction Circles* (*Zhonghua Xiaoshuo Jie*) edited by some important Butterfly writers, made a poignant remark about the vogue:

Our paramount intention is to save fiction from vice ... Since fiction became popular, its influence has penetrated into every corner of society ... Imitating the Western style, some people wear fancy hats and white robes to get married according to their own free will; worshipping the nihilists, some people carry guns or bombs and to assassinate in public ...[16]

They thought that Western fiction was to bear the blame for all the changes in society and none of the changes was good. Jin Songcen struck a more moralistic tone in his criticism of the 'Western wind': 'The wind from Europe has intoxicated so many people. I really fear that in several decades' time, the habit of shaking hands and kissing will be practised in Chinese society, and waltz will become so fashionable that people will ignore their job in order to learn dancing.'[17] Here, Western influence on social customs was ascribed to Western fiction,

---

[14] A Ying 1937: 80.

[15] Qian Zhongshu recalls an interesting incident in his essay on Lin Shu: in the early 1930s when Lin Shu was already dead, he talked with Lin Shu's close friend Chen Yan, who greatly deplored the fact that Qian, then a young student, was studying foreign literature, as he saw no merit in foreign literature comparable to that of Chinese. Qian told him that it was Lin Shu's translations that had aroused his interest in Western literature, upon which Chen said angrily, 'This is totally wrong. Lin Shu, if he knew that, would not be glad. In reading his translations, what you should do is to admire and learn from his elegant prose in literary Chinese. How could you, on the contrary, admire the foreign originals?' (Qian Zhongshu 1981: 32).

[16] A Ying 1960: 174.   [17] Ibid. 175.

which was regarded as the main culprit for the moral degeneration of Chinese society.

Many important figures of late Qing fiction seemed to be caught in a dilemma over whether to welcome or reject Western influence. Wu Jianren was a typical case. On the one hand he helped to found the Translation and Communication Society (*Yishu Jiaotong Gonghui*), and urged his friends to translate Western novels, for some of which he wrote appreciative prefaces. He even declared that his own story 'Preparing for the Constitution' ('Yubei Lixian') was 'an effort to make the readers believe that this is a translation', because Western fiction 'has a special charm . . . with many agreeable aspects'.[18] On the other hand he drew a clear demarcation line between himself and Western fiction by declaring, 'I always disagree with my translator friend as he is for importing foreign ideas and I uphold the old morality'.[19] On another occasion he launched an even fiercer attack on translated fiction: 'The enormous number of newly translated novels . . . are all blind repetitions. They (the translators) pursue only personal interests, totally neglecting their duty to the masses.'[20] Even though his novels such as *Strange Events* and *Nine Murders* were undeniably influenced by Western fiction in narrative technique, Wu Jianren consistently denied that he had learned anything from Western literature, accusing the translators of Western detective novels of 'discarding our strong points while worshipping the short-comings of the Westerners.' In order to correct this mistake, he wrote *Chinese Detectives* (*Zhongguo Zhentan An*) so as 'to gag those worshippers of foreigners.'[21] The surprising self-contradiction can only be understood as the manifestation of the anxiety of late Qing writers toward the changes that were taking place in their own writing. Even such seemingly insignificant 'utilizable' things as narrative devices in fiction could hardly be assimilated, for they would surely give rise to disruptive changes to vernacular fiction still in its traditional mode. No matter how much he had learned from Western fiction, Wu Jianren had to maintain a clear distance from it so as to preserve his habitual channel of communication with the reading public.

Thus we arrive at a conclusion: Western influence in the late Qing period was extensive but not decisive. It was limited by an inconvenient medium, by the reluctance of the readers, by the apprehension of the authors, and by the pragmatic attitude of the reformist critics. As a

---

[18] 'Introducing "Yubei Lixian"' YYXS 1, no. 2 (1906).
[19] Wei Shaochang 1982*b*: 85.   [20] Ibid. 132.
[21] *Zhongguo Zhentan An*, Shanghai: Guangzhi Shuju, 1906, p. vi.

result of such an attitude there was no sufficient driving force from outside Chinese culture to push late Qing fiction out of the Chinese narratological conventions.

III

Almost none of the late Qing fiction writers before the 1911 Revolution read foreign literature in the original. There were only a few exceptions: Liang Qichao knew Japanese, but he was too occupied with reformist propaganda to read much Japanese fiction. Though Zeng Pu knew French and translated Hugo, his knowledge of French was not enough for abundant reading.[22] Su Manshu is reported to be a polyglot, yet he led too precarious a life to make translating Western literature his career.[23]

Direct access to foreign sources, nevertheless, was not a decisive factor for the reception of foreign influence. The Butterfly fiction writers knew foreign languages better than the earlier late Qing writers, and many of the Butterfly writers were productive translators of Western popular literature such as romance and detective novels. The trouble with them was that they were too busy catering to the public demand to care for a serious study of Western literature.

In contrast to the situation in the late Qing, almost all the May Fourth writers started their writing careers when studying abroad,[24] and the generation after them were mostly students of foreign literature. The first generation of modern Chinese writers were, almost without exception, also the first generation of Chinese scholars of foreign literature. They did an enormous amount of reading in foreign literature, taking it as part of the preparations for their own writing career. Yu Dafu

[22] According to the short biography of Zeng Pu written by his son Zeng Xubai, Zeng Pu attended the Tongwen Guan (School of Foreign Languages) run by the Zongli Yamen (Foreign Ministry) in 1895. There were altogether two students of French, and three of English. None of them worked hard as it was not their knowledge of the foreign language that decided whether or not they would be able to enter the Ministry. The school itself did not last longer than a few months before it was closed. Later, Zeng Pu taught himself French during his convalescence from an illness. (Wei Shaochang 1962b: 159, 166)

[23] It seems that Su Manshu cared more about Western poetry than fiction, though he translated some fiction, including the first Chinese rendition of *Les Misérables* in collaboration with Chen Duxiu.

[24] Some May Fourth writers, e.g. Tao Jingsun, had stayed abroad too long, or had gone so deeply into foreign literature that they were not even able to write good Chinese. These were very rare cases, however. Most of them had received a solid training in the Chinese classics before they went abroad.

states that before he tried his hand at fiction, he 'had read about one thousand works of fiction by Russian, German, English, Japanese, and French authors'.[25] Lu Xun acknowledged 'what I have been relying upon is more than one hundred foreign fiction works and a little know-ledge of medicine'.[26] But his was undoubtedly an understatement. Ac-cording to Zhou Zuoren's recollection, during their four-year stay in Tokyo (1906–9), he and his brother (Lu Xun) devoted themselves to the study of literature and spent most of their time and money on fiction in Japanese, German, and English. The bookshop in Tokyo specializing in Western books had to order directly from Europe at their request since the books in stock were too few for their needs.[27]

It is easy to make a long list of statements made by the May Fourth writers about their reading, but what I would like to point out specifically is that, unlike the late Qing writers who were indiscriminate in receiv-ing Western influence (as can be seen in the awkward imitation of the detective story in *The Travels of Lao Can*, and in the large number of third-rate fiction works Lin Shu translated), May Fourth writers were very selective. Lu Xun acknowledged that 'the profundity of presenta-tion and the strangeness of form' of his early stories that shocked the Chinese literary circle was attributable partly to his reading of certain Western works.

But the reason for the excitement was in fact due to the long neglect of the literature of the European continent. As early as 1834, Gogol of Russia wrote a story, 'The Madman's Diary'. In 1883, Nietzsche had his character Zarathustra say: 'You have already walked the path from worms to men, but there are still many among you who are worms. You were once monkey-like, but even now many of you are more monkeyish than any monkeys.' And the ending of my story 'Medicine' has the coldness of Andreev.[28]

According to himself, Yu Dafu was influenced by foreign writing rang-ing from the newly emerging Japanese confessional fiction *Watakushi-Shosetsu*, to the *Erzahlungen* of Germany,[29] to the works of Edgar Allen

---

[25] Yu Dafu 1927: 25. He used the Chinese measure word *bu* which is ambiguous when denoting fiction—it may be 1,000 'books' or 1,000 'pieces'. No matter which, the amount was surprising.

[26] Lu Xun 1956: v. 246.   [27] Zhou Zuoren 1980: 234.

[28] Zhao Jiabi 1935: Volume 2 of Fiction, pp. i–ii. This was confirmed by his brother Zhou Zuoren who stated that when reading avidly in Tokyo before they started writing themselves, both of them were fond of reading Eastern European fiction. (Zhou Zuoren 1980: 89).

[29] Preface, *Yu Dafu Selected by Himself (Yu Dafu Zixuanji Xu)*, Shanghai: Tianma Shudian, 1933, 4.

Poe,[30] and to Jean-Jacques Rousseau.[31] His greatest admiration, however, seems to have been reserved for Turgenev who perhaps reinforced
the characteristic touch of melancholy found throughout his works.[32]
The other writers of the Creation Society seem to have been more
fascinated with some German short novels—Goethe's *Die Leiden des
jungen Werthers* and Storm's *Immensee*, both good models for the world-
weariness of over-sensitive young members of the gentry class.

Other writers had other preferences. Ye Shengtao, for instance, stated
repeatedly that the writer who pulled him out of the Butterfly fiction
was Washington Irving, who taught him 'to write more of the ordinary
men and women'.[33] Lao She's first novel, *Zhang's Philosophy*, was
strongly reminiscent of *The Pickwick Papers* and *Nicholas Nickleby*,
and he himself mentioned that he read much nineteenth-century English
literature before he had started his writing career.[34]

IV

Paradoxically, it was under Western influence that Regionalist fiction
(*Xiangtu* fiction) germinated in the May Fourth period. Lu Xun first
used the term to group a number of young authors:

All those writers who write about their minds become Regionalist writers, no
matter whether they claim their own approach is subjective or objective. As
viewed by the natives of Beijing, what they produce is exile literature, which
is different from what Georg Brandes called Exile Literature in that it is the
authors themselves, not their works, that are exiled.[35]

[30] A character in Yu Dafu's story 'The Evening When the Spring Breeze Was In-
toxicating' ('Chunfeng Chenzui de Wanshang'), very probably his surrogate, is said to
write stories *à la* Poe.

[31] Jean-Jacques Rousseau is largely responsible for Yu Dafu's sentimentalism. Yu
Dafu tells us that '*Les Rêveries du promeneur solitaire* was definitely the most profound
and most sentimental book. This is the cry of a wounded soul . . . No one who is lonely
could resist shedding tears for Rousseau or for himself when reading the book.' (BZJ,
78)

[32] Yu Dafu wrote in 1927: 'Among all the major and minor writers of the world, the
one whom I feel is the most lovable, the most familiar, and whom I shall never be tired
of though I have been reading him for long is Turgenev. This might be a personal
preference not shared by many. But it was no other than he, that giant of the northern
country with an amiable countenance, sad eyes and long beard, who aroused me to read
and write fiction.' (GQJ, 45)

[33] Ye Shengtao, Preface to *Ye Shengtao Xuanji* Xu (*Selected Works of Ye Shengtao*),
(Shanghai: Kaiming Shudian, 1952), 2.

[34] Wu Huaibin and Zeng Guangcan 1985: 54.

[35] Zhao Jiabi 1935: Volume 2 of Fiction, p. ix.

His last modification is a little difficult to understand. What Lu Xun
means, I think, is that the works of those Chinese writers do not focus
on their exile life in Beijing but the life in their hometowns which they
miss—the life of the peasants and small-town folk. The first example
he mentions is Xu Qinwen, one of his closest disciples and imitators,
whose first collection of short stories 'Hometown' ('Guxiang') obviously takes its title from Lu Xun's celebrated short story. It is of great
interest to see how Lu Xun's comments on this title: 'The fact that Xu
Qinwen named his first collection 'Hometown' is, perhaps without he
himself realizing it, an acknowledgement that he was a Regionalist
writer, and that before sitting down to writing Regionalist fiction, he
had already been expelled from his hometown and exiled.'[36] If this title
means so much, then Lu Xun is acknowledging that he himself is the
precursor of Regionalist fiction. Considering the huge number of May
Fourth authors who could be grouped under this heading,[37] it is safe to
say that Regionalist fiction is an essential component part of May Fourth
fiction.

Zhou Zuoren stated, 'I do not like regionalism in most things, but in
art I feel differently'.[38] Strange though it may seem, the Regionalist
trend of May Fourth fiction emerged under Western influence. At the
turn of the century, the European 'lesser nations' developed a powerful
nationalism in literature, with a strong local flavour. The winning of the
Nobel Prize by Henri Sienkiewicz further fuelled this trend.

We can see that even those May Fourth regionalist writers who felt
they had their roots deep in the Chinese soil were also profoundly
influenced by Western literature. Regionalist writers did not hesitate to
confess their indebtedness: Li Jingming and Jian Xian'ai owed much to
Sienkiewicz; Wang Luyan translated a collection of Sienkiewicz's short
stories, but felt more indebted to Nemerov the Bulgarian; Peng Jiahuang
expressed his thanks to K. Miksziath of Czechoslovakia; Xu Qinwen
was indebted to Chekhov; Li Qiye owed much to Andreev; Fei Ming
was inspired by George Eliot and Thomas Hardy, two English writers
who have strong local flavour. But it seems that Sienkiewicz had
more admirers than anyone else. His short novel *The Charcoal Sketch*,

---

[36] Zhao Jiabi 1935: Volume 2 of Fiction, p. ix.

[37] The May Fourth writers whom scholars of modern Chinese literature consider to be
Xiangtu writers include Xu Qinwen, Wang Luyan, Jian Xian'ai, Li Jingming, Feng Wenbing,
Huang Pengji, and other young writers dwelling in Beijing, and Peng Jiahuang, Xu Jie,
and others in Shanghai. They belonged to different coteries.

[38] Zhou Zuoren 1932: 84.

translated by Zhou Zuoren, was a continuous source of excitement for Chinese writers.[39]

This Regionalist fiction, mostly writing about the life of the peasants, was something new in China, and definitely not subcultural despite its 'socially low' subject-matter. It was an artistic expression basically belonging to the new *intelligentsia*. Before modern times, there had hardly been in China a truly regionalist literature. Regionalist colour existed more in orality than in literacy. Only oral narrative performance is locally divided. The few collections of folk poetry or local drama were intentionally preserved as expressions of orality, and kept at a distance from the established modes of literature. Though it is said that *Jin Ping Mei* is written in Shandong dialect, *The Scholars* in Anhui dialect, and *The Dream of the Red Chamber* in Beijing dialect, regional influence was limited to the use of some particular words. One reason is to be be found in the Chinese language which, because it is not phonetic, was a powerful unifying force that discouraged any local variations. But this is not the main reason, since the Chinese vernacular was much more flexible and capable of recording vivid local dialects such as the Suzhou dialect of Shanghai prostitutes in *Lives of Shanghai Flowers* and some prostitution novels in the late Qing period. In most of these novels, only the directly quoted reported speech of the prostitutes, who were after all culturally marginal people, was recorded in Suzhou dialect. The heroes, even when talking with these prostitutes, had their speech reported in good Mandarin.

Against the background of such a tight grip of Chinese culture over possible diversification, the rise of Regionalism in the May Fourth period was really significant. It indicates a powerfully decentralizing current.

V

May Fourth fiction was not very far behind the latest developments in European literary trends. Many writers of the time were fascinated with *fin-de-siècle* literature. Yu Dafu's first story 'The Silver Death' ('Yinhui Se de Si') was in fact a recasting of Ernest Dowson's life. The hero in the story, when found dead in the street, has in his pocket a volume of

---

[39] Many regionalist writers acknowledged their indebtedness to *The Charcoal Sketch*. Jian Xian'ai, for instance, recalled that, when young, he spent two weeks copying out the whole text of the novel by hand. In 1926 he bought the new translation. Ten years later he recommended it to readers again 'with an extreme passion'. This short novel seemed to be his life-long favourite.

Dowson's prose and poems, the only property he has left. When a story by Teng Gu was printed in *Chenbao Fukan* on 17 September 1925, there was an editor's note attached to it, possibly written by Teng Gu himself: 'All the works of Mr Teng Gu carry a flavour of decadence. He loves best the works of Symons and Gautier . . . He is neither as wild as Wilde, nor as eccentric as Gautier, since he only wants to use the decadent to show his revolt against the times.'[40]

Revolt, or a pose of revolt, was the key note in Western avant-garde literature, as May Fourth writers understood it. As a result, many heroes in May Fourth fiction bear a striking resemblance to the decadent heroes of nineteenth-century Western literature.

After reading Turgenev's 'Diary of a Superfluous Man' for the third time, Yu Dafu feels that each time he had 'gained more from it'.[41] In his short story 'Moving South' ('Nan Qian'), the hero is said to behave like this: 'All year round, he refused to talk with others, always sitting by himself in his bedroom and musing. The books he read were all by those who were defeated on the battlefield of life. He loved best James Thomson, Heine, Leopaldi, Ernest Dowson, and the like.' A clearer pronouncement of Yu Dafu's affinity with the Western avant-garde can be seen in his long essay of 1923, 'Class Struggle in Literature' ('Wenxue shangde Jieji Douzheng'),[42] in which he accuses naturalism (at that time the term was interchangeable with realism) as being 'incapable of demonstrating individuality to the full', and goes on to praise modernist writing in France (the decadence and nihilism of Baudelaire and Verlaine, the social protest of Maeterlinck and Rodenbach, the 'dolorism' of Duhamel), in Germany (the expressionism of Georg Kaiser, Fritz von Unruh, Ernst Toller, and others), and in Russia (the symbolism of Garshin and Blok). For, as he sees it, all these were writings of 'class struggle against the establishment'.[43]

In another of his essays, the realist methods of the nineteenth century are considered a 'blind alley'. Only by 'employing the innovative technique' of 'New Sensualism, Expressionism, and Psychoanalysis' is it possible 'to contract the breath of modern man, the panorama and the rhythm of modern life into literature'.[44]

---

[40] Quoted in Yang Yi 1986: 652.

[41] Yu Dafu 1927: 45.   [42] CZZB no. 3 1923.

[43] For English literature he had nothing but contempt, as he saw 'only stale air', with H. G. Wells and George Bernard Shaw offering 'false' socialism 'as a lullaby for the proletariat'. Only Jack London and Upton Sinclair had 'a little modern spirit'.

[44] 'Some Words about Fiction' ('Guanyu Xiaoshuo de Hua'), in Yu Dafu 1983: vi. 86.

A more telling proof of the closeness of May Fourth writers to the Western avant-garde is Lu Xun's preferences among Russian writers. Feng Xuefeng recalls an extremely interesting incident: in 1936 Feng was writing a preface for the Czech translation of Lu Xun's short stories. As a returnee from Moscow, he emphasized that Lu Xun was influenced by Tolstoy and Gorky, the two 'masters of realism' canonized by Soviet ideologues. Lu Xun crossed out the two names, saying, 'They had little influence on me. It was Andreev who exerted some influence.'[45]

If we examine Lu Xun's works carefully, we find that all his life he kept mentioning four Russian writers far more than others—Dostoevsky, Garshin, Andreev, and Arzhibashev. These four form a continuous line of Russian decadent fiction, with the first as the path-breaker. The last two left Russia and went into exile after the 1917 Bolshevik Revolution.[46] Arzhibashev was condemned by Gorky and Vorlosky (an active diplomat-critic in early Soviet years) as individualist, decadent, and hedonist, a verdict with which Lu Xun agreed, as he himself once remarked that Arzhibashev was 'world-weary, egocentric, and often carnal'.[47] The condemnation of Soviet ideologues did not stop him reading, translating, and loving the works of those decadent Russian writers.

This affinity between May Fourth fiction and European Modernism has been noticed by some critics. Prusek finds that 'what then arose in China was certainly in its essence closer to modern European literature after the First World War than to the literature of the nineteenth century'.[48] This is not very exact as we have found in May Fourth fiction more influence of Western modernism around the turn of the century, than of the post-war Modernism represented by James Joyce, Thomas Mann, Virginia Woolf, and others. But Prusek is correct in pointing out the closeness between the two fictions.[49]

[45] Feng Xuefeng 1981: 15.

[46] The profound influence on Lu Xun of these 'decadent' Russian writers has not received sufficient study. Hanan (1974: 53–96) provided a detailed comparison of Andreev's *A Red Laugh* (which Lu Xun began to translate as early as 1909 but did not finish) and Lu Xun's 'The Madman's Diary'. Sun Fuyuan tells us (1980: 72) that Andreev's story 'Toothache' (translated by Lu Xun's brother Zhou Zuoren) inspired Lu Xun's 'Medicine'.

[47] Lu Xun 1956: vi. 234.   [48] Prusek 1980: 56.

[49] Chen Pingyuan arrives at a more startling conclusion: 'The fiction produced by May Fourth writers was more "modernized" than the Western fiction works translated into Chinese at the time.' (Chen Pingyuan 1988: 14). What he wanted to say was that Chinese fiction could have been modernized without the influence of Western fiction. I think that Chen is correct in his observation that Chinese fiction was in closer contact with the latest Western fiction than a list of the translations of the time might demonstrate, as translators generally feel safer in translating already established authors.

Thus there is a basic difference between the late Qing reception of Western literature, which had sinicization of the foreign elements as its main concern, and May Fourth literature, which took the modernization of Chinese literature as its central issue. 'To make Chinese literature part of world literature' is the ideal shared by many May Fourth writers. The publishing editorial of the magazine *Literature Every Ten Days* (*Wenxue Xunkan*) run by the Literary Study Society States: 'We regret to say that we, who speak Chinese, are farthest from the mainstream of world literature. We have not contributed anything, nor have we benefited from it in any manner . . . To be isolated from world literature is to be cut away from the spirit of mankind. This is indeed our disgrace and great loss.'[50]

It was Yu Dafu who most explicitly endorsed the slogan of 'Chinese literature going to the world'.[51] In the mind of the May Fourth writers, the absorption of many European literary works did not mean the submergence of May Fourth Chinese fiction in European literature. Instead, it was to bring Chinese literature to the mainstream of world literature.

The metaphors used by late Qing writers and May Fourth writers on this issue show an interesting contrast: in 1902, Liang Qichao said, 'The twentieth century will be the time for the marriage of the two civilizations . . . The Western beauty will surely give birth to a lovely baby to make our lineage stronger.'[52] Twenty years later, Wen Yiduo used a similar metaphor when he praised Guo Moruo's poetry collection *The Goddesses* (*Nushen*) as 'The lovely baby from the marriage of Chinese and Western art' (CZZB, no. 4). Liang's metaphor, China-centring in the guise of male-centring, betrays a condescending attitude, whereas Wen's metaphor shows much more the confidence with which Chinese literature could now meet Western literature.

VI

The term *Quanpan Xihua* (Wholesale Westernization) was first invented by Hu Shi in an article written in English for the 1929 issue of the American journal *Christian Year-Book*, after the May Fourth period had already ended. Ever since then it has caused a long and bitter controversy in China, and evoked more emotional response than judicious

[50] Zhao Jiabi 1935: Volume of Historical Documents, 82.
[51] *Hongshui*, 2, no. 13 (1926).   [52] Liang Qichao 1941: iii. 67.

discussion. Hu Shi, regretting his use of the term, tried in 1935 to replace it with '*Chongfen Shijiehua*', which used to be translated as 'sufficient internationalization'.[53] Hu Shi's new term is a partial improvement, as in the original term the word 'wholesale' is really too absolute, and unnecessarily provocative. What is more, a wholesale cultural transformation is impossible, as no culture can be totally replaceable as long as the nation remains. But the second word 'Westernization' is by no means a misnomer, and there is no point in changing it to the euphimistic 'internationalization', only for the purpose of avoiding hurting national pride. If we let Hu Shi's two terms collapse into one—*Chongfeng Xihua* (sufficient Westernization), we then can see better that Hu Shi was trying to sum up a trend which had lasted for almost fifty years by the time he made the statement, and which should be considered as the most crucial issue in the history of modern China.

Among the opponents of Hu Shi's stand, some are for modernization without Westernization, while some others are against modernization with or without Westernization. Hu Shi and people like him are actually supporting a modernization through Westernization.

I understand that this is too broad an issue to be dealt with in this book—modernization is a notorious word with a multitude of fuzzy edges. What I intend to discuss in this book is whether Chinese fiction needed a certain degree of Westernization at the time of May Fourth, or, since this Westernization actually happened, as we have seen above, how to evaluate it.

Prusek and Dolezelova-Velingerova seem to be advocates of the first attitude—modernization without Westernization—as both of them maintain the theory of 'natural growth'. They argue that Chinese fiction has modernized, or could have modernized, itself without Western influence. Milena Dolezelova-Velingerova insists that the technique of late Qing fiction was more advanced than literary historians usually agree, and that the advancement was due not to Western influence but to the natural growth of Chinese fiction itself. She draws the following interesting conclusion from an exhaustive study of late Qing fiction:

[53] The term *Shijiehua* differs slightly from the English word 'internationalization', which sounds too political and is the equivalent of the Chinese phrase *Guojihua*. A better translation might be 'globalization'. Cyril Birch, in personal communication with me, expressed dissatisfaction with the translation of the word *chongfen*, suggesting that the English equivalent should be 'adequate'. So Hu Shi's new term could be translated as 'Adequate Globalization'. In this book, however, I shall retain the already established translation so that my argument will not be regarded as being based only on a different semantic interpretation.

Western literary technique, such as the first-person narrator or the inversion
of narrative time, was introduced only because Chinese fiction had developed
similar techniques or had evolved to a stage where the integration of the element from outside was only completing the previous evolution.[54]

This is actually an extension of the Prusek proposition I quoted in
Part I—i.e. Chinese fiction would have by itself been undergoing a
process of subjectivization, which had already been developed in the
great masterpieces of the eighteenth century.

For Prusek, the source of subjectivization within Chinese culture was
Chinese poetry. Dolezelova-Velingerova identifies another 'internal'
source of evolutionary motivation force in Chinese vernacular fiction—
literary-language fiction. She put forward an unflinching argument: 'The
importance of the late Qing period to the modernization of fiction should
not therefore be sought in the process of Westernization. Rather, the
period should be seen as the culmination of the long and complex
interaction between *Wenyan* [literary language] and Baihua [vernacu-
lar] fiction.'[55] This is an acute observation. May Fourth fiction did push
Chinese fiction up the discursive hierarchy to the level of the literati
genres by freeing Chinese fiction from the bondage to subculturalness,
and the self-expressive paradigm which used to belong to those genres
is now effectively implemented in fiction. But since the great achievements of Chinese fiction in the eighteenth century did not stop Chinese
fiction from sinking deeper into narratological conventionality, how can
we be sure that elements of subjectivization, already long existent in
poetry and in literary-language fiction, would have been able to pluck
Chinese vernacular fiction out of its communal mode by the time of the
1920s? Since resorting to literary language did not prevent Butterfly
fiction from slipping back into the subcultural communal mode, how can
we be so sure that Chinese vernacular fiction could have modernized
itself without a motivation force from without? We must remember that
Butterfly fiction survived even the drastic cultural disturbances occurring
in the first half of the twentieth century without becoming modernized
apart from some very superficial changes.

I submit that narratological characteristics and personalization of the
narrators are symptomatic only of the general cultural status which,
after all, is ultimately decisive in the narrative mode. It would not have
been possible for Chinese fiction to move out of its basic traditional

[54] Dolezelova-Velingerova 1984: p. xiv.
[55] Ibid. p. xv. Italics and notes in brackets mine.

subcultural position into the counter-cultural position if it had not been
for the general cultural crisis.

VII

Let us return to the examination of the process of 'modernization' in
Chinese fiction early this century, to see how the European influence
played its role in transforming Chinese fiction from a subcultural discourse into a counter-cultural discourse.

Tan Sitong's *Ren Xue* (A Treatise on Benevolence) has all along been
praised by all kinds of revolutionaries for its vehement condemnation
of the old social structure, and praised by today's critics of Westernization (Y. S. Lin, for instance)[56] for having re-affirmed the basic concept of Confucian ethics as the central issue of a Chinese cultural
revival. However, there was not much difference between Tan Sitong's
stand and Liang Qichao's.[57] The same was true of Kang Youwei's
efforts to return to what he thought were the real Confucian texts before
the 'Han fabrication', and his combination of this 'original Confucianism' with his promotion of Western constitutional monarchy.

The same attitude can be observed in late Qing fiction, where the
conventionalized narrative situation and the stereotyped personality of
the narrator were retained, while accepting many of the devices of
Western fiction. This was a kind of Westernization, but was insufficient

[56] Yu-sheng Lin (1979: 34–5) claims that Tan Sitong's *Ren Xue* offered an ideal
answer as to how to preserve the basic principles of Confucianism and traditional Chinese culture in a time of cultural crisis: 'Tan stated in 1894, "How can one blame
Confucianism for being useless? What is used today is by no means Confucianism." This
suggests that he was basically oriented toward a creative transformation of Confucianism
even before he began to work on *Ren Xue*, where his negative attack on *li* [rites] was
directed toward a positive reconstruction of the traditional Confucian vision of morality.'

[57] Liang Qichao recalls his attitude toward the relationship between modernization and
Westernization around the turn of the century:

To put it in simple terms, at that time we held that nothing of Chinese learning since
the Han Dynasty was any good, and that Western thought was all good. Since there was
nothing good from the Han time on, the only Chinese texts we read were the originals
of the Confucian Scriptures and the pre-Qin philosophers. Since everything foreign
was good but we did not know foreign languages, the only thing we could do was to
delve into some Western books translated by missionaries, added with some of our
own ideals. Quasi-religious, quasi-philosophical, quasi-scientific, and quasi-literary,
such were our new but naïve ideals. The New Learning (*Xinxue*) we flaunted was a
mixture of these three elements. ('In Memory of Mr Xia Huiqin' ('Wangyou Xia
Huiqin Xiansheng'), in Liang Qichao 1941: xliv. 18–23)

Liang wrote these words many years after the late Qing, in repentance over adolescent
follies, so the wording was markedly exaggerated.

as proved by the history of Chinese fiction. Soon the time called for another degree of 'sufficiency'. If we review the statements made by May Fourth writers out of the context of the controversy of the times, we might find them naïvely extreme.[58]

Lu Xun's advice to aspiring young writers was 'Do not read Chinese books'.[59] Shen Yanbing (Mao Dun) recalled in an article written in 1936 for high-school students, 'At one time I believed that the old fiction was completely useless to us ... and I still doubt its usefulness today.'[60]

In contrast, May Fourth writers turned to Western literature for new ideas. Wang Tongzhao insisted emphatically: 'I think that in our present situation, in order to bring more force and profundity to our writing, our studies should follow the principles: 1. Read more works by Western writers; 2. Study more works on basic theory and critical approaches to literature.'[61]

Of the moderate right-wing May Fourth writers, Chen Xiying declared, 'We have to read, but not necessarily read Chinese books,'[62] and Hu Shi used no less emotive words than Lu Xun to express the May Fourth writers' harsh criticism of Chinese culture:

I tell you people with all frankness: I believe that there are many old ghosts who are able to eat or bewitch people, and that they are more harmful to people than the pathogenic bacteria discovered by Pasteur; and I believe that though I am unable to sterilize bacteria, I am capable of 'catching the ghosts', and 'beating the demons' ...[63]

This radical refusal of Chinese culture and Chinese fiction by the May Fourth generation has come under attack by many Western and Chinese scholars since the 1950s. A typical critique is provided by Hsia. I shall quote Hsia's stern denunciation verbatim because he is the most outspoken in blaming modern Chinese literature (including May Fourth literature) for the damage it has done to the 'Chinese mind':

[58] e.g. Qian Xuantong calls for 'putting away all Chinese books': 'In order to discontinue Confucianism, and eradicate Taoism, the only method is to put away all Chinese books. Why? Because ninety-nine per cent of Chinese books are of these two kinds, and Chinese literature has all along been a tool to propagate Confucian doctrines and Taoist nonsense ... None of these texts is useful to the new era of the 20th century.' After that he concluded that Chinese characters could now be done away with since there was no more use for Chinese written texts. (XQN 4, no. 4 (1918).)

Qian Xuantong's stand on the Chinese classics sounds impractical even today. But in comparison with the call of Wu Zihui, the leading ideologue of the Kuomintang—'throw all Chinese books into the cesspool'—his was not the most extremist one.

[59] Lu Xun (1956): iii. 78.

[60] 'On My Own Study' ('Tan Wode Yanjiu'), *Zhong Xuesheng*, no. 61 (1936).

[61] Quoted in Zeng Xiaoyi (1985): 342.   [62] Chen Xiying 1928: 285.

[63] Zhao Jiabi (1935): Volume of Theory, 229.

In discarding the traditional religious safeguards and in feeding upon Western positivism, the modern Chinese mind has become increasingly rationalist and increasingly coarsened ... The superficiality of modern Chinese literature is ultimately seen in its intellectual unawareness of Original Sin or some comparable religious interpretation of evil ... In view of the absence of tragedy in traditional Chinese drama and of the strong satiric tradition in Ming and Qing fiction ... one may legitimately wonder whether the study of Western literature has in any significant manner enriched the spiritual life of the Chinese.[64]

As Hsia sees it, the 'absence of tragedy', the neglect of Original Sin or religious interpretation of evil makes learning from Western literature a hopeless task (thus Westernization is *impossible even if the Chinese want it*), and 'the discarding of the traditional religious safeguards' increased the damage of 'feeding on Western positivism' (thus Westernization, *already in practice*, has caused great damage).

We can see that both Hsia and Prusek, the former an unequivocal conservative and the latter a forthright 'progressive', both often engaged in fierce argument, have arrived at virtually identical conclusions: learning from Western literature is unnecessary and has not done much good if not yet inflicted irreparable damage, to Chinese fiction. To deny the benefit of Western influence seems to be the vogue among most scholars of modern Chinese history today.[65]

Another important point in Hsia's critical evaluation of May Fourth fiction is that it was too 'rationalist'. I assume that by this he means that there was too much realism in it.[66] There is indeed a powerful realism in the May Fourth fiction, yet, as I suggested before, it was not the most influential trend in this period. Certainly May Fourth fiction as fiction tends to be less 'realistic' compared to that of the previous periods. Even if we ignore the statements by those confessed anti-realists like Yu Dafu, the leading critic and literary theorist of the period Shen Yanbing insisted in 1921:

[64] Hsia 1971: 504.

[65] In this book I cannot deal with what I call the Neo-Conservative Trend among Chinese intellectuals in the recent years. I have written on this topic in several essays, e.g. 'Xinchao Wenxue: Wenhua Zhuanxing Qi de Chun Wenxue' ('New Wave Literature, A Pure Literature in a Cultural Reorientation Period'), *Jintian*, no. 1 (1991), 83–93. I shall offer a more systematic discussion in a long essay that I have been preparing.

[66] On this point, Prusek again seems to echo Hsia in his criticism of May Fourth fiction, only changing 'rationalist' to 'factual': 'I think that this clinging to the fact, this unwillingness to get away from the specific, individual reality, is perhaps the most striking, and, at the same time, the most noteworthy feature of the new Chinese literature linking it with the old.' (Prusek 1980: 91). Recalling his insistence that May Fourth fiction was nearer to post-World War I European literature, we can see that there is a self-contradiction in Prusek's argument.

Realism is only a passage in the evolution of literature, not the ultimate goal of literature. . . . New Romanticism[67] is definitely a superior method of writing.[68]

The only literature that can help the new thinking must be the literature of New Romanticism. The only literature that can lead us to a correct view of life is that of New Romanticism. Therefore the literature of the future is a literature of New Romanticism.[69]

More than half a century later, in his late years, when he recalled his life during May Fourth period, he still acknowledged, 'I did hold that the translation of the literature of realism and naturalism was necessary. But I firmly opposed any promotion of it . . . I held that New Romanticism was what was needed by the new Chinese literature.'[70]

This repeatedly stated stand of his was echoed by many leading May Fourth writers. Lu Xun took a definite turn towards symbolism with his prose-poem collection *Wild Grass* (*Yecao*). We find in his early fiction more influence of 'decadent writers', as I discussed above. His approval was not only demonstrated by his translating of *Symbols of Agony* (*Kumon no shocho*), Kuriyagawa Hakuson's advocacy of symbolism in literature, but by his using it as the textbook for his course in Beijing Normal University. Indeed we do not find any serious critical effort endorsing realism before 1925.

It is more than obvious that May Fourth fiction took a big step back from the late Qing obsession with factual reality, with the representation of objective truth of the society, and with immediate political issues. In comparison with late Qing fiction, May Fourth fiction is certainly less in accordance with the basic requirements of realism.

VIII

We cannot help noticing that there is a basic paradox in the May Fourth writers' attitude toward Chinese culture. Their advice 'not to read anything Chinese' is not to be taken literally. It was meant more as as a

<hr>

[67] This term is hardly used now. Between 1910 and the early 1920s it was much used by continental European critics, and by May Fourth critics too, to describe all the new movements since the late 19th cent., i.e. the various trends of Modernism.

[68] *Zhongguo Wenxue Bianqian Shi* (*The Evolution of Chinese Literature*), Shanghai: Xin Wenhua Shushe, 1921, 87.

[69] 'Wei Xin Wenxue Yanjiu zhe Jin Yijie' ('A Suggestion for Students of New Literature') *Gaizao*, 3, no. 1 (1921).

[70] Mao Dun 1981: 242.

gesture as it did not apply to the proponents themselves. Lu Xun was one of the most learned scholars in Chinese traditional literature in modern China, and his *A Brief History of Chinese Fiction*[71] is still considered the best work in this field after more than half a century. He and Yu Dafu are regarded as the two greatest modern poets of the classical form. As for Hu Shi and many who followed him, they devoted their whole life to a critical reappraisal and reinterpretation of Chinese culture using Western analytical methods. In early 1920, the movement 'Re-Examining Chinese Cultural Heritage' (*Zhengli Guogu*), with Hu Shi as the leader, was already in full swing, mustering a large number of students from whom emerged a whole generation of new scholars well-versed in both Chinese cultural heritage and Western methodology. Chen Xiying, an admirer of Hu Shi, complained that because of Hu Shi's advocacy of the Re-Examination movement: 'The most obvious result of the New Literature Movement is the soaring price of old Chinese books. A set of 24 *Histories* used to cost 100 *yuan* a few years ago, but now costs 300 *yuan*.'[72]

If, as Hsia noted, tragedy was absent in Chinese narrative art, this was mainly ascribable to its subculturality. It was none other than May Fourth fiction that turned Chinese narrative art toward the tragic, and the exposure to Western literature certainly helped this process.

If Hsia's discussion is narrowed down to Chinese fiction *after* the May Fourth Movement, his argument may be on firmer ground. Unfortunately, he, and some other scholars of modern Chinese literature and culture, try to trace all the troubles of modern China back to the cultural criticism movement of the May Fourth period. As early as the 1950s, Hu Shi fell under similar attack in Taiwan when he was held responsible for throwing the first snowball with his 1917 proposal for a new literature that finally rolled into the avalanche of 'losing China'.

I think that all this springs from a misunderstanding of the nature of the May Fourth Movement which is basically a counter-cultural movement, and should be understood as such in order to do it justice. The best we can expect from a counter-cultural movement is that it renders the rigid old cultural structure flexible. The conflict between the counter-culture and the mainstream culture may develop in many different ways, but would definitely go in the direction desired by the counter-culture.

May Fourth fiction was fortunate in that it developed in the years

---

[71] *Zhongguo Xiaoshuo Jianshi* (1923–4). English transl. Lu Xun 1959.
[72] Chen Xiying 1928: 291.

from 1916 to 1925, when no one political force was able to dominate
China. The warlords were busy fighting for control of the Beijing
Government, and none of them was seriously concerned about ideology.
Neither the Nationalists, then the major opposition party, nor the group
of Soviet-influenced intellectuals was able to provide a set of feasible
policies for ideological leadership. The new intelligentsia, as a whole,
was left 'masterless'. The May Fourth Movement remained a non-
political movement of pure cultural criticism even after the political
incident in 1919 that gave it its name. The central magazine of the
movement, *New Youth*, vowed repeatedly that it would never allow
itself to discuss political issues, so as to maintain its stand of pure
criticism.[73] The various magazines run by young intellectuals generally
followed the example of pure cultural criticism. As for the numerous
literary magazines, they kept even more aloof from politics. As late
as the mid-1920s *Yusi*, supported by Lu Xun and many other May
Fourth leading writers, stressed repeatedly that it refused to discuss
politics.

Detachment from actual political issues is essential for a counter-
cultural movement. It is impossible for the practitioners of the counter-
culture to engage in political activities or the running of government
while claiming that theirs is still a counter-cultural movement.

In 1934, when recalling the May Fourth period, Mao Dun, now a
'proletarian' writer, offered a sharp class analysis of the cultural stance
of the May Fourth cultural critique movement:

The effort to debunk feudal ideas was apparent in the early years of the May
Fourth period. But what new culture should be constituted after the debunking?
There was no definite answer at the time . . . There was, however, a more or
less predominant attitude which was to 'diagnose without prescribing'. This
was not a solution since it was an escape from answering the problem directly.
But this attitude had a social foundation—it represented the consciousness of
the intelligentsia who were poorer than the upper classes but better off than the
lower classes.[74]

[73] *New Youth* abandoned this stand after 1920. In 1919 Chen Duxiu was arrested by
the Government for political activities, and imprisoned for three months. During his
imprisonment, members of the editorial board began to divide on whether they should
steer the journal toward politics. After his release, Chen was angry with the non-political
members, represented by Hu Shi, and decided to get rid of them by moving the journal
back to Shanghai, where the first issue of vol. 8 (May 1920) carried an editorial declaring
that it was now a political magazine following the revolutionary principles of Marxism.
Soon after it became the organ of the newly founded Chinese Communist Party. For a
detailed discussion, please refer to Wang Xiaoming's essay 'Yifeng Zazhi he Yige Shetuan'
('A Magazine and a Coterie') *Jintian*, no. 3/4 (1991), 94–114.
[74] Zhao Jiabi 1935: Volume 1 of Fiction, p. iii.

Despite the doctrinaire Marxist terms he used, his observation was correct. The no-prescription attitude was typical of a cultural critique launched by young intellectuals who formed a counter-cultural deviant sector.

In any case, no counter-cultural movement could hope, or could be hoped, to remould the established cultural structure completely to its own design, otherwise it would cease to be a counter-cultural movement and become a 'natural growth' of the culture itself. To make it simpler, a counter-cultural movement cannot last long, and the outcome of the conflict is always a result of forces. In what fashion this result should take place depends more on the cultural system than on the counter-cultural criticism. It is hardly fair to heap all the blame upon the counter-cultural movement, as Hsia and other critics of May Fourth movement have been doing.

The tragedy of the May Fourth movement lies in the fact that while the cultural criticism of the May Fourth writers successfully kept the movement at the margins of Chinese culture, there appeared a cultural void at the centre, a lack of a valid interpretative system. The temptation to fall into the centrality, symbolized by the writers' participation in politics and by the impatient promotion of revolutionary literature, proved to be too great for many writers to resist. As a result, the counter-culture movement disappeared around 1925, replaced by the revolutionary actions to build a modern nation with weapons and such spiritual weapons like fiction.

If, in retrospect, we find that Chinese culture followed an unsatisfactory path after the May Fourth Movement, and the prospect it created did not come true, the cause might be found in the fact that, after the May Fourth Period, the counter-cultural movement submerged, or let itself become part of mainstream culture, willingly giving up its counter-culturalness. Nevertheless, by refusing to provide a solution to the social conflict, and keeping a distance from the control of a monolithic ideological dominance, May Fourth fiction successfully maintained its counter-culturalness for a certain period. This is a great contribution Chinese fiction made at a critical moment in the history of Chinese culture.

However, it is unlikely that a counter-cultural movement can maintain this stand for long, especially when the pressure for it to become ideologically committed is so high. Yet during the short period that May Fourth fiction withstood the pressure, it accomplished a task which no discourse at any other time could hope to accomplish—the loosening-up of the rigidly established cultural structure, thus creating the possibility of a cultural reorientation. What more can we ask?

After May Fourth

I

For as long as half a century after the May Fourth period a utilitarian and exemplary literature dominated in China. This ideologically committed literature claimed itself to be both 'revolutionary literature' and 'realist literature', though there has never been a satisfactory proposal to reconcile the two diametrically different terms. These are only euphemisms for a political utilitarianist literature.

This literature, seemingly new but quite traditional in discursive mode, started in the last years of the 1920s when May Fourth literature took a sharp turn from its original course. The Revolution of Literature (*Wenxue Geming*) was forcibly pushed into a Literature for the Revolution (*Geming Wenxue*). The new motto was first put forward by the early communist ideologues Yun Daiying, Deng Zhongxia, and Shen Zemin (Shen Yanbing's brother) in 1923–4. They called upon poets to 'engage in practical revolutionary activities', if they wanted to produce the poems needed by the time.[1]

But this call of theirs did not receive an enthusiastic response from writers as the proponents did not belong to literary circles, and could not produce influential works to support the call. The majority of important writers did not begin to incline toward the Literature for the Revolution until 1925–6, months after the incident of 30 May 1925 when British police shot Chinese demonstrators in the International Settlement in Shanghai. In 1925 Shen Yanbing wrote the essay 'Lun Wuchan Jieji Wenxue' ('On Proletarian Literature'), but he later admitted that it was a patchwork of English material on Soviet literature he had gathered, and the article was more a discussion of Soviet literature than of Chinese literature. In 1926 Guo Moruo published his essay 'Revolution and Literature' ('Geming yu Wenxue'), which is generally regarded as the manifesto about the change of direction of the Creation Society. His manifesto sounds not only naïve but arbitrary:

---

[1] Deng Zhongxia, 'Suggestions to the New Poets' ('Gongxian yu Xinshi Ren Zhiqian'), *Zhongguo Qingnian*, 10 (Dec. 1923).

There are two kinds of writings, both called literature: revolutionary literature and counter-revolutionary literature. *After making this point clear, all disputes on the problem should be resolved*, and our attitude toward revolution can be settled ... The only kind of literature we need is the literature of socialist realism which sympathizes with the proletariat.[2]

Yet there were still many May Fourth writers who kept their distance from this call to revolutionize literature. Lu Xun ridiculed the call bitingly:

The literary circle in Shanghai is preparing to welcome the envoy of Proletarian Literature. Everybody is saying that he is coming. I asked the rickshaw-man about the matter, and he told me that he has not sent any envoy. His class consciousness must be distorted. The class consciousness of the proletariat must be in the hands of someone other than the workers.[3]

Lu Xun seemed to be especially put off by the arrogance of the newly converted revolutionaries like Guo Moruo. In another essay, he was more pessimistic about the whole situation, as he protested angrily:

Revolution, Counter-Revolution, Non-Revolution.
The Revolutionaries are killed by the Counter-Revolution. The Counter-Revolutionaries are killed by the Revolutionaries. The Non-Revolutionaries are either killed by the Counter-Revolutionaries as Revolutionaries, or by the Revolutionaries as Counter-Revolutionaries, or by the Revolutionaries or the Counter-Revolutionaries as nobodies.
Revolution. Re-Revolution. Re-Re-Revolution, Re-Re ...[4]

Yu Dafu, who had at this time left Shanghai and his Creation Society friends there and became a close friend of Lu Xun in Beijing, sharply ridiculed the call for a 'proletarian literature full of blood and tears' with his short story 'Blood and Tears' in which he held that the slogan was not sincere. They collaborated in a satirical essay 'Geming Guanggao' ('A Revolutionary Advertisement'), in which Yu Dafu wrote: 'I know an unrevolutionary old man Lu Xun who ... told me not to walk into the cafe of another class. "Before going into any cafe", he said, "you have to make clear to which social class it belongs, to avoid making the tragical mistake of confusing the classes."' (YS, no. 33)

As late as 1927 Lu Xun still openly declared his doubt about the 'Literature for the Revolution'. 'Some people hold that literature is powerful in promoting revolution. I personally have always doubted

---

[2] CZYK 1, no. 3 (May 1926). Italics mine.
[3] Lu Xun 1956: iv. 345.   [4] Ibid. 189.

this, as literature is only writings for enjoyment after labour, though it is true that literature can be a representative of the culture of a nation.'[5] By that time his was perhaps the only voice left among the major figures of May Fourth literature who resisted being carried away by the turmoil of the political events—the Northern Expedition jointly launched by the Nationalists and the Communists. At that time, even Yu Dafu declared his identification with the proletarian literature.

II

Chinese fiction turned rapidly ideologically-committed immediately after the anti-Communist purge in 1927 which drove a large number of young revolutionaries out of the newly-established institutions. Their anger and frustration were expressed in the highly romanticized revolutionary novels produced by authors around the Sun Society (*Taiyang She*) and the reorganized Creation Society in the last years of the 1920s. This trend was soon reinforced by the world-wide 'Proletarian Literature' incited by the Depression devastating Western countries in the early 1930s, and the Soviet literature inspired by the apparent success of the first socialist state. But faced with the serious political crisis and the Japanese military invasion, Chinese literature would inevitably have become highly ideological or polemic even without the international backdrop.

To justify the new start, the theoreticians of the Proletarian Literature felt the need to depreciate the May Fourth Movement. Li Chuli wrote in 1928 'The cultural movement ten years ago was actually a conflict between capitalism and feudalism ... Mr Democracy and Mr Science are representatives of the capitalist ideology'.[6] In October 1931, in his important essay 'The Real Problems Facing the Proletarian Mass Literature' ('Puluo Dazhong de Xianshi Wenti'), Qu Qiubai, the Chinese Communist leader most concerned with literature, declaimed against May Fourth literature as being 'a bourgeois liberal movement of enlightenment', and he added 'We need a proletarian May Fourth which should be a proletarian, revolutionist, socialist literary movement ... a soviet revolutionary literary movement'.

There appeared later another argument which played down the cultural

---

[5] Ibid., v. 78.

[6] Li Chuli, 'How to Build Revolutionary Literature' ('Zenyang de Jianshe Geming Wenxue'), ed. Institute of Literature of the Chinese Academy of Social Sciences, *Geming Wenxue Ziliao Xuebian*, Beijing, 1981, 159.

criticism of the May Fourth Movement. Mao Zedong, in the early 1940s, tried to depict the May Fourth Movement more as a political movement than a cultural movement. 'As the May 4 Movement carried out precisely the task of opposing a government of traitors, it was a revolutionary movement.'[7] Therefore it was not a bona fide cultural movement. 'The May Fourth Movement, which turned into a movement for cultural reform, was but one of the manifestations of Chinese bourgeois-democratic revolution against imperialism and feudalism.'[8]

Beginning from 1927, the pressing need for a revolutionary literature became the hottest topic in literary circles. The members of the Creation Society and the Sun Society seemed to be the most eager apologists for this new literature. So often quoted was the statement 'All literature is propaganda', supposedly made by Upton Sinclair, that it became a truism in those years. Guo Moruo, for instance, declared, 'In this society, there is no such thing as personality or individuality'. Li Chuli contended that literature is 'the weapon of a class', and self-expression should be regarded as 'the spectre of idealism, the raving of individualism'.

In such a situation, few authors were able to hold to their individual stance and their belief in the independence of artistic activity. Take the leading author of the May Fourth period, Lu Xun, as an example: Lu Xun was regarded in the years from 1926 to 1930 by the apologists for Revolutionary Literature as 'the best agent for the bourgeoisie' and 'the most evil demagogue against the proletariat',[9] 'the stumbling block' on the road of revolutionizing Chinese literature. As we pointed out, he was openly against the 'Literature of Revolution' in 1926 and 1927. After the Nationalist Purge, he moved to Shanghai, and was relentlessly attacked by the already revolutionized Creation Society and the Sun Society as a backward writer. Lu Xun's attitude of diagnosis without prescription was considered most threatening to revolutionary literature. In his well-known 1928 essay 'The Dead Age of A Q', A Ying made the accusation that Lu Xun's mind 'stopped moving by late Qing' because he was 'only crying about dejection while refusing to find a way out. This is the poison with which Lu Xun killed himself.'[10]

---

[7] 'The Orientation of the Youth Movement' ('Qingnian Yundong de Fangxiang'), in Mao Zedong 1953: ii. 550.

[8] 'May Fourth Movement' ('Wusi Yundong'), in Mao Zedong 1953: iii. 545.

[9] Li Chuli, 'Please Look at the Farcical Dance of the Chinese Don Quixote' ('Qingkan Women Zhongguo de Don Quixote de Luanwu'), ed. Institute of Literature of the Chinese Academy of Social Sciences, *Geming Wenxue Ziliao Xuebian*, Beijing, 1981, 300.

[10] Qian Xingcun, 'Si Qule de A Q Shidai', in Ibid., 186–8.

Lu Xun stubbornly held to his stand and returned the attack with scathing sarcasm, but the label of 'backward old man' must have hurt him intensely as he used to play the role of the spiritual leader of the young people. He later recalled 'There is one thing for which I really must thank the Creation Society: they "forced" me to read some scientific theory of literature,'[11] as he wanted to outplay those aggressive young men at their own game. It was not the persuasion of Communist Party members that converted Lu Xun into an apologist of the proletarian literature; it was the situation that did not allow the proud man to justify his independent stand as he himself confessed in 1929: 'Since the 1927 revolution the room for speech is really too narrow: you are either a "radicalist", or a "reactionary".'[12]

This conversion was costly: the novelist Lu Xun disappeared, and his pen now was used solely to write the highly propagandist and polemic *feuilletons* and reviews. So far as we know, in the 1930s, on several occasions he planned to write novels, but none of the plans materialized. Though he was now the leading ideologically committed critic, he was unable to write fiction any more. Lu Xun tried to explain away, in his letters to friends, his discontinuation of fiction writing by such excuses as 'fatigue', 'low spirit', 'lack of freedom', or 'lack of time'.[13]

A more or less similar case is Yu Dafu, the other most outstanding fiction writer of the May Fourth period, and, like Lu Xun, a one-time opponent to revolutionizing literature. Yu's passionate temperament made his conversion to revolutionary literature less painful but also less lasting. As early as 1927 he announced his conversion to revolutionary literature in high-flown language.[14] But, again like Lu Xun, he never learned how to write revolutionary fiction and never intended to. In the politically eventful year of 1927, he wrote his most erotic short novel *The Lost Lambs* (*Mi Yang*), in which there is not a hint of revolutionary ideas, and in the same year split away from the revolutionized Creation Society. Though in 1930 he joined the Left-Wing Writers Association together with Lu Xun, he finally moved to Hangzhou in 1933 and gave up fiction writing, leaving the stage of Chinese literature for good.

[11] '*Sanxian Ji* Xuyan' ('Preface to the *Three Leisures*'), Lu Xun 1956: iv. 16.
[12] 'A Survey of New Literature Today' ('Xianjin de Xin Wenxue de Gaiguan'), Lu Xun 1956: vi. 78.
[13] Wang Xiaoming, 'Shuangjia Mache de Qingfu', ('The Overturn of the Two-Horse Cart'), *Purple Mountain*, no. 5 (1989), 170.
[14] 'Our complaint and hatred are the same as the complaint and hatred of the proletariat against the bourgeoisie; our joy or anger is the same as that felt by the proletariat.' ('Gongkai Zhuang Da Riben Shankou Jun', *Hongshui*, no. 30 (1927))

Totally opposite is the case of Shen Yanbing. As the leading literary critic of the May Fourth period, he never endorsed a literature of revolution, though he was one of the very earliest members of the Communist Party and responsible for propaganda work.[15] After he escaped arrest in the 1927 Purge, he resettled in Shanghai, and embarked upon a new career of a novelist, giving himself the pen-name Mao Dun. His fiction works in the late 1920s, almost all on the subject of the 1925–7 Revolution, were hardly revolutionary. In his novels the *Erosion* (*She*) trilogy and *Rainbow* (*Hong*), and in the short stories in the collection *Wild Roses* (*Ye Qiangwei*) there are no 'positive heroes', no indication of the correct road of revolution, no Marxist analysis of the classes in Chinese society. Much space is devoted to sexual relations among the revolution-inspired young people, and the frustration they experienced, not necessarily from the failure of the revolution. His first essay on literature in this period, 'From Kuling to Tokyo' ('Cong Kuling dao Dongjing') was, at that time, severely criticized as 'acutely opposing the Proletarian Literature'.[16]

Chinese left-wing literature came of age in 1932 with the publication of Mao Dun's novel *Midnight* (*Ziye*) which can be said to be Mao Dun's first attempt to apply Marxist class-struggle theory to fiction. The original design was an all-round class analysis of Chinese society, and the prediction of the victory of Chinese revolution. Fortunately, this plan of his was given up and the novel is limited to the life of the Shanghai industrialists, and the inevitable failure of this class sandwiched between the pressure from the Chinese proletariat and foreign capital. This novel remains the greatest achievements of modern Chinese fiction mainly because of his narrative talent.

Most typical works of the Proletarian Fiction, beginning with Jiang Guangci's *Sans-Culottes* (*Duanku Dang*, 1927), Hong Lingfei's *Exile* (*Liu Wang*, 1929), Yang Hansheng's *Fountain in the Earth* (*Diquan*, 1930), or the best among them, Ding Ling's *Water* (*Shui*, 1931) are hardly satisfactory as narrative art.[17]

---

[15] In 1925, for a short while, he was the secretary to Mao Zedong, then the deputy Director of the Propaganda Department of the Kuomintang in co-operation with the Communists. Neither he nor Mao seemed to like to mention the fact, for whatever reasons. Shen Yanbing wrote briefly about it only after Mao's death, in his last memoir. (Mao Dun 1981).

[16] e.g. the Editor's Note of *Chuangzao Yuekan* (*Creation Monthly*), 2, no. 5 (Dec. 1928).

[17] It is hard to say that the left-wing fiction came from the direct and careful planning and co-ordinated leadership provided by the Communist Party, though there were party

They finally brought an end to anything that May Fourth fiction had been. We can see that the individualistic self-expressive paradigm gradually lost its grip on modern Chinese fiction, and a communal mode set in again.

III

This whole process was inevitably reflected in the narratological characteristics of May Fourth fiction. We can get an idea of this from a single narratological feature in plot composition—the ending. In the early years, the May Fourth writers refrained from providing solutions. Theirs was a fiction of diagnosis without prescription, produced by rebels without a cause, at least without a clearly delineated cause. I can quote Yu Dafu's confession as a witness to this 'rebellion for rebellion's sake': 'The inclination to dissent and revolt is shared by everyone. It was this inclination that made Adam eat the apple. But modern men are even more inclined toward this. That is why we are likely to take action opposing what the others are doing.'[18]

Most fiction works remained open-ended after the clash of the characters. Hu Shi in his play *The Marriage* (*Zhongsheng Dashi*) lets his heroine, who defies the family-arranged marriage, leave triumphantly in her lover's limousine. This was laughed at by Lu Xun in a trenchant speech delivered in 1924 'What Happened After Nora Left Home',[19] in which he pointed out that society could not even be figuratively remoulded in art by such a solution, and that 'Ibsen was only writing a poem, *not raising a problem, let alone providing a solution*' (Italics mine).

In his own writing, Lu Xun remained the perfect 'diagnoser but not prescriber'. His only story on the sexual relations theme, 'Regret for the Past' (Shangshi, 1925), allowed the young couple who married for love to separate on account of the economic pressure. Lu Xun admits:

Since my stories are all 'Battlecries' [the title of Lu Xun's first collection], I had to obey the orders. That was why I added a wreath to the mound of Yu'er

members working among the leading bodies of various left-wing organizations, such as the group around Zhou Yang in the leadership of the Left-Wing Writers' Association. Their role seemed motivated mostly by their own enthusiasm in promoting Marxism for literature. There was still a certain freedom to state one's own interpretation of Marxism and to discuss related problems.

[18] 'Wenyi Jianshang shang de Pian'ai Jiazhi' ('The Value of Preference in Literature'), CZZB no. 14 (1923).

[19] 'Nala Chuzou Hou Zenyang', in Lu Xun 1956: i. 159–65.

in 'Medicine', and in 'Tomorrow', I did not want to mention that Shansi Sao
fails to see her lost child in her dream, since the general commander of the time
did not support pessimism.[20]

This 'general commander' could be Chen Duxiu, the editor of *New
Youth*. What Lu Xun did was still far from providing solutions but, as
he said, 'added a little touch of bright colour',[21] such as, for instance,
the wreath left on the beheaded martyr's grave. In this way, his open-
ended stories were made even more open as the 'little touch' was too
ambiguous to be a closure, only adding to the sense of tragedy.

As I mentioned in the previous part when discussing the structure of
plot endings, fiction works with and without end-solutions have entirely
different narratological structures. This might sound an exaggeration,
but I can cite the admission of the pre-eminent woman writer Lu Yin
to bear out this point. In her autobiography she declared that in the
early years of her writing career:

Because I was reading Schopenhauer and believed his words 'Human life is
nothing but a sea of bitterness', sorrow was in my very bones at that time. No
thought would come to my mind that did not have some tint of sadness ... I
did not want to resolve the sorrow, nor did I want to point out a new road for
others.[22]

But she began to change as the May Fourth movement evolved from
its earlier 'no-solution' period to its more solution-providing period.
She described how she passed from the first stage to the other:

In the past I felt sorrowful, but I did not want to resolve this sorrow; in the
second stage I was still dissatisfied with everything in the world, but I wanted
to resolve this sorrow; in the third stage, my dissatisfaction with the world and
my sorrow for life became deeper, but I found a way to overcome this sorrow
or dissatisfaction.[23]

Indeed she was praised by critics for 'turning firmly to realism' by the
end of the 1920s.

Many May Fourth writers sooner or later followed a similar path. Ye
Shengtao, who specialized in depicting the life of schoolmasters and
teachers, had produced excellent stories about their misery and spiritual
dilemmas. But in his 1926 story 'In the Town' ('Chengzhong') his hero,
a schoolmaster who heads the teachers' struggle for their unpaid salaries,

---

[20] 'Preface to *Battlecries* ('*Nahan* Zixu'), Lu Xun 1956: i. 419.
[21] Lu Xun 1956: iv. 348.   [22] Lu Yin 1934: 76.   [23] Ibid. 76–7.

comes to understand that in the end the only outcome is that 'We teachers must unite to settle accounts with them!' (CZ, 12).

With this change of attitude toward solution-providing, a new approach to different trends in Western literature was suggested. Decadence and other *fin-de-siècle* trends were now no longer respected. Shen Yanbing, who had firmly endorsed Modernism in early 1920s, turned his back on it in an essay 'On the Proletarian Art' ('Lun Wuchan Jieji Yishu') of 1925:

The true inheritance of the proletariat is the traditional literature, e.g. revolutionary romanticism and classics that are considered out-dated by the new schools. Why? Because revolutionary romanticism was the product of the bourgeoisie when it was in its ascension. It was the product of the healthy mind of a social class. What we should take as our model should not be the rotten and the perverse. Take Russian literature for example, the achievements of the masters of the past like Pushkin, Lermontov, Gogol, Nekrasov and Tolstoy should be cherished, and carefully preserved. Newly emerged schools such as Futurism or Imagism are of no use to us. (WXZB, no. 196)

This Soviet-invented guideline for returning to safe 'national heritage' while rejecting modernism was to be strictly followed by Chinese Communist Party ideologues throughout the following half century. It is understandable that Modernism was abhorred by the Soviet ideologues, as it is by nature a potential counter-culture which no established cultural order would like to accept, no matter how revolutionary the culture claims itself to be.

Why, then, should the Chinese left-wing writers who were still far from obtaining political power be afraid of Modernism? The main reason has to be found in the fact that traditional literature is more likely to provide a communal mode, while Modernist schools, against their Western and therefore reactionary background, are generally too individualistic for propaganda purposes.

IV

A programme for literature thoroughly controlled by the political party came into being during the anti-Japanese war, when Mao Zedong gave his speeches at the Forum on Art and Literature held in 1942 in Yan'an. The new line was, in fact, a natural growth in the anti-May Fourth argument of the 1930s, left-wing literary circles.

A time of national war is a difficult time for literature as the propagandist use of literature is undeniably justified. In December 1938,

Professor Liang Shiqiu suggested that it was still allowable to write on themes that had nothing to do with the anti-Japanese war.[24] He was deserted by everyone, even his liberal friends, in the ensuing dispute. The war certainly created an atmosphere in which extreme views were given a moral halo.

But Mao's speeches go far beyond the needs of war propaganda. He stipulates the fundamental principles in handling the relationship between the Party and men of letters, between political and artistic standards for judging the values of literary works, and put forward the demand that art and literature serve the cause of the revolution, as 'all art and literature belong to definite classes and follow definite political lines'.[25] All these can be said to be only an extension of the credos of 'socialist realism' laid down by Zhdanov for Soviet literature. But another point in Mao's speech, perhaps much more important, is uniquely his: to achieve an art and literature 'intended primarily for the workers, peasants and soldiers', it is imperative to use 'forms that the common people find pleasant to hear and see'.[26]

Mao ridiculed the former left-wing writers now gathered in Yan'an as 'people from the garrets of Shanghai' who knew nothing but the life of 'petty bourgeois intellectuals'.[27] Since they had cared little about the popular forms, they should now 'go among the masses', and think less of refinement than of popularization.

Mao's demand of a reversal of the development of Chinese fiction was implemented, and the 'Realist' trend of modern Chinese fiction took another abrupt turn. Many fiction writers began to write in the traditional mode, and works recovered traditional narratological features: semi-explicit narrator, omniscient focalization, tidy temporal sequence with a time-brimming scheme, abundant narratological intrusions, *ab ovo* beginnings with closed endings in plots, etc. In some works, even the 'Story-Teller' narrator and traditional chapter dividing formulas re-emerged. Narratorial unreliability became inappropriate since clear-cut value judgement and norm-sharing have to be ensured for effective propaganda. Apart from the events of revolutionary heroism, typical novels of the immediate post-Yan'an period, such as Zhao Shuli's *Li*

---

[24] Liang Shiqiu said in the Editor's note of the literature section of the *Central Daily* of 1 Dec. 1938, 'Works that have nothing to do with the War of Resistance, so long as they are genuine and graceful, they should be considered good literature. It is unnecessary to graft the War of Resistance onto them.' Quoted in Lan Hai *Zhongguo Kangzhan Wenyi Shi* (*A History of Literature in the War of Resistance*), Changsha: Hunan Renmin Chubanshe, 1984, 335.

[25] Mao Zedong 1953: iii. 867.   [26] Ibid. 864.   [27] Ibid. 877.

Youcai's Story-Telling (*Li Youcai Banhua*) or Kong Jue and Yuan Jing's *Lives of New Heroes and Heroines* (*Xin Ernu Yingxiong Zhuan*), read as if they were written in the late Qing, and this is exactly the effect they wanted to achieve. Even their titles are reminiscent of traditional Chinese fiction.

Post-Yan'an fiction, therefore, showed a distinct retrogression to the narratological conventions of Chinese fiction. This is a repetition of the situation in the late Qing period when conventionality is intentionally maintained to facilitate propaganda.

V

With the Communist victory over the whole nation in 1949, Chinese fiction was put completely under Party surveillance to ensure its strict accordance with the guidelines laid down by Mao in 1942. Yet it was a difficult task to deter aberrant tendencies, and criticism movements had to be repeatedly whipped up even before the nationwide victory was secured.

In the 1950s, the slogan 'to serve the workers, peasants, and soldiers' was replaced by 'to serve socialism', which sounds less restrictive but was actually more difficult to cope with as literature was now forced to illustrate whatever happened to be the Party's 'socialist' policies of the moment. Many authors fell victim to criticism campaigns because they offered their works as illustrations to certain policies which were later labelled as 'opportunistic' in the inner-Party power struggle. To be on the safe side, they became writers of 'Sing-Praise Literature' (*Songge Wenxue*) eulogizing the Great Leader and his cause. Almost none of the former left-wing writers was able to remain an active writer in the 1950s. 'Why can't you sing for socialism?' became a challenging question that those writers had to face in the numerous brain-washing movements, and the post-May Fourth writers of revolutionary fiction who had spent their lives in providing solutions in fiction were now overwhelmed by the solutions they had provided.

Not insignificantly, subculture was being liquidated in China during this period too, as truly subcultural discourses like folk-songs, folktales and local operas, in the process of collection, underwent serious tailoring by Chinese folklorists to meet the purist ideological demand. One of the craziest movements in the feverish 1958 Great Leap Forward was to make every member of the masses a poet writing eulogizing poems to the Party. With such an unreasonable politicizing of literature,

Chinese fiction was virtually brought to a halt in the mid-1960s, even before the Cultural Revolution turned the whole of China into a cultural desert.

This does not mean that the May Fourth spirit of cultural criticism has never appeared in any form in Chinese fiction since the 1950s. In 1956 and 1957, many young Chinese writers, together with more than half a million other intellectuals, fell into the trap of the Anti-Rightist Movement. Their fiction works were said to be anti-Communist, yet all we can see in those stories and short novels is an attempt to break from the guidelines mapped out by Mao long ago. Cyril Birch once made the sharp observation that the 'particular interest' of the works of those Rightist writers lies not in 'any cynical glee on our [Westerners'] part that they dig the dirt, nor even that they seem more real, less idealized, but that they seem specifically to be addressed to the cadre community rather than to the masses'.[28] Birch states that his conclusion is drawn not only from the content but from 'their complex language'. This possible narratological restart was, regrettably, nipped in the bud.

Another deviant trend from total Party control of literature was the underground literature of the early 1970s among young people who were culturally starved by the Cultural Revolution. These secretly cir-culated manuscripts belonged to either subcultural mode, e.g. porno-graphy, or to the counter-cultural mode, and were highly experimental fiction and poetry that became the embryo of the new Chinese fiction waiting for a thawing time, a new fiction that could resume the lost cause of the May Fourth fiction after more than half a century. The day finally came, not immediately after the end of the Cultural Revolution but in the mid-1980s, when the political excitement about Reform finally gave way to a sober re-evaluation of Chinese culture. The post-1985 New Wave fiction has shown all the typical signs of a counter-cultural movement, and has been functioning as such in the reorientation Chinese culture—but this interesting topic lies beyond the scope of the current study, and should be handled in another book.

[28] Goldman 1977: 396-7.

Glossary

A Q Zhengzhuan	阿Q正傳
A Ying	阿英
'All Will Be Past'	將過去
Ban Gu	班固
Bao Tianxiao	包天笑
Battlecries	吶喊
Bing Xin	冰心
Bitter Society	苦社會
Bureaucrats, The	官場現形記
Butterfly fiction	鴛鴦蝴蝶小說
Cao Xueqin	曹雪芹
Cases of Lord Shi, The	施公案
Chen Hengzhe	陳衡哲
Chen Sen	陳森
Chen Tianhua	陳天華
Chen Xianghe	陳翔鶴
Chen Xiying	陳西瀅
Chen Zhen	陳枕
Cheng Fangwu	成彷吾
Chenlun	沉淪
China Now	中國現在記
Chongji Qi Huashi	沖積期化石
Chuangzao She	創造社

Chuanying Lou Huiyi Lu	釧影樓回憶錄
Chuanzai Yuekan	創造月刊
Chuanzao Jikan	創造季刊
Creation Monthly	創造月刊
Creation Quarterly	創造季刊
Creation Society, The	創造社
Da Song Xuanhe Yishi	大宋宣和遺事
'Day, A'	一日
Deng Zhongxia	鄧中夏
Ding Ling	丁玲
Dong Yue	董説
Dongya Pofo	東亞破佛
Dream of the Green Chamber	青樓夢
Dream of the Red Chamber, The	紅樓夢
Duanku Dang	短褲黨
Duijing Kanhua Ke	對鏡看花客
Eight-legged essays	八股文
Ershi Nian Mudu zhi Guai Xianzhuang	二十年目睹之怪現狀
Fei Ming	廢名
Feng Menglong	馮夢龍
Feng Shen Yanyi	封神演義
Feng Wenbing	馮文柄
Feng Yuanjun	馮沅君
Fiction Every Month	月月小説
Fiction Forest	小説林
Fiction Monthly	小説月報
Fiction of Detection	公案小説
Fiction of Gods and Devils	神魔小説

Fiction of Private Life	身邊小説
Fiction of Prostitution	狹邪小説
Five Fully Illustrated Pinghua Tales	全相平話五種
Flower and the Moon, The	花月痕
Flower in the Sinful Sea, A	孽海花
Flowers in the Mirror	鏡花緣
Forgotten History of the Xuanhe Reign	大宋宣和遺事
Forgotten Texts of the Sui Dynasty	隋史遺文
Fossils of the Alluvial Age	沖積期化石
Frost in July	六月霜
Fu Ling	傅霖
Future of New China, The	新中國未來記
Gao E	高鶚
Geming Wenxue	革命文學
Golden Lotus	金瓶梅
Gong'an Xiaoshuo	公案小説
Gu Wen	古文
'Gu Xiang'	故鄉
Guanchang Xianxing Ji	官場現形記
Guo Moruo	郭沫若
Guoqu	過去
Hai Bing Guren	海濱故人
Haishang Hua Liezhuan	海上花列傳
Hanhan Zi	憨憨子
Hell for the Living, The	活地獄
Hen Hai	恨海

Hong Lingfei	洪靈菲
Hong Lou Meng	紅樓夢
Hong Tian Lei	轟天雷
Hu Jichen	胡寄塵
Hu Shanyuan	胡山源
Hu Shi	胡適
Hu Yinglin	胡應麟
Huaben	話本
Huang Moxi	黃摩西
Huang Xiaopei	黃小配
Huang Xiuqiu	黃繡球
Huo Diyu	活地獄
Illustrated Fiction	繡像小説
'In the Tavern'	在酒樓上
Investiture of Gods, The	封神演義
Ji Yun	紀昀
Jian Xian'ai	蹇先艾
Jian Xing Lu	劍腥錄
Jiang Guangci	蔣光慈
'Jiang Guoqu'	將過去
Jianren Shisan Zhong	跰人十三種
Jin Ping Mei Chongzhen	金瓶梅崇禎本
Jin Ping Mei Cihua	金瓶梅詞話本
Jin Shengtan	金聖嘆
Jin Shinian zhi Guai Xianzhuang	近十年之怪現狀
Jin Songcen	金松岑
Jing Hua Yue	鏡花緣
Jiu Ming Qiyuan	九命奇冤

Jiu Wei Gui	九尾龜
Journey to the West, The	西遊記
Kanguan	看官
Kangzhan Wenxue	抗戰文學
Ku Shehui	苦社會
'Kuangren Riji'	狂人日記
Lao Can Youji	老殘遊記
Lao She	老舍
Lao Zhang de Zhexue	老張的哲學
Leng Yan Guan	冷眼觀
Li Chuli	李初梨
Li Dingyi	李定夷
Li Jinming	黎錦明
Li Ruzhen	李汝珍
Lian Mengqing	連夢青
Liang Qichao	梁啟超
Libai Liu	禮拜六
Lin Nu Yu	鄰女語
Lin Ruji	林如稷
Ling Mengchu	凌夢初
Ling Shuhua	凌淑華
Lion Roars, The	獅子吼
Literature of Revolution	革命文學
Liu Bannong	劉半農
Liu E	劉鶚
Liu Lengtie	劉冷鐵
Liuyue Shuang	六月霜
Lives of Shanghai Flowers	海上花列傳

Lu Xun	魯迅
Lu Yin	廬隱
Luo Ye	羅燁
'Madman's Diary, The'	狂人日記
Mandarin Duck and Butterfly	鴛鴦蝴蝶派
Mao Dun	茅盾
Mao Zedong	毛澤東
Mao Zonggang	毛宗崗
Marriage to Awaken the World, A	醒世姻緣
Martial Art Novel	武俠小說
'Medicine'	藥
Meiyue Xiaoshuo	每月小說
Memoirs of the Hairpin House	釧影樓回憶錄
Meng Yao	孟瑤
Mengjue Daoren	夢覺道人
Mirror of Flowers	鏡花緣
'Misanthrope, The'	厭世者
More Chapters of the Journey to the West	西遊補
'Mr Pan in Disaster'	潘先生在難中
Mundane Romances	世情小說
'My Old Home'	故鄉
Nahan	吶喊
New Fiction, The	新小說
New Wave	新潮
'New Year's Sacrifice'	祝福
New Youth, The	新青年
Newly Compiled Pinghua Tales of the Five Dynasties	新編五代史平話

Ni Huaben	擬話本
Ni Yide	倪貽達
Nie Hai Hua	孽海花
Nine Murders	九命奇冤
Nine-Tailed Tortoise, The	九尾龜
Notes of a Drunken Old Man, The	醉翁談錄
Old Friends of the Beach	海濱故人
Omnibus of New Chinese Literature	中國新文學大系
Ouyang Juyuan	歐陽鉅源
'Pan Xiaosheng Zai Nanzhong'	潘先生在難中
Pan Xun	潘訓
Pang Huang	彷徨
'Past, The'	過去
Peng Jiahuang	彭家煌
Pinghua	平話
Pinghua Bao Jian	品花寶鑑
Proletarian Literature	普羅文學
Pu Songling	蒲松齡
'Public Example, A'	示眾
Puluo Wenxue	普羅文學
Qian Xingcun	錢杏村
Qian Xuantong	錢玄同
Qian Zhongshu	錢鐘書
Qianze Xiaoshuo	譴責小說
Qiliao Sheng	戚廖生
Qing Lou Meng	青樓夢
Quanxiang Pinghua Wuzhong	全相平話五種
Regionalist Fiction	鄉土小說

'Regret for the Past'	傷逝
Reprimanding Fiction	譴責小説
Resistance Literature	抗戰小説
Revolution of Literature	文學革命
Rulin Waishi	儒林外史
Sanguo Yanyi	三國演義
Sanguo Zhi Pinghua	三國志平話
Sans Culottes	短褲黨
Sanxia Wuyi	三俠五義
Saturday	禮拜六
Scholars, The	儒林外史
Sea of Remorse, A	恨海
'Separated only by a Barred Window'	一欄之隔
'Shangshi'	傷逝
Shen Congwen	沈從文
Shen Mo Xiaoshuo	神魔小説
Shen Yanbing	沈雁冰
Shen Zemin	沈澤民
Shenbian Xiaoshuo	身邊小説
Shengshui Aina Jushi	聖水艾衲居士
Shi Gong An	施公案
'Shi Zhong'	示眾
Shiqing Xiaoshuo	文明小史
Shizi Hou	獅子吼
Short History of Civilization, A	文明小史
Shui Hu Zhuan	水滸傳
Shuo Tang	説唐
Shuo Yue	説岳

Shuobu	說部
Shuohuade	說話的
Shuoshude	說書的
Sing-Praise Literature	頌歌文學
Sinking	沉淪
Society of Literary Studies, The	文學研究會
Songge Wenxue	頌歌文學
Stench of the Sword, The	劍腥錄
Strange Events of the Last Ten Years	近十年之怪現狀
Strange Events Witnessed in the Last Twenty Years	二十年目睹之怪現狀
Su Manshu	蘇曼殊
Su Xuelin	蘇雪林
Suishi Yiwen	隋史遺文
Sun Society, The	太陽社
Tai Jingnong	臺靜農
Taiyang She	太陽社
Tale of Tang, The	說唐
Tale of Yue Fei, The	說岳
Tao Jingsun	陶景孫
Teng Gu	滕固
Tenggu Guxiang	藤谷古香
Thirteen Stories by Jianren	趼人十三種
Three Heroes and Five Gallants	三俠五義
Three Kingdom Yanyi, The	三國演義
Three Kingdoms Pinghua, The	三國志平話
Thunder That Breaks the Sky, The	轟天雷
'Tomorrow'	明天

'Trace of Spring'	春痕
Travels of Lao Can, The	老殘遊記
True Story of A Q, The	阿Q正傳
'Undelivered Letters'	無法投遞的信
Unofficial History of the Embroidered Bed	繡榻野史
Viewed with Cold Eyes	冷眼觀
Wandering, The	彷徨
Wang Luyan	王魯彥
Wang Tongzhao	王統照
Wang Yunqing	王濬卿
Water Margin, The	水滸傳
Wei Xiuren	魏秀仁
Wenming Xiaoshi	文明小史
Wenxue Geming	文學革命
Wenxue Yanjiu Hui	文學研究會
What the Ladies Next Door Say	鄰女語
Wu Cheng'en	吳承恩
Wu Jianren	吳趼人
Wu Jingzi	吳敬梓
'Wufa Toudi de Xin'	無法投遞的信
Wuxia Xiaoshuo	武俠小説
Xi You Bu	西遊補
Xi You Ji	西遊記
Xia Ren	俠人
Xia Zengyou	夏曾佑
Xiang Liangpei	向良培
Xiangtu Wenxue	鄉土小説
Xiao Ming	小銘

Xiaoshuo	小説
Xiaoshuo Lin	小説林
Xiaoshuo Yue Bao	小説月報
Xiaxia Xiaoshuo	狹邪小説
Xin Bian Wudai Shi Pinghua	新編五代史平話
Xin Chao	新潮
Xin Qingnian	新青年
Xin Xiaoshuo	新小説
Xin Zhongguo Weilai Ji	新中國未來記
Xingshi Yinyuan	醒世姻緣
Xiuta Yeshi	繡榻野史
Xiuxiang Xiaoshuo	繡像小説
Xizhou Sheng	西周生
Xu Dishan	許地山
Xu Jie	許杰
Xu Nianci	徐念慈
Xu Qinwen	許欽文
Xu Zhenya	徐枕亞
Xu Zhimo	徐至摩
Xu Zhonglin	許仲琳
'Yanshi Zhe'	厭世者
Yanyi	演義
'Yao'	藥
Ye Shengtao	葉聖陶
Yellow Embroidered Ball	黃繡球
'Yi Lan Zhi Ge'	一欄之隔
Yi Suo	頤瑣
'Yi Tian'	一天
Yinban Sheng	寅半生

Yu Da	俞達
Yu Dafu	郁達夫
Yu Yue	俞樾
Yuan Hongdao	袁宏道
Yuan Yuling	袁于令
Yuanyang Hudie Pai	鴛鴦蝴蝶派
Yun Daiying	鄆代英
Yusi	語絲
'Zai Jiulou Shang'	在酒樓上
Zeng Pu	曾樸
Zeng Xubai	曾虛白
Zhang Chunfan	張春帆
Zhang Zhupo	張竹坡
Zhang Ziping	張資平
Zhang's Philosophy	老張的哲學
Zhao Shuli	趙樹理
Zhongguo Xianzai Ji	中國現在記
Zhongguo Xin Wenxue Daxi	中國新文學大系
Zhou Guisheng	周桂笙
Zhou Quanping	周全平
Zhou Shoujuan	周瘦鵑
Zhou Shuren	周樹人
Zhou Zuoren	周作人
Zhu Dingchen	朱鼎臣
'Zhu Fu'	祝福
Zhu Renhuo	諸人獲
Zhu Ziqing	朱自清
Zhuang Zhe	壯者
Zui Weng Tan Lu	醉翁談錄

Abbreviations of Fiction Works and Magazines Cited in the Book and Their Publication Details

BPHDOL	Bu pingheng de Ouli 不平衡的偶力 Unbalanced Forces, by Zhang Ziping 張資平, 上海: 商務印書館, 1926.
BZJ	Bi Zhou Ji 敝帚集, by Yu Dafu 郁達夫. 上海: 北新書局, 1932.
CH	Chun Hen 春痕 Traces of Spring, by Feng Yuanjun 馮沅君, 上海: 北新書局, 1926.
CJQHS	Chongji Qi Huashi 沖積期化石 Fossils from the Alluvial Age, by Zhang Ziping 張資平, 上海: 泰東書局, 1926.
CKPAJQ	Chu Ke Pai An Jingqi 初刻拍案驚奇 The First Collection of Amazing Stories, by Ling Mengchu 凌濛初, 上海: 古籍出版社影印明尚友堂刊本, 1985.
CL	Chenlun 沉淪 Sinking, by Yu Dafu 郁達夫, 上海: 泰東書局, 1921.
CYZY	Chun Yu Zhi Ye 春雨之夜 A Night of Spring Rain, by Wang Tongzhao 王統照, 上海: 商務印書館, 1924.
CZ	Cheng Zhong 城中 In the City, 葉聖陶, 上海: 開明書店, 1926.
CZJK	Chuangzao Jikan 創造季刊 The Creation Quarterly.
CZYK	Chuangzao Yuekan 創造月刊 The Creation Monthly.
CZZK	Chuangzao Zhoukan 創造週刊 The Creation Weekly.

EKPAJQ   Er Ke Pai An Jingqi 二刻拍案驚奇 The Second Collection of Amazing Stories, by Ling Mengchu 凌濛初, 上海: 古籍出版社影印明尚友堂刊本, 1965.

ESNMDZGXZ   Ershi Nian Mudu zhi Guai Xianzhuang 二十年目睹之怪現狀 The Strange Events Witnessed in the Last Twenty Years, by Wu Jianren 吳趼人, 北京: 通俗文藝出版社, 1954.

GCXXJ   Guanchang Xianxing Ji 官場現形記 The Bureaucrats, by Li Boyuan 李伯元, 台北: 廣雅書局, 1984.

GJXS   Gu Jin Xiaoshuo 古今小說 Stories Ancient and Recent, by Feng Menglong 馮夢龍, 北京: 文學古籍刊行社據日本內閣文庫藏本整理, 1956.

GL   Ganlan 橄欖 Olive, by Guo Moruo 敦沫若, 上海: 創造社出版部, 1926.

GM   Gemo 隔膜 Barriers, by Ye Shengtao 葉聖陶, 上海: 商務印書館, 1922.

GQJ   Guoqu Ji 過去集 The Past, by Yu Dafu 郁達夫, 上海: 北新書局, 1929.

HBGR   Hai Bin Guren 海濱故人 The Friends of the Sea Beach, by Lu Yin 盧隱, 上海: 商務印書館, 1925.

HDY   Huo Diyu 活地獄 The Hell on Earth, by Li Boyuan 李伯元, 台北: 廣雅書局, 1984.

HH   Hen Hai 恨海 The sea of Remorse, by Wu Jianren 吳研人, 台北, 廣雅書局, 1984.

HLM   Hong Lou Meng 紅樓夢 The Dream in the Red Chamber, by Cao Xueqin 曹雪芹, 中國藝術院據庚辰本整理, 北京: 人民文學出版社, 1982.

HSHLZ   Hai Shang Hua Liezhuan 海上花列傳 Flowers in Shanghai, by Han Bangqing 韓邦慶, 台北: 廣雅書局, 1984.

HTL   Hong Tian Lei 轟天雷 The Thunder that Breaks the Sky, by Tengu Guxiang 藤谷古香, 台北: 廣雅書局, 1984.

HXQ	Huang Xiuqiu 黃繡球 The Yellow Embroidered Ball, by Yi Suo 頤瑣, 台北: 廣雅書局, 1984.
HYH	Hua Yue Hen 花月痕 The Flowers and the Moon, by Wei Xiuren 魏秀仁, 台北: 廣雅書局, 1984.
HZ	Huo Zai 火災 The Fire, by Ye Shengtao 葉聖陶, 上海: 商務印書館, 1923.
HZS	Hua Zhi Si 花之寺 The Temple of Flowers, by Ling Shuhua 凌淑華, 上海: 新月書店, 1926.
JGQG	Jin Gu Qiguan 今古奇觀 Tales Old and New, by Bao Weng Laoren 抱甕老人, 北京: 人民文學出版社據明刊本整理出版, 1957.
JHY	Jing Hua Yuan 鏡花緣 Flowers in the Mirror, by Li Ruzhen 李汝珍, 北京: 人民文學出版社據原刊初印本整理出版, 1982.
JMQY	Jiu Ming Qi Yuan 九命奇冤 The Murder of Nine Lives, by Wu Jianren 吳趼人, 台北: 廣雅書局, 1984.
JPM Cihua	Jin Ping Mei Cihua 金瓶梅詞話 Golden Lotus Cihua Version, by Xiaoxiao Sheng 笑笑生, 北京: 文學古籍刊行社影印萬曆本, 1957.
JPM Chongzhen	Jin Ping Mei Chongzheng 金瓶梅崇禎本 (新刻繡像金瓶梅), stored in the East Asiatic Library of the University of California Library.
JS	Jiushi 卷葹 Curly Burwood, by Feng Yuanjun 馮沅君, 上海: 北新書局, 1924.
JSNZGXZ	Jin Shinian Zhi Guai Xianzhuang 近十年之怪現狀 Strange Events of the Last Ten Years, by Wu Jianren 吳研人, 台北: 廣雅書局, 1984.
JSTY	Jing Shi Tong Yan 警世通言 Stories to Warn Men, by Feng Menglong 馮夢龍, 北京: 作家出版社據明葉敬池刻本整理, 1956.
JWG	Jiu Wei Gui 九尾龜 The Nine-Tailed Tortoise, by Zhang Chunfan 張春帆, 台北: 廣雅書局, 1984.

JXL

Jian Xing Lu 劍腥錄 The Stench of the Sword, by Lin Shu 林紓, in 庚子事變文學集, 阿英編: 上海: 中華書局, 1959.

KSH

Ku She Hui 苦社會 Bitter Society, by Yi Ming 佚名, 上海: 中華書局, 1959.

LBL

Li Bai Liu 禮拜六 Saturday.

LCYJ

Lao Can Youji 老殘遊記 The Travels of Lao Can, by Liu E 劉鶚, 台北: 聯經出版社, 1976.

LNY

Lin Nü Yu 鄰女語 What the Ladies Next Door Say, by Lian Mengqing 連夢青, in 阿英編: 庚子事變文學集, 上海: 中華書局, 1959.

LP

Lun Pan 輪盤 The Roulette, by Xu Zhimo 徐志摩, 上海: 中華書局, 1930.

LY

Luo Ye 落葉 The Fallen Leaves, by Guo Moruo 郭沫若, 上海: 創造社出版部,

LYG

Leng Yan Guan 冷眼觀 Viewed with Cold Eyes, by Wang Yuqin 王濬卿, 台北: 廣雅書局, 1984.

MG

Mi Gan 蜜柑 Orange, by Shen Congwen 沈從文, 上海: 新月書店, 1927.

NH

Nahan 吶喊 Battlecries, by Lu Xun 魯迅, in 魯迅全集, 北京: 人民文學出版社, 1956.

NHH

Nie Hai Hua 孽海花 The Flower in the Sinful Sea, by Zeng Pu 曾樸, 上海: 真善美書店, 1933.

NLX

Niao Luo Xing 蔦蘿行 The Cypress Vine, by Yu Dafu 郁達夫, 上海: 泰東書局, 1921.

PH

Panghuang 彷徨 Wanderings, by Lu Xun 魯迅, in 魯迅全集, 北京: 人民文學出版社, 1956.

PHBJ

Ping Hua Bao Jian 品花寶鑑 The Mirror of Theatrical Life, by Chen Sen 陳森, 台北: 廣雅書局, 1984.

QPSTHB

Qingping Shan Tang Huaben 清平山堂話本 The Hua Ben Stories of the Qingping Shan Studio 台北: 世界書局影印日本內閣文庫本, 1958.

QXPHWZ	Quanxiang Pinghua Wuzhong 全相平話五種 Five Fully Illustrated Pinghua Novels 台北: 世界書局影印日本內閣文庫本, 1958.
RLWS	Rulin Waishi 儒林外史 The Scholars, by Wu Jingzhi 吳敬梓, 北京: 作家出版社據臥閑堂本整理, 1955.
SGYY	San Guo Yanyi 三國演義 Romance of Three Kingdoms 北京: 作家出版社據毛宗崗評點本整理, 1955.
SHZ	Shui Hu Zhuan 水滸傳 Water Margin 北京: 人民文學出版社據容與堂本整理, 1982.
SSYW	Sui Shi Yiwen 隋史遺文 Forgotten Texts of the Sui History, by Yuan Yuling 袁于令, 台北: 幼獅月刊社據名山聚藏本翻印, 1975.
STYY	Sui Tang Yanyi 隋唐演義 Romance of Sui and Tang History 上海: 古籍出版社據清四雪堂本整理, 1956.
SZH	Shizi Hou 獅子吼 The Lion Roars, by Chen Tianhua 陳天華, 台北: 廣雅書局, 1984.
T	Ta 塔 The Tower, by Guo Moruo, 郭沫若, 上海: 商務印書館, 1926.
TRXX	Tangren Xiaoshuo 唐人小說 Stories by the Tang Authors, ed. by Wang Pijian 汪辟疆, 上海: 中華書局, 1956.
WMXS	Wenming Xiao Shi 文明小史 A Short History of Civilization, by Li Boyuan 李伯元, 台北: 廣雅書局, 1984.
WXXK	Wenxue Xun Kan 文學旬刊 Literature Every Ten Days.
WXZB	Wenxue Zhoubao 文學周報 Literature Weekly.
XDCX	Xue de Chuxi 雪的除夕 The Snowy New Year's Eve, by Zhang Ziping 上海: 商務印書館, 1926.
XQN	Xin Qingnian 新青年 The New Youth.

XSHY   Xing Shi Heng Yan 醒世恆言 Stories to Awaken
                Man, by Feng Menglong 馮夢龍, 北京: 作家出
                版社據明葉敬池刻本整理, 1956.

XSL   Xiaoshuo Lin 小説林 Fiction Forest.

XSYB   Xiaoshuo Yuebao 小説月報 Fiction Monthly.

XX   Xian Xia 線下 Under the Frontline, by Ye Shengtao
                葉聖陶, 上海: 商務印書館, 1925.

XXS   Xin Xiaoshuo 新小説 New Fiction.

XXXS   Xiuxiang Xiaoshuo 繡像小説 Illustrated Fiction.

XYJ   Xi You Ji 西遊記 The Journey to the West, by Wu
                Cheng'en 吳承恩, 北京: 人民文學出版社據明金
                陵世德堂本整理, 1990.

XYB   Xi You Bu 西遊補 Supplement to the Journey to
                the West, by Dong Yue 董説, 上海: 上海古籍出
                版社據崇禎本整理, 1983.

XZGWLJ   Xin Zhongguo Weilai Ji 新中國未來記 The
                Future of New China, by Liang Qichao 梁啟超,
                台北: 廣雅書局, 1984.

YS   Yu Si 語絲.

YY   Yi Ye 一葉 A Leaf, by Wang Tongzhao 王統照,
                上海: 商務印書館, 1922.

YYXS   Yue Yue Xiaoshuo 月月小説 Fiction Every
                Monthly.

YZ   Ya Zi 鴨子 The Duck, by Shen Congwen 沈從文,
                上海: 北新書局, 1926.

ZGXZJ   Zhongguo Xianzai Ji 中國現在記 China Today,
                by Li Boyuan 李伯元, 台北: 廣雅書局, 1984.

ZLDGS   Zhu Lin De Gushi 竹林的故事 Stories of the
                Bamboo Bush, by Fei Ming 廢名, 上海: 北新書
                局, 1925.

ZWLZ   Zhui Wang Lao Zhu 綴網勞蛛 The Vain Labour
                of a Spider, 許地山, 上海: 商務印書館, 1925.

ZZ   Zhou Zhong 舟中 In the Boat, by Li Jingming 黎
                錦明, 上海: 泰東書局, 1924.

Bibliography of Secondary Sources

A YING 阿英. 1937. *Wan Qing Xiaoshuo Shi* 晚清小説史 *A History of Late Qing Fiction*. Shanghai: Commercial Press.

—— 1959. *Gengzi Shibian Wenxue Ji* 庚子事變文學集 *Literary Works on the Boxer Rebellion*. Shanghai: Zhonghua Shuju.

—— (ed.) 1960. *Wan Qing Wenxue Congchao, Xiaoshuo Xiqu Yanjiu Juan* 晚清文學叢鈔, 小説戲曲研究卷 *Late Qing Critical Papers on Fiction and Drama*. Shanghai: Zhonghua Shuju.

—— 1981. *A Ying Wenji* 阿英文集 *Collected Works by A Ying*. Beijing: Sanlian Shudian.

—— 1981. *Xiaoshuo Sitan* 小説四談 *Four Papers on Fiction*. Shanghai: Shanghai Guji Chubanshe.

ALTER, ROBERT. 1975. *Partial Magic: The Novel as a Self-Conscious Genre*. Berkeley: University of California Press.

BAO JING 鮑晶. 1985. *Liu Bannong Yanjiu Ziliao* 劉半農研究資料 *Studies on Liu Bannong*. Tianjin: Tianjin Renmin Chubanshe.

BAO TIANXIAO 包天笑. 1971. *Chuanyinglou Huiyilu* 釧影樓回憶錄 *Memoirs in the Chuanying Chamber*. Hong Kong: Dalu Chubanshe.

BARTHES, ROLAND. 1975. *S/Z*, tr. Richard Miller. London: Cape.

—— 1977. 'Introduction to Structural Analysis of Narrative'. *Image-Music-Text*, ed. and tr. Stephen Heath, 156–274. Hill and Wang.

BEIJING DAXUE ZHONGWEN XI 北京大學中文系. 1960. *Zhongguo Xiaoshuo Shigao* 中國小説史稿 *A History of Chinese Fiction*. Beijing: Renmin Wenxue Chubanshe.

BIRCH, CYRIL. 1972. 'The Language of Chinese Literature'. *New Literary History*, 4: 141–150.

—— (ed.), 1974. *Studies in Chinese Literary Genres*. Berkeley: University of California Press.

BOOTH, WAYNE. 1983. *The Rhetoric of Fiction*. Chicago: University of Chicago Press.

CAO JUREN 曹聚仁. 1957. *Lu Xun Pingzhuan* 魯迅評傳 *A Biography of Lu Xun*. Hong Kong: Xinwenhua Chubanshe.

CARLITZ, KATHERINE. 1987. *The Rhetoric of Chin P'ing Mei*. Bloomington, Indiana University Press.

CASSIRER, ERNST. 1946. *Philosophy of Symbolic Forms*, tr. Ralph Manheim. New Haven: Yale University Press.

CAWS, MARY ANN. 1985. *Reading Frames in Modern Fiction*. Princeton, NJ: Princeton University Press.

CHAMBERS, ROSS. 1984. *Story and Situation: Narrative Seduction and the Power of Fiction*. Minniapolis: University of Minnesota Press.

CHATMAN, SEYMOUR. 1978. *Story and Discourse, Narrative Structure in Fiction and Film*. Ithaca, NY: Cornell University Press.

—— 1986. 'Character and Narrator: Filter, Center, Slant, and Interest Focus'. *Poetics Today*, 7/2: 189–224.

CHEN DUXIU 陳獨秀. 1937. *Duxiu Wechun* 獨秀文存 *Collected Works of Chen Duxiu*. Shanghai: Yadong Tushuguan.

CHEN PINGYUAN 陳平原. 1988. *Zhongguo Xiaoshuo Xushi Moshi de Zhuanbian* 中國小說敘事模式的轉變 *The Transformation of the Narrative Models of Chinese Fiction*. Shanghai: Shanghai Wenyi Chubanshe.

CHEN SONG 陳崧 (ed.). 1985. *Wusi Qianhou Dongxi Wenhua Wenti Lunzhan Wenxuan* 五四前後東西文化問題論戰文選 *Selected Papers on East–West Cultural Relations around May Fourth*. Beijing: Zhongguo Shehui Kexue Chubanshe.

CHEN XIYING 陳西瀅. 1928. *Xiying Xianhua* 西瀅閑話 *Idle Talk by Chen Xiying*. Shanghai: Xinyue Shudian.

CHEN ZISHAN 陳子善 and WANG ZILI 王自力 (eds.). 1985. *Yu Dafu Yanjiu Ziliao* 郁達夫研究資料 *Studies on Yu Dafu*. Beijing: Sanlian Shudian.

CHENG FANGWU 成彷吾. 1985. *Cheng Fanwu Wenji* 成彷吾文集 *Collected Works of Cheng Fanwu*. Jinan: Shandong Daxue Chubanshe.

DOLEZELOVA-VERLINGEROVA, MILENA (ed.). 1984. *The Chinese Novel at the Turn of the Century*. Toronto: University of Toronto Press.

DUCROT, OSWALD, and TZVETAN TODOROV. 1972. *Dictionnaire encyclopédique des sciences du language*. Paris: Gallimard.

ECO, UMBERTO. 1976. *A Theory of Semiotics*. Bloomington, Ind.: Indiana University Press.

ETIEMBLE, RENÉ. 1974. *Essais de littérature (vraiment) générale*. Paris: Gallimard.

FANG MING 方銘 (ed.). 1983. *Jiang Guangci Yanjiu Ziliao* 蔣光慈研究資料 *Studies on Jiang Guangci*. Yinchuan: Ningxia Renmin Chubanshe.

—— (ed.). 1986. *Jin Ping Mei Ziliao Huibian* 金瓶梅資料彙編 *Materials for the Study of Jin Ping Mei*. Wuhu: Huangshan Shushe.

FENG XUEFENG 馮雪峰. 1981. *Lu Xun de Wenxue Daolu*. 魯迅的文學道路 *Lu Xun's Literary Career*. Changsha: Hunan Renmin Chubanshe.

FORSTER, E. M. 1927. *Aspects of the Novel*. London: Edward Arnold.

FRIEDMAN, NORMAN. 1955. 'Point of View in Fiction: The Development of a Critical Concept'. *Publications of the Modern Language Association*, 70: 1160–84.

—— 1975. *Form and Meaning in Fiction*. Athens, Ga.: University of Georgia Press.

GALLIE, W. B. 1964. *Philosophy and Historical Understanding*. London: Chatto and Windus.

GARVIN, HARRY G. (ed.). 1977. *Literature and History*. London: Bucknell University Press.

—— (ed.). 1982. *Literature and Ideology*. London: Bucknell University Press.

GE GONGZHEN 戈公振. 1955. *Zhong Guo Baoye Shi* 中國報業史 *A History of Chinese Newspapers*. Beijing: Sanlian Shudian.

GENETTE, GERARD. 1980. *Narrative Discourse*, tr. Jane E. Lewin. Oxford: Blackwell.

GOLDMAN, MERLE (ed.). 1977. *Modern Chinese Literature in the May Fourth Era*. Cambridge, Mass.: Harvard University Press.

GRIEDER, JEROME B. 1970. *Hu Shih and the Chinese Renaissance: Liberalism in the Chinese Revolution, 1917–1937*. Cambridge, Mass.: Harvard University Press.

APPENDIX III

GUO MORUO 郭沫若. 1979. *Wenyi Lunji* 文藝論集 *Debates on Literature*. Beijing: Renmin Wenxue Chubanshe.

HANAN, PATRICK D. 1967. 'The Early Chinese Short-Story: A Critical Theory in Outline'. *Harvard Journal of Asiatic Studies*, 27: 168–207.

—— 1973. *The Chinese Short Story: Studies in Dating, Authorship, and Composition*. Cambridge, Mass: Harvard University Press.

—— 1974. 'The Technique of Lu Hsun's Fiction'. *Harvard Journal of Asiatic Studies*, 34: 53–96.

—— 1981. *The Chinese Vernacular Story*. Cambridge, Mass.: Harvard University Press.

HEGEL, ROBERT E. 1981. *The Novel in Seventeenth-Century China*. New York: Columbia University Press.

HELL, VICTOR. 1976. 'L'Art de la breveté, short story et Kurzgeschichte', *Revue de littérature comparée*, 50: 88–109.

HERNADI, PAUL. 1972. *Beyond Genre*. Ithaca, NY: Cornell University Press.

HSIA, C. T. 夏志清. 1968. *The Classical Chinese Novel: A Critical Introduction*. New York: Columbia University Press.

—— 1971. *A History of Modern Chinese Fiction*. New Haven: Yale University Press.

—— 1975. 'Suishi Yiwen Chongkan Xu' 隋史遺文重刊序 'Introduction to the Reprint of Suishi Yiwen'. *Suishi Yiwen*, 1–20. Taipei: Youshi Chubanshe.

—— 1976. 'Ping Lao Can Youji' 評老殘遊記 'Concerning Lao Can Youji'. *Lao Can Youji*, 121–34. Taipei: Jinglian Chubanshe.

—— 1977. *Ren de Wenxue* 人的文學 *Human Literature*. Taipei: Chun Wenxue Chuban Youxian Gongsi.

—— 1983 'Zhongguo Xiaoshuo, Meiguo Piping Jia' 中國小説, 美國批評家 'Chinese Fiction and American Critics', tr. Liu Shaoming. *Mingbao Yukan*, July: 41–7, and August: 85–90.

HU SHI 胡適. 1929. *Hu Shi Wencun* 胡適文存 *Collected Works by Hu Shi*. Shanghai: Yadong Shuju.

HU SHIYING 胡士瑩. 1980. *Huaben Xiaoshuo Gailun* 話本小説概論 *An Introduction to Huaben Fiction*. Beijing: Zhonghua Shuju.

HU YINGLIN 胡應麟. 1958. *Shaoshi Shanfang Bicong* 少室山房筆叢 *Essays Written in Shaoshi Shan House*. Beijing: Zhonghua Shuju.

HUANG LIN 黃霖 and HAN TONGWEN 韓同文 (eds.). 1982. *Zhongguo Lidai Xiaoshuo Lunzhi Xuan* 中國歷代小說論著選 *Essays on Fiction in Ancient China*. Nanchang: Jiangxi Renmin Chubanshe.

IDEMA, WILT L. 1974. *Chinese Vernacular Fiction: The Formative Period*. Leiden: E. J. Brill.

JI YUN 紀昀. 1965. *Siku Quanshu Tiyao* 四庫全書提要 *Digests of Siku Quanshu*. Beijing: Zhonghua Shuju.

KANG YOUWEI. 1990. *Kang Youwei Shiwen Ji* 康有為詩文集 *Selected Essays and Poems by Kang Youwei*, ed. Shu Wu 舒蕪 *et al.*, Beijing: Renmin Wenxue Chubanshe.

KELLOG, ROBERT. 1972. *Novel and Narrative*. Glasgow: University of Glasgow Press.

KONG JINGLING 孔境另. 1957. *Zhongguo Xiaoshuo Shiliao* 中國小說資料 *Studies on Chinese Fiction*. Shanghai: Gudian Wenxue Chubanshe.

KROEBER, KARL. 1971. *Styles in Fictional Structure*. Princeton, NJ: Princeton University Press.

KUHN, THOMAS. 1970. *The Structure of Scientific Revolution*. Chicago: Chicago University Press.

LEE, LEO OU-FAN. 1973. *The Romantic Generation of Modern Chinese Writers*. Cambridge, Mass.: Harvard University Press.

LEMON, L. T. and REIS, M. J. (eds.). 1965. *Russian Formalist Criticism: Four Essays*. Lincoln: University of Nebraska Press.

LI, PETER. 1980. *Tzeng P'u: A Literary Journal*. Boston: Twayne Publishers.

LI ZONGYING 李宗英 and ZHANG MENG YANG 張夢陽 (eds.). 1982. *Liushi Nian lai Lu Xun Yanjiu Lunwen Xuan* 六十年來魯迅研究論文選 *Selected Papers on Lu Xun in the Last Sixty Years*. Beijing: Zhongguo Shehui Chubanshe.

LIANG QICHAO 梁啟超. 1941. *Yinbingshi Heji* 飲冰室合集 *Collected Works Written in Yinbin Room*. Shanghai: Zhonghua Shuju.

LIN, YU-SHENG. 1979. *The Crisis of Chinese Consciousness: Radical Anti-Traditionalism in the May Fourth Era*. Madison: University of Wisconsin Press.

LINK, PERRY E., JR. 1981. *Mandarin Ducks and Butterflies: Popular Fiction in Early Twentieth-Century Chinese Cities*. Berkeley: University of California Press.

LIU DAJIE 劉大杰. 1957. *Zhongguo Wenxue Fazhanshi* 中國文學發展史 *A History of the Development of Chinese Fiction*. Shanghai: Gudian Wenxue Chubanshe.

LOTMAN, YURI. 1977. *The Structure of Artistic Text*. Ann Arbor: University of Michigan Press.

LOWENTHAL, LEO. 1961. *Literature, Popular Culture and Society*. Englewood Cliffs, Prentice-Hall.

LU XUN 魯迅 1956. *Lu Xun Quanji* 魯迅全集 *Complete Works of Lu Xun*. Beijing: Renmin Chubanshe.

—— 1959. *A Brief History of Chinese Fiction*, tr. Yang Hsien-yi and Gladys Yang. Beijing: Foreign Languages Press.

—— 1976. *Lu Xun Shuxin Ji* 魯迅書信集 *Letters by Lu Xun*. Beijing: Renmin Wenxue Chubanshe.

LU YIN 盧隱. 1934. *Lu Yin Zizhuan* 盧隱自傳 *Autobiography of Lu Yin*. Shanghai: Diyi Chubanshe.

LUBBOCK, PERCY. 1957. *The Craft of Fiction*. New York: Viking.

LUCID, DANIEL P. (ed.). 1977. *Soviet Semiotics*. Baltimore: The Johns Hopkins University Press.

LUO YE 羅燁. 1957. *Zuiweng Tanlu* 醉翁談錄 *Talks of a Drunken Old Man*. Shanghai: Shanghai Guji Chubanshe.

MACHEREY, PIERRE. 1966. *Pour une théorie de la production littéraire*. Paris: F. Maspero.

MADDEN, DAVID. 1980. *A Primer of Novel*. Methuchen, NJ: Scarecrow Press.

MAI, YINGFA 麥穎發. 1936. *Quanpan Xihua Yanlun* 全盤西化言論 *Opinions for a Wholesale Westernization*. Guangzhou: Lingnan Daxue.

MAO DUN 茅盾. 1984. *Mao Dun Weh* 茅盾文集 *Collected Works of Mao Dun*. Beijing: Renmin Wenxue Chubanshe.

—— 1981. *Wo Zouguo de Daolu* 我走過的道路 *The Road of My Life*. Hong Kong: Sanlian Shudian.

MAO ZEDONG 毛澤東. 1953. *Mao Zedong Xuanji* 毛澤東選集 *Selected Works of Mao Zedong*. Beijing: Renmin Chubanshe.

MATEJKA, LADISLAV, and KRYSTYNA POMORSKA (eds.). 1971. *Readings in Russian Poetics*. Cambridge, Mass.: MIT Press.

—— and IRWIN TITUNIK (eds.). 1976. *Semiotics of Art*. Cambridge, Mass.: MIT Press.

MENG YAO 孟瑤. 1966. *Zhongguo Xiaoshuo Shi* 中國小説史 *A History of Chinese Fiction*. Taipei: Wenxing Shudian.

MENG YUANLAO 孟元老. 1935. *Dongjing Menghua Lu* 東京夢華錄 *Dreams of the East Capital*. Shanghai: Commercial Press.

METZ, CRISTIAN. 1974. *Film Language A Semiotics of the Cinema*, tr. Michael Taylor. New York: Oxford University Press.

NIE GANNU 聶紺弩. 1981. *Zhongguo Gudai Xiaoshuo Lunji* 中國古代小説論集 *Essays on Classical Chinese Fiction*. Shanghai: Shanghai Guji Chubanshe.

PHARIS, DAVID A. 1985. *Charles S. Pierce and the Lingustic Sign*. Amsterdam: J. Benjamins.

PLAKS, ANDREW H. (ed.). 1977. *Chinese Narrative, Critical and Theoretical Essays*. Princeton, NJ: Princeton University Press.

PRUSEK, JAROSLAV. 1980. *The Lyrical and the Epic, Studies of Modern Chinese Literature*. Bloomington, Ind.: Indiana University Press.

QIAN ZHONGSHU 錢鐘書 *et al*. 1981. *Linshu de Fanyi* 林紓的翻譯 *The Translations by Lin Shu*. Beijing: Commercial Press.

RAO HONGJING 饒鴻競 *et al*. (eds.). 1982. *Chuangzao She Ziliao* 創造社資料 *Studies on the Creation Society*. Fuzhou: Fujian Renmin Chubanshe.

RIMMON-KENAN, SHLOMITH. 1983. *Narrative Fiction*. London: New Accent.

ROLSTON, DAVID L. (ed.). 1990. *How to Read the Chinese Novel*. Princeton, NJ: Princeton University Press.

SCHOLES, ROBERT. 1962. *Approaches to the Novel: Materials for a Poetics*. San Francisco: Chandler.

—— and ROBERT KELLOGG. 1966. *The Nature of Narative*. London: Oxford University Press.

SCHULZE, LEONARD, and WALTER WETZELS (eds.). 1983. *Literature and History*. Lanham: University Press of America.

SCHWARTZ, BENJAMIN I. (ed.). 1972. *Reflections on the May Fourth Movement: A Symposium*. Cambridge, Mass.: East Asian Research Center, Harvard University.

SEBEOK, THOMAS (ed.). 1986. *An Encyclopaedic Dictionary of Semiotics*. Berlin: Mouton de Gruyter.

SUN FUYUAN 孫伏園. 1942. *Lu Xun Xiansheng Ersan Shi* 魯迅先生二三事 *A Few Things about Lu Xun*. Repr. 1980, Changsha: Hunan Renmin Chubanshe.

SUN KAIDI 孫楷第. 1931. *Riben Dongjing Suojian Zhongguo Xiaoshuo Shumu Tiyao* 日本東京所見中國小説書目提要 *Digests of Books of Chinese Fiction seen in Tokyo, Japan*. Beiping: Guoli Beiping Tushu Guan.

—— 1932. *Zhongguo Tongsu Xiaoshuo Shumu* 中國通俗小説書目 *A Bibliography of Chinese Popular Fiction*. Repr. 1957, Beijing: Zuojia Chubanshe.

—— 1956. *Sujiang, Shuohua yu Baihua Xiaoshuo* 俗講, 説話與白話小説 *Popular Narrative and Vernacular Fiction*. Beijing: Zuojia Chubanshe.

—— 1990. *Xiqu Xiaoshuo Shulu Tijie* 戲曲小説書錄題解 *An Annotated Bibliography of Chinese Drama and Fiction*. Beijing: Renmin Wenxue Chubanshe.

SUN ZHONGTIAN 孫中田 and ZHA GUOHUA 查國華. 1981. *Mao Dun Yanjiu Ziliao* 茅盾研究資料 *Studies on Mao Dun*. Beijing: Zhongguo Shehui Kexue Chubanshe.

TATE, ALLEN. 1955. *The Man of Letters in the Modern World*. New York: Meridian.

TAY, WILLIAM. 1984. 'Wang Meng, Stream of Consciousness and the Controversy over Modernism'. *Modern Chinese Literature*, 1: 3–17.

T'IEN, JU-K'ANG. 1988. *Male Anxiety and Female Chastity*. Leiden: E. J. Brill.

TODOROV, TZVETAN. 1968. 'Poetique'. *Qu'est-ce que le structuralism?* ed. O. Ducrot *et al.*, 98–116. Paris: Editions du Seuil.

USPENSKY, BORIS. 1973. *A Poetics of Composition: The Structure of the Artistic Text and Typology of a Compositional Form*, tr. Valentina Zavarin and Susan Wittig. Berkeley: University of California Press.

WANG CHUANXIAO. 王傳曉 (ed.). 1958. *Yuan Ming Qing Sandai Jinhui Xiaoshuo Xiqu Shiliao* 元明清三代禁毀小説戲曲史料. Documents Concerning the Censorship of Fiction and Drama in the Yuan, Ming and Qing Dynasties. Beijing: Zuojia Chubanshe.

WANG FUREN 王富仁. 1983. *Lu Xun Qianqi Xiaoshuo yu Eluosi Wenxue* 魯迅前期小説與俄羅斯文學 *Lu Xun's Early Fiction and Russian Literature*. Xi'an: Shanxi Renmin Chubanshe.

WANG PIJIANG 汪辟疆. 1958. *Tangren Xiaoshuo* 唐人小説 *Stories by Tang Authors*. Shanghai: Shanghai Guji Chubanshe.

WANG XUNZHAO 王訓昭 *et al.* (eds.). 1981. *Guo Moruo Yanjiu Ziliao* 郭沫若研究資料 *Studies on Guo Moruo*. Beijing: Zhongguo Shehui Kexue Chubanshe.

WATT, IAN. 1957. *The Rise of the Novel: Studies in Defoe, Richardson and Fielding*. Berkeley: University of California Press.

WATTS, RICHARD J. 1981. *The Paralinguistic Analysis of Narrative Texts*. Tuebingen: Narr.

WEI SHAOCHANG 魏紹昌. 1962a. *Lao Can Youji Ziliao* 老殘遊記資料 *Studies on Lao Can Youji*. Shanghai: Zhonghua Shuju.

—— 1962b. *Nie Haihua Yanjiu Ziliao* 孽海花研究資料 *Studies on Nie Hai Hua*. Shanghai: Shanghai Wenyi Chubanshe.

—— 1980. *Li Boyuan Yianjiu Ziliao* 李伯元研究資料 *Studies on Li Boyuan*. Shanghai: Shanghai Guji Chubanshe.

—— 1982a. *Yuanyang Hudie Pai Yanju Ziliao* 鴛鴦蝴蝶派研究資料 *Studies on the Butterfly School*. Shanghai: Shanghai Wenyi Chubanshe.

—— 1982b. *Wu Jianren Yanjiu Ziliao* 吳研人研究資料 *Studies on Wu Jianren*. Shanghai: Shanghai Guji Chubanshe.

WHITE, HAYDEN. 1983. 'The Authoritative Lie'. *Partisan Review*, 50: 307–12.

WONG, KAM-MING. 1974. *Narrative Art of* The Dream of the Red Chamber. Ithaca, NY: Cornell University Press.

WU HUAIBIN 吳懷斌 and ZENG GUANGCAN 曾廣燦 (eds.). 1985. *Lao She Yanjiu Ziliao* 老舍研究資料 *Studies on Lao She*. Beijing: Shiyue Wenyi Chubanshe.

WU XIAORU 吳小如. 1982. *Gudian Xiaoshuo Mangao* 古典小説漫稿 *Scattered Papers on Chinese Classical Novels*. Shanghai: Shanghai Guji Chubanshe.

XU KE 徐柯. 1918. *Qing Bai Lei Chao* 清稗類鈔 *Anecdotes in Qing Unofficial History*. Shanghai: Commercial Press.

XUE SUIZHI 薛綏之 and ZHANG JUNCAI 張俊才 (eds.). 1982. *Lin Shu Yanjiu Ziliao* 林紓研究資料 *Studies on Lin Shu*. *Fuzhou*: Fujian Renmin Chubanshe.

YANG YI 楊義. 1988. *Zhongguo Xiandai Xiaoshuo Shi* 中國現代小説史 *A History of Modern Chinese Fiction*, vol. i. Beijing: Renmin Wenxue Chubanshe.

—— 1988. *Zhongguo Xiandai Xiaoshuo Shi* 中國現代小説史 *A History of Modern Chinese Fiction*, vol. ii. Beijing: Renmin Wenxue Chubanshe.

YOU GUO'EN 游國恩 *et al.* 1979. *Zhongguo Wenxue Shi* 中國文學史 *A History of Chinese Literature*. Renmin Wenxue Chubanshe.

YU, ANTHONY. 1975. 'Narrative Structure and Problems of Chapter Nine in the Hsi-yu chi'. *Journal of Asian Studies*, 34: 295–311.

YU DAFU 郁達夫. 1927. *Guoqu Ji* 過去集 *The Past*. Shanghai: Kaiming Shudian.

—— 1978. *Dafu Wenyi Lunwen Ji* 達夫文藝論集 *Critical Essays by Yu Dafu*. Hong Kong: Gangqing Chubanshe.

—— 1983. *Yu Dafu Wenji* 郁達夫文集 *Collected Works by Yu Dafu*. Hong Kong: Sanlian Shudian.

YU PINGBO 俞平伯 (ed.). 1960. *Zhi Yan Zhai Honglou Meng Jiping* 脂硯齋紅樓夢輯評 *Marginal Commentaries on* The Dream of the Red Chamber *by Zhi Yan Zhai*. Shanghai: Zhonghua Shuju.

ZENG, XIAOYI 曾小逸 (ed.). 1985. *Zouxiang Shijie Wenxue* 走向世界文學 *Toward a World Literature*. Changsha: Hunan Renmin Chubanshe.

ZHANG, GUOGUANG 張國光. 1981. *Shuihu yu Jin Shengtan Yianjou* 水滸與金聖嘆研究 *A Study of* Water Margin *and Jin Shengtan*. Zhengzhou: Zhongzhou Shuhua She.

ZHANG, JINGLU 張靜盧. 1953. *Zhongguo Jindai Chuban Shiliao* 中國近代出版史料 *Materials Concerning the Publication Business of Modern China*, vol. i. Beijing: Commercial Press.

—— 1957. *Zhongguo Jindai Chuban Shiliao* 中國近代出版史料 *Materials Concerning the Publication Business of Modern China*, vol. ii. Beijing: Commercial Press.

ZHANG SHENGYI 張聲怡 and LIU JIUZHOU 劉九洲 (eds). 1985. *Zhongguo Gudai Xiezuo Lilun* 中國古代寫作理論 *Theories on Writing in Ancient China*. Wuhan: Huazhong Gongxue Yuan Chubanshe.

ZHAO JIABI 趙家璧 (ed.). 1935. *Zhongguo Xin Wenxue Daxi* 中國新文學大系 *An Omnibus of Chinese New Literature*. Shanghai: Liangyou Tushu Yingshua Gongsi.

ZHAO JINGSHEN 趙景深. 1980. *Zhongguo Xiaoshuo Congkao* 中國小說叢考 *Papers on Chinese Fiction*. Jinan: Qilu Shushe.

ZHAO XIAQIU 趙遐秋 and ZENG QINGRUI 曾慶瑞. 1984. *Zhongguo Xiandai Xiaoshuo Shi* 中國現代小說史 *A History of Modern Chinese Fiction*. Beijing: Zhongguo Renmin Daxue Chubanshe.

ZHENG FANGZE 鄭方澤. 1983. *Zhongguo Xiandai Wenxue Shi Biannian* 中國現代文學史編年 *A Chronology of Modern Chinese Literature*. Changchun: Jilin Renmin Chubanshe.

ZHENG YIMEI 鄭逸梅. 1981. *Nan She Congtan* 南社叢談 *Anecdotes about Nan She*. Shanghai: Shanghai Renmin Chubanshe.

ZHENG ZHENGDU 鄭振鐸. 1954. *Zhongguo Su Wenxue Shi* 中國俗文學史 *A History of Popular Chinese Literature*, 2nd edn. Beijing: Zuojia Chubanshe.

ZHONGGUO SHEHUI KEXUEYUAN WENXUE YANJIU SUO 中國社會科學院文學研究所. 1981. '*Geming Wenxue' Lunzheng Ziliao Xuanji*' 革命文學論爭資料選集 *Controversies on 'Literature of Revolution'*. Beijing: Renmin Wenxue Chubanshe.

ZHOU LIANGGONG 周亮工. 1958. *Yinshuwu Shuying* 因樹屋書影 *Shadows of Books in Yinshu House*. Shanghai: Zhonghua Shuju.

ZHOU RUCHANG 周如昌. 1976. *Hong Lou Meng Xin Zheng* 紅樓夢新證 *New Arguments about* The Dream of the Red Chamber. Beijing: Remin Wenxue Chubanshe.

ZHOU SHOUJUAN 周瘦鵑. 1926. *Xiaoshuo Congtan* 小說叢談 *About Fiction*. Shanghai: Dadong Shuju.

ZHOU ZUOREN 周作人. 1932. *Zhongguo Xin Wenxue de Yuanliu* 中國新文學的源流 *Sources of Chinese New Literature*. Beiping: Renwen Shudian.

—— 1980. *Zhitang Huixiang Lu* 知堂回想錄 *Memoires of Zhi Tang*. Hong Kong: Tingtao Chubanshe.

Index